THE HISTORY OF THE TYRANTS OF SICILY
BY 'HUGO FALCANDUS' 1154-69

MANCHESTER
UNIVERSITY PRESS

Manchester Medieval Sources Series

series advisers Rosemary Horrox and Janet L. Nelson

This series aims to meet a growing need amongst students and teachers of medieval history for translations of key sources that are directly usable in students' own work. It provides texts central to medieval studies courses and focuses upon the diverse cultural and social as well as political conditions that affected the functioning of all levels of medieval society The basic premise of the new series is that translations must be accompanied by sufficient introductory and explanatory material and each volume therefore includes a comprehensive guide to the sources' interpretation, including discussion of critical linguistic problems and an assessment of the most recent research on the topics being covered.

already published in the series

J. A. Boyle   *Genghis Khan: history of the world conqueror*

John Edwards   *The Jews in Western Europe, 1400–1600*

Paul Fouracre and Richard A. Gerberding   *Late Merovingian France*

Chris Given-Wilson   *Chronicles of the Revolution, 1397–1400: the reign of Richard II*

P. J. P. Goldberg   *Women in England, c. 1275–1525*

Janet Hamilton and Bernard Hamilton   *Christian dualist heresies in the Byzantine world c. 650–c. 1450*

Rosemary Horrox   *The Black Death*

Janet L. Nelson   *The Annals of St-Bertin: ninth-century histories, volume I*

Timothy Reuter   *The Annals of Fulda: ninth-century histories. volume II*

R. N. Swanson   *Catholic England: faith, religion and observance before the Reformation*

Jennifer Ward   *Women of the English nobility and gentry, 1066–1500*

forthcoming titles in the series will include

Mark Bailey   *English manorial records, c. 1180–1520*

Ross Balzaretti   *North Italian histories, AD 800–1100*

Brenda Bolton   *Innocent III*

Richard Fletcher and Simon Barton   *El Cid and the Spanish Conquest*

Judith Jesch and Bridget Morris   *The Viking Age*

Simon Lloyd   *The impact of the crusades: the experience of England, 1095–1274*

Alison McHardy   *The early reign of Richard II*

Edward Powell   *Crime, law and society in late medieval England*

Ian Robinson   *The pontificate of Gregory VII*

Richard Smith   *Sources for the population history of England, 1000–1540*

Elisabeth van Houts   *The Normans in Europe*

THE HISTORY OF THE TYRANTS OF SICILY BY 'HUGO FALCANDUS' 1154–69

Translated and annotated by
Graham A. Loud and Thomas Wiedemann

MANCHESTER UNIVERSITY PRESS
Manchester and New York
Distributed exclusively in the USA by St. Martin's Press

Copyright © Graham A. Loud and Thomas Wiedemann, 1998

The right of Graham A. Loud and Thomas Wiedemann to be identified as the authors of this work has been asserted by them in accordance with the Copyright, Designs and Patents Act 1988

Published by Manchester University Press
Oxford Road, Manchester M13 9NR, UK
and Room 400, 175 Fifth Avenue, New York, NY 10010, USA

Distributed exclusively in the USA by
St. Martin's Press, Inc., 175 Fifth Avenue, New York, NY 10010, USA

Distributed exclusively in Canada by
UBC Press, University of British Columbia, 6344 Memorial Road, Vancouver, BC, Canada V6T 1Z2

British Library Cataloguing-in-Publication Data
A catalogue record for this book is available from the British Library

Library of Congress Cataloging-in-Publication Data applied for

ISBN   0 7190 4894 X *hardback*
          0 7190 5435 4 *paperback*

First published 1998

05 04 03 02 01 00 99 98   10 9 8 7 6 5 4 3 2 1

Typeset in Monotype Bell by Carnegie Publishing, Lancaster
Printed in Great Britain by Bell & Bain Ltd, Glasgow

CONTENTS

Series editor's foreword	vi
Preface	vii
List of abbreviations	ix
Maps	xi
Genealogical tables	xiii
Introduction	1
The historical background	2
The *History of the Tyrants of Sicily* and the history of Sicily in the years 1154–69	13
The authorship of the *History*	28
Classical resonances in the *History*	42
The manuscripts of the *History*	50
The *Chronicle* of Romuald of Salerno	51
The translation	53
The History of the Tyrants of Sicily	55
Additional texts	219
I Romuald of Salerno, *Chronicon sive Annales*, 1153–69	219
II From Boso's *Life of Pope Adrian IV*	243
III The Treaty of Benevento, 1156	248
IV A letter concerning the Sicilian tragedy to Peter, Treasurer of the Church of Palermo	252
Bibliography	265
Index	277

SERIES EDITOR'S FOREWORD

The Norman Kingdom of Sicily has long attracted international scholarship. Among Britons, the redoubtable Evelyn Jamison was a pioneer editor of sources, while in recent years, an increasing quantity of distinguished work has confirmed the *regno*'s central place on the historiographical map of the Middle Ages. Anglophone undergraduates, however, have not hitherto had the source materials they need for independent study. The gap is filled, for key decades of the twelfth century, by the present book. Combining unsurpassed knowledge of the Normans in southern Italy, with expert appreciation of medieval latinity, Graham Loud and Thomas Wiedemann offer a set of translations as learned as they are readable, along with an introduction and notes that place the texts securely in their political, cultural and literary setting. The jewel in this crown in the *History* of 'Hugh Falcandus', whose Sallustian relish in political reportage ensures that (as the author hoped) 'glory glows with vitality': at the same time Loud and Wiedemann provide indispensable guidance to a historian's craft that included skilful distortions and suppressions of evidence. While thus offering several kinds of exercise in methodology, this welcome addition to the Manchester Medieval Sources Series gives an entrée into an intriguingly complex, and centrally important, Mediterranean world.

Janet L. Nelson, King's College London

PREFACE

None of the principal contemporary narrative sources for the history of the 'Norman' Kingdom of Sicily have hitherto been translated into English. Given the intrinsic interest of the subject, that circumstance would by itself justify the present work. But the *History* of the so-called 'Hugo Falcandus' is also a most important text for students of the classical heritage in the Middle Ages. It is therefore entirely appropriate that this translation and its accompanying material should be the product of a collaboration between a medieval historian and a classicist. As we have discovered while working together, the two disciplines do not always share the same priorities, and there have been a number of animated discussions as to the principles of translation and the type of critical apparatus required. We hope that the results will prove satisfactory both to students of medieval history and to those of classical civilisation. What follows is the product of a true collaboration. The original translation of the main text and the *Letter to Peter* was done by T.E.J.W., as was the section of the introduction on the classical resonances in the *History*, while the rest of the introduction, the translations of the other subsidiary texts, and the notes to all the sources, were the work of G.A.L. But each of us has read, commented upon, and sometimes rewritten, the other's sections. What follows may therefore be seen as fusion rather than jigsaw.

However, scholars do not exist in a vacuum, nor indeed should they; and a number of other people have contributed materially towards the completion of this project. Richard Purslow first commissioned this book, and his successor as the history editor at Manchester University Press, Vanessa Graham, showed exemplary patience with unexpected delays. Dominic Berry, Errico Cuozzo, Horst Enzensberger, Lindy Grant, John McGuckin, Ian Moxon, Alan Murray, Ian Netton, and above all Kathleen Thompson, patiently answered queries on the most arcane subjects: many of their answers have been incorporated in the footnotes. Without Dr Thompson's generous help we should have remained bemused by the complicated kin-grouping of the twelfth-century Counts of Perche. Hubert Houben and Hiroshi Takayama sent gifts of their publications which proved extremely useful both to this work and to other projects as well. The encouragement of Professor Sally Vaughn led to many of the ideas in the introduction being first aired before the Haskins Society conference at Houston in 1995, while discussion with two final-year students at Leeds, Nick Handforth and Danny Hodgson, helped to refine and clarify the section on the authorship of the *History*. At Nottingham, Michael Pucci helped to prepare the final MS. most efficiently. Last, but certainly not least, we are grateful to Diane Milburn and Margaret Hunt-Wiedemann. Among many other ways in which they contributed to this enterprise, D.B.M. drew the maps and proved herself adept at the repair and refurbishment of ageing word processors, while M.H.-W. laboured to improve the translation. However, none of those who have assisted us should share the authors' responsibility for any defects that remain.

G.A.L. and T.E.J.W.
Leeds and Nottingham.

ABBREVIATIONS

Al. Tel.	Alexandrini Telesini Abbatis Ystoria Rogerii Regis Siciliae, Calabriae atque Apuliae, ed. L. De Nava (Fonti per la storia d'Italia 112), Rome 1991.
BAS	Biblioteca Arabo-Sicula, ed. M. Amari, 2 vols, Turin 1880.
Cat. Bar.	Catalogus Baronum, ed. E. M. Jamison (Fonti per la storia d'Italia 101), Rome 1972.
Chron. Cas.	Chronica Monasterii Casinensis, ed. H. Hoffmann (MGH SS xxxiv), Hanover 1980.
Chron. Casauriense	Chronicon Casauriense auctore Johanne Berardi, in L. A. Muratori, Rerum Italicarum Scriptores, ii(2), Milan 1726, 775–1018.
Cod. Dipl. Aversa	Codice diplomatico normanno di Aversa, ed. A. Gallo, Naples 1927.
Cod. Dipl. Bar.	Codice diplomatico barese, 19 vols, Bari 1897–1950.
Documenti inediti	I Documenti inediti dell'epoca normanna in Sicilia, ed. C. A. Garufi (Documenti per servire alla storia di Sicilia, Ser. I. xiii), Palermo 1899.
Falco	Falconis Beneventi Chronicon, in G. Del Re, Cronisti e scrittori sincroni napoletani i, Naples 1845, 161–252.
Guillelmi I Diplomata	Guillelmi I Regis Diplomata, ed. H. Enzensberger (Codex Diplomaticus Regni Siciliae, Ser. I. iii), Cologne 1996.
Italia Pontificia	Italia Pontificia, ed. P. F. Kehr, 10 vols, Berlin 1905–74.
Malaterra	De Rebus Gestis Rogerii Calabriae et Siciliae Comitis auctore Gaufredo Malaterra, ed. E. Pontieri (Rerum Italicarum Scriptores), Bologna 1927–8.
MGH	Monumenta Germaniae Historica (following the usual conventions, SS = Scriptores, SRG = Scriptores Rerum Germanicarum, etc.)
MPL	J. P. Migne, Patrologia Latina, 221 vols, Paris 1844–64.
Rogerii II Diplomata	Rogerii II Regis Diplomata Latina, ed. C.-R. Brühl (Codex Diplomaticus Regni Siciliae, Ser. I. ii(1)), Cologne 1987.
Romuald	Romualdi Salernitani Chronicon, ed. C. A. Garufi (Rerum Italicarum Scriptores), Città di Castello 1935.
Siragusa edn	La Historia o Liber de Regno Sicilie e la Epistola ad Petrum

Panormitane Ecclesie Thesaurium di Ugo Falcando, ed. G. B. Siragusa (Fonti per la storia d'Italia 22), Rome 1897.

Ughelli, *Italia Sacra* F. Ughelli, Italia Sacra sive de Episcopis *Italiae*, 2nd edn by N. Colletti, 10 vols, Venice 1717–21.

The above abbreviations are those used in the notes for sources to which there will be frequent reference. Other primary sources used less often will be cited by editor/translator and short title in the notes, but full details may be found in the bibliography. An exception has been made for non-Sicilian sources to which there is only a single reference, which for the sake of space have been omitted from the bibliography. For these works full bibliographical details will be given with the citation. We have, however, omitted such bibliographical details of well-known classical texts which are available in a number of different editions and translations, citing simply the generally accepted chapter and paragraph divisions. Since this volume is primarily intended for students, references in the notes have been made to English translations of certain well-known medieval sources, such as the *History* of William of Tyre, rather than to editions of the original Latin or Greek texts. Reference to all secondary publications is given in the notes by the author/date system.

The Kingdom of Sicily in the twelfth century.

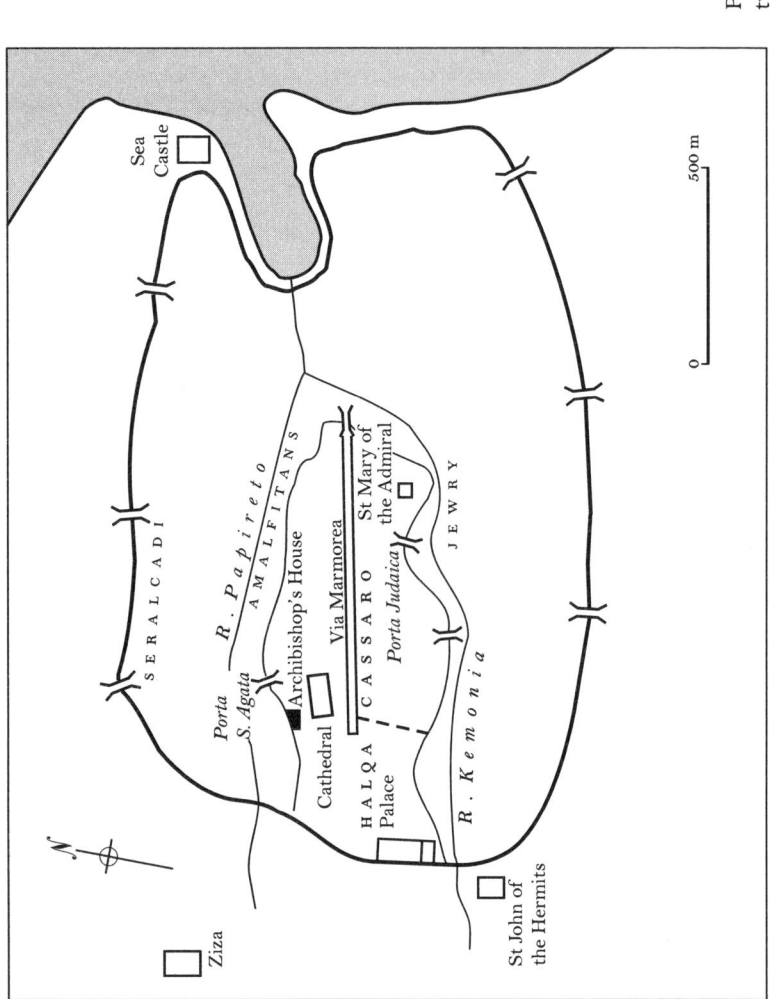

Palermo in the twelfth century.

I. The Sicilian royal family

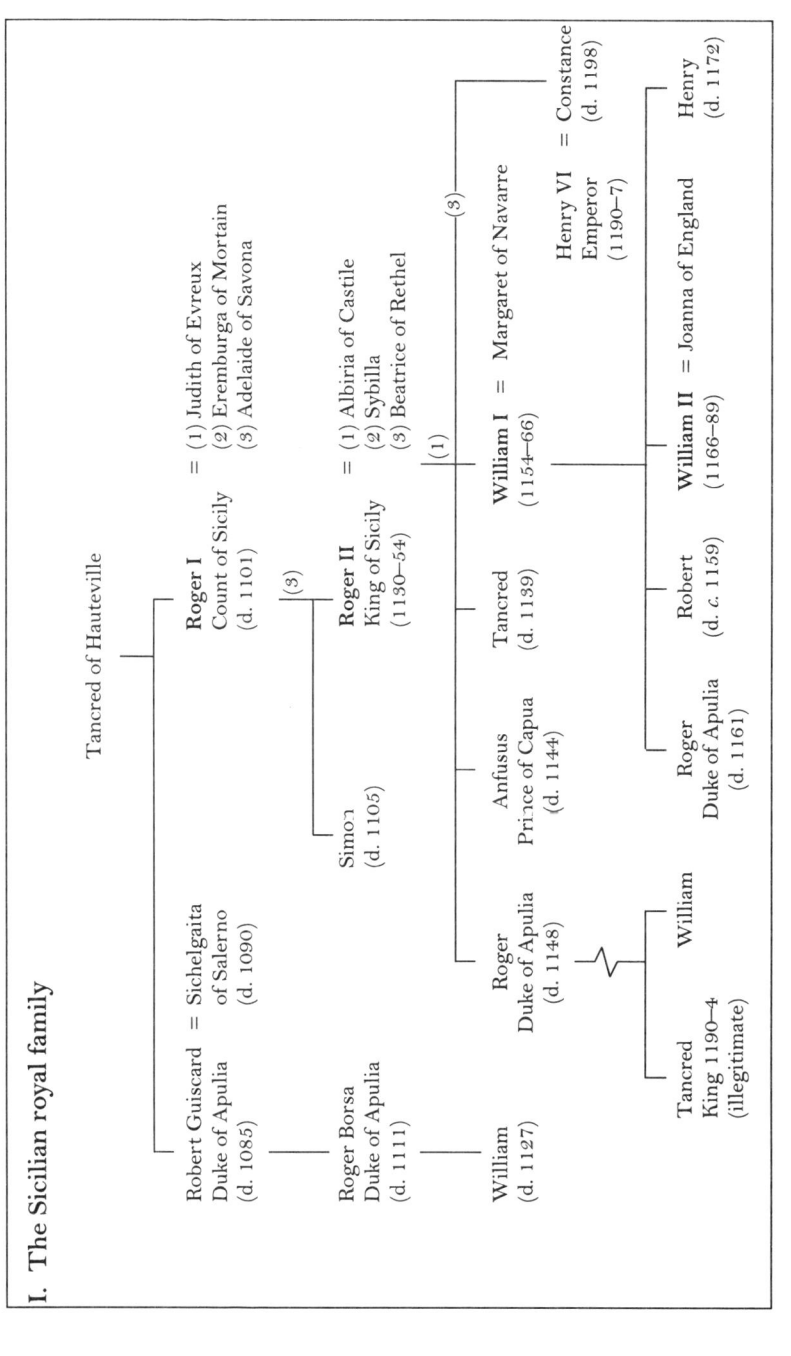

II. The French and Spanish relatives of Queen Margaret

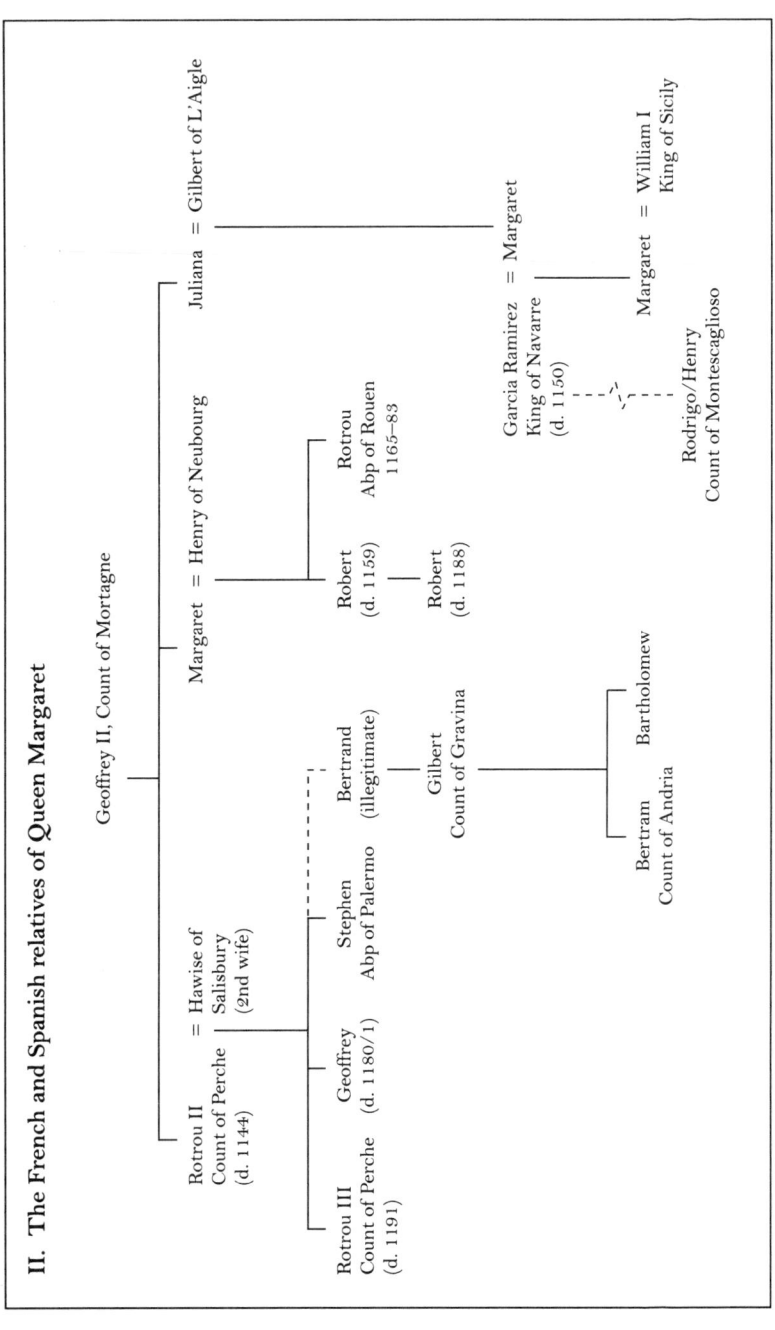

III. The family of Archbishop Romuald II of Salerno

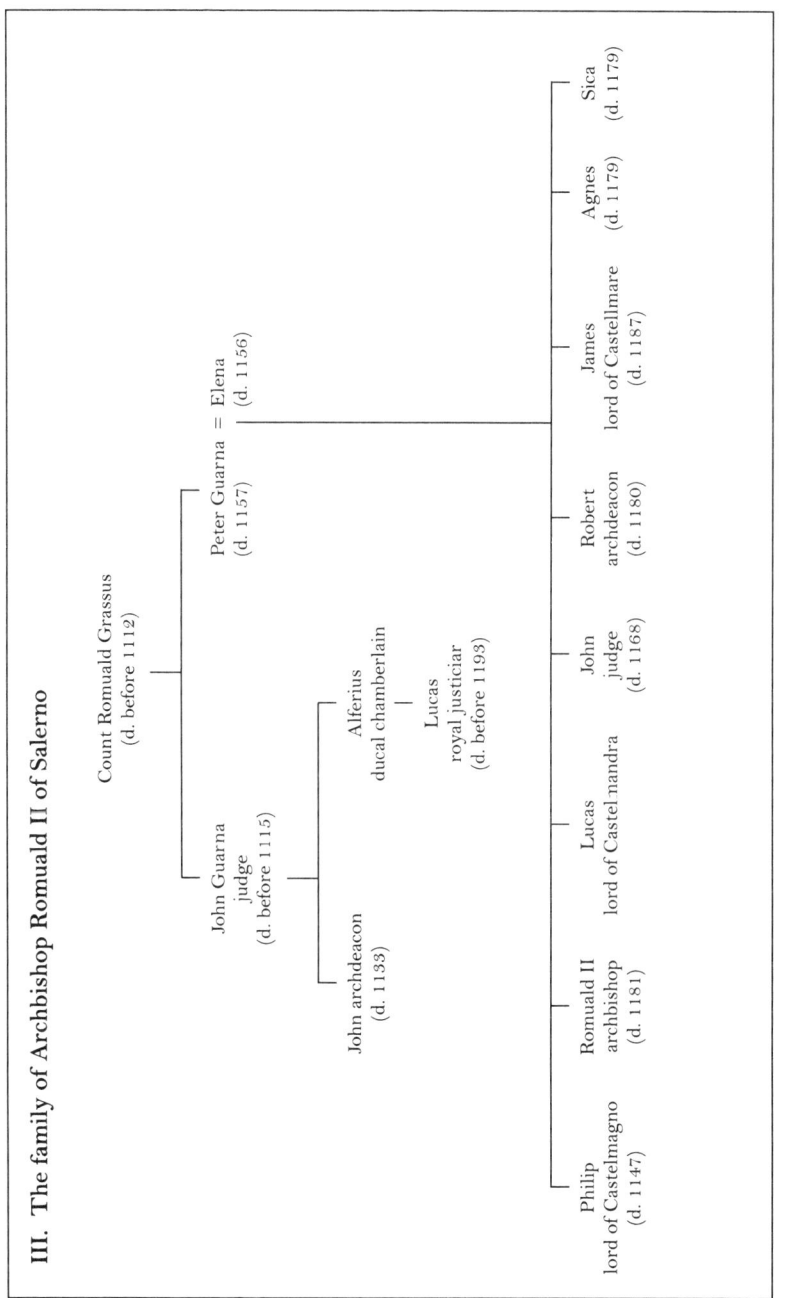

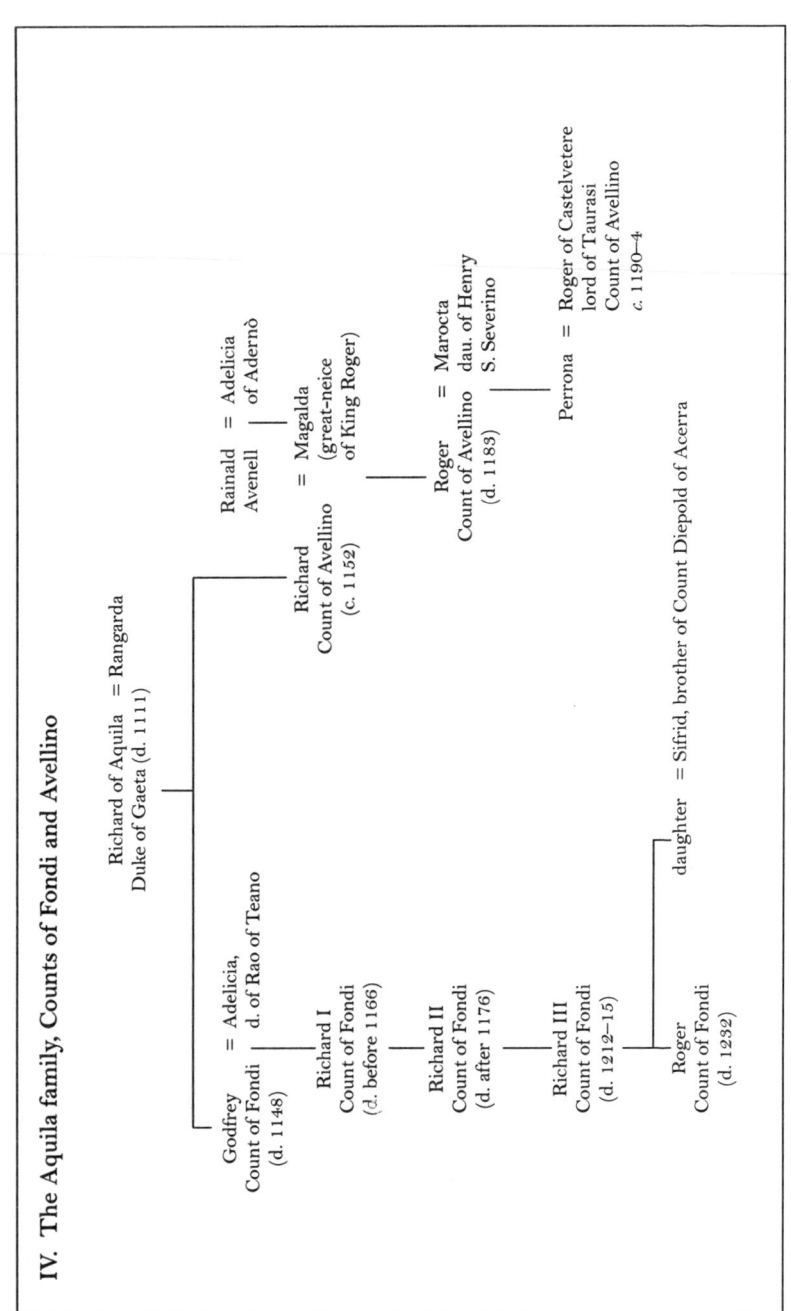

IV. The Aquila family, Counts of Fondi and Avellino

V. The Counts of Catanzaro

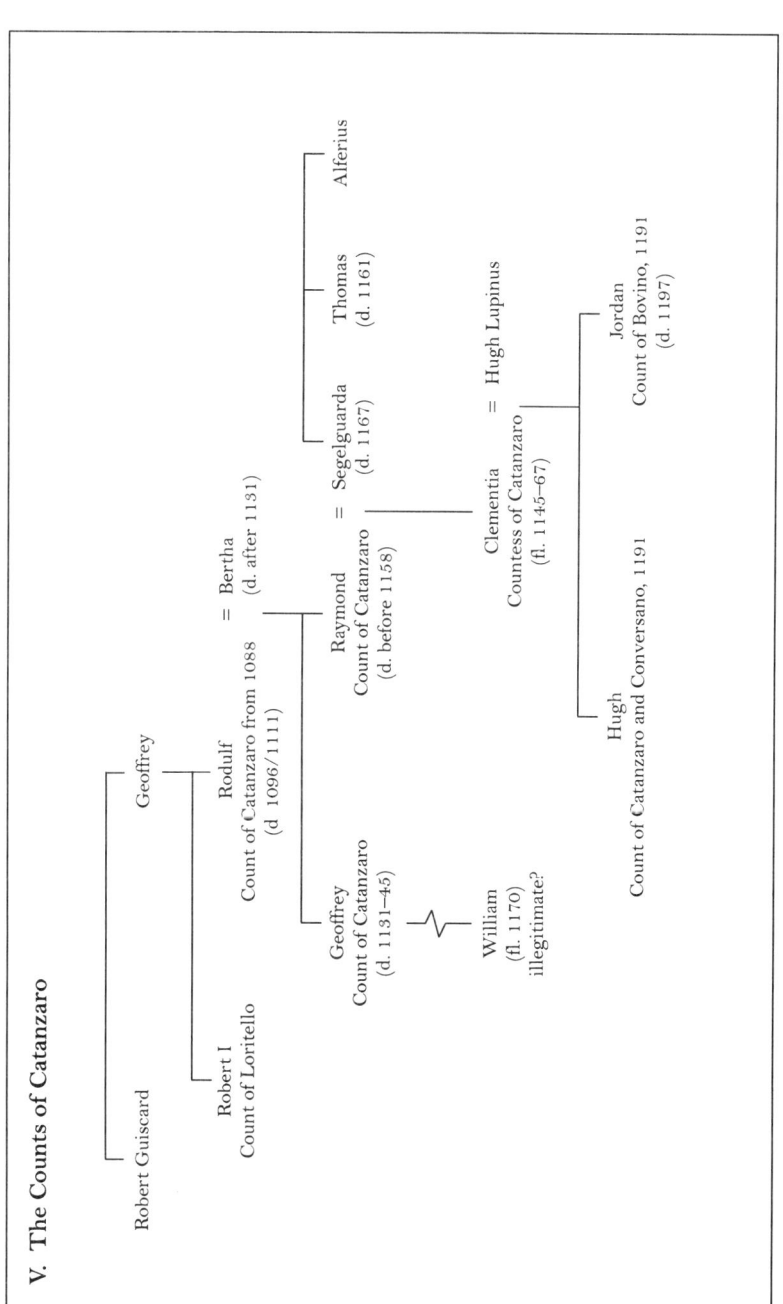

INTRODUCTION

The *History of the Tyrants of Sicily* attributed to 'Hugo Falcandus' is our principal source for the history of the kingdom of Sicily in the troubled years between the death of its founder, King Roger, in February 1154 and the spring of 1169. It covers the reign of Roger's son, King William I, known to later centuries as 'the Bad', and the minority of the latter's son, William II 'the Good'. The *History* of 'Falcandus' is also one of the most important texts illustrating the revival of classical learning during the twelfth-century renaissance.

However, this text also poses many problems, not least in that neither its authorship nor its date of composition have been satisfactorily established. Furthermore, the geographical scope of its coverage is relatively limited, for its author concentrated almost exclusively on events within the bounds of the kingdom of Sicily, and primarily on what happened at the royal court. While this narrow but powerful focus undoubtedly enhances the reader's interest in the story told, and the fluent and polished style carries that story along in one of the most literary of medieval historical sources, the wider background to the events described is largely neglected. We learn little or nothing of outside occurrences which impinged upon the Sicilian kingdom. In addition, 'Falcandus' (whoever he was) is a patently prejudiced and partisan witness, who loathed most of the people whose actions he described, and roundly denigrated their every deed and motive. The factual framework employed by our author may be perfectly true, and many of the details which he provides are confirmed by other sources, but the interpretation which he placed upon them is such that the *History* must be treated with more than usual critical attention. Furthermore, the author's classical learning permeates his *History* and is in itself a distorting factor, not least in his consciousness, shared with other well-educated twelfth-century authors, that Sicily had historically (before its conquest by the Roman republic) been ruled by tyrants, and that the rule of the new Norman kings could be seen, for a variety of reasons, as a revival of that classical tyranny.[1]

Hence, to provide a more balanced view of Sicilian history at this period, that section of the contemporary world chronicle ascribed to Archbishop Romuald II of Salerno, who died in April 1181, which described the years 1153–69 has been included as an appendix to this translation. To this has been added the text of the important treaty concluded between King William I of Sicily and Pope Adrian IV at Benevento in June 1156, which 'Falcandus' did not even mention, and the section of Cardinal Boso's *Life of Adrian* which describes the background to the treaty as seen from the papal court. Romuald's chronicle – if indeed he was the author of this section of the work – not only provides another opinion, but shows much more interest than does 'Falcandus' in affairs elsewhere in Italy and the Christian West. In particular the chronicle of Romuald enables us to see how the papal schism of 1159 and the simultaneous dispute between the German Emperor Frederick Barbarossa and the north Italian cities affected the destiny of the kingdom of Sicily. These additional sources allow the reader to gain a fuller and more balanced picture of the history of Sicily during the reign of William I and the minority of his son William II than is obtainable from the pages of 'Falcandus' alone. One further text is also translated here: the *Letter to Peter*, a propaganda pamphlet written in the spring of 1190, not long after the death of King William II, opposing the claims to the succession of his aunt Constance and her German husband, the future Emperor Henry VI. This tract was copied in all the known manuscripts of the *History of the Tyrants*, and has usually been ascribed to the same author. Since this tract has been central to discussions of the date and authorship of the *History*, both texts clearly need to be studied together.

The historical background

Southern Italy was first infiltrated and then conquered by groups of French immigrants, primarily but not exclusively from Normandy, during the early to mid-eleventh century. By 1059 this process was sufficiently far advanced for Pope Nicholas II formally to recognise the two principal Norman leaders, Robert of Hauteville (known as

1 Wieruszowski (1963).

'Guiscard' – 'the cunning') and Richard Quarrel as the rulers of, respectively, the Duchy of Apulia and the Principality of Capua. Thereafter, at least in theory, they both held their lands as papal vassals, although in practice the Gregorian Reform papacy needed their military and political support a great deal more than they needed it. Guiscard in particular extended his conquests despite considerable opposition from his papal overlord. In 1071 he conquered Bari, the headquarters of what had been the Byzantine provinces in southern Italy and the last town in the peninsula to be held by the empire of Constantinople. In 1076–7 he captured Salerno and what remained of its hitherto-independent principality – despite the protests of, and excommunication by, Pope Gregory VII – and at the same time the forces of his nephew, Robert of Loritello, made inroads into papal lands (or lands over which the papacy had claims) in the Abruzzi. In 1081 Guiscard launched a full-scale attack on the Balkan lands of the crumbling Byzantine Empire, and it was while he was pursuing this ambitious project that he died in the summer of 1085.

While Robert Guiscard was thus occupied, his younger brother Roger was leading the conquest of the island of Sicily from its Muslim rulers. He and Guiscard had captured Palermo, the island's principal town, in 1072, but the conquest of the rest of Sicily was a slow process. It was only finally completed with the capture of the last Muslim enclave around Noto in the south-east in 1091. Roger ruled the island himself, albeit as the vassal of his brother, and then of the latter's son (another Roger), with the Duke of Apulia retaining direct control only of Palermo and half of Messina. In addition the Count of Sicily had a half share of Calabria, the toe of mainland Italy. Capua meanwhile remained an independent principality under the rule of Richard Quarrel's descendants.

What the Norman conquest had not therefore done was to unite southern Italy and Sicily as one territorial state. Indeed, the years after Guiscard's death in 1085 and that of Prince Jordan I of Capua in 1090 saw the collapse of central authority and the decentralisation of power in both the duchy of Apulia and the principality of Capua. Though Guiscard's son and grandson, Dukes Roger Borsa (1085–1111) and William (1111–27), made efforts to enforce their authority in inland Apulia, the focus of their activities came to be more and more in the principality of Salerno on the west coast. The towns along the Adriatic coast of Apulia escaped entirely from their jurisdiction. Bari, for example, was by the 1120s under the rule of an independent prince called Grimoald, who to judge by his name was from the native population of southern Italy, who still called themselves 'Lombards'. In 1122 Duke William had also surrendered his share of Calabria and the Sicilian towns in return for military and financial assistance from his cousin, Count Roger II of Sicily, especially against the rebel count of Ariano in Apulia. The princes of Capua had meanwhile lost control of the northern part of their principality, and their authority became limited to the plain in the south around the town of Capua. Such was the situation on the mainland when Duke William died childless in July 1127.[2]

The unification of southern Italy and the creation of the new Kingdom of Sicily was the work of Roger II of Sicily in the years 1127–30. Despite considerable opposition in Apulia, and initially also from Pope Honorius II, who was by no means anxious to see the south of the peninsula united under such an independently-minded ruler as Roger, the latter enforced his claim to succeed his cousin, receiving formal investiture as duke from the pope in August 1128. Less than a year later the Prince of Capua acknowledged his overlordship, and Roger was therefore ruler over the whole of southern Italy – except for the city of Benevento, which had since 1073 been a papal possession. In September 1130 Pope Anacletus II granted him the right to rule over his lands as a kingdom 'and to have by hereditary right all royal dignities and regalian rights'.

Anacletus's bull said that this grant of royal status was a reward for Roger's and his father's loyalty to the papacy, and because 'divine providence has granted [to you] greater wisdom and power than the rest of the Italian princes',[3] or in other words as a consequence of the extent of his new dominions, which, one might suggest, was for Roger much more to the point. Certainly this latter idea was repeated in Alexander of Telese's propagandist biography of King Roger, written c. 1136, which described the creation of the kingdom as follows:

> Those close to Count Roger, and particularly his uncle Count Henry by whom he was loved more than anyone, began very frequently

---

[2] There is no good modern discussion of the government of the duchy of Apulia after 1085, apart from the very thematic one of Martin (1993), 715–67, which does not look at the Principality of Salerno. For Capua, see Loud (1985), 86–95.

[3] Deér, *Das Papsttum*, 62–4.

to suggest to him the plan that he, who with the help of God ruled so many provinces, Sicily, Calabria, Apulia and other regions stretching almost to Rome, ought not to have just the ducal title but ought to be distinguished by the honour of kingship. They added that the centre and capital of this kingdom ought to be Palermo, the chief city of Sicily, which once, in ancient times, was believed to have had kings [who ruled] over this province; but now, many years later, was by God's secret judgement without them.[4]

Alexander's account, it should be noted, made no mention of the papacy. But it did raise the supposed precedent of the Greek kings in Sicily during the early classical period (none of whom had ever in fact been ruler over the island as a whole). The king's enemies viewed this precedent in a very different light, however. Thus the German chronicler Bishop Otto of Freising denounced King Roger's 'cruel works on the model of the ancient Sicilian tyrants'.[5] For the circumstances in which the kingdom of Sicily was created meant that it was from the first embattled, and that the legitimacy of the new monarchy was immediately questioned.

First of all, Anacletus was but one of two rivals for the throne of St Peter in 1130, albeit the one who was in possession of Rome and who had had a narrow majority among the cardinals during the disputed pontifical election which had followed the death of Pope Honorius in February 1130.[6] The clear if unspoken bargain made between him and the new king of Sicily was that the grant of the royal title was in return for recognition as the rightful pontiff and, if necessary, military support. The latter was forthcoming in the spring of 1132 when Roger dispatched his principal vassal, Prince Robert II of Capua, still at that point loyal to him, with 200 knights to aid Anacletus in Rome.[7] Not

---

4 *Al. Tel.*, lib. II, c. 1, pp. 23–4. Among other discussions of the significance of this passage, see Fuiano (1956); Brown (1992), 199, 202–4.

5 A. Hofmeister, *Ottonis Episcopi Frisingensis Chronica*, lib. VII, c. 23, p. 346. Cf. the remarks in the early thirteenth century by the Swabian chronicler Otto of Sankt Blasien, who described Sicily as *nutrix tyrannorum* (Hofmeister, *Ottonis de Sancto Blasio Chronica*, 56).

6 Amid the huge literature on the schism, see Stroll (1987), especially 65–81 on the southern Italian ramifications, and Robinson (1990), 65–78 for a useful summary. On the schism and the kingdom of Sicily see also Deér (1972), 203–30; Loud (1985), 143–9.

7 *Falco*, 206–7.

surprisingly therefore the ecclesiastical supporters of the rival pope, Innocent II (the eventual victor in the schism), denied the legitimacy of the new Sicilian kingdom. Bernard of Clairvaux, for example, denounced Roger's 'usurped crown procured by outrageous bribery'. They found a ready audience at the court of the German emperor, Lothar, who regarded the south of Italy as a part, albeit a distant one, of his own dominions, and for whom the creation of the new kingdom was therefore, as St Bernard once again pointed out, a direct challenge. 'There can be no doubt', he wrote, 'that anybody who makes himself king of Sicily opposes the emperor.'[8] The eastern emperor John Comnenus was equally hostile, for the Byzantines had never forgotten that they had ruled both Apulia and Calabria until their expulsion by Robert Guiscard. An alliance was concluded between the two empires against the King of Sicily (or, as one contemporary German chronicler, described him 'a semi-pagan tyrant') in the summer of 1135, and Lothar launched an unsuccessful, but for a time very menacing, invasion of the Sicilian *regno* in 1137.[9]

This external threat was doubly dangerous because Roger's determination to enforce his rule effectively on the mainland, which included such measures as the prohibition of private warfare (enacted in 1129 even before his coronation) roused significant and long-lasting opposition from within his kingdom. This came in particular from a coalition of powerful nobles in southern Apulia, a number of the more important Apulian towns, and from the Prince of Capua and the latter's cousin and strongest vassal, Count Rainulf of Caiazzo. Rainulf, despite the fact that he was also the king's brother-in-law, became by far his most active and effective opponent. From 1132 onwards the king was forced to conduct a series of annual campaigns on the mainland and to resort to such brutal measures as the destruction of the rebel town of Aversa in 1135, the sack of Capua in 1137, and the execution of Prince Jacquintus of Bari and his counsellors in 1139, in breach of the terms on which that city had surrendered. It was to such deeds as these that the author of the *History of the Tyrants of Sicily* referred when he wrote in his preface of Roger's administration of 'justice in its full rigour on the grounds that it was particularly necessary for

8 MPL clxxxii, 282, 294, epp. 127, 139.
9 For the 1135 Treaty of Merseburg, see the Erfurt Annals (*Annales Erphesfudenses*), MGH SS vi, 540–1, and the *Annalista Saxo*, MGH SS vi, 769. For the 'semi-pagan tyrant', *ibid.*, 774.

a newly-established realm'. He continued: 'if perhaps he seemed to have acted somewhat harshly against some, I suppose that he was forced to it by necessity'. Other commentators were less forgiving. Falco, a notary from Benevento whose chronicle reveals a growing loathing for Roger, after describing the sack of Venosa by the king's Muslim troops in the spring of 1133, exclaimed that 'he demonstrated such cruelty towards Christian people as has scarcely ever been heard of in our time'.[10]

It was only in 1139, after Count Rainulf's death, that King Roger finally triumphed over the south Italian rebels. In July of that year he secured the reluctant recognition of his royal status from Innocent II, after the pope had attempted a further, and catastrophically unsuccessful, invasion of the kingdom of Sicily. But while from then onwards his position within his kingdom was secure, and reinforced by the development of an effective structure of local administration within the mainland provinces, the external situation remained threatening. Neither the eastern nor the western emperors were prepared to acknowledge the new kingdom. Peace talks with Byzantium c.1143 broke down when the new emperor, Manuel Comnenus, refused to accept Roger's status as a king, and the Sicilians launched a naval attack on Byzantium in 1147 – which, among other things, contributed significantly to the failure of the Second Crusade. The war with Byzantium, and Sicilian naval operations in the lower Adriatic, also incurred the hostility of Venice. Pressure from the western emperor led Genoa, one of the other principal maritime powers of northern Italy, into war with the kingdom of Sicily.[11] While a cessation of hostilities was eventually secured with the Italian mercantile powers, the German emperors' hostility to the kingdom of Sicily continued down to the conference at Venice in 1177 where a general peace was made between the empire, papacy, north Italian cities and Sicily. Even then German opinion was still not wholly reconciled to the recognition of the Sicilian monarchy. An early thirteenth-century chronicler

10 *Falco*, 218. On Falco's attitude towards the king, see Loud (1993), especially 186–9. Cf. below, p. 58.

11 However, Pisa, the third major maritime power of northern Italy, would not seem to have been at war with Sicily at this period, having made peace with King Roger in October 1137. When William I seized Pisan property in the *regno* in October 1162, the Pisan chronicler Maragone complained of a breach in the long-established peace between Sicily and his city; Lupo Gentile, *Annales Pisani* 11, 28.

remarked that the marriage in 1186 of Frederick Barbarossa's son Henry with the Sicilian princess Constance, seen as the heiress to her nephew, the childless King William II, 'recovered for the Roman empire what had, after the death of the Emperor Lothar, been taken away from the empire by Roger when he had captured Pope Innocent and extorted the name of king from him'.[12] For some years after 1139 the German court provided a refuge for dispossessed rebels such as the Prince of Capua, Count Roger of Ariano and (probably) the relatives of Rainulf of Caiazzo.[13] One of the latter, the count's nephew Andrew of Rupecanina, was to become a thorn in the flesh of the Sicilian government during the 1150s and 1160s, launching several attacks on its northern border. Another exile, Alexander, the former count of Conversano, who had fled to Byzantium in 1132 and was thereafter frequently employed in the diplomacy between the two empires (not least during the Second Crusade), was described by the German ruler Conrad III in a letter of 1150 as 'accustomed to serve both empires with unbroken loyalty', and by a contemporary Greek historian as 'extremely devoted to the Romans [i.e. Byzantines] and the emperor's affairs'.[14] The activities of these Sicilian exiles helped to ensure that the two great empires of medieval Christendom remained actively hostile to King Roger's kingdom. At the same time the king of Sicily was believed to be fomenting discontent within Germany. Indeed, according to Otto of Freising, Conrad's death in 1152 was suspected by some to have been caused by his Italian doctors, who had been suborned by Roger 'because of his fear of the king [i.e. Conrad]'.[15] Far-fetched as such suppositions may have been, the external threats to the kingdom of Sicily, and especially that from the western empire, were undoubtedly taken seriously in King Roger's last years. Round about 1150 a register was drawn up of the military strength of the

12 Hofmeister, *Ottonis de Sancto Blasio Chronica*, 39.
13 Robert II of Capua and the Count of Ariano witnessed a diploma of Conrad III at Würzburg in April 1144; *MGH Diplomatum Regum et Imperatorum Germaniae* ix, ed. F. Hausmann, 176–7, no. 99; and Robert undertook diplomatic missions to Byzantium in 1142 and again in 1145; Mierow, *Deeds of Frederick Barbarossa*, 56, 59. Both he and Count Rainulf's brother Richard were in Germany in 1148; Jaffé, *Monumenta Corbeiensia*, 228–9, no. 147 a letter which refers to King Roger's bribery of the German princes.
14 Wibald of Korvey, *Epistola* no. 164, in Jaffé, *Monumenta Corbeiensia*, 365; Brand, *Deeds of John and Manuel Comnenus by John Cinnamus*, 115.
15 Mierow, *Deeds of Frederick Barbarossa*, 110. Cf. note 13 above.

mainland provinces, the 'Catalogue of the Barons', which imposed a new and uniform system of military obligation on landowners deemed sufficiently important to hold their property directly from the king. Not only did they owe a normal quota of military service, but in addition they were made subject to the *augmentum*, an extra levy, usually doubling their normal quota of service, which was designed as an emergency measure in case of invasion, a *levée en masse* of the military potential of the kingdom.[16]

Nor were relations with the papal court particularly smooth after the settlement of 1139; an agreement into which, as we have seen, Pope Innocent had been forced by military defeat. Some at the Curia, notably Innocent's successor Celestine II (pope 1143–4), were extremely reluctant to accept this concession to the principal secular ally of the despised Anacletus.[17] In addition, the incursions by Sicilian troops, led by King Roger's elder sons Roger and Anfusus, into the territory claimed by the papacy in the Abruzzi in the early 1140s raised a new bone of contention. There were also a number of ecclesiastical issues outstanding: notably the rights over the Church which Roger claimed as a consequence of a grant to his father by Urban II in 1098,[18] and the status of the bishoprics on the island of Sicily.

This last issue is complicated and needs some explanation. Roger I had converted the existing Greek archbishopric at Palermo (the only Christian see on the island when the Normans arrived) to the Latin rite. Between 1081 and 1093 he had created, with papal agreement, five further dioceses in Sicily and another one for the newly-conquered island of Malta. However, in 1130–1 Anacletus had at Roger's request undertaken a considerable reorganisation of the Sicilian bishoprics. He had raised Messina to be an archbishopric and grouped the other existing sees into two metropolitan provinces subject to Palermo and Messina. He had also sanctioned the foundation of two new bishoprics at Cefalù and Lipari (to be part of the province of

---

16 Jamison (1971), especially 3–7.
17 *Romuald*, 227; Gaudenzi, *Chronicon Ferraria* 27–8; *Annales Casinenses*, ad ann. 1144, MGH SS xix, 310; Robinson (1990), 386–8. However, cf. Loud (1982), 152–3 and (1985), 192–4, for some qualifications.
18 *Malaterra*, IV. 29, p. 108; Deér (1972), 235–44, although this author's emphasis on the 'feudal' aspects of the relationship between the papacy and the south Italian rulers should be treated with caution.

Messina).[19] Innocent and his successors naturally refused to accept these measures (as they considered them illegal), and the episcopal structure on the island remained in limbo for almost twenty years after the death of Anacletus in 1138 and the subsequent conclusion of the schism. Even when an agreement on most of the political problems between Sicily and the papacy was reached between King Roger and Pope Eugenius III at a meeting at Ceprano, on the kingdom's northern border, in 1150, the pope still refused point-blank to sanction any changes to the pre-schism ecclesiastical structure on Sicily. Nor did the good will of the Ceprano agreement last very long. Roger secured the succession of his only surviving son, William, by having him crowned as co-ruler at Easter 1151, without consulting his nominal papal overlord, which was deeply resented by the Curia.[20]

Hence the situation of the Sicilian monarchy on the death of King Roger in February 1154 was by no means favourable. Both the German and the Byzantine empires remained hostile. Relations with the papacy were poor, and 'Romuald' informs us that the new pope, the Englishman Adrian IV, enraged the king by refusing to address him by his royal title but only as 'lord of Sicily'.[21] The exiled nobles saw the accession of the new ruler as their opportunity to attack the kingdom and regain their lost lands, and Manuel Comnenus prepared a military expedition to recover the former Byzantine territories in Apulia. Nor was the internal situation of the *regno* entirely stable, for King Roger appears to have left a legacy of discontent both among the patriciate in the larger towns, who had seen their stirrings towards civic independence firmly suppressed, and among at least some of the mainland nobility. For not only had a number of important men fled or been exiled during the 1130s and been replaced by new men, but after 1139 the king had launched a considerable reorganisation of the upper ranks of the mainland aristocracy. Some of the most powerful lordships were suppressed, notably the counties of Ariano, Caiazzo and Loritello, and other new counties were created, the function of which was military rather than administrative, though sometimes a grant of increased status must have been a reward for proven loyalty. (However, none of the new counties

---

19 *Italia Pontificia* x, 230, no. 25, 339, no. 23, 357, no. 4, 364, no. 1. Helpful discussion in White (1938), 88–9, 189–91.

20 Chibnall, *The Historia Pontificalis of John of Salisbury*, 67–9; Deér (1972), 244–7.

21 See below, p. 222.

had such extensive resources as those suppressed.) Many of the new counts were either related to the king or came from Calabria and Sicily, the dominions which he had ruled before 1127, where he could rely on the aristocracy's loyalty. In the short run this policy was successful in ensuring stability, but it is notable that the mainland nobles who rebelled in 1155 were almost all of them (Robert de Bassonville excepted) from families whch had been prominent for several generations. This suggests that Roger's reorganisation of the nobility and the intrusion of new men had led to tensions and resentment.[22] It was these problems left over from the previous reign, just as much, if not more than any misgovernment by William I and his advisers, which led to widespread revolt within the kingdom in 1155–6.

Furthermore, the internal stability of the island of Sicily was by now under threat. This was caused by the immigration of Latin Christians, who came both from the southern mainland and, in the south-eastern part of the island in and around the lands of King Roger's maternal relatives, the Aleramici family, also from northern Italy.[23] The resulting change in the demographic balance of a population which had in 1100 comprised almost exclusively Muslims and Greek Christians not surprisingly led to tensions. The early thirteenth-century Iraqi historian Ibn al-Athir, who was well informed about Sicily, praised Roger for the use he made of Muslim officials and administrative practices, and the judicial protection he accorded them; hence, he said, the king's Muslim subjects loved him.[24] But at the very end of his reign the king's attitude may have been changing, as shown by the execution three months before the king's own death of the converted official Philip of Mahdia, on suspicion of apostasy back to Islam. The Romuald chronicle's obituary notice of King Roger claimed that 'towards the end of his life ... he laboured in every conceivable way to convert Jews and Muslims to the faith of Christ'.[25] Assuming that this opinion

---

22 Cuozzo (1989), 105–20; Loud (1998).

23 Peri (1978), 74, 80; Abulafia (1983) 11–13; and on the Aleramici family, Garufi (1910). For a former inhabitant of Bari, now resident in Palermo, *Cod. dipl. bar.* v. 183, no. 107 (1122).

24 *BAS*, i, 114–15. Houben (1994) provides an important discussion of royal policy towards non-Christians.

25 See below, p. 220. The trial and death of Philip of Mahdia is recorded in a later interpolation to Romuald's chronicle, *Romuald*, 234–5, and by Ibn al-Athir, *BAS*, i, 122.

reflects truth rather than a clerical writer's sense of Christian propriety, a change in official attitude may have been the product of the growing influence at court of Latin Christians such as Maio of Bari, after the death of King Roger's Greek minister George of Antioch (dated by Ibn al-Athir to the 546th year after the Hegirah (April 1151–April 1152)). The reign of William I saw the clear dominance of this Latin element within the administration, although Muslim converts continued to be employed, notably the Caid Peter who was to be a royal *familiaris* in the 1160s. The growth of the Latin element in the royal administration was, to some extent anyway, at the expense of the Greek officials who had hitherto been so important.[26]

However, the growing immigration from the mainland posed a more direct threat to the Muslim inhabitants, even though neither William I nor William II appears to have been intrinsically hostile to them. Where Muslims and Christians came into contact, as they did especially in the east of the island and also in Palermo, there was a growing risk of violence. This was to erupt in Palermo during the attempted coup against King William in March 1161, as 'Falcandus' described, and shortly afterwards in a pogrom launched by the north Italian immigrants in south-eastern Sicily against the Muslims in that area. This hostility on the part of the new Latin settlers led to a partial displacement of the Muslim inhabitants from the east of the island, while the population of the western part of the interior remained overwhelmingly Islamic. It also undoubtedly contributed to that sense of unease among the Muslims, despite royal protection and material prosperity, which is abundantly clear from the account of his visit to Sicily in the winter of 1184–5 by the Spanish Muslim traveller Ibn Jubayr. These tensions came into the open after the death of William II in November 1189, when another attack on the Muslims of Palermo by their Christian neighbours led to a general revolt among the Saracens of western Sicily which was only finally suppressed more than thirty years later.[27] Yet earlier, although Ibn Jubayr referred to Muslims being forced to convert to Christianity by royal pressure, this would seem to have applied only to a few prominent individuals,

---

26 Jamison (1957), 39–47; *BAS*, i, 121.

27 For the 1189 revolt, see *Annales Casinenses*, ad ann. 1189, MGH SS xix, 314. More generally see Peri (1978), 83–9, 117–27. An undated charter of Bishop Gentile of Agrigento (1154–71) recorded his purchase of four villages from various Muslims who had been expelled from Sicily; see Collura, *Più antiche carte di Agrigento*, 61, no. 25.

especially those involved in the royal administration. There is some evidence for more widespread conversion, primarily from the north-eastern part of the island, but it is rather for conversion to Greek Orthodox Christianity than to the Latin Church. This may reflect the fact that the ancestors of many of these converts were themselves Greeks who had converted to Islam during the two centuries of Islamic rule in Sicily. 'Falcandus', whoever he was, was by no means immune to this anti-Islamic feeling, though he reserved his particular dislike for the royal officials who had converted to Christianity but who, he considered, were still Muslims at heart – an opinion which was, interestingly, shared by Ibn Jubayr.[28]

The *History of the Tyrants of Sicily* and the history of Sicily in the years 1154–69

The *History* of the so-called 'Hugo Falcandus' falls into two distinct parts. The first describes the reign of William I of Sicily from the king's accession early in 1154 until the suppression of rebellion on the mainland in 1162. The tone is throughout consistently hostile to the king and to his chief minister, Maio of Bari, who was murdered in November 1160. The last three and a half years of the reign are then ignored, as though nothing worthy of note – or germane to the author's theme of the tragic misgovernment of Sicily – had occurred. This is all the more unfortunate since other evidence for the actions of the royal court is equally sparse. Only thirty-five charters of William I now survive, and of these only four date from after 1160. (There are, by contrast, 156 surviving royal charters from the reign of William II).[29] The second half of the *History* commences with the death of William I in May 1166, leaving as his successor a child just short of his thirteenth birthday. 'Falcandus' describes the rivalries at the royal court which followed the king's death: the Queen Mother Margaret's summoning of her cousin, Stephen of Perche, to become her chief minister; the growing dislike among many of the great men of the realm for Stephen's pre-eminence and of the populace of Sicily as a

28 Broadhurst, *The Travels of Ibn Jubayr*, 340–3, 357–8, and below, p. 78. For Greek Christian converts, see Johns (1995). One prominent convert to the Latin faith was Roger, godson of Count Roger I, 'formerly called Ahmed', for whom see Pirro, *Sicula Sacra*, i, 85–7 (1141).

29 Enzensberger (1981), 111–12.

whole for his French followers; and the uprising which led to his expulsion in the summer of 1168. The *History* concludes with a brief discussion of the arrangements for sharing power at court after Stephen's flight, and an account of the earthquake which devastated eastern Sicily in February 1169. The abruptness of the ending has led some scholars to think that the work was left incomplete.

The work is very much a history on the classical model, that is to say, a coherent prose work of literature with an underlying theme, but with little or no overt attention to chronology. In this respect it presents a complete contrast with Romuald's chronicle, which utilises a much more conventional annalistic format, albeit not absolutely on a year-by-year basis. Like his classical exemplar Sallust, 'Falcandus' rarely mentions dates, one of the few exceptions being that of the royal court's return from Messina to Palermo in 1168, where we are told that King William II left Messina on 12 March and arrived at Palermo on 20 March, and that a plot was hatched to murder Stephen of Perche on Palm Sunday.[30] Even here the year is not specifically mentioned and must be inferred. Normally the author preferred to indicate time by such phrases as 'in the meantime', 'after a few days', or 'after these events'. It is noteworthy that no date is given for one of the great dramatic climaxes of the book, the murder of Maio of Bari, although we are then informed that on the day after the murder the king appointed the famous classical and scientific scholar Henry Aristippus to replace his deceased minister, and the account goes on to suggest that this was not long before the New Year. It is Romuald's chronicle which gives the date of the murder, St Martin's Eve (10 November) 1160, and similarly dates the attempted coup by the prisoners in the palace dungeons, in the course of which William I came within an ace of assassination, to the fifth day of Lent (9 March) 1161. 'Falcandus' says that this occurred on the day after the plot was leaked to a knight loyal to the king, but does not say when that day was. He then interrupts his account of the aftermath of the failed coup to recount an incident in the career of one of the few officials of whom he approves, the notary and canon of Palermo, Robert of S. Giovanni, which clearly occurred several years earlier, probably in 1156/7.[31]

'Falcandus' is usually reliable enough on factual details, in so far as

---

30 See below pp. 196–7.

31 Jamison (1913), 286–8, and see below, note 94 to the text of the *History*.

these can be checked from other sources. For example, his figure of 160 galleys for the royal fleet sent to relieve Mahdia late in 1159 tallies quite closely with that given by the (admittedly later) Islamic historian Ibn Khaldun of 150 vessels.[32] He displays an intimate acquaintance with both the personnel and the workings of the royal administration. The royal officers whom he mentions and the titles which they held can almost all be attested from charter evidence, and such passages as his account of the trial of Richard of Mandra in 1168 show his clear grasp of legal matters. That two very prominent men discussed in the *History*, Count Everard of Squillace – important at the beginning of William I's reign – and Count Roger of Gerace, one of the *familiares* of the regency council of 1168, cannot be otherwise attested from documentary sources, is quite explicable given the relative paucity of surviving charters (especially in Latin) from Calabria, whence they both came.

None the less, in spite of its many virtues, the *History* is a treacherous and often misleading source. The bias within it is often clear from the vituperative abuse directed at certain individuals, and the almost universal suspicion of men's motives. Count Everard of Squillace and Robert of S. Giovanni are two of the few exempted from such criticism, though the author's attitude to Stephen of Perche, despite the latter's tactical mistakes, is also generally favourable. More typical of his opinions was, for example, his view of Archbishop Roger of Reggio: 'a man whose avarice and cupidity were inexhaustible, who while he was very restrained in his own expenses, could all too easily be impressed by the splendours of someone else's table'. Yet the archbishop was clearly a trusted servant both of the crown and of the papacy, being charged with the highly responsible task of escorting Alexander III from Messina back to Rome in November 1165, and by the pope with the consecration of Walter of Palermo in 1169.[33]

The lack of balance in the account is nowhere more apparent, and significant, than in the treatment of King William I and Maio of Bari. 'Falcandus' portrayed the king as cruel, suspicious to the point of paranoia, but also foolish and indolent, easily manipulated by his Svengali-like minister. Our author claimed that King Roger himself had a poor opinion of William and had hardly thought him fit even to be Prince of Taranto. Quite what this meant is a good question:

---

32 *BAS*, ii, 203.
33 Duchesne, *Liber Pontificalis*, ii. 413, *Italia Pontificia*, x. 232–3, no. 32.

it is unlikely that King Roger's younger sons played any significant part in the administration of the mainland, and their titles were therefore largely honorific, sources of income certainly, but not of power. But the surviving royal charters at least imply a different picture from that suggested by 'Falcandus', for from 1142 onwards, when he was 22, William was present on a regular basis at his father's court, along with his elder brother Roger (who died in 1148), and was not in any sense marginalised.[34] Furthermore, Henry Aristippus, in the dedicatory letter accompanying his translation of Plato's *Phaedo*, written in 1156, portrayed William as a veritable philosopher–king 'whose court is a school ... whose solutions leave nothing undiscussed, and whose zeal leaves nothing untried'.[35] Doubtless such an idealised portrait was the product of a courtier's flattery and an excess of Platonic enthusiasm, but it still presents a remarkable contrast to the view of the king expressed in the *History*, and perhaps should not be entirely ignored. King Roger had been a patron of scholars, and probably William I was too.

Maio meanwhile was shown as a complete and accomplished villain, vicious, treacherous and sexually depraved, plotting to supplant the ruler who depended on his advice. But while Romuald reports this charge as mere allegation by Maio's enemies, 'Falcandus' treats it as established fact, and gives a long and circumstantial account of the minister's plotting with his co-conspirator Archbishop Hugh of Palermo. Far from being original, this story was, so Evelyn Jamison suggested, based upon an oriental folk-tale called 'Stephanites and Ichnelates' then circulating in Greek translation at the Sicilian court. Furthermore Jamison argued that the maxims of good and just government held up for emulation in the collection of fables of which 'Stephanites and Ichnelates' was a part were precisely those of which 'Falcandus' approved, and whose absence in Sicily he lamented. The parallels between this section of the *History* and the fable are not so close as to make Jamison's case absolutely conclusive, but her

---

34 *Rogerii II Diplomata*, 265–6, appendix no. 3 (= Collura, *Più antiche carte*, 35–7, no. 12) (May 1142); 166–70. no. 59 (November 1143), 187–9, no. 65 (October 1144), 189–97, nos. 66–7 (both November 1144), 205–6, no. 71 (September 1146), 214–16, no. 75 (February 1148). And in April 1146, William and Duke Roger presided over a court settlement between the churches of Bagnara and Cefalù; *ibid.*, 271–3, appendix no. 6.

35 Minio-Paluello, *Phaedo interprete Henrico Aristippo*, 90. (Engl. trans. Berschin (1988), 232–3).

suggestion as to where this seemingly absurd libel was derived from is certainly interesting, and warns the reader to exercise great caution in assessing the veracity of this 'historical' account.[36] One might also point to other parallels for such an accusation: thus in the sixth century the Emperor Justinian's unpopular minister John the Cappadocian was accused of having designs on his master's throne.[37] Moreover, there is further evidence which suggests that 'Falcandus' traduced Maio. Certainly he exaggerated his humble origins. Maio's father Leo was a long-serving judge, one of the civic leaders of Bari, not just 'a man who sold olive-oil' in that city. If he was involved in that trade it was probably as a major entrepreneur in the booming export business from Bari, which was at this period turning the city's hinterland into a region almost exclusively devoted to olive cultivation, and which was the kingdom's principal source of that crop. He was certainly not, as the *History* seems to imply, merely a shopkeeper or street-trader.[38] Maio's sister, Eustochia, was the Abbess of the nunnery of St Scholastica in Bari, although we do not know exactly when she was chosen for this post and thus whether her position was the result of her family's importance within the city or of Maio's own role as royal minister.[39] Furthermore, for an alleged monster of sexual depravity Maio displayed some peculiar interests. He was, although a layman, the author of a commentary on the Lord's Prayer, written for his son Stephen, in which he displayed close knowledge both of the Bible and of the works of Gregory the Great. This text may be pedestrian and derivative, and his knowledge of Christian Fathers other than Gregory probably derived at second-hand from *florilegia* rather than actual study of their works, but it provides a sharp contrast to the portrait of Maio which 'Falcandus' painted. Furthermore, the canon lawyer and subsequently (from 1173) cardinal, Laborans, who was a canon of Capua cathedral, quite possibly appointed by Maio's ally Archbishop Hugh, who was translated from the see of Capua to Palermo *c.*1150, dedicated a treatise *Concerning*

36 Jamison (1957), 251–67.
37 A. Cameron, *Circus Factions. Blues and Greens at Rome and Byzantium* (Oxford 1976), 95.
38 For the relationship, *Cod. dipl. bar.* v, 190–2, no. 112, at p. 190 (1155, by which time his father, Leo, was dead). He can be attested earlier from 1119 to 1147; *Cod. dipl. bar.* i, 75–8, no. 40, v, 174–6, no. 101. For the growth of olive cultivation, see Martin (1993), 362–6.
39 Siragusa (1929), 175; Martin (1993), 480, 671.

justice and the just man to Maio.[40] Similarly Henry Aristippus claimed that his (now lost) translation of the *Lives of the Philosophers* by Diogenes Laertius was done at the request of Maio and Archbishop Hugh.[41] The religious connections and (probably) patronage of Maio's family were reflected in the contemporary necrology of the important Benedictine abbey of Holy Trinity, Venosa, in which both his parents and those of his brother-in-law the Seneschal Simon were commemorated.[42] The evidence other than 'Falcandus' suggests therefore that Maio was rather more than conventionally pious, and something of an intellectual. The allegations of sexual depravity made in the *History* were probably a reflection of the classical learning with which its author was imbued. To classical writers sexual licence was a particular hallmark of the actual or would-be tyrant, as for example Sallust's Catiline or the wicked Caesars of Suetonius: Caligula, Nero and Domitian.[43]

This is not the only way in which the picture of Maio and William I in the *History* is misleading. Certainly the former's pre-eminence as the king's chief minister, his 'emir of emirs' (Latin *admiratus admiratorum*), was no invention: the description of Maio in the Treaty of Benevento as the king's *familiarissimus* (using the superlative), whereas other later ministers, however eminent, were only *familiares*, shows this.[44] But while 'Falcandus' portrays Maio's influence as entirely malign, a more balanced assessment of the years 1154 to 1160 suggests that he was a man of considerable ability. Given the difficult situation which William I inherited in 1154, his and Maio's government was by no means unsuccessful. The rebellions both on the mainland and in Sicily were suppressed. The Byzantine expeditionary force sent to south Apulia in 1155–6 was routed. Peace was made first with Genoa and the papacy, then with Venice (though these last negotiations may

---

40 Siragusa (1929), 171 and (especially) Matthew (1992a).

41 *Meno interprete Henrico Aristippo*, ed. V. Kordeuter (London 1940), 6.

42 Houben, *Il Libro del capitolo del monastero della SS. Trinità di Venosa*, 142–3, 158–9.

43 Sallust, *Catiline* 14–15; Suetonius, *Caligula* 36 (his seduction and shame of respectable married women, among other vices), *Nero* 28–9, *Domitian* 22. Cf. also Cicero, *In Verrem* 1. 5.14, 2. 54.142 and *In Pisonem* 29. For this theme in late Antiquity see also Cooper (1992), especially 152–7.

44 MGH *Constitutiones* i, 589 (see below, p. 249); cf. Takayama (1989) and (1993), 98–101, 115–25.

have been begun at the end of Roger's reign), and in 1158 with Byzantium, an agreement which secured peace with the eastern empire for more than a quarter of a century, until the Sicilians themselves chose to initiate hostilities once more with William II's attack on the empire in 1185. The external threat had thus been greatly diminished. Although the German emperor Frederick Barbarossa remained hostile, the peace agreements with the north Italian maritime powers greatly hampered his chances of launching a successful invasion of the kingdom. These diplomatic successes were completely ignored by the writer of the *History*.

The Treaty of Benevento of July 1156, which secured peace with the papacy, was especially notable. This was not merely a fragile and temporary accord, like that made by Roger at Ceprano in 1150, but a comprehensive settlement of almost all the problems at issue between Rome and Palermo, including the king of Sicily's right to the lands in Marsia conquered in the early 1140s and the sending of papal legates into the kingdom. The king's right to allow legates on to the island of Sicily only when he chose, as granted in 1098, was confirmed, but legates were to have free access to the mainland provinces. The king's right of veto, but not of appointment, in episcopal elections was also sanctioned. Similarly, while the 1156 treaty did not deal specifically with the problem of the episcopal structure on Sicily, measures were taken simultaneously and also soon afterwards to regulate this. During the July 1156 negotiations Adrian IV assigned to the archbishop of Palermo the suffragans which had been sought in vain from Eugenius III in 1150, allocating the bishops of Agrigento and Mazzara to his province. By January 1159 the status of Messina as an archbishopric had also been recognised.[45] Only the problem of the two sees created by Anacletus (Lipari and Cefalù) lingered on, until in 1166 Alexander III finally gave formal sanction to their existence, and the prelates who for many years had held the title only of 'elect' could at last receive episcopal consecration.[46]

---

45 *Italia Pontificia* x, 231, no. 27; Starrabba, *I Diplomi della cattedrale di Messina*, 20–3, nos. 14–15.

46 *Italia Pontificia* x, 340–1, no. 26. Bishop Boso of Cefalù had been consecrated by December 1166; *Documenti inediti*, 93–4, no. 40; White (1938), 97, 196. One consequence of the anomalous status of Cefalù for so many years was the burial of King Roger in Palermo cathedral, even though he had founded Cefalù to be his mausoleum. The canons of Cefalù made an impassioned (but unsuccessful) plea for the return of his body *c*. 1169;

The real and immediate importance of the Treaty of Benevento was, however, in the change which it created in Siculo–papal relations. Though these had not been uniformly bad between 1139 and 1156, periods of *détente* such as the pontificate of Lucius II (1144–5) and the middle part of Eugenius III's pontificate (1148–51) had alternated with periods of considerable tension and even, as in the first eighteen months of Adrian's pontificate, outright hostility. But the treaty and the concessions made in its immediate aftermath with regard to the Sicilian church structure solved nearly all the contentious issues between king and pope. Whereas before 1156 there was a strong party in the Curia hostile to the kingdom of Sicily, thereafter German chroniclers perceived there to be a strong and growing 'Sicilian party' in its ranks.[47] The disputed papal election of 1159 and the support given by Frederick Barbarossa to the pro-imperial minority candidate Octavian (Victor IV) completed the *rapprochement* between Sicily and Alexander III, the pope recognised by all of Christendom outside the German empire. Indeed, the king of Sicily emerged as Alexander's most important temporal supporter. Royal ships carried him from Terracina to Genoa in 1161. In the autumn of 1165 Alexander left France by sea and travelled to Sicily, and then in November Sicilian ships escorted him onwards from Messina to Rome. Two years later, during the minority of William II, Barbarossa advanced on Rome with a powerful army. The Sicilian government sent two ships to rescue Alexander, who then retreated to Benevento, which (as we said above) was papal property but actually within the kingdom of Sicily, and remained in exile there from August 1167 until February 1171 when he was finally able to return to Rome. Almost as important was the monetary support of the Sicilian kings, for Alexander's inability to control the papal lands around Rome effectively had had disastrous consequences for his finances. The treaty of 1156 had specified that not only should William I continue the annual payment to the papacy made by his predecessors (first promised by Guiscard back in 1059), but also that he should add an extra payment for the territory in Marsia which Roger had annexed in the 1140s. In addition William made a very substantial further donation of 60,000 *tari* on his death-bed

---

Documenti inediti, 106–9, no. 46. Cf. Deér (1959), 1–14, for an important discussion.

47 Robinson (1990), 388–9, 470–3. One example: Gerhoh of Reichersberg, *De Investigatione Antichristi*, MGH *Libelli de Lite* iii, 361–2.

in May 1166, and the two ships which the minority government sent to rescue Alexander in the summer of 1167 contained a large sum of money to assist him. The gratitude felt at the Curia towards the Sicilian king was made clear in Boso's official biography of Alexander in the *Liber Pontificalis*, which recorded William I as 'the faithful and devoted son of the Roman Church'.[48]

Yet of all this 'Falcandus' says nothing. The growing significance of relations with the papacy can only be inferred in his narrative from the presence of members of the college of cardinals at the Sicilian court, notably John of Naples, a native of the kingdom of whom 'Falcandus' had no very high opinion. By contrast Romuald's account devotes close attention to papal affairs, which is indeed to be expected if the archbishop himself was the author of this part of his chronicle (as we believe he was), given the important role which he played in Sicilian diplomacy in the 1170s (which will be discussed below). But the attention of the *History* is devoted exclusively to events inside the kingdom, and very largely to those in Sicily itself and to a lesser extent Calabria.

This is very apparent from the author's account of the renewed series of revolts against William I in 1160–2, with his vivid and detailed discussion of the murder of Maio by Matthew Bonellus and the rising by the prisoners in the royal dungeons which almost led to the king's death in March 1161. Brief as Romuald's narrative of these events is, it provides both corroboration of the *History*'s account of what happened in Palermo (though stressing the role of the archbishop himself) and also something of a corrective by laying rather more emphasis on the troubles which were simultaneously occurring on the mainland. It is Romuald, not 'Falcandus', who gives a list of the mainland counts who had banded together against Maio. It is notable that these included not merely members of families whose titles went back before the creation of the kingdom in 1130 (such as the rebels of 1155), but also some like Roger of Avellino and Roger of Tricarico who owed their dignities to King Roger – though both they and some of the others came from families long prominent in the south. Indeed two of those Romuald named, Bohemond II of Manopello and the queen's relative Gilbert of Gravina, had only very recently been granted their counties by William. However, while both opposed Maio, neither actually

---

48 Duchesne, *Liber Pontificalis*, ii, 414.

rebelled; they remained entirely loyal to the king after Maio's murder, and Gilbert was indeed to be the Master Captain of Apulia and Terra di Lavoro, effectively the viceroy on the mainland during William I's later years.[49] The *History* undoubtedly traduces Maio, but the concentration of power in the hands of one all-powerful minister and his family was a major factor in destabilising the kingdom, as it was to be once again in 1167–8 when Stephen of Perche was chancellor.

None the less, it must be stressed that this was not the only reason why the government of William I took strong measures against the disloyal and reacted very harshly to the rebellions of 1160–2. There was still a significant external threat. Frederick Barbarossa's continued determination to attack the kingdom was made clear by his treaties with Pisa and Genoa in April and June 1162, promising those cities extensive rewards in return for naval aid once Sicily had been conquered.[50] Even if the participation of the Genoese in such schemes may have been reluctant, given their growing trade with the *regno* and their long-standing rivalry with the Pisans, these agreements largely nullified earlier Sicilian diplomacy, and it was not surprising that, once the campaign against the mainland rebels in 1162 was concluded, frontier fortresses like the abbey of Montecassino were strongly garrisoned.[51] In the autumn of 1163 Alexander III wrote to his ally King Louis VII of France, asking him to warn the king of Sicily that

> since his enemies are preparing themselves and devoting their whole purpose towards entering his lands and wearing him out with their continual harassment, he should in consequence make himself and his lands ready, and take careful measures to prevent the plots and strategems of his enemies from doing him any injury.[52]

In the circumstances such advice was probably superfluous.

Nor was this threat lessened thereafter, even though the combined

---

49 Jamison (1913), 289. For the detailed evidence for this paragraph, Loud (1998).
50 MGH *Constitutiones* i, 282–7, nos. 205, 211. Cf. Belgrano, *Annales Genovesi*, i, 64–5. Summaries and comment, Abulafia (1977), 123–31; Epstein (1996), 76–7.
51 *Annales Ceccanenses*, ad ann. 1162; *Annales Casinenses*, ad ann. 1162; MGH SS xix, 285, 312.
52 MPL cc, 269, ep. 211.

INTRODUCTION

Genoese and Pisan fleet which Barbarossa had ordered to be prepared by May Day 1164 for service against Sicily never actually sailed.[53] An imperial army under Archbishop Christian of Mainz raided deep into the papal territories around Rome in 1165, and a Sicilian army under Richard de Say was dispatched there to aid the papal forces. King William's death in 1166 was followed by renewed pressure on the frontier of the principality of Capua by two of the exiles, Andrew of Rupecanina and Richard of Fondi.[54] According to John Cinnamus, at about the same time a brother of William I (unnamed in his account, but clearly King Roger's illegitimate son Simon) asked Manuel Comnenus for Byzantine assistance to make himself king in his nephew's place. The emperor, however, refused, not wishing to breach the peace which had been made in 1158. Indeed, according to Romuald he went further, and offered his only daughter in marriage to the young king. It is not clear how serious this proposal was, but undoubtedly the 1158 peace treaty had proved its worth.[55] Barbarossa's capture of Rome in July 1167 marked the culmination of the external danger, but after his retreat, with his army devastated by an epidemic (probably amoebic dysentery), the threat to the *regno* receded. None the less, it did not entirely disappear, and as late as 1176 an imperial army was active in Lazio, and Sicilian troops were sent to oppose it.[56] Only with the truce concluded at the Venice peace conference in 1177 (of which Romuald of Salerno provides the most detailed account) was the kingdom of Sicily entirely secure.

There were thus good reasons why the government of William I cracked down hard on internal dissent and disloyalty. These were not necessarily the product of any tyrannous inclinations on the part of the ruler, or even of Maio, but were the result of the difficult situation which the king had inherited in 1154 and the continuing conflict with the powerful German Empire. Yet the atmosphere of suspicion, paranoia and factional dispute at the royal court which the *History* so

---

53 Lupo Gentile, *Annales Pisani*, 30–1.

54 *Annales Ceccanenses*, ad ann. 1165–6; MGH SS xix, 285.

55 Brand, *Deeds of John and Manuel Comnenus*, 134. The marriage proposal was linked with Manuel's approach to the pope to secure recognition as the one and only emperor in Christendom, disregarding the claims of Frederick Barbarossa; see Parker (1956). But whether this proposal was more than very speculative appears doubtful.

56 *Annales Ceccanenses*; *Annales Casinenses*; MGH SS xix, 286, 312.

vividly evokes cannot be entirely discounted. Among the most important evidence for this is another letter written by Alexander III to his ally Louis VII of France, in February 1165, requesting him to make representations to the king of Sicily on behalf of an exiled nobleman called Florius of Camerota (whom other sources show to have been a royal justiciar in the principalities of Salerno and Capua from 1150 onwards). The terms of this letter are instructive:

> He [Florius] has posed this defence – and he has often been pointed out to us as a religious and honest person – that some people of his land have prepared plots against him before the king and have suggested that he was committing the sin of treason. We sent a letter to our venerable brother the Archbishop of Capua, whom we knew to be, even more than others, loyal and devoted to the king, ordering him to warn the king about this and to render him more cautious. But since the archbishop had already made this plain for himself on behalf of Florius, [who is] his nephew, the king did not believe what he said on our behalf, but rather treated him [Florius] as one of the men whom he held suspect: [and] he forced him to leave his land and travel to the Jerusalem region.

Significantly the pope went on to ask Louis not only to approach King William but also, in case that plea was not successful, to recommend Florius to the support and protection of the emperor at Constantinople.[57] One suspects that the pope's estimate of William's character was a realistic one, and Romuald's comments about Queen Margaret's reversal of her husband's policy towards the aristocracy after his death are also suggestive. None the less, one should note that the soubriquet 'the Bad' which has traditionally been attached to William I was not a contemporary one; indeed it seems to date only from the later fourteenth century.[58]

The second half of the *History*, dealing with the first two and a half years of the minority of William II, is more difficult to assess critically than the description of the reign of William I, because we are so dependent on 'Falcandus' for knowledge of the factional disputes which split the court, and it is less easy to point to obvious omissions and distortions in his account. The factual details are once again largely supported by charter evidence and Romuald's chronicle, though the

57 MPL cc, 332–3, ep. 303.
58 Enzensberger (1980), 394–6.

archbishop (or his ghost-writer) tactfully omitted his own involvement in the manoeuvring at court in the summer of 1166. The queen's invitation to her cousin Stephen of Perche was precisely to secure the services of an outsider who would be independent of the interest groups at the court, even if, perhaps inevitably, such independence did not last. What is perhaps more surprising, and not explained by our sources, is why Stephen himself was the agent chosen. He was almost certainly still a young man, born at the earliest in 1137/8 and quite probably later.[59] He was elected as Archbishop of Palermo a few months after his arrival in Sicily – the *History* telescopes the chronology here – but not consecrated, which is almost certainly explained by his not yet having reached the canonical age of 30. The *History* implies that he was the queen's second choice from among her French relatives as an adviser; it is probable that the other man named, Robert of Neubourg, was rather older and more experienced.[60]

Yet there were other reasons for the problems of the years 1166–8 besides any inexperience of Stephen (of whom the *History* has for the most part a good opinion) or the dislike which the *History* ascribes to the arrogant and greedy conduct of his French followers. The greatly increased role of the senior Latin clergy provided a new element among the contending parties at court; by contrast they had played little or no role in government under King Roger, or indeed during Maio's predominance. But perhaps the key to the tensions comes in Romuald's comment that Queen Margaret 'restored their lands to those freed ... recalled to the kingdom the counts and barons who had been exiled and restored lands which had been confiscated to them'.[61] For this brief summary obscures how difficult and prolonged a process this was. Despite the creation of eight new counts in the summer of 1166, by no means all the exiles were immediately restored. Indeed while in some cases, such as those of the Counts of Loreto and Marsico, the new creation was simply the restoration of the son of a former count, and Richard of Mandra's appointment to Molise filled a county which had been vacant through the extinction (through natural causes) of the former holders, other promotions were at the expense of families who had lost out during William I's reign.

---

59 Thompson (1995), 22. He may well have been named after King Stephen of England, who was then in control of Normandy.

60 See note 169 to the *History*, p. 159 below.

61 See below, p. 239.

Thus while the creation of Richard de Say as Count of Fondi rewarded one of the most loyal and active agents of the old king, it was at the expense of the son of the former count who had died in exile.[62] If the exiled Counts of Acerra and Avellino recovered their lands and positions immediately, others did not, and in some cases could not without dispossessing a new holder. Hence it was only with the exile of Stephen of Perche's ally Gilbert of Gravina and his son Bertram of Andria in 1168 that some of those exiled under William I could be fully restored – with Richard de Say's transfer to Gravina, Richard of Aquila's restoration to Fondi, Roger fitz Richard of Alba's transfer to Andria and the reversion of the county of Alba to the son of the previous holder.[63] Similarly the first evidence for the restoration of Richard of Carinola to his father's two counties was in June 1168; we can be fairly certain that it did not follow immediately after William I's death, for the *History* did not name him as one of the new counts of 1166.[64] And was the transfer of the queen's brother Henry from the county of Montescaglioso to that of the Principate in 1168 due to a desire to recompense the former Count of Montescaglioso, Godfrey, blinded in 1156 but still alive, and perhaps more to the point to endow his nephew (and the king's cousin) Tancred, found in our sources as Count of Lecce from the autumn of 1169 and heir to Godfrey's family lands in that region?[65] The most important of the exiles, Robert of Loritello, was only recalled and restored to his position in March 1169, almost a year after Stephen of Perche's flight.[66] In that same year Roger of Rupecanina, brother of Andrew, was restored to the county of Alife, though that was only a part of the extensive lordship which his uncle Rainulf of Caiazzo had held before 1139.[67] The restoration of the exiles and the resolution of

62 Cuozzo (1984), 283.
63 Cuozzo (1981), 143; Cuozzo (1984), 283, 337. The dating of the restoration of Fondi to Richard II of Aquila in 1168 is hypothetical, and might have been even later. The first charter surviving from him as count is only from July 1173; Archivio secreto Vaticano, Archivio S. Angelo, Arm. I. xviii. 118 (the donation to the papacy of a site for building a church and hospice).
64 Archivio secreto Vaticano, Archivio Boncompagni Ludovisi, Prot. 270, no. 9, a donation of the count to the monastery of St Mary of Elci.
65 *Cat. Bar.* 28, art. 155; Garufi (1912), 339–40; Reisinger (1992), 24–7.
66 *Annales Ceccanenses*, ad ann. 1169; MGH SS xix, 286.
67 Cuozzo (1984), 266, 281.

conflicting claims among the aristocracy therefore took some three years after the death of William I.

The enlarged council of ten *familiares* established after Stephen of Perche's flight comprised five senior ecclesiastics, three counts and two court officials, one of whom was a converted Muslim. It was clearly an attempt to strike a balance between the different interest groups at court. However, a governing group of this size may well have proved impracticable, and from the autumn of 1170 the number of *familiares* (in a Sicilian context to be translated as 'chief ministers', not simply courtiers or intimates) was back down to three, as it had been in William I's later years. It was to remain at only three or four throughout William II's reign.[68] After 1168 the kingdom remained internally peaceful, and one of the former exiles, Tancred of Lecce, became a key figure in the governing regime as one of the two Master Justiciars on the mainland from 1176. Yet we cannot assume that the tensions at court so graphically described by 'Falcandus' disappeared. A letter of Peter of Blois (formerly one of Stephen's entourage), which must be dated to the summer of 1171, suggested that the king, 'a most ill-advised youth', was taking 'treacherous counsel' rather than the wise advice of Archbishop Romuald of Salerno and Count Roger of Avellino. Was this a covert jibe at Peter's former friend Archbishop Walter of Palermo, whose dominance at court was mentioned right at the end of the *History*?[69] A later chronicler recorded how the court was divided between its 'two columns', Walter and the vice-chancellor Matthew, who 'hated each other and, while they appeared friendly in public, they freely criticised each other (through envy) in private'. It was their rivalry, he claimed, which led to the disputed succession after the king's death, with Matthew supporting the king's cousin Tancred and Walter a partisan of the claims of Constance and Henry VI.[70] All this is reminiscent of the situation as described by the *History*. Were we to possess a detailed account of events at court after 1169, it is quite possible that it would reveal a picture of internecine rivalry

---

68 Takayama (1989) and (1993), 119–23.

69 MPL ccvii, 27–32, ep. 10, col. 29. The letter can be dated, since it refers to the vacancy in the church of Agrigento (after the death of Bishop Gentile, last attested in March 1171, and before the election of Bartholomew, in office in December of that year).

70 *Ryccardi de Sancto Germano Chronica*, 5–6.

undoubtedly less overtly violent but not necessarily less bitter than that shown by 'Falcandus'.

In hindsight the reign of William II came to be seen as an age of peace and prosperity. William himself was portrayed as 'the flower of kings, the life and strength of his people ... a paragon upholding the ideals of law and justice; everyone in his kingdom was content with his lot, and everywhere was safe'.[71] But it must be stressed that these comments were written half a century after the king's death. The war of succession in the 1190s, and the problems of Frederick II's long minority and then absence in Germany between 1212 and 1220, had been so traumatic that the period before 1189 seemed therefore a golden era when all was well (certainly by comparison with what came after). The myth of William 'the Good' indeed began early, but we should be wary of allowing such hindsight to colour our own assessment too strongly.[72]

The authorship of the *History*

We know neither when the *History* was written nor who wrote it. The one thing which is certain is that the author was not called Hugo Falcandus. The surviving medieval manuscripts give no authority for this name, which occurs for the first time in the earliest printed edition, produced by Gervaise of Tournai and published in Paris in 1550. Since the editor wrote that the binding of the manuscript which he used for this edition was perished and rotten – and presumably therefore the flyleaves also – the suggestion by Evelyn Jamison that the name Hugo Falcandus resulted from the misreading of a damaged inscription or title seems inherently plausible.[73] Furthermore, no such person can be found in the considerable number of surviving Sicilian charters from the later twelfth century.

The *History* itself gives many clues, if not to the exact identity of the author (to whom we shall refer from now on as Pseudo-Hugo), then at least to his background and attainments. He was clearly a man of education, steeped in the Latin classics, and especially the works of Sallust, and one of the finest Latin stylists of the twelfth century, just

---

71 *Ibid.*, 4. Cf. Gaudenzi, *Chronicon Ferraria*, 31–2.
72 Enzensberger (1980), 390–2; Abulafia (1979); Loud (1998).
73 Jamison (1957), 194–7.

as much a classically educated and orientated writer as, for example, John of Salisbury. His classical models – and, it has been argued, at least one other more exotic source – influenced parts of his exposition, as in his portrayal of Maio, and some of the great set pieces of his narrative, particularly in their use of direct speech, reflect this classical tradition. But his intimate knowledge of the personnel and accurate rendition of the offices of the court, his use of technical terms such as *familiaris*, *duana* and *defetarii*, and his familiarity with Roman law and interest in legal matters, strongly suggest that he himself belonged to the royal court. (Some seven different trials are discussed in the *History*, and on two occasions actual royal edicts are quoted.)[74] The very partisan nature of the account and the personal (and often unpleasant) details included also suggest an insider's view. Our author was a man who was both well informed – the details about the administration and officials are almost invariably confirmed by the charter evidence – and probably involved in the events described. He was not necessarily one of the principal actors in the story which he told, but he was certainly a contemporary, and probably an eyewitness. The earliest surviving manuscript, Cod. Vat. Lat. 10690 (following the conventions of previous scholars, MS. V), dates from the early thirteenth century, and the carelessness and omissions of that MS., and the survival of a different recension in MSS A and B, suggest one or more stages between MS. V and the archetype, and hence a considerable lapse of time. (See below, 'The manuscripts of the *History*', for details of the MS. tradition.) Thus the *History* was written relatively soon after the events described, though just how long after has been much debated.

The text itself must be our principal evidence, even though links with, and dependence upon, other works either produced by contemporary Sicilian writers or current in court circles have been suggested. Most of these alleged connections will be discussed later. However, there is one text which *must* be considered alongside the *History*, because it may well have been by the same author: the *Letter to Peter*. This tract does not just show stylistic similarities, use of the rhymed prose of the *cursus*, a similar vocabulary and an equal breadth of knowledge

74 *Ibid.*, 244–5. The two specific references to royal laws (of King Roger) are important evidence against the theory of Ménager (1969), that the two manuscripts which purport to contain King Roger's assizes represent early thirteenth-century clerical compilations, rather than actual legislation of the 1140s.

of the Latin classics as the *History*. It also shows some of the same viewpoints. Thus, for example, in the *History* we read that 'the people of Apulia are utterly disloyal, and vainly hope to win their independence (an independence which once achieved, they are quite unable to maintain, since they are neither any good at warfare nor orderly in peace time)'. The *Letter* echoes this: 'For I do not think that any hope or reliance ought to be placed in the Apulians, who constantly plot revolution because of the pleasure [that] they take in novelty'.[75]

Even more tellingly, all four surviving MSS. of the *History* also contain the *Letter*. So too did the now lost MS. which was used for the first printed edition of 1550. Furthermore, the *History* and the *Letter* were in these MSS. treated as part of one and the same work. This is made clear from the internal divisions of the two older manuscripts (V and A) and the first edition, in which the *Letter* formed one of the six sections of the complete combined text. The chapter headings dividing the *History* up into fifty-five decidedly unequal sections were later (thirteenth-century) additions, written as marginal notes to provide a guide to the contents, and then adopted as paragraph headings by the scribe of the fourteenth-century MS. C, a usage followed in the only modern edition, that of G. B. Siragusa of 1897. There is, however, one significant contrast between the two different recensions of our author's work: in one (MSS. V and C, and the 1550 edition) the *Letter* precedes the *History*; in the other (MS. A and its direct copy MS. B) this order is reversed and the *History* precedes the *Letter*, which of course it ought to chronologically, since the *History* deals with the years 1154–69 and the *Letter* must be dated to the early months of 1190.

Previous commentators have sought both to identify the geographical origin of the author and to point to an actual person who may have written the *History*. Was he, despite the view expressed in the preface that Sicily was a terrifying place which was the home of unparalled deeds of wickedness, actually a native Sicilian? Or could he have been from one of the mainland provinces of the *regno*, albeit long resident at the royal court, and hence perhaps the combination of detailed knowledge but apparent disapproval of the inhabitants of the island? Or might he have been one of the foreigners who were attracted to the Sicilian court? One may point to Gentile of Agrigento (a Hungarian), Richard of Syracuse (an Englishman) and Stephen of Perche

---

[75] See below, pp. 66, 254.

(a Frenchman) as obvious examples of such immigrants. Might he have been one of the persons important enought to be mentioned in the narrative, referring to himself in the third person to conceal his own identity, or was he more probably a minor player at the court, not himself directly involved in the political disputes, but a close and horrified observer? Such questions might seem rhetorical, but all of them have been posed by latter-day students of the *History* of 'Hugo Falcandus'.

Two principal candidates have been suggested as the author. The first, Robert of S. Giovanni, was a royal notary, active from 1155 onwards and possibly as early as 1147, and also a canon of the palace chapel at Palermo.[76] He was a seemingly a protégé of King Roger's granddaughter, Adelicia of Adernò (who is mentioned in the *History*), and he held churches and property at Collesano and Polizzi from the Bishop of Cefalù, 'in whose disputes and service', as we are told in a charter of Bishop Boso of 1167, he had 'often laboured'.[77] Robert was himself referred to in the *History*, as a royal envoy to Venice, a candidate for the chancellor's position after the imprisonment of Asclettin in 1156, and one of those loyal to Stephen of Perche. He was one of the few people at the court of whom the *History* had a good opinion, as 'a man of high reputation and proven faithfulness'. But, the author suggested, because of this he had incurred the hatred of the wicked Maio, who had covertly attempted to cause his death by having him sent to sea on an unseaworthy ship. (This last detail, it should be noted, was a cliché derived from classical literature.)[78]

Certainly Robert's background at the royal court and what is known of his career would fit in with what we might surmise of the author of the *History*. It would undoubtedly explain his dislike of Maio and his relatively favourable opinion of Stephen of Perche. That the *History*

---

76 Garufi (1942), 121–2, identified nine royal charters between 1147 and 1169 which he alleged were all written by him, but as Jamison (1957), 212–13, pointed out, there are clear indications that there was more than one royal notary of the same name. However, a charter of 1155 to Montecassino (*Guillelmi I Diplomata*, 16–19, no. 6 = Gattula, *Accessiones*, 258), of which the original survives, was in the same hand as a private charter of Robert of S. Giovanni of 1182, *Documenti inediti*, 173–4, no. 72 (= Garufi (1942), 126–7, no. 3), and thus clearly identifies him as the notary who wrote it.

77 *Documenti inediti*, 100–1, no. 43 (= Garufi (1942), 125–6, no. 2).

78 E.g. Suetonius, *Nero* 34; Tacitus, *Annals* 14.3.6.

suggests that the latter would have done better to have heeded Robert's advice rather than that of his French followers does not contradict this, for the author clearly had no great liking for these followers, and while sympathetic to Stephen, was not blindly so. Nor can the fact that Robert is referred to in the third person, and in flattering terms, be assumed to disqualify him as a possible author. If the work was written in William II's lifetime, while many of the principals of whom the writer disapproved were still alive, this might have been a wise precaution. Furthermore, there is a very probable analogous example from the twelfth century of an anonymous author describing himself in the third person, in the contemporary biography of King Stephen of England. The authorship of this work (another highly 'classical' composition) has been ascribed with some certainty to Robert, Bishop of Bath 1136–66, whose capture by the Empress Matilda's partisans in 1138, and subsequent justification to the king for the measures he took to secure his release, was there described without any personal attribution.[79]

However, there are two important arguments against Robert's authorship of the *History*. First, was it very likely that a person who was himself a royal notary would inveigh against 'the enormous rapacity of the notaries' and implicitly praise Stephen of Perche for trying to set limits to their fees? Secondly, and much more seriously, Robert of S. Giovanni was expressly mentioned as being dead in May 1185, when Bishop Guido of Cefalù granted his son Rainald life tenure of a church in the territory of Polizzi.[80] He cannot therefore have been the author of the *Letter to Peter*, which can only have been written after the death of William II in November 1189, and dates almost certainly from the early spring of 1190. While it cannot be absolutely certain that the two works were written by the same person, the combination of stylistic similarities and the manuscript evidence makes this extremely probable. If the *History* and the *Letter* were by the same author, then this automatically disqualifies Robert of S. Giovanni as a candidate.

The other possible author who has been suggested is an extremely interesting figure. Eugenius, son of the Emir John, was a Greek who came from a family of hereditary royal officials, and is known to have

---

79 *Gesta Stephani*, ed. K. R. Potter and R. H. C. Davis (Oxford 1976), xviii–xl, 58–65.

80 *Documenti inediti*, 202–4, no. 83 (= Garufi (1942), 127–8, no. 4).

been both a poet (in Greek) and the translator into Latin of the *Optics* of Claudius Ptolemy, from Arabic, and of the *Prophecy of the Erythraean Sibyl*, from Greek. The contemporary translator of Ptolemy's *Almagest*, whose identity is unknown but who was working in Sicily between 1158 and 1160, acknowledged his assistance, and described him as 'a man as fully expert in Greek as in Arabic, and with a knowledge also of Latin', and a contemporary poet hailed him as 'Clio's famous offspring', which suggests he had some repute as a historian.[81] But Eugenius was also an important royal official. He was one of the two masters of the *Duana Baronum*, the royal financial office for the mainland provinces, based at Salerno, from 1174 until the death of William II. In 1190 King Tancred recalled him to Palermo, promoted him to the rank of emir, which his father and grandfather had held before him, and (probably) placed him in overall charge of the royal finances.[82] He was subsequently one of those arrested by Henry VI after his coronation as King of Sicily at Christmas 1194 and deported to Germany. But unlike the emperor's other victims, most of whom never returned from their imprisonment north of the Alps (and, indeed, several of whom were later mutilated), Eugenius's spell in confinement was relatively brief, no doubt because his administrative expertise was far too valuable to be dispensed with. By July 1196 he was back in the *regno*, acting as the agent in the Terra di Bari of the imperial chancellor, Bishop Conrad of Hildesheim, who had been left in charge of the kingdom's administration by the emperor.[83] Subsequently, from the summer of 1198 until September 1202, there are a number of references to a Eugenius as Master Chamberlain of Apulia and Terra di Lavoro, although none of them expressly identifies him as the son of the Emir John. However, since this office fulfilled precisely the function which the Emir Eugenius had under William II – that of the principal royal financial officer on the mainland – it is probable that this was still the same man, although as Léon-Robert Ménager

---

81 Haskins (1927b), 191–3; Jamison (1957), 3–32, especially 3–4 and 234, 356.
82 Jamison (1957), 95–7, 333–45 (which lists the documentary evidence). For the *Duana Baronum*, see Takayama (1985) 133–43 and (1993), 145–57, whose discussion of the financial administration supersedes that of Jamison (1957), 49–53, 69–74. For the emirate, a badge of rank rather than an office, see Ménager (1960), especially 86–9.
83 Jamison (1957), 148–52, 349–51.

(who contested the identification) pointed out, he must by then have been very elderly by contemporary standards.[84]

The claims of Eugenius to be the author of both the *History* and the *Letter to Peter* were advanced by Evelyn Jamison in 1957, in a magisterial volume which is still indispensable both to a study of the text and to the closing days of the Norman kingdom. It was her contention that the composition of these two works followed the order established by Recension I of the manuscripts; namely that the *Letter* was the earlier of the two to be written, in the spring of 1190 – she suggested in February. She dated the composition of the *History* to some years later, for she proposed that Eugenius had written it while a prisoner in Germany, from July 1195 until perhaps January 1196 (assuming, as she did, that Eugenius returned to Italy in the suite of the chancellor Conrad at the very beginning of that year). The unhappy circumstances in which it was written would explain, she thought, the marked air of pessimism in the *History*, and the stress on the capricious operations of the Wheel of Fortune, an image also associated with the downfall of King Tancred's family in the illustrations in the unique surviving manuscript of the contemporary poem on Henry VI's conquest by Peter of Eboli, and in another sycophantic contemporary poem in praise of Henry VI by Godfrey of Viterbo.[85]

The arguments advanced for Eugenius as the author of the *History* are complex and can only be summarised here. They rest fundamentally on four grounds. First, there was his background in the royal administration. In default of any other evidence this would indicate his fluency in Latin as well as his native Greek, especially since much of his career was spent on the mainland, in the provinces of Apulia and Terra di Lavoro, where Latin was universally employed as the language of record. But, more to the point, his family background and career would undoubtedly have furnished him with the knowledge of law and the institutions of government displayed by the author of the *History*. During most of the period described by that work, 1154–69, Eugenius must have been a junior member of the royal administration; he could not have been appointed as Master of the *Duana Baronum*, in or a little before 1174, without considerable prior experience –

---

[84] *Ibid.*, 161–71, 351–6; Ménager (1960), 76–7.

[85] Jamison (1957), 125–7, 237–40 and plate IV; Siragusa, *Liber ad Honorem Augusti di Pietro da Eboli*, 150; *Gotifredi Viterbiensis Gesta Henrici VI*, MGH SS xxii, 337.

which one would expect anyway, since both his father and grandfather had been royal officials. He is likely, therefore, to have been an eyewitness to the events described, as the author was, and must have known those mentioned, in some cases very well indeed. There are two very good examples of this in Walter of Moac (see below, p. 195), who was Eugenius's apparently senior colleague in the *Duana Baronum* in 1178–9, and Darius the Usher, whom the *History* reported as being rumoured to be responsible for the tragic death of William I's eldest son in 1161 (see below, p. 113), who succeeded Eugenius at the head of the *Duana Baronum* in 1190, and to whom the emir sent instructions in that year concerning problems to do with royal revenues from the city of Salerno.[86]

Second, Eugenius was a partisan of Tancred, who after William II's death was the candidate for the throne supported by the court officials led by the vice-chancellor Matthew. His importance among these supporters was shown by his later arrest and imprisonment in Germany, and by the fact that he was depicted among the emperor's prisoners in one of the illustrations to Peter of Eboli's poem.[87] That he might have been the author of the *Letter*, a propaganda tract urging the Sicilians to resist the impending German invasion in support of the claims to the throne of Henry VI and Constance, is therefore perfectly plausible.

Third, and the most difficult of the arguments to evaluate, are the links which have been suggested between the *History* and the *Letter* and the other works attributed to Eugenius or associated with him. Jamison suggested that the interest in natural history and phenomena shown in the *Letter* was also displayed in the poetry of Eugenius and the translations of Claudius Ptolemy, the one from his own pen and the other to which he provided assistance. She also identified marked similarities in tone and content between the *History* and verses written by Eugenius while a prisoner, and also resemblances between his poetry and the *Letter*. Finally she suggested that the account of Maio's alleged conspiracy against William I in the *History* was based on the oriental folk-tale of 'Stephanites and Ichnelates', and that the general concepts of good and bad government enunciated in the collection of fables to which this story belonged were reflected in the two Latin

---

[86] Jamison (1957), 323–32, 343–5.

[87] Jamison (1957), 123 and plates V–VI; Siragusa, *Liber ad Honorem Augusti di Pietro da Eboli*, 143.

works under discussion. The translation of 'Stephanites and Ichnelates' from Arabic into Greek may not have been directly attributable to Eugenius, but it was certainly known to him, for an inscription in the translation names him as possessing a copy.[88]

Finally, it may be argued that the fall of the independent Sicilian kingdom to its German enemies in 1194 and the emir's subsequent imprisonment provides a plausible context for the work, and explains its generally pessimistic and unfavourable tone.

But although this is a most interesting and suggestive thesis, these arguments are far from conclusive, and it must be said that both the reviewers of Jamison's book when it was first published, and subsequent commentators, have greeted her identification of Eugenius as the author with universal scepticism.[89] One must accept that his administrative career and support of Tancred would make him a feasible candidate. But the alleged links with Eugenius's known works cannot be considered as more than, at most, possible. There are some resemblances, but also considerable divergences, between the account of Maio in the *History* and the 'Stephanites and Ichnelates' fable. Furthermore, Eugenius may have had little or no part in the Greek edition of that story, for the inscription suggests that he simply gave someone a copy of that work.[90] Nor, indeed, does the reference in the *Letter* to 'the arrogance of the Greeks', albeit presumably meaning the Byzantine Empire, seem entirely plausible for an author who was, supposedly, a Greek himself.

There are, moreover, three other, very strong, arguments against the authorship of Eugenius. These relate to the context in which the *History* was allegedly written, the culture of the author, and the date of composition in so far as this may be deduced from the internal evidence of the text. (Despite some contradictory indications, the dating of the *Letter* to the spring of 1190 is accepted.)[91]

---

88 Jamison (1957), 220–77, *passim*, especially 251–67 for the folk-tale.
89 E.g. the reviews by L. T. White, *American Historical Review* lxiii (1957–8), 645–7 and M.-T. Alverny, *Cahiers de Civilisation Médiévale* i (1958), 381–3. Cf. Fuiano (1960), 130–7; Ménager (1960), 78; Hoffmann (1967), 140–2; Capitani (1977), 20.
90 Berschin (1988), 234–5.
91 The author has only recently heard of the death of the King of Sicily (William II died on 18 November 1189), and wonders whether the Sicilians will choose a king for themselves or opt for the 'yoke of slavery',

One must ask whether the relatively brief period in which, according to Jamison's reconstruction, Eugenius was imprisoned at the castle of Trifels was sufficient for the composition of the *History*, or indeed whether he would have had either access to the books which she suggested he may have read then, or time both to read them *and* write the *History*, even though, since he was able to write poetry during his imprisonment, its conditions are unlikely to have been too arduous. Nor can the argument that the stress in the *History* on the workings of Fortune and her wheel was a product specifically of the circumstances of 1194–5 be accepted. The author's principal model was Sallust, to whom the workings of Fortune were a crucial intellectual underpinning: 'There can be no question that Fortune is supreme in all human affairs. It is a capricious power, which makes men's actions famous or leaves them in obscurity without regarding their true worth.'[92] Sallust did not himself refer to the Wheel of Fortune, but this image was well known in the Roman world. The first recorded use is by Cicero in 55 BC, although he clearly did not invent the metaphor, and by the early empire it was already becoming a cliché.[93] From the *Consolation of Philosophy* of Boethius, it passed into widespread use in the Middle Ages.[94] In particular it was employed by many of the leading historical writers of the twelfth century, notably Orderic Vitalis, Abbot Suger of St Denis and Otto of Freising, as well as by that archetypal twelfth-century renaissance man, John

---

i.e. submission to Constance and her German husband Henry VI. Tancred of Lecce was elected on 8 December, and crowned on 18 January 1190. The delay before the coronation was due to the wish to secure the agreement of Pope Clement III, and perhaps for the pope to coerce the reluctant Archbishop Walter of Palermo into accepting the new king; Clementi (1967), 59–64. And yet the author writes of 'spring replacing the cold of winter'. Jamison (1957), 83, suggests that this might indicate a date as early as February (1190), though one might feel that February was somewhat early for spring. But though the author fears a German attack, this had not yet occurred, as it did for the first time in May 1190. Hence the *Letter* must have been written before that month.

92 Sallust, *Catiline* 8.1.

93 Cicero, *In Pisonem* 22; Tacitus, *Dialogus de Oratoribus* 23.1, who wrote that he did not want to laugh at the term, even though every speaker trotted it out. The Wheel of Fortune can also be found in Tibullus 1.5.70, Propertius 2,8.8 and Ammianus Marcellinus 26.8.13.

94 *Consolatio* 2.2. 28–31; Patch (1927), 149–77; Capitani (1977), 13–14.

of Salisbury.[95] The image had also been used by two earlier south Italian authors, both writing in the last years of the previous century: William of Apulia in his verse *Deeds of Robert Guiscard*, and Geoffrey Malaterra of Catania's *Deeds of Count Roger [I] of Sicily*.[96] So general was its employment that one can hardly associate it with any particular context – it was part of the intellectual terms of reference of any reasonably well-educated contemporary author.

Furthermore, the general culture displayed by our author, though undoubtedly impressive in terms of its absorption of the classical heritage, was an exclusively Latin one, and one must question how probable it would have been for a Greek like Eugenius, however proficient he may have been at reading and writing Latin, to have absorbed Latin literary culture to this extent. By contrast there is no direct reference to Greek texts whatsoever, whereas there is quotation from or allusion to Latin writers: above all Sallust, but also Lucan and Cicero, at least those parts of his *œuvre* which were known at this period, and perhaps too knowledge of Juvenal, Martianus Capella and Quintilian (especially in the *Letter*). (See below, 'Classical resonances in the *History*', for more detailed discussion.) For all Pseudo-Hugo's polished prose, his classical reading is what one would expect from a well-educated man in western Christendom, although he profited from it more fully and less self-consciously than many others. All the classical authors whom he knew were, for example, also known to John of Salisbury; and all were available in the library of Montecassino during the Norman period.[97] There is, however, no

95 Chibnall, *The Ecclesiastical History of Orderic Vitalis* iv, 14–15, iv, 290–1 ('So the Wheel of Fortune turns each day'), vi, 242–3 ('Fortune is like a turning wheel'), 544–5 (on the capture of King Stephen of England, 1141); Suger, *Vie de Louis VI le Gros*, ed. H. Waquet (Paris 1929), 168 (= Suger, *The Deeds of Louis the Fat*, trans. R. C. Cusimano and J. Moorhead (Washington, DC 1992), 103); Mierow, *Deeds of Frederick Barbarossa*, 219; Millor, Butler and Brooke, *The Letters of John of Salisbury*, i. 49, ep. 31.

96 'The Wheel of Fortune had turned and began to raise up the sons of Tancred', Mathieu, *Guillaume de Pouille, La Geste de Robert Guiscard*, 134 (lib. II, lines 36–7). Cf. *Malaterra* II. 24, III. 9, pp. 37, 61, among other more general examples of Fortune in this work, identified by Capitani (1977), 38–40.

97 Liebeschütz (1950), *passim*; for Montecassino, Bloch (1972); and for knowledge of the classics in southern Italy generally at this period, Cavallo (1975).

sign, certainly in the main text, of the Greek authors whom Henry Aristippus claimed were known in Sicily.[98] And whereas Jamison suggested that the hostile portrait of Maio was derived from an oriental folk-tale, another commentator has pointed rather more plausibly to Cicero's *In Catilinam* and Boethius' *The Consolation of Philosophy*.[99] In addition, there is the reference already quoted to Eugenius as 'a man as fully expert in Greek as in Arabic, and with a knowledge also of Latin'. Yet whoever Pseudo-Hugo was, he was more than a man with 'a knowledge of Latin' – he was one of the great Latin stylists of the twelfth-century renaissance.

Finally there is the question of the date of composition. Direct indications in the text are few. There is a reference to Pope Alexander III, 'who at that time [*tunc*] was head of the Roman Church', suggesting that this was written after his death on 30 August 1181. But even that may be ambiguous. Hartmut Hoffmann has argued with regard to this passage that *tunc* could in medieval Latin sometimes mean 'now' or 'in the very recent past' (like the modern German *jetzt*), as well as its more common classical meaning of 'then'/'at some time in the (more distant) past'.[100] There is, however, one other very interesting passage which has a direct relevance to this question. It comes in Pseudo-Hugo's account of the attempted coup of 1161 during which the king's eldest son Roger met his death, probably through an arrow-wound – though our author cannot resist adding the rumour that the youth was in fact kicked to death by his own father, in a fit of jealous rage because the conspirators had tried to install him as king in his father's place. Pseudo-Hugo saw the death of the young Duke Roger as having occurred 'lest [this island] should ever be short of tyrants', for he claimed that the boy resembled his uncle and namesake, King Roger's eldest son, who had died before his father (in 1148), 'a man of unparalleled humanity and sweetness', whereas William II resembled the character of his father of the same name, who 'put as much effort into enslaving himself to cruelty and stupidity as his brother had in embracing wisdom and humanity' (see below, p. 113). Highly artificial and rhetorical as this passage is, it shows, interestingly in the light of later views of him as 'the Good' and of

---

98 Minio-Paluello, *Phaedo interprete Henrico Aristippo*, 89–90.

99 Fuiano (1960), 148; from Boethius, *Consolatio* 3.5 and Cicero, *In Catilinam* 1.30, 2.1.

100 Hoffmann (1967), 130–2.

his reign as one of good government and peace, that Pseudo-Hugo had no very high opinion of William II. Both this and the phraseology employed suggest therefore that it was written during his lifetime, and indeed, as Hoffmann has argued, quite possibly relatively early in his reign.[101] Had it been composed after his death, with the knowledge of the disasters of civil war, foreign invasion and the downfall of the dynasty which had ensued, surely this opinion would have been different? Later writers lamented William II, rather than criticising him.

This indeed raises a more general reflection. If the *History* was composed in 1195, as Jamison suggested, why is there no reference at any point to events after 1169, apart from, as she argued, the general tone of doom and gloom? Yet even if the work was left incomplete, which is in itself arguable – not least since the histories of Pseudo-Hugo's exemplar Sallust have similarly abrupt endings – it is difficult to think that there would not have been some references made in the light of hindsight; perhaps to William II's premature and childless death, or to Tancred of Lecce as the future king, or perhaps to the unpleasant irony (which would would surely have appealed to Pseudo-Hugo's mordant tendency) that the latter's long-time colleague as mainland governor, Count Roger of Andria, was to become his rival and was to die (probably by violence) as Tancred's prisoner.[102] But there is no trace of such knowledge, and this surely therefore points to a date of composition before the death of William II in November 1189.

We may thus conclude that the identification of the Emir Eugenius as the author of the *History* and the *Letter to Peter* is not only unproven, but very unlikely. Both works were probably by the same person – the manuscript tradition would certainly suggest as much.[103] But who that person was must remain unknown: he was probably a member of the court, but perhaps only a minor functionary, possibly someone whose name is entirely unknown to historical record, or mentioned just in passing in one or two charters. It is, however, more or less certain that the *History* was written during the lifetime of King William II, on which more recent commentators than Miss Jamison are agreed.

---

101 *Ibid.*, 136.
102 Garufi, *Ryccardi de Sancto Germano Chronica*, 10.
103 Fuiano (1960), 109–21, agrees with Jamison as to common authorship, if not as to the identity of that author. Hoffmann (1967), 139–40, is not entirely certain.

Quite when before 1189 it was composed (or perhaps, for reasons which will be explained in a moment, one should say completed), is a good question. Hartmut Hoffmann has suggested that the last part of the work must have been finished very soon after the conclusion of the narrative, in the early 1170s. He argued that the precision of the details given about the events of the royal court's sojourn at Messina in the winter of 1167–8 and the subsequent rising against Stephen of Perche (the only part of the narrative where exact dates are given) suggests a nearly contemporary author, and that the air of pessimism permeating the *History* as a whole makes more sense in the early 1170s than later on, given that William II's reign was generally peaceful.[104]

But Hoffmann takes this argument one step further. He also suggests that it is possible that the first part of the work, the twenty-four chapters (according to the later headings of MS. C) dealing with events up to 1162, may have been written actually during the last years of William I, and that the author recommenced his work some, but not many, years later to describe the minority of William II. This would explain the yawning chronological gap between the two sections, with the omission of the last three and a half years of William I's reign, and Hoffmann suggests also the contrast between the two parts: 'up to 1166 the tragedy of an over-harsh and wicked regime, after 1166 the tragedy of a mild and good one'. However, while this theory cannot be entirely discounted, it too presents potential difficulties. Thus the passage discussed above about William II copying his father's bad qualities would have to be a later interpolation, for it cannot have been written before 1166 about a boy who was only 12 when his father died. And a further argument that Hoffmann adduces for the very early date of this part of the *History* may be problematic. Writing of the destruction of Bari in 1156, Pseudo-Hugo concluded that the city 'now lies transformed into piles of rubble'. Hoffmann criticised Jamison's contention that this was a use of the historic present, and suggested that at the time when Pseudo-Hugo was writing Bari had still not been rebuilt, and indeed it remained unrebuilt until the 1170s.[105] But in fact the repopulation and therefore,

---

104 Hoffmann (1967), 134–5, 138.

105 *Ibid.*, 133–4, 136–8 (quote from p. 138); *contra* Jamison (1957), 236. However, with regard to the Bari passage Hoffmann was returning to an idea suggested long ago by Hartwig (1883), 416–17.

one presumes, the rebuilding of Bari seems to have taken place only a very few years after its destruction on the orders of William I. The religious communities may not have been disturbed at all; people were moving back to the town from 1159 onwards, and its judges were functioning once again in the early to mid-1160s, precisely at the time when, according to Hoffmann, this passage was written.[106] Nor indeed is this phrase the only example of our author dropping into the historic present, seemingly for emphasis. This comment cannot therefore be a sure indication that the first half of the *History* was written almost contemporaneously with the period it describes, and certainly does not suggest a date in the early 1170s. Given the conciliatory policy pursued by Queen Margaret after her husband's death, the rebuilding of Bari must surely have been permitted after 1166, but it seems more probable that it was already well under way, and most unlikely that the town was still in ruins in the early 1170s. Indeed, the recovery of Bari appears to have begun sufficiently early to make it very doubtful that this use of the present tense is a reliable pointer to the passage having been composed while William I was still alive.

Therefore the case for the composition of the *History* in two stages, and its completion in the early 1170s, remains speculative. But we may be sure that it is a genuinely contemporary text, in the sense that it was composed within twenty years of the last event which it mentioned, at a time when many of those whose actions were described so cuttingly were still alive. Given that circumstance, the author may have been wise to remain anonymous, and so he must remain today.

Classical resonances in the *History*

Whoever he was, Pseudo-Hugo remains one of the finest and most compelling writers of the Middle Ages. In terms of medieval historical writing he is unusual in telling us a structured story on a single coherent theme (even if Hoffmann is correct in his supposition that the *History* was composed at two different times). This was something hardly ever attempted in secular Latin historiography from late

---

[106] *Annales Palidenses* ad ann. 1156, MGH SS xvi, 89; *Cod. Dipl. Bar.*, v, 200–2, no. 117 (February 1159); and *ibid.*, 202, no. 118 (December 1160), 209–11, no. 120 (January 1164), 215–16, no. 124 (August 1166), for the judges.

antiquity until the beginning of the twelfth century.[107] Classical Latin texts were of course known to anyone who was literate throughout the Middle Ages. Their influence can be traced in quotations, but access to such quotations was frequently through grammarians' handbooks or *florilegia* (selections of excerpts), and need not indicate any interest in narrative technique or even in content. There seems to be only one actual verbatim quotation from a classical text in the *History* (from Lucan's epic poem, the *Pharsalia*; see below). The influence of classical writing on Pseudo-Hugo was of a very different order. The very idea of writing a historical monograph, and many of the concepts he uses and types of episode he chooses to narrate, are clearly derived from Sallust (Gaius Sallustius Crispus, *c.* 86–35 BC), whose accounts of the *Conspiracy of Catiline* and the *Jugurthan War*, two relatively short monographs dealing with particular aspects of Roman history, provided suitable material for the author of the *History of the Tyrants* – warfare certainly, but warfare fought to a great extent through conspiracy and subterfuge.

The *Conspiracy of Catiline*, Sallust's first work, deals with an attempt by a Roman nobleman to seize power from the lawful consul Cicero in 63 BC. His *Jugurthan War* tells the story of a conflict fought by various Roman commanders against a king of Numidia in north Africa from 112 to 105 BC. While the *Catiline* explains civil strife in terms of moral decline, the *Jugurtha* emphasises the importance of concord in achieving success in war. In addition, Sallust wrote the *Histories*, a continuous narrative of the period from 78 to at least 67 BC, of which only excerpts survive. Sallust rapidly became a paradigm of Latin prose-writing; by the fourth century AD he had become one of the four standard authors on the school syllabus, along with Cicero and the verse writers Terence and Vergil. That syllabus continued into the post-Roman period and beyond. There are admittedly relatively few manuscripts of Sallust surviving from the Carolingian period, but from the eleventh century onwards the previous trickle becomes a flood, and these texts became even more influential. Consequently there is nothing surprising about a twelfth-century writer being imbued with both Sallustian vocabulary and some of the ideas

---

107 Nithard and (to some extent) Widukind of Korvey might be seen as exceptions. From *c.* 1100 there were various historians of particular crusades, from southern Italy Geoffrey Malaterra, and especially Galbert of Bruges (*c.* 1130) and the *History of the Papal Court* of John of Salisbury (*c.* 1165).

to which he gave expression, especially on moral decline and civil discord.[108]

Pseudo-Hugo uses Sallust, but he does not plagiarise him; indeed he hardly ever uses more than one Sallustian word at a time. He moulds his own sentences out of vocabulary that is Sallustian, but originating from several different Sallustian phrases (and sometimes phrases from other Latin writers, such as Cicero). Frequently Pseudo-Hugo changes the case and number of a classical word, and switches active verbs to passive.

These echoes occur especially in character descriptions and in the first few pages of the text, where Pseudo-Hugo makes use of material from the Sallustian 'prefaces'. Many of the ideas in his preface are reminiscent of Sallust, but are expressed in a completely reshaped form. The first chapter of the *Jugurtha*, like the first paragraph of Pseudo-Hugo, associates the concepts fortune, glory, effort and danger, but while Sallust goes on to say that it is beauty, wealth and physical strength that slip away (*dilabuntur*),[109] pseudo-Hugo instead talks of glory slipping away, and uses a different verb (*evanescat*). Directly Sallustian is Pseudo-Hugo's reference to the idea that later generations are inspired to act virtuously by being reminded of their ancestors, in the case of the Romans through the *imagines*, busts of ancestors who had held public office, which were kept in the entrance-hall of Roman houses.[110]

Classical narratives frequently begin by defining their subject-matter, as was essential when a text was broadcast either through oral delivery to an audience or from a scroll which the reader needed to unroll. In typical classical fashion, Pseudo-Hugo begins his history with the phrase *rem in presenti me scripturum propono quae* ... ('It is my intention in the present [work] to write down a story which ...'). At *Jugurtha* 5.1, having brought his prefatory remarks to an end, Sallust announces his subject-matter to his readers: *Bellum scripturus sum quod* ... ('I am going to write about the war which ...'). *Res* meaning subject-matter is a common usage in classical Latin (e.g. *Jugurtha* 79.10); but the only word in this clearly Sallustian reminiscence which actually occurs in Sallust's text – where it is in a different case – is *scripturum*. *Propono*

---

108 Haskins (1927a), 226; Smalley (1971), 165–75; Reynolds (1983), 345–7.
109 Sallust, *Jugurtha* 2.2.
110 *Ibid.* 4.5.

INTRODUCTION 45

occurs again in the form *propositum* in the sentence with which Pseudo-Hugo introduces his character-sketch of King Roger: *Placet ante, nec a proposito quidem dissidet, de moribus eius pauca summatim perstringere, cum satis incivile sit tanti viri mentione habita, virtutem eius silentio praeterire.*[111] This sentence recalls the words with which Sallust introduces his character-sketches of the *mores* (the character or habits) of Caesar and Cato at *Catiline* 53.6: *Quos quoniam res obtulerat, silentio praeterire non fuit consilium* ('Since the story has mentioned these men, it has not been my intention to pass them over in silence'). But Pseudo-Hugo's sentence shows that he has other passages in mind as well. At *Jugurtha* 95.2, Sallust introduces the Roman commander Sulla: *Sed quoniam nos tanti viri res admonuit, idoneum visum est de natura cultuque eius paucis dicere* ('Since the material has drawn our attention to that great man, it seems fitting to say a few things about his character and habits'). Pseudo-Hugo's use of this sentence is rather more than simply a borrowing of the words *pauca* and *tanti viri*. The borrowing lies in the very fact of emphasising character in a secular text – something central to classical literary culture, where courtroom oratory required vivid positive or negative representations of those involved on either side of a case. Rhetorical character-sketches of this kind were one of the sources of classical secular biography like *The Lives of the Caesars* by Suetonius – known, but with the exception of Einhard's *Life of Charlemagne* not copied since late antiquity. Other words used in this sentence are reminiscent of Suetonius and Cicero: *summatim perstringere* recalls the phrase *celeriter perstringam* ('cover quickly'/'summarise') used by Cicero in *Philippic* 2.47, as well as Suetonius' frequent use of *summatim*[112] – and we may note that Pseudo-Hugo has just used the phrase *breviter ac succincte transcurram* ('I shall summarise briefly and concisely') a few lines before. Pseudo-Hugo's claim to brevity is itself indicative of how he sees his relationship to Sallust, for brevity was a characteristic for which Sallust was renowned among Roman writers.[113]

The language with which Pseudo-Hugo describes the bad character of Maio shows that Pseudo-Hugo was thinking of the classical arch-intriguer Catiline. The use of the word *monstrum* was probably drawn

---

111 Siragusa ed. 5.

112 E.g. *summatim breviterque composuit*, of Tiberius' autobiography; *Tiberius* 61.1.

113 *Sallustiana brevitas;* Quintilian, *Institutio Oratoria* 4. 2.45, 10. 1.32 and 102.

directly from Cicero's representation of Catiline, both in his speeches *Against Catiline* (1.30 and 2.1) and *On Behalf of Caelius* (*Pro Caelio* 5.12).[114] Maio has 'the ability to pretend and dissemble whatever he pleased' (*simulandi ac dissimulandi*), like Sallust's Catiline (*Catiline* 5.4). But once again it is Pseudo-Hugo who controls his classical material, not vice versa. Thus Sallust's description of human nature, *praeceps ad explendam animi cupidinem* ('eager to gratify its mind's desire'; *Jugurtha* 6.3), has been transformed into *praeceps in libidinem animus* ('a mind keen on sexual gratification'), and Maio's *aestuantis animi tempestatem* ('the tempest within his seething mind') is a long way from its source in Marius' troubled mind, *aestuans* (*Jugurtha* 93.2).

Other Sallustian elements are the speeches and the digression-endings. Hence Pseudo-Hugo cuts short his account of the disaster (or divine punishment) which overtook the notary Matthew's relatives and the Salerno civic elite in 1162 with a reference to the 'licence to digress' (*evagandi licentiam*). The idea – but not a single actual word – is taken from the concluding sentence of the prefatory remarks of the *Jugurtha*, where Sallust apologises for digressing.[115] On the other hand, after he has described the confirmation of Stephen of Perche's election as archbishop, Pseudo-Hugo's vocabulary is entirely Sallustian: *ad rei seriem revertamur* ('let us now return to the sequence of events').[116]

Further passages could be mentioned to illustrate the extent to which Sallust is part of Pseudo-Hugo's literary armoury. Compare, for example, the first sentence of chapter 5 (according to the later divisions), *Comite vero longe alia mens erat aliudque volvebat in animo*, with Sallust's comment on Jugurtha's reply to the dying King Micipsa, *ipse longe aliter animo agitabat* ('he had very different thoughts on his mind', *Jugurtha* 11.1). But our author's use of classical vocabulary shows that his borrowing was not restricted to Sallust. Thus at the end of chapter 7 he writes of a Byzantine army being 'scattered and slaughtered' (*fusi caesique*). The standard Latin phrase used by both Sallust and Livy (and probably in formal reports of victories in battle by Roman commanders) was *fusum fugatum*, but *caesum fusumque* occurs at the beginning of Cicero's fourteenth *Philippic*, which Pseudo-Hugo must have read. A similar recasting of a Sallustian with a Ciceronian usage occurs when we are told that King William 'resigned [*abdicavit*] his

---

114 Wiedemann (1979), 479–84.
115 *liberius altiusque processi*; *Jugurtha* 4.9.
116 Siragusa ed. 115; cf. *Jugurtha* 4.9, 42.5, 79.10; Wiedemann (1993), 150–9.

life and his realm together',[117] which combines Cicero's condemnation of Antony placing a diadem on Caesar's head: 'he has given up [*abdicavit*] the consulship together with his freedom' (*Philippic* 3.12), with Sallust's description of the death of King Masinissa: 'his reign and his life ended together' (*Jugurtha* 5.5).

With Vergil, too, we have reminiscences rather than citations. Thus the description of the youthful appearance of Matthew Bonellus, *qui prima lanugine genas vestiret*,[118] recalls Vergil, *Aeneid* 8.160, but the words *prima lanugine* for the first growth of facial hair come from elsewhere – perhaps *Aeneid* 10.324 or Juvenal 13.59. It is interesting that the phrase was also used by Suetonius, in his life of the Emperor Otho (c. 12). Some other passages in Pseudo-Hugo also suggest that he had read Suetonius, such as the use of the rare word *strena* for a New Year's gift,[119] which occurs three times in Suetonius, but elsewhere only in relatively obscure late antique authors such as Symmachus and Maximus of Turin. Similarly the phrase *nullo sexus aut aetatis habito discrimine* used in the account of the slaughter of Muslims in 1161[120] suggests both Sallust, *Catiline* 52.22, *inter bonos et malos discrimen nullum*, and Suetonius, *Caligula* 8, *sine ullo sexus discrimine*. The theme of the wicked ruler who caused the death of his nearest and dearest by kicking them was a topos of classical invectives against tyrants; it occurs in Suetonius, *Nero* 35.3.[121] More problematic is the extent to which Pseudo-Hugo's account of Maio's attempt to kill Robert of San Giovanni by providing him with an unseaworthy ship is indebted to the story of Nero's unsuccessful attempt to dispose of his mother Agrippina in this way.[122]

Yet the possible, even probable, use of Suetonius raises a real difficulty. The revival of interest in the classics during the eleventh and twelfth centuries saw some diffusion of this hitherto rare text, but apparently only north of the Alps, and even there within a relatively restricted

---

117 Siragusa ed. 88.
118 *Ibid.*, 31.
119 *Ibid.*, 48, and see the *History*, note 75.
120 Siragusa ed. 70.
121 Cf. Nero's murder of Poppaea, Tacitus, *Annals* 16.6. More generally, see Ameling (1986), 507–8.
122 Suetonius, *Nero* 34.2. Could 'Maio' have reminded Pseudo-Hugo of 'Baiac'? Cf. Tacitus, *Annals* 14.3–5.

area, principally the Loire valley and the Anglo-Norman kingdom.[123] We do not know where Pseudo-Hugo might have seen a copy.

Another unresolved question is the relationship, if any, between the story of how Stephen of Perche put on a breastplate to protect himself at the trial of Count Henry of Montescaglioso (see below, p. 187) and the breastplate which Cicero claimed to have worn to protect himself against Catiline. Cicero's breastplate is mentioned in detail in Plutarch's *Life* of Cicero (14.5); but although some Plutarchan writings (probably the Pseudo-Plutarchan *Institutio Trajani*) were, according to Henry Aristippus,[124] known in twelfth-century Sicily, there is no evidence that the *Lives* were. The breastplate was also referred to in passing by Cicero himself in his speech *Pro Murena*, but this was an exceptionally rare text, preserved only a single manuscript at Cluny which remained there unread until its discovery by Poggio Bracciolini in 1415.[125] The story was not mentioned by Sallust, and it is hard to see how it could have reached Pseudo-Hugo. This is a pertinent reminder that just because episodes described by later historians may have classical resonances, that does not automatically mean that the later author invented them. Like the story of Robert's unseaworthy ship, that of Stephen's breastplate may simply have been true.

As regards actual quotations from classical authors, all we seem to have are two lines of Lucan, which Pseudo-Hugo not only cites but gives the correct context for (Cato's remarks about Pompey when he hears of the latter's death).[126] Lucan's epic on the civil war between Caesar and the Pompeians was a favourite text throughout the Middle Ages. There are other verbal reminiscences in the *History*: the phrase *carbasa ventis exposuit* ('he exposed his sails to the winds') comes from Lucan 3.596.[127] Like Vergil, Lucan seems to have been well-known in southern Italy during this period. William of Apulia used both authors in his verse epic on Robert Guiscard, and although we only have information about a few south Italian libraries in the Middle Ages, we know that both Montecassino and the monastery of Tremiti

---

123 Reynolds (1983), 399–403. And we should note that even John of Salisbury only knew of Suetonius through the excerpts made in the ninth century by Heiric of Auxerre.

124 Minio-Paluello, *Phaedo interprete Henrico Aristippo*, 89.

125 *Pro Murena* 51; Reynolds and Wilson (1974), 121.

126 Siragusa ed. 103. Below, p. 151.

127 *Ibid.*, 26.

possessed copies of both epics.[128] Similarly Sallust was used, or at least quoted, in Geoffrey Malaterra's account of the conquest of Sicily, and was also in the libraries of Montecassino and Tremiti. The latter indeed possessed two copies. There is furthermore Cod. Vat. Lat. 3327, an Apulian manuscript of *c.* 1100 (the exact provenance of which is unknown) which contains Sallust's two monographs.[129] In addition Montecassino possessed several Ciceronian MSS., including one of the *Philippics* (now Cod. Vat. Lat. 3227).[130]

The *History* also contains two legal maxims for which no parallels are cited in standard medieval Latin lexicons, but which are likely to have been coined by the glossators: *superabundantem non nocere cautelam* ('an excess of caution does no harm') and *quod vi metuve gestum fuerit ratum non habere praetorem* ('no judge would consider what had happened as a result of force or threats as legitimate').[131] The use of *praetor* for judge goes back to the classical Latin of the *Digest*. Another indication of our author's awareness of legal vocabulary is that Caid Martin's office was referred to as a *praetorium*, a term used very rarely in medieval texts, and then to refer to the office of the quaestor, the Byzantine emperor's chief judicial officer.[132] Given Pseudo-Hugo's interest in legal matters, and the importance of Roman law in the twelfth-century Sicilian kingdom, where royal legislation was largely a reworking of Justinian's law books, this is hardly surprising. But there was no wholesale and deliberate classicisation of official terminology: hence Arabic borrowings such as *duana* and *defetir* were retained, and not expressed by means of classicising periphrasis as occurs so often in the work of other well-educated medieval writers, such as the author of the *Gesta Stephani*.[133]

Finally, as Michele Fuiano pointed out, the marked difference in tone

---

128 Mathieu, *Guillaume de Pouille, La Geste de Robert Guiscard*, 61–2; Bloch (1972), 579, 593; Cavallo (1975), 395–6. Petrucci, *Codice diplomatico del monastero di Tremiti* iii, 369–71, lists the library of that monastery *c.* 1175. More generally, see Schanz and Hosius (1935), 500.

129 *Malaterra*, preface and I.26, pp. 4, 20, from *Catiline* 1.1, *Jugurtha* 3.3; Cavallo (1975), 395–6, 402; Lowe (1980), i, 152. There are six Sallust quotations in the Montecassino Chronicle.

130 Lowe (1980), i, 72; Reynolds (1983), 75.

131 Siragusa ed. 54, 163.

132 *Ibid.*, 80.

133 *Gesta Stephani* (see note 79 above), xxix–xxx.

between the *History* and the *Letter to Peter* is not necessarily proof of different authorship.[134] The *Letter* is of a different rhetorical style (the 'grand' style), and much of it is in the form of a series of panegyrics praising particular places (especially Syracuse and Palermo), utilising relatively few of the commonplaces which one would expect in a classical panegyric, namely those which medieval writers would have found in the *locus amoenus* descriptions found in poets like Horace and Ovid. In the *Letter*, too, there are phrases which suggest knowledge of Cicero, especially the *Tusculan Disputations*, but Fuiano's suggestion of direct use of Quintilian is more problematic.[135]

The manuscripts of the *History*[136]

Recension I (with the Letter to Peter followed by the *History*)

V. Cod. Vat. Lat. 10690, written *c.* 1230. It is divided, not into the chapters of the later MSS., but into six unequal sections, of which the *Letter* is the first. Among the several later hands which have made annotations is that of the early humanist Zanobi della Strada (*c.* 1312–1361). This MS. was later in the library of the monastery of S. Nicolò dell'Arena of Catania, and was acquired by the Vatican Library in 1903.

C. Paris, B. N. MS. Lat. 5150, a composite MS. of the mid-fourteenth century, containing the *Letter* and the *History* (fols. 64r–104v), and also papal biographies: the *Deeds of Innocent III*, Boso's twelfth-century section of the *Liber Pontificalis*, and the only copy of Nicolò of Calvi's biography of Innocent IV. The text of Pseudo-Hugo here was a direct copy of V, but with the addition of chapter headings derived from marginal notes in V. The irrelevance of some of these, such as that of c. 29, 'The fickleness of women', would show, even in default of other manuscript evidence, that these cannot have been part of the

---

134 Fuiano (1960), 109–110.

135 Siragusa ed. 169: *flebiles modos* (*Tusculans* 1.106), and *lugubre carmen* (*Tusculans* 3.46); Quintilian: Fuiano (1960), 167, but this was described by Hoffmann (1967), 117, as *haltlos*. Furthermore, while there was some limited knowledge of Quintilian in twelfth-century France, he was virtually unknown in Italy until the Renaissance; Reynolds (1983), 332–4.

136 This section is a summary of Jamison (1957), 182–91, 358–73, not the product of an independent examination of the MSS.

original text. MS. C was written before 1361, when it was acquired by Petrarch, who made extensive annotations. There are also a few annotations by Giovanni Boccaccio.

Recension II (with the *History* preceding the *Letter to Peter*)

A. Paris, B. N. MS. Lat. 6262, *c.* 1300 or perhaps slightly earlier, preserving the sixfold section division, albeit with the *Letter* as the last, not the first, part. This may have been the MS. from which Guillaume de Nangis, a monk of St Denis, copied the preface into that of his *Life of St Louis* (King Louis IX of France), written between 1286 and the king's canonisation in 1297.[137] This is generally the fullest and most accurate text, but with a couple of apparently deliberate changes and some damage caused by fire.

B. Paris, B. N. MS. Lat. 14357, a late fourteenth-century composite MS. made for the abbey of St Victor in Paris. The text of Pseudo-Hugo was copied from A.

In addition there must have been one further MS. of recension I (P*), now lost, on which the *editio princeps* of 1550 was based, and probably V as well.

The only modern edition, that by G. B. Siragusa in 1897 in the Fonti per la storia d'Italia series, was based on MS. A − V being then unknown − with the chapter headings based on C. After V was acquired by the Vatican Library, Siragusa published a pamphlet listing variant readings. Should a new edition be undertaken, then V, the earliest surviving MS., would probably be the basis, despite the carelessness of its copyist.

The *Chronicle* of Romuald of Salerno

In contrast to the shadowy figure of Pseudo-Hugo, the putative author of the other principal narrative of mid-twelfth-century Sicilian history, Romuald II, Archbishop of Salerno 1153–81, is well-documented.[138]

---

137 Jamison (1957), 370–1; Capitani (1977), 15.
138 See Garufi's introduction to *Romuald*, v–x. A selection of documents from Romuald's archiepiscopate are published by Ughelli, *Italia Sacra* vii, 399–407. See also Balducci, *Archivio della curia arcivescovile di Salerno*, i: *Regesto delle pergamene*, 22–30.

He was descended from the Guarna, an important Salernitan family of Lombard descent, prominent as city judges, in the Church, as ducal, and later royal, officials, and as landowners in the Principality of Salerno. (See genealogical chart III.) The account of the years 1153–69 translated below is part of a lengthy history from the creation of the world up to 1178, which concludes with a detailed eyewitness account of the peace conference at Venice in 1176–7 which brought the dispute between Frederick Barbarossa and his various enemies to a close, and at which Archbishop Romuald and Count Roger of Andria were the chief Sicilian negotiators. At the end of the description of the conference Romuald's authorship is expressly declared.[139]

Needless to say, most of this chronicle was in fact a compilation of older authorities, notably Orosius, Isidore of Seville, Bede and Paul the Deacon. Donald Matthew has shown that much of the more recent history, up to 1126, was derived from a set of contemporary Apulian annals, probably written at Troia. From 1127 onwards, however, the chronicle is original, albeit relatively brief. The account of William I's reign and the early years of William II is a valuable check on Pseudo-Hugo, although much of the author's attention was devoted to events concerning the papacy and northern Italy. Given the archbishop's role as a diplomat – he was one of the Sicilian representatives at the Treaty of Benevento in 1156 as well as at the Venice conference – such an interest might be considered quite predictable. However, even this text presents problems. Professor Matthew points not merely to the significance of the Troia annals, but to the errors and inconsistancies which are signs of more than one person revising the older, historical, parts of the chronicle, and suggests that in fact Romuald himself wrote only the account of the Venice conference, for in his acknowledgment of authorship he refers to the truth of his account of events at which he was present and saw for himself (which would apply rather to the conference than to the rest of the history). While acknowledging the Salernitan bias of the section after 1127, Matthew is doubtful whether the archbishop himself was responsible for this part, not least because, while Romuald's political role is given more emphasis than in Pseudo-Hugo's account – for example, he is alleged to have crowned William II – there is no detailed discussion of the Treaty of Benevento at which he was one of the royal delegation. But

---

139 *Romuald*, 293–4. A very brief account of the aftermath of the conference follows.

this argument is hardly conclusive, and one might equally well suggest that the emphasis on foreign affairs was a reflection of Romuald's own concerns. If the archbishop was not the author himself, the writer was probably one of his entourage.[140]

The translation

Any translation is a matter of judgement and preference. What follows represents our choice of vocabulary and terminology, sometimes only decided after considerable discussion. Though Pseudo-Hugo was much influenced by Sallust, his vocabulary is less classical than it would at first sight appear to the reader brought up on the great Roman historian. Thus his *miles* is very clearly a mounted knight: the account of the siege of Taverna expressly contrasts *milites* with footsoldiers, *pedites*.[141] The term has thus been rendered 'knight', not 'soldier'. The distinction between *Lombardi* and *Longobardi* has been made clear by rendering these as 'North Italians' and 'South Italians' respectively, rather than translating one or other of these terms as 'Lombard' (although the use of 'Lombard' has been retained in the translation of *Romuald*, when this refers to the north Italian opponents of Frederick Barbarossa – the townsmen of the 'Lombard League'). *Sarraceni* has been rendered as 'Muslims', and *Masmudi* as Almohads, in deference to modern readers. In a south Italian context *castellum/castrum* could mean a castle, urban citadel or keep (as it regularly does in Malaterra's history), but often, and in charters almost invariably, was used to refer to a fortified village or even a small town, as opposed to unfortified villages (*casales/villae*). When used in this last context, *castellum/castrum* has been left untranslated. So too has *familiaris*, which in Sicily had a precise technical meaning as 'chief minister', and *stratigotus*, one of several contemporary terms for the principal royal official in a town (see the *History*, notes 96, 102). The *Ostiarius* was clearly a junior palace official. The term might be translated as 'doorkeeper' or even 'sentry', but has here been rendered as 'usher'. Terms derived from Arabic have been left untranslated, but are explained in the notes.

---

140 Matthew (1981), especially 267–70.
141 Siragusa ed. 76. See below, p. 127.

THE HISTORY OF THE TYRANTS OF SICILY

It is my intention in the present work to write down a story whose frightfulness would be enough, indeed more than enough, either to make it completely unbelievable or at any rate to cast suspicion upon its reliability, were it not that in Sicily there is nothing amazing about the performance of deeds of such extreme wickedness that they should rather be lamented by the bellowing of writers of tragedies than narrated in accordance with historical truth. Nowhere else does Fortune give her wheel a more sudden twist, or sport more hazardously with mortal men.[1] So it will be the terrifying nature of the place itself that will give credit to the things which I am about to write about; and it will be worth while to pass on to the memory of future generations political changes that were as terrible as they were sudden, in order that those who, tied to Fortune's strings, measure their status by abundance of riches should be warned by what happened to others and cease boasting of their success; otherwise they might find themselves complaining of their misfortunes on each occasion when they either fall from a position of honour or in some way or other lose their material wealth. And I shall also do my best to ensure that those few men whose honesty shone memorably among so many great crimes committed by extremely wicked men should not be deprived of the praise they deserve, and that the glory which virtue deserves should be passed down through the ages with uninterrupted recognition. Just as that glory glows with vitality, as one might put it, from the moment when outstanding deeds are done, so it grows old and slips away when later generations do not speak of it. And thus it comes about that the glory which someone achieves as a result of immense effort and hard

---

1 The image of Fortune's wheel was used several times by the author, e.g. p. 94 below. Jamison (1957), 140–1, 236–40, suggests that its use in the *History* is both an indication of the date when the work was written, after the fall of Sicily to the Germans in 1194, and of Eugenius's authorship. However, cf. the introduction, p. 37 above, which contests this view.

work will die down and disappear in a short time, just as embers do. So it is to the advantage of many that any brave deeds that are done should be handed down to the consciousness of later generations. Not only does this mean that brave men will get the due reward for their effort, but also that all future generations will benefit, especially as children are often induced to behave well by the example of paternal excellence. It is as though a spark which has been transferred to the children but which in some lies asleep and, so to speak, prematurely dead, may easily recover when it is reminded of inherited virtue. And if there are any whose own excellent nature makes them crave to perpetuate their name, the memory of their fathers will itself increase that craving and add strength to their intention to realise whatever it is that they hope for, making them more active in both respects. That was why the ancient Romans kept all those masks of their fathers in their homes, so that the achievements of their predecessors would always be before their eyes, so that they would be ashamed to turn to wanton degeneracy and waste their lives in dishonourable idleness, so that they would have before their eyes what one might call a compulsion to strive for virtue.[2]

Consequently I too will not allow the events that recently occurred in the Kingdom of Sicily – not without great danger to many people – to be forgotten by being left fallow. Some of these events I saw myself, and others I learnt about from trustworthy accounts by men who had taken part in them. But it is not my intention to narrate in individual detail every hazard of war or military conflict or what took place in each city and town. It will be enough for my intentions if I do not remain silent about those men who were worthy of praise, and summarise major events briefly and concisely, paying particular attention to what happened at court.

First of all[3] therefore it is well known that when Count Roger of Sicily, the brother of Robert Guiscard the Duke of Apulia, departed this human life, his son Roger first obtained the whole of Sicily and part of Calabria by right of succession; then, when he had learnt of

---

2 Sallust, *Jugurtha* 4.5. See introduction, p. 44 above.

3 In the early MSS. this is the beginning of a new section, in Recension I it was part III of the whole work, part II of the *History*; Jamison (1957), 184. See the introduction, 'The manuscripts of the *History*'.

the death of his blood-relative William, Duke of Apulia,[4] he crossed over to Apulia, overcame all those of its cities and princes who attempted to resist him, and added the whole of it to his empire, finally taking the title of Duke of Apulia. Thinking that it was unsuitable for such enormous and widespread power to be constricted in the status of its title, he preferred to be called King rather than Duke; and consequently he made Sicily a kingdom. Let me begin with a few summary remarks about his habits (nor is this irrelevant to my stated aim), since it would be unjust to refer to such a great man and then pass over his excellence in silence.

Among the other natural gifts with which Nature herself had endowed this man of great vitality, he had a keen intellect and never lacked confidence in himself, so much so that if he was ever asked about anything at all he never made the slightest delay in giving a reply. Whenever there was a discussion of more important matters, he was not embarrassed to call his court together and first hear the opinion of each person in order to choose the one that was better. And if there was any point that he had considered more deeply or carefully concerning the matter in hand, he would give his own opinion last of all, and immediately explain the reason why that seemed to him to be the best course of action. Although the man's spirit was always awake and on the lookout for greater things, leaving him no time for inactivity or idle leisure, he nevertheless undertook nothing thoughtlessly or on the spur of the moment, and the application of discretion restrained the impulses of his great spirit, so that nothing at all trivial should be present in the works of this wisest of kings; and it was not easy to judge whether he was wiser in speech or action. He took enormous care both to sort out present problems with care and to make careful provision for the future out of present conditions, and he made certain that he would use wisdom not less than power both in destroying his enemies and in increasing his kingdom by extending its territories. For he subjugated Tripoli in Barbary, Africa, Sfax, Gabes and numerous other barbarian cities through many personal efforts and dangers.[5]

4 Duke William died on 28 July 1127; Garufi, *Necrologio di S. Matteo di Salerno*, p. 102.

5 *Africa* refers to the town of Mahdia and its hinterland (cf. p. 78 below). Tripoli was captured in June 1146 (after a first attack in 1143 had failed), Mahdia and Gabes in June and Sfax in July 1148. See Abulafia (1984), especially 33–5, for discussion.

He also made every effort to find out about the customs of other kings and peoples, in order to adopt any of them that seemed particularly admirable or useful. When he heard that any persons were either effective counsellors or famous warriors, he would honour them with gifts to encourage their virtue. Since he derived his own origin from the Normans and knew that the French race excelled all others in the glory of war, he chose to favour and honour those from north of the Alps particularly. In short, he made efforts to administer justice in its full rigour on the grounds that it was particularly necessary for a newly-established realm, and to exercise the options of peace and war by turns, with the result that he omitted nothing that virtue requires, and had no king or prince as his equal during his lifetime. Now as regards the fact that some writers categorise many of his actions as tyrannical and call him inhuman because he imposed on many men penalties that were severe and not prescribed by the laws, it is my opinion that as a prudent man who was circumspect in all things, he intentionally behaved in this way when his monarchy was only recently established so that wicked men should not be able to wheedle any impunity for their crimes; and that while those who deserved well (to whom he showed himself mild) should not be discouraged by excessive severity, there should nevertheless be no place for contempt as a result of excessive mildness. And if perhaps he seemed to have acted somewhat harshly against some, I suppose that he was forced to it by some necessity. For there was no other way in which the savagery of a rebellious people could have been suppressed, or the daring of traitors restrained.[6]

When after many efforts and dangers he had brought a peace to his kingdom that remained unshaken for as long as he lived, he also made provision for the future and prepared a vast treasure for the defence of the realm, which he stored at Palermo. Thereafter he devoted himself to peace and leisure, thinking that he was happy in successful offspring, and entrusted participation in the care of the realm to his

---

[6] A very similar verdict about King Roger was (surprisingly) reported by the otherwise hostile German chronicler Otto of Freising: 'There are, however, those who say that he did these things for reasons of justice rather than tyranny, and they say that he loved peace more than any other prince. They assert that it was to preserve this [peace] that he treated rebels with such severity.' However, he went on to allege that others believed the king was primarily driven by avarice; Hofmeister, *Ottonis Episcopi Frisingensis Chronica* VII c. 23, pp. 346–7.

sons Roger, Duke of Apulia, and Anfusus, Prince of Capua, in whom the image of their father's virtue was reflected most truly. But later they both paid the debt due to fate, not without unbelievable pain on the part of their father and the greatest grief throughout the kingdom, leaving as a survivor William, Prince of Tarento, whom his father had hardly thought worthy of the same princely status.[7] Since there was no one else left, his father placed the diadem on his head and made him a partner in sovereignty.[8] Not long afterwards he himself surrendered to fate, overcome by early old age, both worn down by his immense efforts and more devoted to sexual activity than the body's good health requires.[9] His son William, whom he had made king while he still lived, suceeded him, and took control of the palace and the treasure and the responsibility for the realm. It was a time when the kingdom of Sicily was rich in hard-working and famous men, had the greatest power by land and sea, was feared by all the peoples round about, and enjoyed complete peace and all possible tranquillity.

But after only a short time, all this tranquillity slipped away and suddenly disappeared, in such a way that you will easily comprehend that the fortune and condition of kingdoms submits to the character of their rulers, and you will have no doubt that the glory of any realm

---

7 Anfusus died on 10 October 1144, Roger on 2 May 1148 (the Salerno cathedral necrology mistakenly dates this 1149); Garufi, *Necrologio di S. Matteo di Salerno*, 60, 158; Inguanuez, *Necrologio di Cod. Cas.* 47, 59; *Romuald*, 231, n. 4. The year of Anfusus's death, not specified in the necrologies, is clear from the last documents which mention him as Prince of Capua; Inguanez, *Regesto di S. Angelo in Formis*, 196–200, nos. 68–9 (May 1144, September 1144), while in December of that year William was described as Prince of Capua; *ibid.*, 201–5, no. 70.

8 William was crowned as co-ruler at Easter 1151; Chibnall, *The Historia Pontificalis of John of Salisbury*, 69. However, the only two documents which describe him specifically as Prince of Taranto, both from the abbey of Montevergine, are (at least in their present form) forgeries; *Rogerii II Diplomata*, 125–9, no. 46 ('1137'), 145–7, no. 52 ('1140'). None the less it seems clear that an authentic tradition was preserved, and William was described in other charters as 'prince', though without any specific territorial title. The charter evidence shows William regularly associated both with his father and with his elder brother Roger (see introduction, note 34).

9 Roger died on 27 February 1154; Garufi, *Necrologio di S. Matteo di Salerno*, 30; Inguanez *Necrologio del Cod. Cas.* 47, 60.

can be increased to the same extent as you can identify virtue in its prince. For King William, the heir only to his father's power and not to his character, went wild with such a degree of lunacy that he ignored the decisions of his excellent father, and allowed the organisation of the court (reformed by his efforts) to deteriorate, and even either sent into exile the advisers his father had looked to, or locked them within the confines of prisons. And he appointed as great admiral Maio of Bari, a man of humble origins who had first been a notary at court and then step by step reached the post of chancellor.[10] This man was a beast than whom no more repellent pest could be found, none more effective in achieving the destruction and the overthrow of the realm. For he had an intellect that could grasp anything; his eloquence was equal to his intellect; he had the ability to pretend and dissemble whatever he pleased; his mind, keen on sexual gratification, contrived intercourse with women married and unmarried, especially noble ones. He was particularly keen to overcome the chastity of those who had a reputation for decency. Once he had tasted the desire for power, he turned over many plans in his mind, he exhausted his spirit with many schemes, and was borne forward by constant incitements to wickedness; yet he managed to hide the tempest within his seething mind behind a calm appearance.

This was the man upon whom the greatest honour was bestowed, and to whom the care and government of the whole realm was committed. It quickly happened that the king gave absolute credence to his words, and wished to believe no one else, to hear nothing at all from anyone else. Maio excluded everyone else, and would confer with the king alone each day; he alone dealt with the affairs of the realm, and turned the king's mind in whichever direction he pleased, sometimes presenting lies as truth and sometimes soothing the king's fears with flattery. From this the hope came upon him that he might achieve the result which he already aimed at, and might put his plan into action when an opportune moment appeared. He was pushed

10 Maio was attested as *scrinarius* (archivist?) in a number of royal charters from October 1144 onwards; *Rogerii II Diplomata*, 183–9, nos. 64–5, 205–6, no. 71 (September 1146), 214–16, no. 75 (February 1148). Two charters of September 1149 and October 1151 refer to him as vice-chancellor, and while both are in their present form forged, the editor suggests that both are based on genuine originals; *ibid.*, 224–33, nos. 78–9. Cf. *Romuald*, 234–5. He first appeared as 'Great Admiral of Admirals' in October 1154; *Guillelmi I Diplomata*, 7–8, no. 2.

headlong by the desire to rule, and considered any delay a loss. Meanwhile his mind was granted no rest, no peace; he went around everywhere, planned ahead, carefully looked at every option to see by what scheme and by what means he could seize control of the realm. Thinking about this over a long period, he came to the conclusion that the noblemen (with whom Sicily was flourishing at this time) would stand in the way of his plan. Those of whom he was particularly afraid were Count Robert of Loritello, who was the king's maternal cousin,[11] Count Simon of Policastro[12] and Count Everard of Squillace.[13] Their good character was known to him, and he knew that he could corrupt their loyalty by no deceit and no bribes; if they survived unharmed, he had no hopes of a successful outcome to his plan.

So he decided to scheme for their destruction first, as the first-fruits of his wickedness. He also decided to make Archbishop Hugh, who at that time headed the church at Palermo, a partner and participant in his plot, and he strove for this with all the power he had; with his support, he would realise his hopes the sooner.[14] For he knew that

11 Robert of Loritello (died 15 September 1182) was the son of Robert de Bassonville, who was granted the county of Conversano in 1133 and who died before 1142, and King Roger's sister Judith; Cuozzo (1984) 28. According to Romuald he was given the County of Loritello at King William's (second) coronation at Easter 1154. His first charter as Count of Loritello dates from July 1154; Ughelli, *Italia Sacra*, vii, 706–7, whereas in March of that year he styled himself only 'Count of Conversano and Lord of Molfetta'; Petrucci (1959), 116, no. 5.

12 Simon of Policastro was the son of King Roger's maternal uncle Count Henry of Paterno, who died between 1136 and 1141. He was made Count of Monte Sant'Angelo in 1135; *Al. Tel*, III. 33, p. 77, and was attested in charters in Sicily from 1143 onwards; *Rogerii II Diplomata*, 156–62, no. 57, at 158; Garufi (1910) 49–52.

13 Everard of Squillace is mentioned by no source other than 'Falcandus'. Nor is it clear whether he was related to the later Count Anfusus of Squillace, attested 1176–7 (Garufi, *Tabulario di Monreale*, 10–11, no. 15; Stubbs, *Gesta Regis Henrici II*, i, 170), who was subsequently recorded as a *consanguinus* of King Tancred; Zielinski, *Tancredi et Willelmi III Regum Diplomata*, 30–2, no. 12 (May 1191).

14 Hugh had been translated to Palermo from the archbishopric of Capua *c.* 1150; Chibnall, *The Historia Pontificalis of John of Salisbury*, 67. His predecessor as Archbishop of Palermo, Roger Fesca, was last attested in 1147; Leccisotti, *Troia*, no. 93, no. 27 (March 1147), *Documenti inediti*, 54–62, no. 25.

he was an intelligent and perspicacious man, who was hard-working and suitable material for any plot; furthermore his spirit was proud, he was eager for glory and a slave to lust. The admiral at first tested his views little by little, then opened his mind to him with greater confidence and explained one part of his plan; but he said nothing about his wish to rule himself, and persuaded the archbishop without difficulty that, with the ineffective monarch out of the way, they themselves should take on the obligation of looking after the realm to preserve it free from harm for the children until they should have reached adult years. They both agreed that they should depose the king. Maio kept the rest quiet in order not to deter an ally in the plot by its atrocity. What he was hoping was that if he could become the boys' guardian, there would be no need of anyone else's advice about the next step for seizing the realm.

It is further stated that these two, in accordance with the Sicilians' custom, formed an alliance of blood-brotherhood, and bound themselves with a mutual oath that each would support the other in every way, and that they would be of one mind and purpose both in good and in bad circumstances; anyone who harmed one would become the enemy of both. Having made this alliance, the said archbishop began to enjoy the king's friendship, on Maio's prompting and advice, so that whatever the admiral suggested to the king was confirmed by what his ally told him.

1 The king crosses to Salerno

While these plans were being hatched between them at Palermo, the king decided to cross the Straits, and he proceeded first to Messina and then, a few days later, to Salerno.[15] Many leading men hastened to visit the king from different parts of Apulia and of the Terra di Lavoro. Robert, Count of Loritello, undertook the journey to Salerno with the same intention. Having learnt of his imminent arrival, Maio cleverly turned the king's mind against the count, with the effect that he was unable to get any opportunity to speak to the king, and went

15 King William was at Salerno in March 1155 when he presided over a court there which dealt with various complaints by Abbot Rainald of Montecassino against a royal justiciar, Hervey de la Bolita; *Guillelmi I Diplomata*, 16–19, no. 6 (previously published by Gattula, *Accessiones*, 258–9 = Jamison (1913), 435–6, calendar no. 40).

away sad and angry without having seen him. After having spent some time there transacting a few items of business not worth recording, the king returned to Palermo and thereafter shut himself off as though afraid of the sight of men; but he he allowed the admiral to see him every day, and frequently gave the archbishop the opportunity too, and he learnt about the affairs of the realm from them, not as they actually were, but as they described them in conformity with their own plans.

During this period the Chancellor Asclettin[16] and Count Simon were in Apulia with a large army in order to oppose the German emperor, who was rumoured to be approaching, and making sure that no sudden invasion could take place.[17] Everything was full of fear and suspicion, and it was by no means clear who supported the king and who the admiral; the whole situation was uncertain and ambiguous. For the admiral now had many supporters and partners in his scheme throughout the realm, and his name was feared by all in much the same way as that of the king himself.

2 The Count of Loritello

Given hope by this situation, the desire to rule dug its claws into the man ever more sharply. So he wrote to the chancellor that he should summon Count Robert of Loritello to Capua as though to hear the king's orders, and then take every step to see that he was arrested and sent to Palermo under a reliable guard. He used all sorts of persuasion to make the king agree with this plan, claiming that the count himself had a deep desire to grasp control of the realm, and was claiming that the kingdom itself rightly belonged to him on the grounds that his uncle, King Roger, was said to have directed in one

---

16 Asclettin had been Archdeacon of Catania for at least a decade; *Rogerii II Diplomata*, 267–8, appendix no. 4 (June 1143) (= White (1938), 260–1, no. 18, with date 1144); *Documenti inediti*, 53–4, no. 22 (June 1145), but had only very recently been appointed chancellor in Maio's place. His forces attacked Benevento and ravaged the city's *contado*; Duchesne, *Liber Pontificalis* ii. 390 (translated below, p. 244).

17 Frederick Barbarossa was crowned emperor in Rome on 18 June 1155, but left the city and retreated northwards at the end of July, apparently because of sickness in his army; Mierow, *Deeds of Frederick Barbarossa*, 150–3.

of his wills that if his son William should turn out to be useless or unsuitable, then they should put Count Robert, about whose abilities there was no doubt, in charge of the realm. When he had received the chancellor's letter and learnt from his friends of the plot that was being laid against him, the count decided that the best course of action for him would be not to reject the king's orders openly, while still avoiding the trap that had been set. So he went to Capua with an escort of about 500 well-armed knights, and encamped in the plain outside the city. When the chancellor heard of his arrival, he immediately sent him a message telling him to dismiss his knights and come into the city himself with a few men, since he wanted to talk to him privately and tell him what the king's orders were. The count replied that he was not going to enter the city, but that if the chancellor came out he would be prepared to listen to anything that had been addressed to him from the court. The chancellor realised that his hopes had been thwarted and the count already knew about the plot. He went out to him, saying that it was the king's wish that he should transfer all the knights whom he levied from his fief to the command of Count Bohemond.[18] The count was very put out by this, and replied that it was a disgrace and contrary to accepted custom that his knights should be allocated to another commander as though he himself were either a traitor or an incompetent warrior. When the chancellor repeated the request, advising that he should obey the king's wishes, the count added that these orders came either from a madman or from a traitor, and consequently he would in no way obey them. So the chancellor's vain hope was deluded, and he returned to Capua; the count made his way into the Abruzzi.

Not long after this, there was rioting in the army between the chancellor's knights and those of Count Simon, and it got so bad that the knights' indiscipline spread to their lords as well, and many words and threats were exchanged between them. It is not clear whether this happened at the chancellor's instigation, or developed by chance; but it seems plausible that Maio's orders lay behind it, and that when

18 Bohemond of Tarsia, Count of Manopello in the Abruzzi. He was from a family in the Val di Crati in northern Calabria, and his brother Carbonellus was a royal justiciar in the Val di Crati from 1152 to 1157. He was appointed by King Roger as count in this sensitive northern frontier region in the summer of 1140, and was active as a royal justiciar and military commander. See *Chron. Casauriense*, 888–91 and Cuozzo (1984), 287–91. For his arrest, see below, pp. 75–6.

the chancellor saw no way in which he could lay any charges against the excellent count, he decided to instigate the rioting, to give him something to blame him for. For he also described the situation in hostile rather than objective terms in the reports he sent to court, and was more accusing of the count than the matter warranted, saying that Count Simon had frequently been responsible for discord in the army; that he had incited his knights to sedition; that Count Robert had escaped because he had told him about the plot against him; that messengers frequently passed between them, and it was not clear what plan he was hatching; that, in short, it was extremely dangerous to entrust an army to him. The grand admiral brought this and other intelligence of the same sort which the chancellor had sent him to the king's attention, and added that a great deal of weight should be given to these reports; for he himself had already heard that Count Robert had been conspiring against the king with several others, and that Count Simon was a member of the same party. Now there was clear evidence for this. He thought that consideration should be given to avoiding the danger which this incipient plot represented. It was too late to amputate decaying flesh once it had already infected the adjoining parts.

The king was easily persuaded, since he was suspicious of all his family and blood-relatives. So the count was summoned to court by a royal letter, and another constable was appointed in his place. When he arrived he was given no opportunity to prove his innocence or to reply to the accusations which had been made against him in accordance with legal procedure. For he was immediately arrested and thrown into prison, not without causing Maio a great deal of odium.

3 Rumours of the king's death

When this had happened as described, the king thereafter secreted himself from everyone in such a way that for a long period of time he appeared to no one at all, apart from the admiral Maio and Archbishop Hugh. This was interpreted by many as evidence that he was dead. Some thought that he had been given poison by the admiral, and they did not find this hard to believe, as they had long heard that he was plotting to do this. And many who came to court from various parts of Apulia and were denied their customary opportunity of an audience with the king broadcast absolutely certain stories of his death all over Apulia, saying that there was no cause to question what the rumours had stated.[19]

Since the people of Apulia are utterly disloyal, and vainly hope to win their independence (an independence which, once achieved, they are quite unable to maintain, since they are neither any good at warfare nor orderly in peacetime), they took up arms, made alliances, and turned their attention to fortifying their castles. Some, tired of perpetual peace, were driven by pure capriciousness; hope of plunder incited others to war; not a few were incited to take up arms because they felt that the king's death ought to be avenged. But many took up arms to fight on the admiral's side. So everything was confused and degenerated into violence, and the outcome of the fighting in different places was indecisive. The Count of Loritello took possession of several cities along the coast. The Byzantine emperor was asked for support by the count, and led by the hope of recovering Apulia he sent some extremely noble and powerful persons to Brindisi with an enormous amount of money.[20] You could have seen everything thrown into similar confusion in the Terra di Lavoro; some rebelled from the king, others stood by him. Robert of Sorrento was welcomed by the Capuans, and took possession of the principality of Capua, which belonged to him by right of inheritance.[21]

19 Other sources suggest that the king was seriously ill during the autumn of 1155, e.g. Mierow, *The Deeds of Frederick Barbarossa*, 166, and especially Lupo Gentile, *Annales Pisani*, 15: 'King William of Sicily became extremely ill in the month of September and remained so up to Christmas, and as a result everyone in his land thought him to be dead.' Cf. Chalandon (1907), ii. 219. What happened was very similar to the situation twenty years earlier, at the beginning of 1135, when King Roger was first seriously ill and then prostrated by grief at the death of his first wife, Elvira. It was widely rumoured that he had died, and this led to revolt in Apulia and Capua; *Al. Tel.* III. 1–2, pp. 59–60.

20 The Byzantine expedition was led by Michael Palaeologus and John Dukas. They were later joined by Alexius Comnenus, the son of Nicephorus Bryennius and Anna Comnena and grandson of the Emperor Alexius I. Cf. Brand, *Deeds of John and Manuel Comnenus by John Cinnamus*, 106, 126.

21 Cf here *Annales Casinenses* ad ann. 1155, MGH SS xix, 311: 'Robert of Sorrento captured the whole of the principality of Capua right up to Naples and Salerno.' Prince Robert II of Capua had been in exile at the German court since being driven from his principality in 1137. He had taken part in two embassies from Conrad III to Manuel Comnenus, in

4 Maio

When news of this reached Palermo, the admiral was somewhat perturbed by this unexpected situation, though it was not enough to affect the expression on his face. For he purposely kept a dignified expression even when he was in great danger, so that when there was something to fear the look on his face would not reveal the fact: that would give his enemies hope, and equally strike fear into his own supporters. He adopted what was the best policy in this crisis, sending frequent letters from the king and from himself to those who had not yet rebelled, exhorting them to remember their good qualities and fight bravely against the traitors to confirm the good opinion that had so far been held of them; they should remember that rewards and praise were offered for virtue, while penalties and everlasting disgrace were inflicted on traitors. In the meantime he rallied everyone he could to his side at Palermo, confiding to them his plan to kill the king, and decided that it should be carried out as soon as possible, since he was afraid that if by any chance the king got to know of his crime, he would be accused of high treason and executed.

At that time there was a person called Godfrey at Palermo, the Count of Montescaglioso. He was both a man of the highest liberality and an outstanding warrior with a very intelligent mind; but he was fickle and disloyal, always looking for new political opportunities.[22] The admiral thought that his support would be essential for him, and that the best way to get him on his side would be to arouse the king's enmity against him first. The count possessed various cities in Sicily, including Noto, Schiafani and Caltanisseta; but he was more especially fond of Noto than of the others. The castle there was particularly

---

1142 and 1145; Mierow, *Deeds of Frederick Barbarossa*, 56, 59; Brand, *Deeds of John and Manuel Comnenus by John Cinnamus*, 37–8. His mother was the daughter of the Duke of Sorrento, hence the appellation. He was still in possession of Capua in April 1156, when he made a donation to the nunnery of St John the Baptist in that city; M. Monaco, *Sanctuarium Capuanum* (Naples 1630), 646–8.

22 Godfrey was made Count of Montescaglioso only at the very end of King Roger's reign, in 1152/3. His family had, however, been lords of Ostuni and Lecce, in the Salento peninsula, since the late eleventh century. His sister had been the mistress of Duke Roger of Apulia, by whom she had had two sons, Tancred and William (for whom see note 38 below); Cuozzo (1985) 30–2; Martin (1993), 741–2.

well fortified both because of its large garrison and because of the nature of the terrain, and the place was ideal for protection.[23] So Maio began by persuading the king to let him take this castle for himself, saying that it was dangerous for the count to hold it. Then, when he had heard that the count was extremely vexed at having lost the town, he asked him to come to see him in secret.

He swore that he was more upset by this affair than anyone might easily believe, and that he had objected strongly to the king when he had given the order; but that the man felt so insecure and was so mad that he was now no longer ready to accept advice from anyone, and that there was no way of persuading him to rescind an order he had once given. Even more shamefully, he was saying that Solomon had not known as much as he, and while he was in fact the most stupid of mortal men, he claimed that he alone was wise and able. Furthermore, it was easy to conclude from his words that this man, a tyrant rather than a king, would plan some frightful wickedness if he were to rule any longer; and soon few noblemen would be left who had not been sent to execution or to prison. 'Worse things deserve to happen to us, for if we were men and not more cowardly than women, if we used our minds and were not like brute beasts, we would long ago have laid our complaints to rest by destroying this great monster. But perhaps the fates are dragging us to our destruction, and the disaster that is unavoidably upon us makes us blind. Certainly this fate lies in our fear, which has already brought us into extreme danger.' The count well understood the intention of this speech, and replied that it was thought by everyone that the king did nothing at all without the admiral's advice. Consequently the responsibility for this affair lay with the man who ought to be making public the king's insane and tyrannous regime, and instead of taking the blame for someone else's actions, he should be exhorting individuals to avenge them all; all would gladly follow him if they understood his intention, and he himself would also shed the king's blood the moment that Maio gave the order.

In reply, the admiral praised the count's prudence, extolled his abilities to the skies, embraced him, and told him that the archbishop and

---

[23] The Arab geographer Edrisi, *BAS* i, 19, said that Noto was eight miles from the sea, and 'among the strongest and highest of fortresses'. It had been the last Muslim-held fortress in Sicily to capitulate to Roger I (in 1091).

several others were in agreement that, after the king's death, he should be appointed admiral in his place. He added – more to try him than because he meant it – that he himself was unworthy to be in charge of so great a realm; he thought it was a more sensible policy for the king's son to succeed his father. But it did not escape Godfrey what his intention was in saying this, and he replied that he would never allow that to happen. For nothing that was not tyrannous could be generated from the seed of a tyrant, and those who were born to a wicked father would themselves inherit their father's wickedness. The one thing that he approved of and desired was that the royal dignity be conferred on the admiral, who responded that that was what would happen if only he agreed. The count promised him his help in this affair, and to encourage him to make up his wavering mind he committed himself to him with an oath. Thereafter the admiral sought a suitable place and opportunity for carrying out the crime, assuming that count Godfrey would give him support in everything.

5 The count's aims and intentions

But the count's intentions were quite different, and he had something else in mind; for he had already made a number of persons from Bari who were then staying at Palermo swear an oath to him, and he had on his side Simon of Sangro[24] and Roger, son of Richard,[25] and several noblemen and knights of their party who were ready to follow him through any danger, who thought it disgraceful, shocking and tragic to allow a man whose father used to sell olive-oil at Bari (for that was what was said) to take over the government. Nor did they have

24 Simon had been made Count of Sangro by King Roger in 1140. He was the son of a man called Theodinus and grandson of Count Mainerius of Trivento; Jamison (1959) 54, 57; Cuozzo (1984), 320–2. By 1160 he had been succeeded by a Count Philip, who according to Romuald was one of the conspirators against Maio. See below, p. 228.

25 Roger, son of Richard was from the family of the lords of Trevico, in Apulia. His grandfather Richard, son of Guarin had been killed in a peasant uprising in 1122; *Falco*, 187. He subsequently became Count of Alba, and in the autumn of 1168 was transferred to the County of Andria. He was a figure of major importance in the reign of William II and was killed in the autumn of 1190 while fighting against the new king, Tancred of Lecce. See Cuozzo (1981), 129–68, and for his father, Cuozzo (1984), 64–6.

any objection to assassinating the king, because of the tyrannous regime he was exercising against the nobility. Their plan was this: that the moment the admiral had killed the king, they themselves would immediately attack him as though they were the assassinated king's avengers; then he would get no further pleasure from his treachery, and they could make the king's eldest son his father's heir. So the count started a secret counter-plot against Maio's scheming, flattering him profusely the meantime, asking him not to be irresponsible in putting off this great matter, always to have some knights ready with him, and to wait from day to day for the admiral to put his plan into action. When he saw that he was acting less decisively and that the matter was being put off, he assumed on reliable evidence that his good faith was not believed by Maio, and that he was distrusted. So he shelved the plan to kill the king, and prepared to attack Maio, whom he decided that he might have to kill in the king's own presence, if he could not do so in any other way.

And there was a day on which this would actually have happened just as he had planned, except that – with the assassins already brought inside the palace – it was suddenly announced in the court that some galleys had arrived from Apulia. This distracted the knights from their undertaking, and Maio escaped by the grace of Fortune. But the count, realising that what had occurred could not be concealed (since many people had seen the knights being brought in with their weapons), decided that for now he should have a secret meeting with the admiral, and he told him the whole story of what had happened to him and how his hope had been frustrated: 'Today', he said, 'we went into the court well prepared, and the tyrant would have completed the last day of his life, if the galleys from Gallipoli, which we heard had just put into port, had not prevented us.'[26] The admiral replied that his fears had been in vain, for the whole of Gallipoli had sworn to follow him and shared his intentions. Later that day it was suggested to him by many of his friends that Count Godfrey had entered the court with weapons to kill him; and he told them that he knew all about that – it had all been done in accordance with his plan; it was the king who had had reason to be afraid, not he.

26 Gallipoli, on the Gulf of Taranto 37 km. SW of Lecce, was the nearest major port to Godfrey's hereditary lordship of Lecce, and the most suitable for a journey to the south (as opposed to Otranto for a voyage across the Adriatic). It was, however, not part of his lordship, being a royal town; Poso (1988), 81.

6 Maio's plot revealed

As political instability was developing in Sicily, Bartholomew of Garsiliato and a few others occupied Butera, an extremely defensible site which could easily resist any attacks by besieging forces because of the advantages provided by its sheer cliffs.[27] Many others went to join him, and began to plunder the fields nearby, devastate adjoining places and make alliances with various powerful men. This almost brought Maio to the depths of despair, to the extent that he thought that the crime he was planning would unavoidably have to be postponed; for there was no other way to deal with this crisis except by explaining the whole matter to the king himself, while he still had the strength to go and fight his enemies; otherwise the whole of Sicily would in a short time go over to the enemy. When the king learnt about this, he first put the matter off and did nothing, saying that the men who dared to hold out were not very important, and they would quite soon return home from the fortification they had occupied. For that was what the king was like: he was unwilling to leave the palace, though when necessity forced him to leave it, he acted with an impetuousness as great as his previous indulgence in laziness. He threw himself into any kind of danger, not bravely so much as rashly and thoughtlessly. He did not calculate what forces he had, and what the opponent had; he attacked the enemy without any concern as to whether he was equal to them or not.

He soon realised that those who were at Butera had no desire to give up, but were pursuing their aims more actively, and sent Count Everard to them as his representative, to find out from them with what intention and objectives they had occupied his castle, and what they intended to do next. They said that they would not give the count an answer unless he swore an oath to them, that he would himself tell the king in due order everything that they told him. The count gave them the oath that they had asked for, and they said that they were doing and had done nothing in opposition to the king, but were inspired by the intention of uncovering the treachery of the admiral Maio and Archbishop Hugh, and of preventing the plot which they knew with absolute certainty had been hatched against the king, and that Maio himself was striving to be king with all his powers. They would willingly go

---

27 Edrisi described Butera as 'a very strong fortress, of great importance and very well known', *BAS* i, 19.

to Palermo to throw themselves at the king's feet once they had heard that the traitors had been punished.

Count Everard was a man of unshakeable loyalty: when he brought the king news of all this, bravely but ineffectually, the king first began to reflect, amazed at the unprecedented affair; but then he thought that it was churlish to believe that the man whom he had raised to such a height of dignity should be plotting his death, and passed all that the count had said on to the admiral, adding that he was never going to believe anything of the sort about him. From then on the admiral was suspicious of Count Everard, and bitterly hostile to him, but he was wise enough not to show it until he might find a suitable time for revenge. Meanwhile Count Godfrey fled to Butera, leaving knights to garrison several of his castles.

Tremendous disturbances followed at Palermo, and the entire city was afraid and resentful; the populace seethed and murmured in opposition to Maio. With one voice they all called for Count Simon, as unjustly imprisoned. When the admiral saw that the situation was deteriorating and could no longer easily be controlled except by giving the populace what it demanded, he persuaded the king to have Count Simon taken out of the dungeon. When he was released at the king's command, the situation in the city reversed completely, so that peace and security seemed to have been restored with him. So the king, reluctantly and at Maio's insistence, led out his army to make it seem that there was no question of inactivity in such a crisis, and no good cause for delay, and laid siege to Butera; he would have wasted considerable time there if he had not brought Count Simon with him. After he had attacked the castle with his entire forces for some time, the townspeople continued to resist him just as bravely, and there seemed to be no way of forcing them to surrender. In the end negotiations took place, on the advice and exhortation of Count Simon; and the admiral, the archbishop and several counts took an oath to Count Godfrey and his associates by the king's soul, that the king should allow them to leave the realm unharmed, freely and securely and without hindering them in any way. In this way the town was retaken and peace restored throughout Sicily, and a few days later the king reached Messina, intending to cross over to Apulia.

7 The king crosses to Apulia and fights the Greeks

At that time Count Simon, at Maio's instigation, attacked the chancellor with a variety of accusations when he visited the court.[28] When he bravely stated that he would reply to each of them, he was not allowed to proffer his arguments; for he was suddenly arrested, condemned, and sent to prison, where he died some years later.

As the king was about to cross the Straits, he gave orders that Count Godfrey (who was waiting at Messina, having prepared a ship and all the other arrangements required for the passage) should not be allowed to cross over, and should be kept under careful guard until he himself had returned. Increasing the size of his army along the way, he reached Brindisi, where he ordered his knights to prepare to do battle against the Greeks. When the Greeks saw that they were cheated of the help of Count Robert (whose arrival they were expecting), they decided to try their luck; this was the only course left open to them. The first stages of the battle were inconclusive; but then the Greeks were not strong enough to resist their enemy's attacks any further, and they were scattered and cut down. A large number of them were transported to Palermo with their commanders.[29]

8 The destruction of Bari

Having won this victory, the king led his army up to Bari; the population of the city came out to meet him without weapons, and begged him to spare them. But looking at the ruins of the royal citadel which the people of Bari had destroyed, he said, 'My judgement against you

---

28 Count Simon was at Messina in April 1156 when he made a donation to the church of St Leo at Pannachio on the slopes of Mount Etna; Pirro, *Sicula Sacra* ii, 1157.

29 *The Deeds of John and Manuel Comnenus by John Cinnamus*, 127, blamed the Byzantines' defeat on Robert's abandonment of their army. The *Annales Pisani*, 15–16, date the king's campaign to May and June 1156, and the *Annales Casinenses*, MGH SS xix, 311, date the capture of Brindisi to 28 May 1156. William I mentioned his victory in a charter confirming the privileges of the see of Brindisi in August 1156, in which the various punishments inflicted on traitors and the 'depopulation' of Brindisi were recorded in gruesome detail; *Guillelmi I Diplomata*, 42–4, no. 15 (= Monti, *Codice diplomatico brindisiano*, i, 32–3, no. 17).

will be just: since you refused to spare my house, I will certainly not spare your houses; but I will allow you to leave freely with your property.'[30] They were allowed a truce for two days, during which period they were to leave, taking all their things with them. When that had happened, the walls were first brought down to ground level, and the destruction of the entire city followed. That is why the most powerful city of Apulia, celebrated by fame and immensely rich, proud in its noble citizens and remarkable in the architecture of its buildings, now lies transformed into piles of rubble.[31]

News of this event quite terrified Count Robert and the other remaining rebels, especially when they saw that everyone was going over to the king from the towns of all Apulia. It would not now be easy to offer resistance to such forces, and the king's cruelty excluded any expectation of pardon. So many abandoned the castles, towns and cities which they held and emigrated beyond the borders of the kingdom. Several fled to the territory of the Abruzzi along with Count Robert. Robert of Sorrento, the prince of Capua, could think of no course that would be safer to him than flight. He travelled through the territory of Count Richard of Aquila without coming to any harm, but as he was crossing a river he was arrested at his orders and surrendered to the king.[32]

---

30 The royal citadel was hated by the Bariots as the instrument and symbol of royal rule and the loss of their municipal independence; it had already been destroyed once in 1132; *Al. Tel.* ii. 34, p. 39. The king had then, in an attempt to conciliate the citizens, promised not to have the citadel rebuilt; *Cod. dipl, Bar.* v, 137–9, no. 80, but had clearly gone back on his word after 1139.

31 The 'destroyed' city of Bari was recorded in a charter of January 1157, the will of a former inhabitant now living in Giovinazzo; *Cod. dipl. Bar.* v, 195–6, no. 114. The town appears, however, to have been repopulated, at least in part, by February 1159; *ibid.* v, 200–2, no. 117. For discussion of the use of the 'historic present' in this passage, see Jamison (1957), 236; Hoffmann (1967), 133–4; and above, pp. 41–2.

32 Richard of Aquila was Count of Fondi. He was descended from a prominent Norman family from L'Aigle (dépt. Orne), who had been important in the northern part of the principality of Capua since the last years of the eleventh century and had succeeded his father Count Godfrey in 1148; Garufi, *Necrologio di S. Matteo,* 8; Cuozzo (1984), 282–4. He was a cousin of Count Roger of Avellino (see Genealogical Table IV). He had taken advantage of the disorder in the previous year to seize the towns of Suessa and Teano in the central part of the principality of Capua; *Annales Casinenses* ad ann. 1155, MGH SS xix, 311.

He was thrown into chains soon afterwards at Palermo, and the admiral had him blinded. Count Richard had greatly displeased the king before, but he earned his favour by this deed, although he did not completely escape a reputation for infamy. For I have heard many people consider it to have been a criminal act for him to have vilely betrayed his lord, a man of the greatest nobility and humanity, to whom he had in addition bound himself by an oath of loyalty.

But the king had conquered the Greeks and put Count Robert to flight; he pursued his remaining enemies, who all fled from his presence, and put down the disorders throughout Apulia and the Terra di Lavoro. Successful in all his actions, he crossed the Straits and returned to Palermo.[33]

9 The king's return to Sicily

Meanwhile Count Godfrey (to whom the crossing of the Straits had been forbidden) was blinded and imprisoned at Maio's behest.[34] Count Simon, who had remained at Policastro, was summoned to the court for some reason so that he could be arrested as soon as he arrived. But just as he was setting out for the journey, he was prevented by an opportune death.[35] Count William of Lesina,[36] Bohemond of Tarsia and several others were also already being held in chains at

33 William I was still at Salerno in July 1156 when he issued a charter there confirming the property and rights of the bishopric of Troia; *Guillelmi I Diplomata*, 38–41, no. 14 (= Martin, *Les Chartes de Troia*, 239–41, no. 75). He probably returned to Sicily soon afterwards.

34 However, Godfrey only died on 8 April 1174. He was buried in Palermo cathedral; Garufi (1912), 339–40; Poso (1988), 57.

35 Count Simon was dead by October 1156, when a charter referred to his unjust alienation of lands belonging to a dependency of the see of Lipari; *Guillelmi I Diplomata*, 44–6, no. 16 (= Kehr (1902), 433–4, no. 15). But to infer, as Garufi (1942), 59–60 does, that this was in fact the reason why he was summoned to court, contradicting the *History*, is going beyond the evidence. Though the comital title lapsed, his family was not dispossessed. Simon's son Manfred gave the bishopric of Lipari some houses at Butera for his father's soul in December 1158; Garufi (1910), 84, no. 10.

36 William had been Count of Lesina since at least 1141. But by October 1156 a new count had been appointed, Geoffrey de Ollia, the son of a former royal justiciar, Henry de Ollia; Petrucci, *Cod. dipl. Tremiti* iii, 287–91, no. 103, 300–3, no. 108.

Palermo;[37] among them was Robert of Bova, who was said to be a maternal uncle of Count Everard. He was a good warrior, but disloyal, and the king of France had ordered him to go into exile for a time after he had perpetrated some act of treachery there. Tancred and William, the sons of Duke Roger by a nobly-born mother with whom the duke had consorted, were kept under arrest within the palace compound.[38] But Maio's mind did not rest and cease from its unspeakable plan when he saw the prisons full of famous and noble men. He ordered some to have their eyes gouged out, others to be beaten with cudgels, and some to be put into foul snake-pits. He took their wives and daughters away from their houses and shut them up in different places; he forced some to serve his own lust, and others to offer their bodies for sale indiscriminately under pressure of poverty. The traitor's rage could not be sated by all these events, and he thought he had achieved nothing while he saw Count Everard surviving unscathed. But he was at a loss to know what charge to lay against so great a man, whose loyalty was obvious to all. Therefore he spied on all that the count did and said in order to find grounds for slandering him.

So one day when the count went out to hunt with a few followers, the admiral went straight to the king and announced that Count Everard had left court without permission with a large force of knights; this was clear proof of rebellion, and if he were to be allowed to leave freely he would have many who supported his plan. He persuaded the king to send messengers without delay to call the count back from his journey. When the count heard the king's command, he abandoned his hunting expedition and returned to Palermo. He was immediately

37 According to the *Chron. Casauriense*, 895–7, which confirms that he was imprisoned, in punishment for his failure to resist Robert of Loritello's invasion, Bohemond was then (unlike the others) released, but died soon afterwards. His sons were not allowed to succeed him in his county. The new count was a certain Walter. (For Bohemond's career and family, see above, note 18.)

38 Tancred and William were the illegitimate sons of Duke Roger by a daughter of Accardus, lord of Lecce and Ostuni, whose son Godfrey became Count of Montescaglioso *c.* 1152/3. Tancred was born *c.* 1134, William *c.* 1138. Subsequently, under William II in 1176, Tancred became one of the two Master Constables and Justiciars of Apulia and Terra di Lavoro, commanded the expedition against Byzantium in 1185, and was crowned king in January 1190 after William II had died childless. He died in January 1194. For his career before 1190, see Reisinger (1992), 10–18.

summoned to court, arrested and put in chains. At first he had his eyes gouged out, and soon after the admiral had his tongue cut off as well. At that point opposition died down throughout the kingdom; all those brave men whom the admiral thought he had cause to fear had either been imprisoned or forced into exile.

When Maio saw that no one was now left who was able to or dared to oppose his will, he again laid plans to carry out the crime which circumstances had forced him to postpone. He thought that this would be easiest to do if he first won the love of the populace and if he appointed his family and relations to the highest offices of the realm so as to protect himself against the pride of the nobility by their support. So he put the seneschal Simon, his sister's husband, in charge of the whole of Apulia and the Terra di Lavoro as Master Captain, and made his brother Stephen admiral of the fleet.[39] Meanwhile he himself distributed much largesse to the poor, made himself sympathetic to everyone, and decided to give much honour to ambassadors, wherever they came from. He put knights who were good warriors from southern Italy and north of the Alps under obligation to him by giving them large payments indiscriminately, and often gave clerics appointments of great honour, as appropriate to each one's status. In this way he was anxious to omit nothing in any way which might seem useful to win the support of ordinary people. While making these preparations to destroy the king, the admiral cleverly disguised his intentions, and the realm appeared to be at peace for a time, except that Count Robert harried the territory of the Abruzzi and adjacent districts of Apulia with constant raiding to such an extent that an army had to be retained in Apulia, where there was frequent fighting, the outcome of which was inconclusive. Meanwhile Richard of Mandra, Count Robert's constable, was captured together with the Bishop of Chieti and brought to Palermo.[40]

---

39 Simon was Master Captain from July or August 1156, at first with Peter of Castronuovo as a colleague (see below, p. 119), and then, from May 1158 at the latest, along with Maio's brother Stephen; Jamison (1913), 287–9. In addition to the evidence cited there, Simon was also recorded as 'royal seneschal and Master Captain of Apulia' in an important court case involving the monastery of St Sophia, Benevento, held at Capua in October 1158; Pergamene Aldobrandini (formerly, until 1990, in the Biblioteca Apostolica Vaticana), Cartolario II, no. 13.

40 The bishop was almost certainly Alan, who received a donation from Count Robert of Loritello in July 1154; Ughelli, *Italia Sacra* vi, 706–7.

10 Africa lost

During this period a treaty was made with the Greek emperor and peace agreed. The Greeks who had been held in chains since the war at Brindisi were sent back to Constantinople. Up till now Maio had overcome every crisis; his power was now so great that he seemed to be endowed with the status not so much of an admiral as of a king. He was now openly making remarks about how mad the king was; he was now making fun of his foolishness in public, and whenever the king gave orders for something tyrannical and barbarous on his advice (such as having people blinded, their tongues cut out and suchlike), he would himself later give instructions that it should not be done, stating that not every order that a tyrant had foolishly or madly issued should immediately be put into effect, or the lives of innocent people would frequently be in danger. What he was aiming to do was to incite public opinion against the king and arouse everyone's opposition against him.

Many think that this was the reason why he allowed Africa [i.e. Mahdia] to be taken by the Muslims. For while a fleet had been dispatched to Spanish waters, the extremely powerful king of the Almohads laid siege to Africa; and when news of this was brought to Sicily, it was decided to recall the fleet in order to assist Africa.[41] At the time it was commanded by Caid Peter, a eunuch. Like all the palace eunuchs, this man was a Christian only in name and appearance, but a Muslim by conviction. It consisted of about 160 galleys. They returned from Spain, and when they could be seen from the Almohad look-out posts, the knights who were in Africa won new heart and began to shout, challenge the enemy, and point to the approaching galleys. The king of the Almohads, on the other hand, was terrified by the unexpected arrival of the galleys, and ordered his army to return to camp; it was so large that it could hardly be controlled.

---

41 The 'king of the Almohads' was Abd-al-Mumin. The Almohads were a Berber confederation who followed the puritanical teachings of an Imam called Mohammed ibn Tumart (d. 1129). They conquered the Maghreb in the 1140s, Tunisia in the 1150s and those parts of Spain still in Islamic hands in the 1160s. See Le Tourneau (1969). Pseudo-Hugo's use of the word *Masmudi* to describe them shows his knowledge of the Islamic world, since the sect was originally based on the Masmuda tribe in the High Atlas mountains.

When the fleet approached land, there was tremendous joy in the city, and the knights raised a battle-cry, and if, as they imagined, the fleet had attacked on one flank and they themselves had opened the gates and attacked the enemy on the other, then the barbarian army would have been defeated and destroyed that day. But that was not done. To everyone's amazement, just as many were already unfurling their sails, Caid Peter (who was commanding the fleet and planned the whole thing) inexplicably turned to flee, exposing his sails to the winds. The other galleys followed their fleeing commander as best they could; and the barbarians, not unaware of the traitor's treachery, manned sixty galleys, which they had earlier beached out of fear of the fleet, and gave chase to the fugitives on the spot. Seven galleys were captured by the Almohads; the others returned to Sicily, having acquitted themselves in a wretched and disgraceful fashion.[42]

This action strengthened the the morale of the barbarians and brought despair to the besieged. Although undefeated in the fighting, the knights were few in number and suffered from lack of food. They achieved whatever heroism could achieve under the impossible circumstances. Not only did they resist frequent attacks by large numbers of enemies with great bravery, but they went out almost every day and threw the barbarians' army into confusion, many of them returning after inflicting considerable casualties. So when the king of the Almohads had used up every means that he thought worth while for capturing the city, looking with amazement upon the bravery of the besieged knights, and full of admiration for their courage and loyalty, he had no hopes that the city could now be captured by force; if he had not learnt on the information of deserters that it was at the point of starvation, he would have withdrawn his army. When he heard that, contrary to human custom, they were now not hesitating to eat horses, dogs and other unclean animals, he tried to persuade the knights to surrender, saying that it was in vain that they were concealing their shortages; he was not unaware of what they were

---

42 The principal Muslim accounts of these events were by Ibn al-Athir and Ibn Khaldun; *BAS* i, 122–5, ii, 203–4. Ibn Khaldun estimated the Sicilian fleet at 150 galleys. Peter had originally been called Ahmed, and taken from Jerba to Sicily as a child, presumably when that island had been captured by the Sicilians in 1135; *BAS* ii, 187; Amari (1933–9), iii, 505. But the Muslim sources do not support Pseudo-Hugo's charge of treachery, instead ascribing the defeat of the Sicilian fleet to the prayers of Abd-al-Mumin.

suffering; no help would come to them from Sicily, for he had recently received letters from the palace eunuchs, from which he had clearly learnt what was really going on. In short, they should have no hope of escape, but he wanted to spare them because of their courage, and if they should prefer to stay with him out of fear of the tyrannous regime of the king of Sicily, he would give bounteous pay to as many of them as there were. If, on the other hand, they opted to return to Sicily, he would allow them free transit and give them the necessary ships.[43]

On considering this proposal, they asked for a few days' truce to send representatives to Sicily to ask for help; and if in the end they failed to get any, they would accept the proposed terms. This too was not denied them. But when their messengers came to Palermo and explained the danger and hunger their city was suffering, and that they had already suffered everything that dire necessity had inflicted upon them, and requested that at least some food should be sent there, they nevertheless achieved nothing with all their arguments. For the admiral had falsely indicated to the king that at his own orders enough grain had been stored in Africa to last for a whole year; and in public he would say openly that the king's opinion was such that he would say that he would suffer no loss if Africa were captured, for the city cost him more than the honour was worth; the knights' pay and the other things needed to defend the city represented major outgoings from a place from which he never expected to receive any income. This was what the admiral was saying, with the intention of showing that the king had gone mad, thinking that it was no loss if his realm was truncated by being deprived of such a fine city; and although help could easily be sent there, nor did he care about the disgrace involved, or the danger that would be posed to Sicily from North Africa.[44]

So when it was realised in Africa that the messengers had been deceived and they had no hopes of any assistance, and were no longer able to put up with the hunger, it was decided to stand by the

---

43 Ibn al-Athir, *BAS* i, 125, claimed that King William sent a message threatening reprisals against the Muslims of Sicily if his men were put to death.

44 Gaudenzi, *Chronicon Ferrariae*, p. 29, has a variant on this story, suggesting that Maio falsely reassured the king that all was well rather than arouse his anger (Cf. Jamison (1957), 288–9).

conditions previously agreed. So the city was finally surrendered to the Almohads, and after they had been given enough ships for the crossing, they sailed over to Sicily.[45]

11 Maio

Maio's intentions could no further or no longer be concealed from the king, and it could not be doubted that he was motivated by a desire to rule. Yet no one came forward to inform of this dastardly scheme; no one dared to reveal such open treason to the king, for everyone knew that he was not going to believe a word of it, and they remembered what had happened to Count Everard and so many others as a result. So they preferred silence to danger, and awaited the outcome with bated breath. Various contradictory rumours about this had now filled the whole of Sicily, and it was broadcast everywhere that the admiral had shown off to many of his associates some sort of diadem and other royal insignia which he had prepared for himself; and there were some who said that the queen had had them sent over to him from the palace. For they thought that the whole business was being undertaken with her consent, and that she was in league with Maio through some disgraceful agreement. To many these rumours seemed to be unfounded; nevertheless there were others who stated that Maio's associate, the notary Matthew,[46] had taken a large sum of money to Pope Alexander, who at that time was head of the

---

45 Mahdia surrendered on 21 January 1160; Ibn al-Athir, *BAS* i, 124. The Muslim historians suggest that the native population of these North African towns were restive under Sicilian rule, despite the relatively mild nature of that rule, and welcomed the Almohads as liberators; Abulafia (1985) 41–3.

46 Matthew came from Salerno. He was first attested in July 1156, when he was the notary who wrote the Treaty of Benevento. He was recorded as *Magister notarius* from March 1164, vice-chancellor from December 1169, was a royal *familiaris* throughout the reign of William II, and chancellor under King Tancred, who made one of his sons Count of Ajello. Another son, Nicholas, was Archbishop of Salerno from 1182 to 1221. Mathew died on 21 July 1193; Enzensberger (1967), 54–7. One of his brothers, Constantine, was abbot of the monastery of Holy Trinity, Venosa, from 1157/9 to 1167; Houben (1995); 158–9. Another brother, John, was Bishop of Catania from 1168 to 1169 (see below, pp. 171–2). His cousin Philip was a royal chamberlain in the Salerno region; Cuozzo (1984), 165.

Roman Church,[47] and on the advice and with the help of John of Naples, who was one of the cardinals, had asked that the king of Sicily be deposed so that the admiral might succeed in his place.[48] There was a precedent in one of the Frankish kings; when he was deposed on the grounds that he was useless, the Roman pontiff appointed Pepin, father of Charles, in his place.[49] The entire people was now saying this and more of the same kind at the street corners. Some were saying that the king was to be struck down with a sword in the palace itself, most that he was to be shut up in a monastery. There were also some who believed that he was to be sent off to an island.

These same rumours were being spread about in Apulia, and the disgrace of the thing turned the minds of all against Maio. So the people of Amalfi (who always used to be incited by new rumours) took the decision, first of all, not to obey any order emanating from Maio, and not to receive into their city anyone at all whom Maio had appointed as captain over Apulia. And the counts and other noblemen who particularly disliked Maio's influence discussed the matter and swore an oath among themselves to strive for Maio's death with all the forces at their command and with all their might, and neither to obey the court any more nor to abandon their new coalition until they had heard either that he had been killed or that he had fled the realm. They also decided that the same oath would be taken throughout

---

47 For the possible significance of this phrase in dating the work, see the introduction, p. 39 above.

48 John of Naples, Cardinal deacon of SS. Sergio e Baccho from 1150 to 1158 and Cardinal priest of S. Anastasia from 1158 to 1182, was one of the most prominent members of the College of Cardinals under Alexander III, in whose election he played a significant part. He was particularly active in affairs concerning the kingdom of Sicily and was also involved in the dispute between Henry II and Archbishop Thomas Becket. He was murdered while Apostolic legate in Constantinople in 1182. See Zenker (1964), 73–7.

49 The deposition of Chilperic in 751, often cited thereafter as a precedent for the deposition of an unsatisfactory monarch, e.g. by Gregory VII with regard to Henry IV of Germany in 1076 and 1080; Gregory, *Registrum* IV. 2, VIII. 21, ed. E. Caspar (MGH, 2 vols., Berlin 1920–3), 294, 563–5; Peters (1970), especially 34–45. Interestingly, while *Romuald*, 143, wrote of Pope Zacharias's agreement to Pepin's accession, he (or whoever wrote this part of his chronicle) omitted any mention of the deposition of the previous monarch; cf. Hoffmann (1967), 146.

the kingdom from those who were willing; if they were unwilling, it would be extracted from them none the less. Many cities and the greatest possible number of towns now joined their coalition. They went round the whole of Apulia and the Terra di Lavoro with an enormous number of knights, forcing everyone to take the oath to them. The coalition consisted of Count Jonathan,[50] Count Richard of Aquila, Count Roger of Acerra[51] and other counts and powerful men, among them the queen's blood-relative Count Gilbert, to whom the king had given the County of Gravina after he had recently summoned him from Spain.[52] At Salerno Marius Borell, a man of very great eloquence, addressed the populace with a very effective speech in which he persuaded the majority of citizens to let the counts in and take the oath to them in the same terms as they themselves had sworn.[53]

50 Count Jonathan of Carinola was the son of Richard, Count of Carinola and Duke of Gaeta (d. 1135) and was descended from a junior branch of the Capuan princely family. King Roger also gave him the new county of Conza, in the south of the principality of Salerno, c. 1145; Cuozzo (1984), 180–1, and for his family Schütz (1995), 372–6; Loud (1996), 332–3, which gives a genealogical chart.

51 Roger of Acerra was more usually known as Count of Buonalbergo (cf. for example a charter of his in June 1158, Cava dei Tirreni, Badia di S. Trinità (henceforth Cava), Arm. Mag. H. 32), though his family also held Acerra, near Naples. His father Robert, who died before 1154, had been given the county of Buonalbergo in Apulia by King Roger c. 1150; see Cuozzo (1984), 220–1. His family, the de Medania, came originally from Anjou and had been landholders in the plain of Naples since the 1090s; Cod. dipl. Aversa, 397, no. 51 (1091); Ménager (1975), 370–1. They were related to the San Severino family. Cf. Schütz (1995), 384–5.

52 Gravina had previously been held successively by two members of the north Italian family of the Aleramici (the relatives of King Roger's mother Adelaide), Silvester son of the margrave Manfred; Cava, Arm. Mag. H. 21–2 (November 1155) and then his uncle, Albert, son of the Margrave Boniface; Cava, Arm. Mag. H. 28 (March 1157). His sister-in-law Philippa continued to hold the nearby lordship of Forenza until her death in 1176/9; Garufi (1910), 53–8; Cuozzo (1984), 20, 22–3.

53 Marius Borell was a relative of the Counts of Sangro and was a vassal of Count Jonathan of Carinola in the principality of Capua; *Cat. Bar.* 152, art. 835; Cuozzo (1984), 230. The *Annales Ceccanenses* (MGH SS xix, 284) recorded that he had burned the town of Arce, on the kingdom's northern frontier, on 21 August 1155. He was therefore already an avowed rebel.

12 Count Andrew

At the same time Andrew of Rupecanina, who was in exile in Campanian territory at that time, when he saw that the realm was so deeply divided into different parties, got together some knights and captured Aquino.[54] He occupied the town of San Germano (which lies beneath Monte Cassino) and marched on from there as far as Alife. Soon afterwards he was surrounded by the same citizens who had welcomed him of their own accord, and escaped with difficulty with a few of his knights; he had found it safer to capture enemy cities than to get out of them once captured.

In the meantime, while Apulia was in turmoil in this way, Sicily remained at peace, and was disturbed by no disorders – for although both peoples are treacherous, shifty, and ready to commit any crime whatsoever, yet the Sicilians are more cautious at hiding their intentions and covering them up, and mollify those they hate with flattering adulation, in order to attack them when they do not expect it and thus do them all the more harm. But in addition the admiral had not allowed anyone to survive in Sicily who had the strength of character to dare to do anything. For Count Silvester was the most timid of men; although he supported the policy of the Apulians and had even promised that he would help them in all possible ways, he did not dare to do anything that would reveal his intentions.[55] And Count Roger of Creon, whose daughter Maio had violated, pretended to bear this insult patiently, and let the Apulians avenge it.[56]

54 Andrew of Rupecanina was the nephew of King Roger's rival, Count Rainulf of Caiazzo (d. 1139). His family had been in exile since his uncle's death, some of which period he had spent at the Byzantine court, whence he returned in 1161; Brand, *Deeds of John and Manuel Comnenus by John Cinnamus*, 130. He had already seized Alife once, in 1155 (*Annales Casinenses*, MGH SS xix, 311); it had been one of the principal centres of his uncle's dominions.

55 Count Silvester of Marsico was a relative of King Roger, for whom this new county in the southern part of the principality of Salerno had been created c. 1150. He was the son of Godfrey of Ragusa and grandson of Roger I of Sicily; Cuozzo (1984), 159–60. His presence at court is attested in December 1157; *Guillelmi I Diplomata*, 60–4, no. 22, p. 63 (= Pirro, *Sicula Sacra*, i, 97–8).

56 Roger of Creon, son of the late William of Creon, and his widowed mother Rocca appeared in a legal case before King Roger in May 1142 when they

When the admiral saw that the counts' forces grew enormously, contrary to his expectations, he first sent letters in the king's name to the maritime cities of Amalfi, Sorrento and Naples, which had not yet rebelled, and thence to Taranto, Otranto, Brindisi and Barletta on the Adriatic coast, warning them not to be affected by any rumours and not to believe the false insinuations of the counts and get mixed up with a crowd of traitors. But things had got to such a point that no one gave recognition to the royal letters; it was said that they were issued by a traitor's hand, and that it was Maio's policy that they set out, not the king's. Maio also repeatedly warned his brother Stephen (who was in command of the knights in Apulia) to resist Count Robert's repeated onslaughts, and advised him to give the knights an increase in pay to bind them more closely to himself, and to incite them to stand firm against the counts with gifts as well as promises. Fear of the counts had forced the seneschal Simon to retire into some well-defended town. He also decided to send the Bishop of Mazzara to Melfi as his representative, to calm the minds of the citizens and appease their anger.[57] But not only did the bishop make no attempt to dissuade the people of Melfi from their course of action, he even reinforced their indignation by telling them more and more frightful things about Maio's treachery than they had heard so far. Even Calabria began to sway, now that storms were shaking Apulia; its loyalty had previously hardly ever been affected.[58] This worried

were in dispute with the canons of Agrigento, *Rogerii II Diplomata*, 265–6, appendix II, no. 3 (= Collura, *Più antiche charte*, 35–7, no. 12). He is also mentioned in a forged charter ascribed to the king in favour of the bishopric of Messina, dated July 1144; *Rogerii II Diplomata*, 163–6, no. 58. He must have been related to Hugh of Creon, who exchanged properties with Abbot Ambrose of Lipari in 1105; White (1938), 248, no. 5, and his brother Matthew, who witnessed this transaction and two charters of Roger II in December 1125 and July 1126; Ménager (1956/7), 169–71, no. 5; *Rogerii II Diplomata*, 18–20, no. 7, and made a donation to the Greek monastery of St Philip at Fragalà in the Val Demone in 1122; Cusa, *Diplomi greci ed arabi*, 413–14. But in none of these documents did any member of this family, which came originally from Maine, have a comital title; Ménager (1975), 369–70.

57 Turstan, Bishop of Mazzara from December 1157; *Guillelmi I Diplomata*, 63, to February 1177, when he was one of those present at William II's marriage; Stubbs, *Gesta Regis Henrici II* i, 169. Cf. *Italia Pontificia* x, 253.

58 Garufi (1942), 50 suggests that this passage points to the author being a Calabrian.

the admiral even more, and he thought that he ought immediately to send a man there as his representative whose arguments the Calabrians were sure to trust.

13 Concerning Matthew Bonellus and how he killed Maio

He thought that no one would be able to carry out this embassy more effectively than Matthew Bonellus. His family was extremely noble, and his reputation was untarnished with everyone. Several Calabrian noblemen were related to him by lineage.[59] But, in addition, the admiral loved him no less than a son. When he looked at him, still young in age like one with his first youthful down still on his cheeks, of noble blood, gracious in appearance, with a strength of body greater than could be expected from one of that age, holding the finest territory in Sicily, he betrothed to him his daughter, who was still very young. Matthew distributed largesse to the knights and made himself liked by everyone; he was also second to none in the equestrian games which they call tournaments. Thus he won for himself the support of the knights, and became very well known. However, his character was unreliable; he was prone to abandon a plan which he had decided upon, willing to make promises but lukewarm when it came to acting upon them.

Matthew was captivated by the beauty of an illegitimate daughter of king Roger, who had been married to Hugh, count of Molise; and so he decided to abandon his marriage to the little girl to whom he was

---

[59] Matthew was lord of Caccamo and Prizzi on the island of Sicily. The *Chronicon Ferrariae*, 29, called him a *consanguineus* of the king, but this seems unlikely Jamison (1957), 289. His father William Bonellus gave some property at Caccamo to the see of Lipari in 1137; White (1938), 256, no. 15. This document refers to William's wife Sybilla and a son called Tancred, but makes no mention of Matthew, who was first recorded in November 1155, confirming his father's foundation of the priory of S. Angelo, Prizzi; Enzensberger (1967), 140–1, Anhang 1 (a forgery based on a genuine original). He witnessed a royal charter to Archbishop Hugh of Palermo in December 1157; *Guillelmi I Diplomata*, 63, and a grant was made by the Bishop of Agrigento at his request late in 1160; White (1938), 264–5, no. 24 (= Collura, *Più antiche carte*, 45–7, no. 18). One of his ancestors, Richard Bonellus, witnessed a charter of Countess Adelaide of Sicily confirming the privileges of the church of Palermo in 1112; Pirro, *Sicula Sacra*, i, 80–1.

betrothed, on the grounds that she was not noble.[60] He was also angered by the fact that the admiral, when he found out, gave orders that the countess's palace should be carefully guarded, thus hindering what they both desired.

He undertook the mission, and having crossed the Straits was explaining the reason for his visit to a number of powerful Calabrians who had come to discuss the situation with him, and arguing that Maio was in every respect harmless. Roger of Martorano, who was very important in Calabria at that time, answered on behalf of all who were present that he found it beyond belief that he could stoop to such a level of insolence as to follow the orders of this most wicked traitor by trying to prove that he was harmless in the face of everybody's opinion, and that he was taking the admiral's side in such a way that he could reasonably be suspected of involvement in his conspiracy: 'I would find it easier to understand that others should follow Maio's lunacy and get mixed up in his evil business, and would not have thought that a matter for such surprise. For a meagre inheritance and insufficient estates force some to abandon the path of honesty so as to make their poverty easier to put up with by any scheme whatsoever. Humble birth prevents others from hoping for any advancement, and makes their situation so miserable that they are prepared to serve those more powerful by flattering them, thinking that it is the height of good fortune if they are allowed to cling to the feet of noblemen, and in consequence they are not afraid to undergo any dangers whatsoever, and fear no accusations of wickedness. Those who wish to hope for great things although they have no nobility themselves and no virtue with which to redeem their descent differ from these, though they labour under a similar delusion when they undergo great dangers in order to be able to deny their humble origins. Many noblemen who have lost their reputation because of wicked deeds give an equal weight to right and wrong, thinking that

---

60 Hugh II of Molise died *c.* 1156; Jamison (1933), 92; he was certainly dead by October 1158; Pergamene Aldobrandini, Cartolario II, no. 13. The *Necrologio di Cod. Cas.* 47, 66, has two Count Hughs listed, on 29 October and 28 December, probably the two Counts of Boiano/Molise, but it is not clear which was which. John of Salisbury described his attempt to secure an annulment of his first marriage; Chibnall, *Historia Pontificalis*, 80–2. Eugenius III refused to allow this, but as Dr Chibnall points out, *ibid.*, 99, this must later have been granted. His widow, Adelaide, was still alive as late as 1206; Kamp (1973–82), i, 240.

there is nothing that they can do in future that could remove the brand of disgrace that has once been put on them. There are also some who are born from the seed of traitors and choose to follow their fathers' footsteps. One can properly put up with men of such a type obeying Maio's orders and frequenting his threshold. But no excuse can permit a young man of the highest nobility and unsullied reputation such as you, with the support of a wealthy patrimony, to gape at filthy lucre. Hold before your eyes the kind of parents who bore you, and you should understand that every approach to wrongdoing is barred to you, and that an obligation to spurn wickedness is imposed upon you. Indeed, if you were to see no one opposing the crimes of this traitor, then you at least ought to avenge the nobility whom this man is so horribly persecuting. Now that everyone has joined the opposition to him with one mind, are you alone going to argue that this man is harmless? So long as you assert his innocence you bring yourself under suspicion, and you ought to be afraid of causing some loss or tarnishing of your reputation.

'Can anyone be thought to be more harmful than he who thirsts for the blood of every good man, who harms no one unless he has found him to be innocent, and finally tries to snatch the realm away by trickery from the man through whom he has attained such a position of power? You call this policy harmless, you approve of this plan, you agree that the king should be killed or deprived of his status, although you are tied to him by an oath of loyalty, you agree that after he has been deposed, this notary who once sold olive-oil should become king?

'Look at the alternative: you will be the second man after the king, so long as he reigns; you will shine with the highest honours, and you will be given the choice of picking whoever you like as royal counts. But this way, if I am not mistaken, you delude yourself. That men's minds should be so blind! Imagine that the king had been deposed. What would happen? Do you think that Maio could impose his rule? On the very same day that he had taken over the realm he and all those associated with him would be, even if not cut down by the sword, then certainly stoned to death.

'Remember also that you are the only one left in Sicily who is thought to have any strength of character. You are the only one whom people look up to; whatever you are going to do, it cannot be concealed. Make your choice: do you prefer your virtue to be broadcast, or your wickedness? At the very least you should be ashamed to disappoint everyone's hopes. You should be ashamed to turn to the study of evil habits after such an auspicious start to your life. Your own nobility cannot but be stained by the contagion of a relationship with such a father-in-law. Reject him. If you are sensible, you will reject a wife who will bear you inferior children whose ambiguous descent will make them unlike their father. Finally, listen to the advice of your friends, and prepare yourself to avenge them all; assert your own freedom together with that of what is left of the nobility, and do not let this insufferable beast run riot any longer to our destruction. It may be that virtue has been put on trial, and that he has forced it underground with his ceaseless persecutions; yet the courage, and the swords, to avenge these crimes are not lacking. The king's own safety and the well-being and freedom of the realm are in your hands. When all others have been condemned for failing to carry out such a glorious deed, Fortune's smile has reserved to you the summit of great fame.

'And there is no need at all to hold back and put things off, or await a suitable opportunity. He thinks that he has enmeshed you so tightly in his snares and plots that there is no one he more freely allows to see him. So whether you approach him armed or unarmed, alone or accompanied by a crowd of knights, neither will give him cause for fear or arouse his suspicions. You will, therefore, be able to cut him down without difficulty wherever you choose. Once he is dead, you need have no fear that he will leave behind anyone who might avenge him. Young man, act now. Strive to attain this degree of happiness, fearlessly follow the path to which virtue summons you, and do not deny the duty you owe and which Fortune demands. If you promise to do this, with our unreserved support, you will not only achieve immortal glory from this deed, but also the well-deserved reward which we will all willingly grant – for we desire and demand in every way that the Countess of Catanzaro be joined to you in the bond of matrimony. To remove any possible shadow of doubt, let us give you the complete assurance of an agreement, whether you prefer the formality of an oath, or whether you think that any other type of contract is necessary for you. I will not waste time by telling you how much higher the countess's nobility is than yours, and how she has refused to marry men of great power. I imagine that none of these things is unknown to you.'[61]

---

61 Clementia, Countess of Catanzaro, was the daughter and heir of Count Raymond of Catanzaro (who died before 1158), a great-nephew of Robert

By means of this speech he set on fire the young man's spirit, ready as it was to be moved by love of glory, and made him hate Maio's crimes. Matthew was already inclined against a marriage alliance with him, although hesitancy of some kind still held him back. But soon, having thought about it a little, and balancing up on the one hand the lowly origin of the girl he was engaged to, her father's infamy, and the danger that was threatening Maio, and on the other hand the promised marriage to the countess, he was ashamed to hesitate about it, and became more convinced of the advantages of this plan. He no longer delayed, but replied to Roger of Martorano and the other noblemen who were present that he would confidently undertake the course to which they had persuaded him, and would carry it out entirely as promised, so long as they adhered to the proposed agreement. Consequently after both sides thought that none of the things they had agreed required substantial changes, and when later the countess herself as well as her relatives confirmed the prearranged marriage contract, and both sides had sworn an oath and confirmed the agreement they had made, a definite date was arranged for Maio's death. Matthew Bonellus added that, should a suitable occasion present itself in the meantime, he had no intention of waiting for the agreed day, and that he would do nothing to prevent the act from being carried out as soon as possible.

One could now see that in other respects too Fortune, tired of the admiral's great successes, had deserted his service. For when the day approached which he had set for the king's murder, he wanted to have a private discussion with the archbishop. As each of them in turn discussed the king's speedy removal, the suppression of popular demonstrations and the condition the realm would soon be in, a disagreement arose about the treasury and about who should be granted custody of the king's sons. The admiral stated that he should be assigned wardship of the children, the treasury and the entire palace, since he needed to wrestle with the administration of the kingdom, and the treasury was absolutely essential if rebel uprisings were to be put down and attacks by external enemies repulsed; and the conflicts and civil wars that would arise could not be controlled

> Guiscard, and his wife Segelguarda. She was first recorded in December 1145, when she witnessed a charter of her aunt Countess Berta of Loritello; Pratesi, *Carte latine di abbazie calabresi*, 41–2, no. 14. She later married Hugh Lopinus, recorded as Count of Catanzaro from 1168. See Jamison (1931), 451–70, and Genealogical Table V.

without major expenditure. But the archbishop said that he would never allow this, for a great deal of ill will would ensue if Maio had wardship of the children, and it would greatly confirm the suspicions the people already held. It would make everyone absolutely certain that his real aim was nothing other than the crown, and opposition to him would harden in every way. The law did not permit a man under such suspicion to be made the boys' ward, and required such a man to be removed if he was their guardian. It would be a more sensible policy to entrust the custody of the children and of the treasury to the archbishops, bishops and other respected men of religion, against whom no suspicions could be harboured. For the income of the entire realm would suffice for the expenditure that was required, and if there was a real need, he would get as much as he needed from the guardians of the treasury.

Their disagreement was dragged out at length in this way with arguments on both sides; the archbishop could not be moved from the position he had taken up, while Maio did not care for it at all, since he had known that he was trying to sabotage his plans; finally he lost his temper and made the point that he had deserved nothing of the archbishop to make him oppose his project. Now he claimed back what he was owed, in that it was from good will alone that he had invited him to be an associate and participant in his plan; for he had no need of his support, and could easily carry his intentions out without his knowledge, or even in the face of his opposition. But the disagreement had done no harm at this juncture, and he was now in no doubt as to what expectations he could have of such an associate. Furthermore, he now regretted his plan and entirely turned his mind away from the undertaking, and would never consider anything of the kind again.

At this the archbishop – although he did not believe that he meant any of what he said – replied, 'That is a proper view, and I entirely agree with it; for the wickedness of the operation repels me too, and it cannot be done without danger to both our personal safety and our honour.'

So Maio went away, having dissolved the agreement of alliance that they had made a little while before, and made every effort to prepare for revenge. First of all he provoked the king's mind against his former associate with the hope of gain (for which he was keen), so as to extort 700 ounces of gold from him. Although a loss of this size might easily have moved the archbishop to become impatient with anguish, and he seethed with anger at the shame and indignity of what had happened, nevertheless he directed his thoughts entirely to avenging the matter. Previously they had been united by such a bond of harmony and devotion that they would call one another brothers; now as vicious but secret enemies they employed all their efforts towards each other's destruction. No longer did one seek the other's good fortune, but they grudged each other their lives and strove to kill each other. The admiral intended to kill the archbishop by giving him some deadly poison to drink, and watched for a suitable place and time to do it. But the latter revealed Maio's shocking crime to many, both in person and through many members of his household, and called for them to avenge such wickedness; deflecting their prejudice against him, he incited the minds of the common people against Maio, as well as aligning many knights and noble persons with himself by all sorts of arguments.

At this time the Logothete Nicholas,[62] who was in the territory of Calabria at the Court's orders, wrote a letter to Maio in which he gave a short account of everything that Matthew Bonellus had done and of the agreement made between him and the Countess of Catanzaro, as he had learnt from what his friends had told him. This at first caused Maio to feel insecure and reflect for some time, and he could not bring himself to believe that the same man was plotting to thwart him whom he had made every effort to raise up, and had treated as a son. But when he had come to put more trust in the story, confirmed as it was by many others, he considered how to avenge himself, and addressed his mind to preventing Matthew from getting away with it unpunished.

After he had acted as described, Matthew Bonellus returned to Sicily and went as far as Termini, a town which is 20 miles from Palermo.[63]

---

62 The Logothete Nicholas can be attested from 1145 and continued in office until the autumn of 1172. He was the son of one of Roger I's chaplains, a Greek priest called Scholaris. His brother Sergius may also have held the same office, probably immediately before he did. There was only one Logothete of the Palace at any one time; the office was of Byzantine origin and up to 1173 was always held by a Greek. The Logothete acted as the king's spokesman and master of ceremonies, and sometimes also officiated as a judge in Calabria; Jamison (1951), especially 13–17.

63 *The Travels of Ibn Jubayr*, 344–5, described Termini as follows: 'This town is strongly fortified, and surmounts and towers above the sea ... [it] is a

Here he was met by one of his knights, whom he had left at Palermo when he set off for Calabria, and from him he learnt about Maio's state of mind and intentions, including the fact that he had prepared a dungeon for him on his return. Although he was urgently summoned by a letter from the admiral, and the short period of time did not allow for longer reflection, he thought it a sensible idea not to leave Termini until he had sent messengers to test Maio's attitude. So he sent Maio a letter in which he said that the Calabrian uprising had been put down by his efforts; instead of being enemies, everyone in Calabria had become very well disposed towards him and ready to do whatever he might order, and they were awaiting nothing else but his instructions. His own loyalty in this matter had been tested sufficiently and more than sufficiently. He had spared no effort in carrying out the admiral's policies, though of course the reason why he had followed his wishes most diligently and obeyed his orders in every respect was the hope and belief that Maio would think that a man whom he saw sweating on his behalf deserved to be embraced with greater good will, and would not postpone the agreed wedding to his daughter. But the opposite had occurred. Instead of favour, he had been repaid with ingratitude as his reward. He had already been kept in suspense by the long wait for the promise to be fulfilled; now he was being tortured even longer, and defrauded of his desire. Now he asked for the following – he demanded it with every possible prayer – he appealed by anything that he might have deserved of him – that Maio should reward the man who had turned his fear into joy and had brought the frightening and dangerous beginnings of a war to a happy outcome by granting him the happiness of the promised marriage on his return.

The admiral looked at this letter and showed it to his friends, especially those who had incited his anger towards Matthew Bonellus, saying that it was now obvious that what they had said to him was false; it was disgraceful that a man should be charged with such an accusation who was requesting marriage to his daughter with such insistent prayers and wishes, and he would never again believe anyone who had anything bad to say about him. So he wrote back to him immediately that he should feel safe to come and discuss his worries with

> high and impregnable fort, and in its lower part is a thermal spring which serves the citizens as baths.' Edrisi, *BAS* i, 16, noted that the town was walled and had the remains of an ancient theatre, the new fortress, and two bath-houses.

him, and that as soon as he came, he would make arrangements to satisfy his desire, and that he would attain the marriage that he had requested in such affectionate terms. When he had seen the content of these letters, Matthew entered Palermo with a happy look on his face, as though he had been mollified by the promise of marriage; and there he was received in a friendly and respectful way by the admiral, and thanked him, and requested that what he had been promised should be effected by a swift consummation. Then he went secretly to the archbishop, who was suffering from a fever, and told him everything that had occurred; he was earnestly warned by him to make all haste he could and set aside any cause for delay, for such a great plot could not be put off without danger.

In the meantime Matthew Bonellus was carefully looking for a suitable time to put the operation into effect; and Fortune did not desert his preparations. Egged on by regret that she had placed a man of low birth, stained by such terrible crimes, almost at the pinnacle of affairs, she now threatened to throw him over the edge, and little by little she began to bring the top of her revolving wheel down to the bottom against him as she described her circuits. For when the admiral had made the archbishop drink poison administered by one of his servants (whom he had suborned with bribes and promises), he was surprised that he took a long time to die and was languishing, and he was affected by terrible anxieties, afraid that the archbishop might be restored to his previous state of health. He saw that this had happened because the poison was not strong enough, and prepared another which had much more power to harm and was more deadly. On a particular day, about the eleventh hour, he took this with him and called on the archbishop,[64] sat down beside him and began by asking him how he was; then he went on to say that he would easily survive, if he trusted the advice of his friends, and asked him to take some medicine which was soothing and highly effective for this kind of illness, which he himself had had prepared most carefully in his presence. But the archbishop swore that he was in such a state of depression, and suffering such weakness of the limbs, that a body as weak as his would not be able to suffer an evacuation of the bowels without considerable danger, and he himself could not bear even to see any kind of medicine whatsoever, and could only eat food with

---

64 Jamison (1957), 290 suggested that the archbishop's house was at the junction of the Via Coperta and the modern Via Celso.

the greatest difficulty. So Maio ordered the potion that he had prepared to be kept for another day, in order not to give the appearance of making the suggestion too insistently and thus to draw suspicion to himself. He sat by his side in a more friendly manner, and contradicted him meekly about this, exhorting him not to have such a negative attitude to his friends' advice, and not to oppose his wishes permanently, since he knew that it was typical of an illness that the mind frequently wanted what was harmful, and similarly rejected things that were beneficial; if he wanted to get better, he would sometimes have to force himself; and he swore that he cared about the archbishop's health just as much as about his own, for if he should happen to die, he did not know what he would do next, where to turn to, what support to look for, whose loyalty to rely upon. He put no trust or reliance in anyone else. The archbishop thanked him, apologised for the weak state he was in, and praised the reliability of his friendship. Replying at great length to each of his points and adding a great many words about other things as well, he quickly sent someone to tell Matthew Bonellus that if he were a real man, he should make haste and prepare to carry out in a manly fashion what he had promised. He should secretly get his knights armed – he should station armed men in appropriate places – in the meantime he himself would keep Maio there by engaging him in various topics of conversation.

As ordered, Matthew Bonellus summoned his knights to the back part of the house, explained the whole matter to them, and said a few words to encourage them to be brave and strong at heart – the plot could be carried out easily with no cause for fear or danger – if Maio left, feeling secure because he had no inkling that this danger was upon him, then it was certain that every escape-route was closed against him; on the other hand, if he was aware of it and afraid to leave, and tried some other plan, then he would be cut down just as swiftly in the residence itself, and he would be granted no time to plan anything. The men did not need to be burdened with long arguments, since they had both been bound by an oath to undertake the operation and were motivated by hatred of Maio, and even more eagerly motivated by hope of gain.

Darkness was now following the setting of the sun, and you could see the whole city paralysed by sudden and strange rumours, the citizens going about in groups, this way and that, and asking each other in turn what fear it was that had suddenly stunned the city in this way. You would see some with their heads bent to one side, but their ears pricked up, forming little groups in the city's squares and proffering different and contradictory comments on the situation. What most people thought about it was that in accordance with Maio's plans, the king would be killed in the street as he went to visit the archbishop that night. But Matthew Bonellus, when he saw that his knights were keen and bold and that Maio was being kept occupied by the archbishop, just as required, and that the night was providing an equally opportune cloak of darkness, began by positioning several knights in suitable places along the Via Coperta, which stretches from the archbishop's residence to the royal palace, along which Maio might be expected to escape.[65] Next he secretly placed ambushes along the road he would have to cross, and carefully placed more of his knights to watch the passageways ('veins', as they are commonly called), in case he tried to pass through them into other parallel streets.[66] And he told some of his own men to mix with the crowd that was in attendance on Maio. He himself planned to encounter the admiral with a few men by the gate of Saint Agatha as he was coming out, and thought that this was a suitable place for an ambush, since the road becomes extremely narrow there, then divides into three and suddenly becomes extremely wide after its previous narrowness.

So when the admiral decided to take his leave after having failed to achieve what he intended, the archbishop ordered the doors to be carefully barred as soon as he had gone. With the bishop of Messina accompanying him,[67] he had reached the narrow section of the street near the place of the ambush when the notary Matthew, a member of his household, and the chamberlain Atenulf came up to him, having made their way through the crowd of followers with some difficulty,[68]

- 65 Cf. Broadhurst, *The Travels of Ibn Jubayr*, 347: 'On leaving the castle [i.e. the royal palace] we had gone through a long and covered portico down which we walked a long way until we came to a great church. We learnt that this portico was the king's way to the church.'
- 66 The *Chronicon Ferraria*, 29–30, said that Maio was murdered as he returned from the bath-house – its author was probably misled because one of these alleyways led to a bath-house; Jamison (1957), 290.
- 67 The bishop (by this date properly archbishop) of Messina was called Robert; for him see Starrabba, *I Diplomi della cattedrale di Messina*, 21–3, no. 15 (January 1159) and Romuald, p. 230 below.
- 68 Atenulf was a Lombard, son of a certain John and grandson of Count Ursus. He had been chamberlain of the principality of Salerno in 1144–6; see Jamison (1913), 391–2 and her calendar of documents, nos. 14, 18,

and murmured into his ear that Matthew Bonellus seemed to be preparing an ambush with a number of armed knights, and that, according to what they had heard, he himself was the intended victim. Maio stopped in shock at this sudden unpleasant news, and asked for Matthew Bonellus to be summoned to him. When he realised that he was being called for, and that his plans were no longer secret from Maio, he jumped out from his hiding-place, and suddenly appeared before him, menacing him with his drawn sword, and said, 'Look, traitor, here I am: I am avenging the nobility you destroyed, even if belatedly, to put a limit to your unspeakable wickedness, and with a single blow against you I will erase both the title of admiral and of false king.' Although Maio was not even allowed a respite for prayer, his wit did not desert him even in the final crisis of his life. He shifted to one side and avoided the blow of the raised sword, turning the striker's force to nothing. But he was not able to avoid the impact as he came at him again with greater power; he sustained a mortal blow, and fell to the ground dying. Those who had been in attendance on him suddenly disappeared, each escaping as he could. The notary Matthew, severely wounded, got away with some difficulty in the darkness of the night.

Matthew Bonellus and his companions, having acted in this way, were afraid to stay in Palermo any longer, since they were not sure what the king would think of what they had done. So they went that same night to Caccamo, one of his fortresses. But once the traitor's death became known, the entire city — which until then had been in a state of suspense with contradictory rumours – exploded with such joy that it was only then that Maio's unpopularity with the people became apparent. For some threw his body into the middle of the street and kicked it with their feet; others unrestrainedly pulled out the hairs of his beard and spat in his face. And there were also some who thought that Maio was still alive, and that such a clever man would never have been lacking in wit to such an extent as to let himself be killed like this – they asserted that the person who was lying there dead had been one of his knights.

20–1. No. 14, for which Jamison could not provide a reference and which has never been published in full, is located in the Archivio diocesano, Salerno (Mensa Archiepiscopalis, Arca I, no. 53). Atenulf had been one of the chamberlains of the royal palace, the first recorded holder of such a post, since 1155; Jamison (1957), 45.

During that night the king, when he heard the people's unprecedented demonstration from his palace, wondered what storm had been raised up in the city, and when he saw Odo, the master of the stable,[69] who had gone to the palace to inform him of what had happened, he learnt everything from him, and was extremely angry that anyone should have tried anything so bold without his orders. For even though it was accepted that the admiral was plotting something against the royal majesty, it ought in the first instance to have been brought before him, and punishment should have been reserved to the king. The queen heard of Maio's death with much greater anger and intolerance, and exploded with even more anger at Matthew Bonellus and his associates. In the meantime, in accordance with the king's instructions, sentries were selected to go round the city throughout the night to prevent any rioting or trouble from arising out of the incident. A number of men were also assigned to guard the admiral's house. Permission was given for the houses of his relatives by blood and marriage to be looted without constraint, since the mob could not easily be hindered from this.

14 The king's capture[70]

On the following day the king selected his *familiaris* Henry Aristippus, Archdeacon of Catania (a man of most humane character and well educated in both Latin and Greek culture), to exercise the admiral's office in his stead for the time being and take control of the royal notaries; and he dealt with the realm's affairs in secret with this man.[71] He and Count Silvester explained the admiral's deceptions

- 69 The *magister stabuli* may have been the official who in other medieval royal households was known as the marshal, effectively the second-in-command of the royal household troops.
- 70 In the early MSS. this was the beginning of a new section (IV, part III of the main text).
- 71 Henry was a key figure in the transmission of Greek learning to the West during the twelfth-century renaissance. He translated the *Meno* and *Phaedo* of Plato (the latter done while he accompanied the king on his mainland campaign in 1156; see *Phaedo interprete Henrico Aristippo*, ed. L. Minio-Paluello (London 1950), 90), the fourth book of Aristotle's *Meteorologica*, and was alleged to have translated some of the works of Gregory Nazianzes. He also brought back important Greek MSS. from Constantinople when he went there as one of the Sicilian envoys in 1158, including

and intention to the king, and tried to mollify his attitude towards Matthew Bonellus; but the king's anger would not have been appeased by any arguments, if certain royal crowns had not been found in Maio's treasure-chests, which provided proof of his crimes; so in the end the king understood from incontrovertible evidence that he had been deceived. On the same day, therefore, Maio's son Stephen was arrested, together with his brother Stephen (both of them were admirals), as well as the notary Matthew, who was his principal assistant. Whatever could be found in his treasure-chests was transferred to the court without delay; and the eunuch Andrew and several others were tortured and forced to tell whatever they knew about Maio's possessions, whether hidden somewhere secretly or placed in the care of friends.[72] A lot of things were found as a result of their disclosures, and in the end his son Stephen, after having been subjected to many terrors and threats, swore that he knew nothing more that he could tell the court about this except that he thought that he had once heard his father say that the bishop of Tropea had received about 300 ounces of gold from him ostensibly as a deposit.[73] So the bishop was summoned to court and ordered to return the stated amount of gold which Maio had deposited with him. He replied that he would return more than they asked for; when he had returned home he handed over to the prison warders who had been sent to accompany him 700,000 *tari*.[74]

> one of Ptolemy's *Almagest* (now Venice, Cod. Marciana gr. 313). He was archdeacon of Catania from the summer of 1156. See Jamison (1957), xvii–xxi; Haskins (1927b), chapters 8–9; Berschin (1988) 232–4. For the *familiares*, see below, note 101.
>
> 72 Maio's houses in Palermo near the church of St Cataldus (which he had founded) were later purchased by Count Silvester from the king; Garufi, *Tabulario di Monreale*, 163–5, no. 2 (1176, a charter of Silvester's son, Count William of Marsico). Stephen as emir had witnessed the royal charter to the Archbishop of Palermo in December 1157; *Guillelmi I Diplomata*, 63.
>
> 73 Hervey, attested as Bishop of Tropea from January 1155; *Guillelmi I Diplomata*, 14–16, no. 5 (= Ughelli, *Italia Sacra* ix, 451), witnessed the December 1157 privilege for the Archbishop of Palermo (as above) and another charter in April 1162; Garufi, *Tabulario di Monreale*, 161–3, no. 1, but by October 1163 was in exile in France; MPL cc. 269, ep. 211.
>
> 74 The *tari* was a gold coin, of Islamic origin, equivalent to a quarter *dinar*, minted in Sicily from the tenth century and also on the mainland at Amalfi from 960 and Salerno after *c.* 1000 30 *tari* were reckoned to be equivalent

After these events messengers were sent to Caccamo to summon Matthew Bonellus and tell him that having learnt of his crimes, the king had been happy to hear of the admiral's death; they were to state this on oath, to remove any cause for fear and suspicion that he might be in danger. Although Matthew had no faith in oaths of this kind, he knew that the king would not dare to do anything against him, both because of his popularity with the common people and because he was relying on the support of all the counts who had rebelled for this very reason together with the whole of Calabria. So he reached Palermo untroubled, accompanied by all his knights. As he entered the city a great crowd of both men and women went out to meet him, and accompanied him right up to the palace gate with enormous joy. There he was kindly received by the king, and unreservedly restored to his favour; and thence he was brought to his own house by the senior members of the court through the same throngs of common people.

By this famous deed, then, Matthew Bonellus won the hearts of the people and of the nobility, not only in Sicily but also across the Straits throughout Calabria, Apulia and the Terra di Lavoro, so that all praised his courage and bravery, and not even in the most distant parts of the realm did his command reach anyone without effect. Now that the reason for their rebellion had been removed, the counts themselves and the cities of Apulia together with all who had been allied to them awaited his intentions and plans for the future. In Sicily, indeed, and especially at Palermo, the entire people was now openly shouting that whosoever had tried to harm Matthew Bonellus should be adjudged a public enemy, and that they themselves would take up arms – even against the king himself – if anyone should try to punish him with any severity for the admiral's death. For everybody ought to follow the man who had restored freedom to everyone by the removal of a public threat to the realm.

The palace eunuchs, however, were afraid of his power because of their evil character and consciousness of their crimes, in that they had not only been aware of the admiral's plots, but had participated

---

to an ounce of gold. Under William I the weight of the Sicilian *tari* was about 1.05 grams, with a gold content of nearly 70 per cent. (Amalfitan *tari* were lighter, *c.* 0.88 g., and with a much lower gold content, 41–3 per cent). Travaini (1995) is now the standard work; see especially chapters 2–3.

in them; so they took steps to incite the king's anger and hatred towards him. Relying upon the advice of the queen herself, they explained the grounds for their fears to the king, and claimed that considerable danger would be hanging over the king's head if steps were not taken in time. For as a result of what had recently happened to him, Matthew Bonellus had been raised to such a height of pride that he thought that there was no one in the kingdom who was his equal in strength or power. When he saw the entire people flowing to his side, led by some rashness, and that even noblemen obeyed all his plans and followed his orders, he would think that nothing was forbidden that his spirit told him to do, and he would wish to be accorded even greater respect, not just by the common people, but by the magnates of the court as well. In the meantime he was binding everyone to himself with oaths and secret agreements. Furthermore, there were all the leaders on the mainland; he himself had got them into a position where they had offended the king to such an extent that they now thought that he would never forgive them. They were constantly inciting his juvenile mind along these lines: that if he wanted to attain the summit of glory and wished to be subject to no danger from now on, then he should make every effort to achieve both complete freedom for the kingdom and safety for himself. He would not be able to do that so long as the king was alive, and he should not let himself be deceived by the lying promises of the court into thinking that someone whose right hand he had cut off could so easily be reconciled to him. (For that was what the king thought and said: Maio's death had deprived him of his right hand.) Thirsty for glory, the young man was being incited even further on these grounds; he was ready to try and dare anything, and unless steps were carefully taken against plans of this kind, he would surely follow wherever the heat of his character and youthful impulse led him, and would not be restrained by any fear of perjury. Those who thought that he would keep faith with anyone were indeed stupid and blind, since he had ignored the claims both of oaths and of family relationship. He had betrayed a father-in-law who had been like a father to him in that he had obtained the restoration of his own patrimony through his help, showing no gratitude for such great benefits, and having the innocent man betrayed and killed. (They asserted that everything that he himself and his companions had nailed on the admiral was false, and he had not in fact prepared the crown that had been found in his treasure-chest for his own use, but for the king's, to be handed over to him on the first of January as the customary New Year's gift.)[75] All of Matthew Bonellus's oaths and alliances could not have been made just for the single purpose of killing Maio. He had another, greater intention, and was aiming at a higher ambition, towards which he thought that the route could appropriately be prepared by means of a first step of this kind.

By constantly suggesting these ideas and more of the same kind to the ears of the king, they brought it about that he would no longer admit Matthew Bonellus among his courtiers, and came to believe that he had killed Maio for no other reason than in order to put into effect the plan for the king's own death which he had shared with a number of traitors. Quick as he was to punish, he could now scarcely tolerate the delay in avenging this affair, but had to put it off to a suitable occasion, until the popular unrest had been sedated and the atmosphere favouring revolution died down. But in the meantime he ordered 60,000 *tari* to be recovered from Bonellus and from those who had stood surety for him, which he had once promised that he would give to the court in order to receive his patrimony; but the admiral, sparing his son-in-law, had deferred payment of the sum without informing the king. So Matthew Bonellus was hard hit by the sudden and unexpected demand to pay this long-dormant debt, and he also saw that he was being invited to court less frequently than before, and was no longer received as he had been accustomed to be; he wondered what this change might mean. And he had another not insignificant cause for fear and suspicion in that the chamberlain Atenulf seemed to be extremely powerful at court. He had had a very friendly relationship with Maio, and both he and Matthew's other enemies were exercising their hostility towards him fiercely and publicly, since they saw that Maio had been overthrown with the support and advice of the archbishop, who had recently succumbed to death,

---

75 *Strena*: a classical Latin word for a New Year's gift (from which derives the French *étrenne*); see especially Suetonius, *De Vita Caesarum, Augustus* 57; *Tiberius* 34; *Caligula*, 42 (and cf. above, p. 47). However, although the Sicilian royal chancery calculated the New Year from either 25 December or 1 January, elsewhere in the kingdom it was usually calculated from 15 March, while at Benevento it was reckoned from 1 March. It is clear from his dating of the Catania earthquake of February 1169 (see below, p. 216) that Pseudo-Hugo himself reckoned the beginning of the New Year to be in March. For the dating of the New Year within medieval Christendom as a whole, the classic discussion is still Poole (1934), 1–27.

exhausted by constant sickness. He assumed that all this could not be happening without the king's agreement, and that men of this kind would never dare to undertake anything against him if they did not think that the king's mind was set against him.

Things had reached such a point of foolishness and audacity that Atenulf's nephew Philip Mansellus paraded along the Via Marmorea at night with some armed knights, and was seen by several persons passing Matthew Bonellus's house particularly slowly.[76] When Matthew learnt of this, he told his own knights to arm themselves on the following night; he first planted ambushes in suitable places around his house, and then told the rest of the knights to go along the Via Coperta as far as the Galcule gate, parading up and down several times, and taking their time as they passed Atenulf's house. He hoped that in this way Philip and his knights, if they were to come out that night as on the previous night, would be discovered either by the one group as they crossed between the streets, or intercepted by the others who were lying in ambush. At the same time it would show that he was not unaware of their schemes, and that he had no lack of numbers or quality of knights, and had the power to destroy them to a man, if respect for the king were not holding back his freedom to undertake such an operation. So they spent about half the night awake, and then returned home without anything happening.

When Matthew Bonellus understood the king's intentions from these and many other indications, he thought he should make other arrangements for himself for the time being. The opportunity to discuss things was still there, and he recounted to his cousin Matthew of Santa Lucia and certain other Sicilian noblemen (who had come to Palermo after he had written to summon them) everything that had happened to him in due order, and that his enemies had conspired with the eunuchs to arouse the king against him and that they had achieved their aim with ease. He was even being forced to repay an old debt by the very same king from whom he had expected a reward for having saved his life. So he appealed to them, requesting that they put into effect the trust of friendship and sworn oaths that had recently bound them

---

76 Philip was the son of Hugh Mansellus, chamberlain of Duke William of Apulia in 1125 and royal chamberlain in the Valle Caudine (SW of Benevento) in 1139, and Atenulf's sister Marocta; Cava, Arm. Mag. F. 25; Bartoloni, *Le Più antiche carte dell'abbazia di S. Modesto di Benevento*, 23–4, no. 8; Salerno, Archivio diocesano, Mensa archiepiscopalis, Arca I, no. 53.

together, that in this his time of need they should not abandon him who had faced danger for the salvation of the entire realm and had not tried fraudulently to escape their common burden; and he warned them that they should make immediate plans to forestall the plots of their enemies and the king's ravings. If they were of one will and remained utterly firm in their intentions so as to sustain anything that might happen by sharing the danger, then they would never lack the support of the people and the favour of the knights. In this way they would easily achieve whatever they attempted. But if there was anyone who preferred to disengage himself by pretending that nothing had occurred, then not one of those who had conspired in Maio's death would escape.

Those present were shocked by the unexpectedness of these reports, and surprised and extremely angry that they were facing danger and ingratitude from the very source where they thought they had deserved well; but what made them most angry was that the chamberlain Atenulf had been so bold as to dare to show open hostility towards Matthew Bonellus. They thought that the matter ought not to be ignored for a moment longer, and that the tyranny and madness of a king of this sort should not be tolerated any further. Some thought that Atenulf himself ought to be attacked immediately, wherever they happened to find him, and that punishment for such insolence should not be put off any longer – for whatever action they set in motion, the people would keenly support. But others said that the matter would be more likely to succeed if they undertook it with more caution and moderation, and that their danger would not now be diminished by Atenulf's death but increased so long as they left unharmed the origin of these evils, which ought to be cut off first. They should take steps to see that with the source of these ills removed, the rest would easily follow; if the outflow from the spring were stopped, the arid streams could be dried up without difficulty. This was the majority opinion among them, and they decided to invite as allies in the operation Count Simon (son of King Roger by a concubine),[77] and Tancred, son of Duke Roger, whom we have mentioned before as outstanding by virtue of his intelligence and diligence rather than

---

[77] His mother was a sister of Count Hugh of Molise; Jamison (1933), 89. He was probably the Simon *comes Mitilene* (Count of Mileto?) at the royal court in December 1157; *Guillelmi I Diplomata*, 63.

bodily strength.[78] For they knew that these men would easily approve of any action that was decided against the king, since the king had taken the principality of Taranto away from Simon in contravention of his father's will, saying that his father had made many mistakes under the influence of his love for his bastards. The Duchy of Apulia and the Principalities of Taranto and Capua ought only to be bestowed on legitimate sons, although it was not unworthy for even natural sons to be granted counties or other royal honours.[79] He had kept Tancred imprisoned within the palace walls, as we have described; his brother William had recently visited him there — much to the king's anger — an extremely good-looking youth, who at the age of 22 found none of the knights his equal in strength. These were the men whom Matthew Bonellus bound to himself and to each other with an oath, as well as many knights and important men; among these he also bound to himself with a similar agreement a noble young man called Roger, Count of Avellino, who was a blood-relative of the king.[80] Their plan was first to capture the king; then once he had been captured, to imprison him on one of the islands or in some other place, until a decision could be taken with general assent; next to make his elder son Roger, Duke of Apulia, a boy of about 9,[81] king, on the assumption that this would be acceptable to the people, and that it would make it clear that they had intended no evil, when,

---

78 Cf. the description of Tancred in the *Liber ad Honorem Augusti di Pietro da Eboli* 22, line 243: 'He has a short body and little strength'; though Peter's extended denunciation of Tancred's physical weakness and deformity should not be taken too literally in what was a propagandist eulogy of Henry VI.

79 These had been the titles bestowed on Roger's legitimate sons, and William himself had successively been Prince of Taranto and Prince of Capua.

80 Roger of Aquila, Count of Avellino 1152–83, was only a very distant cousin of the king. His mother Magalda was King Roger's great-niece, daughter of Adelicia of Adernò, the granddaughter of Roger I. From her he had inherited land in Sicily; Pirro, *Sicula Sacra* ii, 934. He was married to Marocta of S. Severino. His father, Richard, had been granted the county of Avellino by King Roger before 1144 and had died on 24 September 1152; Garufi, *Necrologio di S. Matteo*, 142. See Cuozzo (1984), 100–2, 221–2 and Genealogical Table IV.

81 Roger first appeared as duke in William I's treaty with the Genoese in November 1156; *Guillelmi I Diplomata*, 47–8, no. 17.

having removed the tyrant because of his crimes, they themselves put his son in his place.

They thought that the easiest way to reach their aim would be if they could ensnare the palace castellan Mauger with whatever promises they could make, in order to force him to swear the same oath that they had made among themselves. Their undertaking would not proceed so well otherwise, since he had 300 young men[82] with him who were assigned to guard the palace itself carefully, and they were posted around the narrow gates in such a way that they could not easily be dislodged from the entrance by any number of knights, who would certainly be cut off inside without hope of escape if the exits were not left open to them as they were leaving. But their plans encountered the difficulty that Mauger was an extremely moral man, and was not likely to be easily persuaded by any argument whatsoever to take part in activities of this kind. So they were afraid of the risk of entrusting to his conscience their highly secret operation, and were forced to adopt an alternative plan, hoping that they could obtain the same effect more safely through the palace *gavarettus*.[83] For in order to avoid the necessity and effort of constantly doing his rounds, the castellan had passed the burden of his office over to him, and had entrusted him with the entire responsibility for guarding the palace. It was part of his duties frequently to inspect those who were held imprisoned in the various dungeons, to make their conditions better or worse as he saw fit, and to assign individual guards to each of the dungeons as he chose. The conspirators were confident that this man's cupidity could easily be harnessed to the hope of gain, and that the man's easy-going nature would not long reject their pleas, especially since many of his friends were already involved in the same sworn conspiracy, so that they could tell him about the operation without incurring danger. So his attitude was first explored bit by bit, and then, when his opinion was known quite certainly, they achieved even more than they had hoped, and received an unsolicited oath from him,

82 *Iuvenes*: the medieval sense of this word meant not merely 'young' but unmarried, without responsibilities; Duby (1977).

83 The exact meaning of *gavarettus* is obscure. The Cassinese notary and chronicler Richard of S. Germano in the mid-thirteenth century thought that it was the equivalent of a royal bailiff (*baiulus*); Garufi, *Ryccardi di S. Germano Chronica*, 177, but these were officials in charge of royal property and revenues in a particular district, whereas here the *gavarettus* appears to have been the captain of the guard or chief gaoler.

that he would carry out their orders without deceit exactly as they planned. The details of their plan were as follows. On a prearranged day all the prisoners – those whom they decided should not be excluded from the conspiracy – would have their chains removed, and he would open the dungeons and give each of them weapons so that each one would immediately leap out of his cell when the signal was given. The dungeons were laid out within the palace itself, around the belfry and that part called the 'Greek Tower'.

When these arrangements had been made, Matthew Bonellus went to Mistretta to arrange for food and weapons to be brought there and to prepare his other fortresses with what was needed; as he left, he earnestly warned his associates to behave with prudence and restraint until he got back, and not to broadcast in any rash way the secret that had been entrusted to them. If anything unexpected were to occur in the meantime that needed dealing with, they should write to recall him, for if the situation warranted it, he would appear sooner than they could hope with enormous forces of knights.

But they did not practise the care they had promised, and brought the operation's secure foundations to an extremely dangerous outcome. For one of them, because he wanted a knight who was a very good friend of his to take part in the plot, told him every step of what had been done, and was foolish enough to forget that he had sworn not to pass the plans on to anyone else; perhaps he measured his friend's loyalty by his own, or he was too stupid to understand how dangerous the operation was. When his friend asked him for all the details and he told him both what the time set for it was and who the persons behind it were, he finally realised that the commonly-spoken maxim is true that 'An excess of caution does no harm'. The knight in question thanked him for telling him about this extremely important matter, as though he wanted a respite until the next day to think about it, and drew the attention of another friend of his to what he had heard, saying that such a frightful crime ought not to be kept hidden by pretending ignorance. If it were carried out, it would bring shame on Sicily for ever, and all Sicilians would justifiably be labelled traitors ever after. He would certainly see to it that this should not happen, and would tell the court as soon as he could both who headed the conspiracy and who was involved. Since the other man was in fact himself involved in the plot, he called them traitors, pretended to be utterly appalled at all this, and praised the man's attitude, since he had refused to consent to their crimes. Then he left him as soon as he could and went to Count Simon and the other leaders of the conspiracy, telling them what had happened as a result of their associate's negligence, and exhorted them to look out for themselves that very night, since everything that they had done would reach the ears of the king on the following day.

When they heard how dangerous the situation was and had no time to summon Matthew Bonellus, they decided to finish the work they had begun by themselves. The *gavarettus* was warned that since they could not wait for the agreed date, he should let the prisoners out on the following day, just as they had themselves agreed. He promised to do everything carefully and that every problem that arose in the matter could easily be sorted out. They just had to be ready to appear at about the third hour, so that when the king left the palace building for the rather splendid place where he made a habit of discussing the affairs of the realm every day with the archdeacon of Catania, he could be ambushed there without any disruption or noise. The confidence of this promise turned their wavering spirits towards hope; the unexpected problem had brought them not a little fear and despondency, both because of the absence of Matthew Bonellus and of the others who had gone away with him, and also because they saw that necessity had intervened to force the operation which they had intended to take place in accordance with such careful planning to be put into effect helter-skelter.

On the next day the *gaverettus* swiftly acted to put his promise into effect, with all the speed and prudence with which he had planned it. He led the noble prisoners whom he had provided with weapons out of their dungeons, after first bringing their associates into the palace. These men followed Count Simon, who knew all the passageways of the palace, since he had been brought up there, and they came to the place where the king was talking to Henry Aristippus. As soon as the king saw his brother and his nephew Tancred coming towards him, he was angry that they should have been allowed in, and wondered what their appearance might mean. Then, as he saw the rest of them coming in with their weapons, he realised what the situation was, and tried to flee in terror. But they all suddenly came running, and he was seized by them as he was trying to get to the hidden corners of the palace. By asking him soothingly about the reasons for his tyrannical behaviour and talking of his madness in words which avoided harshness, they left him with the hope that he might escape death. But when he saw William, Count of Lesina, a man of extreme violence, and Robert of Bova, who was just as notorious for his cruelty, coming up to him with drawn swords, he begged those who were holding him not to let him be killed by these men, since he himself wished to abdicate from the throne. He thought that he would not be able to escape the hands of such cruel enemies in any way; and that opinion would not have deceived him, had not Richard of Mandra[84] beaten off an attack made on him by several persons, and ordered the king not to be killed.

After guards had been appointed to watch over him by everyone's agreement, they broke down the doors and went into the interior of the palace again, and began to go through all the rooms, stealing and looting whatever each of them particularly wanted. Some went for gems and rings, since these could be put away in a small space, others greedily took purple garments and [other] royal clothes. Some filled gold and silver vases with talents and gave them to their friends to carry home in the meantime.[85] Some threw vast numbers of coins out of the palace windows to the mob that was standing outside; and there were some who thought that the attractions of the concubines were to be preferred to any material gain. In this way men whose ages, habits and backgrounds were very different busied themselves with activities that were just as varied and contradictory.

None of the eunuchs whom they could find escaped. Many of them had fled to the houses of their friends as soon as the operation began, and many of these were caught in the street and killed by some knights who came out of the Sea Castle, and by others who were beginning to roam through the city. Many of the Muslims who were involved in selling goods from their shops, or who were collecting fiscal dues in the *diwan*,[86] or unwisely going around outside their

---

84 The imprisoned former constable of Robert of Loritello, later (1166) Count of Molise.

85 Cf. the description of the treasures found by Henry VI when he captured Palermo in December 1194; Hofmeister, *Ottonis de Sancto Blasio Chronica*, 63: 'A huge sum in gold and silver was then discovered in the royal treasury which he sent to the public treasury at Trifels and from this he greatly enriched a number of other imperial palaces. For he found there the riches of Apulia, Calabria and Sicily, lands which are very rich in metals, a glorious collection of precious stones and all sorts of gems.'

86 For the *diwan*, see Takayama (1985) and (1993), 81–9. He argues that the *ad-diwan al-ma'mur* was the Arabic name used for the central royal administration as a whole and corresponds to the Latin *curia regis*. The

houses, were killed by the same knights. Afterwards, when they realised the extent of the rioting, and thought that they were not strong enough to resist (since the previous year the admiral had forced them to hand in all their weapons to the court), the Muslims left the homes which most of them had in the centre of the city and withdrew to the suburb which lies across the Papyrus Lake.[87] The Christians attacked them there, and for some time there was indecisive fighting. They could safely repulse our people from the entrances and narrow passageways.

15 The king's son Roger

After these events the counts and their associates took the king's elder son Duke Roger from the palace and made him ride round the whole city, showing him off to everyone and telling the common people not to call anyone else their king and master from now on; he was their lord, he would rule according to the precedent of his grandfather King Roger, he deserved to be crowned by the common will of the entire people. The only thing that they were waiting for was the presence of Matthew Bonellus; there was no doubt that he would arrive either on that very same day or on the next. The boy's teacher Walter, Archdeacon of Cefalù, called a mass of people together

> name was first used at the time of a major administrative reorganisation c. 1145. However, he goes on (confusingly) to suggest that its duties were especially the supervision of the crown lands and the collection of taxes and dues (in other words that it was the crown's fiscal office). There was also a separate subsection of the administration known as the *diwan at-tahqiq al-ma'mur* (Latin *duana de secretis*), created during this reorganisation, which was the office of registration and supervision for non-royal lands.

87 The Papyrus Lake, which was mentioned by the Iraqi traveller Ibn Hawkal in the late tenth century; *BAS* i. 21, was in the north-west of the city, and it seems likely that the Muslims took refuge in the Seralcadi quarter. *The Travels of Ibn Jubayr*, 348–9, noted of the Muslims of Palermo in 1184/5 'in their own suburbs they live apart from the Christians', which suggests that the flight to which Pseudo-Hugo refers was a permanent one. Ibn Jubayr continued that 'these Muslims do not mix with their brethren under infidel patronage, and enjoy no security for their goods, their women, or their children'. However, the Seralcadi quarter was never exclusively Muslim (e.g. the church of St Mark of the Venetians was there, *Documenti inediti*, 149–50, no. 60 (1172)).

and gave a public speech about the king's tyrannical regime.[88] He exacted an oath from them all that they would obey the command of prince Simon (for that was what he called him); many were persuaded by his advice and took the oath, but there were others who said that he was acting disloyally, since if an oath had to be taken to anyone at that time, they ought rather to swear it to the duke, whom they expected to be their next king. So these men managed everything in accordance with their wishes, and there was no longer anyone who either dared or wanted to oppose them; for even the bishops were either praising their deeds in public, or giving the impression of supporting them by keeping silence.

16 The king is set free

When the common people heard that this had been done in accordance with Matthew Bonellus's wishes, they awaited his arrival. But when they had kept this up into a third day and saw that he had not come, and they could see no indication of any kind that he would be coming, they began to protest, saying that it was a disgrace and a great tragedy for the king to have been taken prisoner by a few bandits and to be kept imprisoned in a dungeon. The people ought not to put up with this any longer, seeing the treasures which had been gathered together with much labour for the defence of the realm by the efforts of a most excellent king being carried away and utterly wasted. When these remarks made by a few people had spread among the mass of the crowd, as often happens, they were suddenly transformed, as if by a divine command, or as if they were following the charge of a heroic war-lord; all ran to get their weapons, laid siege

---

88 The later Archbishop of Palermo (February 1169–June 1190). Walter had been archdeacon of Cefalù since 1156, when he witnessed a charter of Adelicia of Adernò; *Documenti inediti*, 76–7, no. 31, and he witnessed an agreement between the Bishop-Elect of Cefalù and the Archbishop of Messina in January 1159; Starrabba, *I Diplomi della cattedrale di Messina*, 21–3, no. 15. A letter to him from Peter of Blois, written after 1173, said that God 'has raised you, a poor man, from the dust'; MPL ccvii, 195–210, ep. 66, at 196, which suggests that he was of humble origin, and went on to say that Walter had taught the young William II 'poetry and the literary arts' (*ibid.*, 198). He was not, however, as is still often claimed, an Englishman; see Loewenthal (1972), and for his career, Kamp (1973–82), iii, 1112–19.

to the palace and demanded that the king be handed over to them, threatening that if the people there held him any longer they would bring ladders and other instruments to capture the palace and would exact the punishment due to traitors from them. The conspirators were taken by surprise by this sudden change in their situation. At first they positioned themselves along the battlements and resisted fiercely, preventing any of the crowd from approaching and forcing them back by shooting rocks down on top of them. But they were very few, and the castle's long circuit required a much greater number of men for its defence. Recognising this, they tried to soothe the anger and the onslaught of the raging crowd, and asked them to put away their weapons for the time being and await Matthew Bonellus and the other leaders in accordance with whose plan all this had been done. But it was not easy to mollify their anger now that it had been aroused; and they attacked again and made much fiercer threats if the king were not shown to them.

Although they saw that they were in no way sufficient to hold out in the palace, the defenders tried hard to keep their resistance up for as long as possible, in the hope that in the meantime Matthew Bonellus would appear. But it did not turn out as they hoped, and they were finally brought to the point of despair, and promised the crowd that they would do as they wished. They went to the king and made an agreement with him that he should allow them to leave safe and unharmed; and then they took him to the windows of the tower called 'Johar'.

The moment they saw the king, an enormous uproar and shouting arose from the entire crowd. They demanded more insistently than ever that the gates be opened, and took the view that the traitors ought not to be allowed to escape. The king, raising his hand for silence, ordered them to be calm, saying that the fact that he had been freed by their efforts was enough to earn the claim of loyalty; now they should put down their weapons and allow those men to leave freely to whom he had himself granted the freedom to go where they pleased – otherwise it might be that they would again lose his gratitude, which they had so thoroughly earned. And so, when the crowd's emotions had been calmed a little, the gates were opened and the conspirators left to take refuge at Caccamo.

Naturally this sudden and unforeseen series of happenings concentrated a great string of dreadful events into a terribly short space of time, and caused significant harm to the entire kingdom. For the realm was not only weakened by the loss of a number of nobles and impoverished by the waste of a considerable portion of the treasury, but it also sustained another loss that could not be made good for a long time to come, namely the death of Duke Roger, whom I mentioned above. He was already beginning to show signs of the character both of his grandfather and of his uncle to a greater extent than his age might lead one to expect. He bore the name of both of them, together with the wisdom of the one and the humanity of the other. Sicily would have been better served if the king had been kept imprisoned for ever, or even suffered sentence of death, instead of losing the promise of such a fine character.

17 The king's son William

But this island, lest it should ever be short of tyrants, claimed for itself the following right with regard to the sons of its kings: that the best of them should die first, and those become kings through whom the privilege of perpetual tyranny might best be maintained. In accordance with this principle, Roger, Duke of Apulia (a man of unparalleled humanity and sweetness) had once been snatched away by an untimely death so as to give William the opportunity to rule; he put as much effort into enslaving himself to cruelty and stupidity as his brother had in embracing wisdom and humanity. In the same way now, too, with the removal of Duke Roger, it made provision for William to reign; no one who knows either of their names will be unaware that they have followed in the footsteps of those whose names they had been given.[89]

18 The king's grief

This boy, then, was shot by an arrow as he was looking out of a window rather carelessly at those who were besieging the palace, and rumour has not identified anyone clearly responsible for the deed. The belief which everyone shared pinned the blame for this great

---

[89] This coded criticism of William II was probably written during his lifetime. See above, p. 39.

crime on the usher Darius.[90] But there were others who claimed that they knew more about the secrets of the palace, and they said that the wound sustained had not been serious enough to be fatal, and held that the guilt for this crime lay with the king himself. Their story was that when the boy ran up to congratulate his father after his release, the father was angry that his enemies had, so to speak, preferred him to himself and acclaimed him as king; so he pushed him away and kicked him, hitting him with as much force as he could. The boy managed to get away with some difficulty, and told the queen what had happened to him; he did not survive for long after that. When the king heard the dreadful news, he was terribly overcome by the shame of the thing. He took off the royal robes and forgot his rank, and sat on the floor and cried inconsolably. His grief left him stunned, and he occupied his memory and his mind, numb with grief, with the awful things that had happened to him, so much so that he took no care of his body, and could not concentrate on formulating any policy, although he was surrounded by his enemies. The gates of the palace were left open and unguarded; he would give audience to all who approached him in a gentle and friendly fashion, thrusting his grief and pain upon them, so that he brought tears to the eyes of many who had hitherto hated him.

19 The king speaks to the people

In the end, having been warned and begged by the bishops and others who had come to console him, he went down to the great hall which adjoined the palace, and gave orders for the people to be called together there, since the place was big enough to take a great crowd. He began by praising their loyalty and thanked them for snatching him from the hands of traitors, then went on to exhort them to remain steadfast in the faithfulness they had chosen if it should happen that his enemies undertook anything against him; it was not absolutely certain, he said, where they had gone, or what supporters they had in Sicily on whose intentions they had relied in carrying out their crime. He added that

---

90 The *hostiarii* (which we have translated as 'ushers') were junior palace officials – their precise function is unclear. Darius was later, in 1190, one of the two, or possibly more, subordinate palace chamberlains in general day-to-day charge of the royal administration, who worked under the direction of the Master Chamberlain; Jamison (1957), 323–32, appendix I, no. 4; Takayama (1993), 102–3, 125–9.

THE HISTORY OF THE TYRANTS OF SICILY   115

this had happened to him because of the many wicked things he had done, and was well deserved; he himself saw this clearly, and admitted it; and from now on he would act in such a way as to show that he accepted the whip of divine correction with a spirit that did not in any way resist. It would not be difficult to concede anything requested by the population subject to him that ought in justice to be granted, and he was pleased utterly to abrogate those customs which had been introduced at various times that either diminished the due liberties of the people or appeared to load them with unjust burdens. On the contrary, he preferred to be loved than feared.

The Bishop-Elect of Syracuse, a most highly educated and eloquent man, reported to the people these and similar things which the king spoke humbly and not without tears.[91] To make them more favourably disposed towards him, he gave them freedom from gate-duties, so that all citizens of Palermo could freely import foodstuffs (whether bought or harvested from their fields and vineyards), and no one could exact any duties on them in the king's name.[92] This was very popular with the people; they had received something which they had long wanted and had never been able to attain.

20 Matthew Bonellus is restored to the king's favour

Meanwhile news was brought to Palermo that Simon, whom they referred to as 'the prince', the duke's son Tancred, William of Lesina, Alexander of Conversano,[93] Count Simon's bastard son Roger

---

[91] Richard, an Englishman, Bishop-Elect of Syracuse from January 1157, though he was only consecrated in 1169, and Archbishop of Messina from January 1183 until his death on 7 August 1195. The surname 'Palmer' with which he is sometimes credited occurs only in very late sources. He was one of the royal *familiares* from Maio's death until 1169 (except perhaps for a brief period during Stephen of Perche's pre-eminence), and then again from 1177 to 1184. For his career, see Kamp (1973–82), iii. 1013–18.

[92] Gate and market duties (*portaticum* and *plateaticum*) were among the most important and profitable revenues of all territorial lords. Palermo was a royal city, so that there these dues would belong to the king, but barons holding fiefs directly from the crown would enjoy such rights in their own towns.

[93] Alexander of Conversano may well have been the former count, who had

Sclavus,[94] and all the others who together were involved in the king's capture, were at Caccamo with Matthew Bonellus, and that a great number of knights had joined them there. So it was decided to send messengers to Matthew himself to ask him what was his attitude towards the king, what was the reason for this great concentration of soldiers, and what he was intending to do; they were to tell him that he ought not to involve himself in the plans of traitors or to receive them when he had heard about the crimes that they had committed. His reply to those who performed this embassy was this: he had never agreed to the crimes committed by those whom they labelled as traitors, nor had he known of, or approved of, their plans; on the other hand it would be tyrannical and cruel not to give refuge to all the noblemen who were fleeing to him and thus expose them to danger of death. Indeed, if the king carefully examined his own deeds, he ought rather to be surprised that the great men of the realm had put up for so long with being virtually enslaved, than that they should finally have been inflamed against him by insufferable grief, provoked by many unjust actions. Not to mention all the other things that they had suffered, it was considered pitiable even in respect of persons of the status of slaves for their daughters to have to stay at home unmarried for the entire period of their lives. But without the court's permission they too were not allowed to arrange marriages among themselves; and it had hitherto become so difficult to get permission for this that some women were only permitted to be given in marriage when their age was so advanced that it removed any chance of bearing children. Others had been condemned to lifelong spinsterhood and had died without hope of being married.[95] Now the

fled into exile in 1132; *Al. Tel.* II. 38, p. 42. He had been present with the Byzantine army defeated at Brindisi in 1156, though we have no specific confirmation that he was captured; Brand, *Deeds of John and Manuel Comnenus by John Cinnamus,* 115. Romuald's account of the 1161 rising refers to an 'Alexander the monk'; see below, p. 229.

94 Roger Sclavus was the illegitimate son of Count Simon of Policastro, and was openly acknowledged as his son. He witnessed two charters of his father, in August 1143 and November 1148, and two other documents of his half-brother Manfred in April 1154; Garufi (1910), 76–8, 80–2, nos. 6, 8–9; Pirro, *Sicula Sacra* i, 621.

95 Cf. Frederick II's 'Constitutions of Capua' of December 1220, c. 17 (Garufi, *Ryccardi di S. Germano Chronica,* 92); ordering that 'no count or baron [is] to contract matrimony without our license, except according to the constitution of King William, and that no son or daughter, on the death

noblemen of the entire realm, and he among them, were asking and demanding the king to abrogate these and other pernicious laws and restore those customs first instituted by Robert Guiscard, which his grandfather Count Roger had respected and ordered to be respected after him. But if on the contrary he wanted to oppose the statutes of his predecessors, they would not put up with it any longer.

When the envoys brought this message back to the king, he replied that he would rather lose his kingdom or, if necessary, bravely meet his death, than let them impose an unworthy agreement on the basis of fear or threats. However, if they put down their arms and sent the traitors away and came to him peacefully to ask for anything, they would quite easily be granted what they wanted. When this was announced at Caccamo, it displeased all those who were there; they criticised Matthew's inactivity and persuaded him to approach the city to lay siege to it. He acquiesced in their plans and advanced on towards Palermo and encamped with his knights about three miles away from the city. In the meantime the king sent messengers to the *stratigotus* and the population of the city of Messina, telling them to man as many galleys as they could carefully with crews and weapons and to send them to him without delay.[96]

But when the knights' approach was learnt of at Palermo, one could see the face of the city become deserted and miserable, its citizens scared, afraid, shocked, gulping down any sound of news with keen ears, and changing their emotions in accordance with the rumours they heard. Some intended to surrender to Matthew Bonellus as soon as he should arrive; others, because they had incurred the enmity of his associates, were afraid that they and their property would be

---

of father and mother, shall dare to usurp any hereditary property or patrimony unless following the custom of this same king' (cf. Powell, *Liber Augustalis*, 117–18 (Bk. iii, tit. 23)).

96 The *stratigotus* or *strategus* was a town governor or royal bailiff, though the term was derived from the Greek *strategos* or general, the usual title for a provincial governor in the Byzantine Empire. The terms *stratigotus*, *catepanus* and *baiulus* tended to be used interchangeably, although the employment of these titles varied in different parts of the kingdom. Thus in Apulia *stratigotus* dropped out of use. See Martin (1993), 818–21. The *stratigotus* of Messina was probably Richard of Aversa, attested in December 1157; Starrabba, *I Diplomi della Cattedrale di Messina*, 17–18, no. 13. See below, p. 183.

plundered by the knights; there was no citizen who placed any hope in armed resistance, and no one had any care for the defence of the city. In addition to these factors, corn was running out, threatening the burden of a prospective famine, since it was no longer possible for grain to be brought in from adjoining places, because the knights controlled the routes on all sides. So everything was confused and uncertain in the city, and if Matthew Bonellus, meeting no resistance on his way, had moved closer, he would have been able to enter the city and occupy the palace without anyone stopping him, and put the king himself in chains.

But he followed a different plan, and marched back to Caccamo. At this point the galleys from Messina suddenly arrived, relieved the citizens of their fears, and restored the king's hopes; and many knights also flowed in from the interior of Sicily in support of the king. As his strength increased, so did the opposing party's lack of confidence and fear. So with his fortunes restored, he regained courage and decided to march out; he abandoned the pleading of his earlier embassy and asserted the dignity of the kingship (nothing was easier for him than to switch from pleading to pride). So he sent a second envoy to Matthew Bonellus, a canon of Palermo called Robert of S. Giovanni, who was a man of high reputation and proven faithfulness, whom no party of conspirators, none of the storms of persecution which had so often shaken the realm, had torn from the straightforward loyalty by which he had always stood. No flattering good fortune had ever raised him to a point where his innate good nature was adulterated by any pride or insolence; and no bad fortune had ever cast him down to the point where he wished to hawk his loyalty for sale in exchange for the favour of powerful men or for the value of any honour. Consequently the archbishop had always secretly hated him, but with little effect, though he set many plans in motion against him. Consequently also the admiral had caused him some harm with hidden plots against him (since he could not attack him openly), but he too could not achieve what he hoped for. When the king – without being advised or warned by anyone – decided to appoint the said Robert to the office of chancellor, and Maio realised this from the king's own indications, he praised his intention in this matter, saying that the decision that those who served him loyally and long should in the end not be denied the favour of the king's liberality was in accordance with justice and worthy of a ruler's majesty; but since the court had decided that an embassy had to be sent to Venice, and it was agreed that the loyalty and ability of this Robert were ideal for this task, it was essential that he should undertake the embassy first. That would give the king a better reason to promote him, and Robert would more thankfully accept the reward for his long service after his labours when the embassy had been completed. When the king had been persuaded of this, Maio immediately wrote to Peter of Castro Nuovo, who was the current Captain of Apulia, to provide Robert of S. Giovanni with an unseaworthy ship that was breaking up with age, and with sailors who were inexperienced, feckless and idle, when he set sail for Venice. The decaying ship would then crack open when any waves broke over it and fail to survive the journey up the Adriatic, and the sailors would not have enough experience to let him survive the journey.[97] When he crossed the Straits and reached Apulia, the archbishop of Trani not only told him about all this, but showed him the admiral's actual letter.[98] Robert took the sensible precaution – since he was not loath to buy his safety with gold – of hiring a ship and sailors at his own expense, and so he escaped Maio's trap even though he was beset by many perils.

This then was the man who went to Caccamo. After long and difficult discussions and disagreements, he brought the negotiations to the following conclusion: that the king provide sufficient galleys for all those who had fled to Matthew Bonellus to allow them to be brought safely and unharmed outside the boundaries of the realm; and that he should take Matthew himself back into his friendship and restore him to his full favour as though he had behaved loyally, and drop any investigation. When this was confirmed by the taking of oaths on the king's side, Matthew entered Palermo to the great applause of the populace, and restored peace to the town. Almost all the others

---

97 This incident would seem to date from 1156 or 1157, while Peter was one of the two Master Captains of Apulia; Jamison (1913), 286–8 and calendar nos. 46–46a. Garufi (1942), 45 would, however, prefer to date it earlier, before the death of Doge Domenico Morosini in February 1155, since Venetian sources record him as making peace with William of Sicily. Robert was certainly in Sicily in July or August 1156, when he witnessed a donation charter of Adelicia of Adernò; *Documenti inediti* 76–8, no. 31. For the echoes of classical literature in this tale, see the introduction, 'Classical resonances in the *History*', p. 47.

98 This archbishop was almost certainly Bertrandus II, attested 1157–87; Kamp (1973–82), ii, 545–7.

were conducted to the galleys and left the boundaries of the kingdom.[99]

21 Matthew Bonellus's arrest; Roger Sclavus

The king pardoned his relative Count Roger of Avellino, thinking that what he would consider a most appalling crime in others ought in his case to be called a mistake rather than a misdeed, because of the infirmity of youth. He was also moved by the appeals and tears of his cousin Adelicia, the same count's grandmother, who was terribly fond of her grandson because she had no other surviving heir.[100] He also retained Richard of Mandra at Palermo and put him in charge of his knights as constable, since he had served him well.[101] At that time the king's *familiares*, through whom he carried out the business of the court,[102] were Richard, Bishop-Elect of Syracuse, Count Silvester of Marsico and Henry Aristippus. However, the king was suspicious of Henry (though he still concealed his hatred), since he believed that he had taken part in the conspiracy that had been directed against him. At the time of the king's capture, this man had also kept some of the palace concubines in his own house for a few days, which made the king particularly angry with him.[103] But since these men

---

99 What happened to them thereafter is unknown, except that Simon, the king's illegitimate half-brother, was at the Byzantine court in 1166; Brand, *Deeds of John and Manuel Comnenus by John Cinnamus*, 134; and Alexander of Conversano was the Emperor Manuel's envoy to the kingdom of Jerusalem in 1168; Babcock and Krey, *William of Tyre: A History of Events beyond the Sea*, 347–8 (Bk. xx. 4).
100 See note 80 above and Genealogical Table IV.
101 The constable of the royal *mesnie* or *masnede* was the commander of the royal military household; Clementi (1967), 68. Richard witnessed a royal charter as constable in April 1162; Garufi, *Tabulario di Monreale*, 161–3, no. 1.
102 In Sicily the king's *familiares* were not simply the trusted men of his court, as the term implied in twelfth-century northern Europe, but his principal ministers. See Takayama (1989), 357–72 and (1993), 98–101, 115–25.
103 We have translated *Palatii puellae* as 'concubines'. *The Travels of Ibn Jubayr*, 340–1, referring to the court of William II, said that 'He [the king] has about him a great number of youths and handmaidens, and no Christian king is more given up to the delights of the realm, or more comfort- and luxury-loving.' He went on to claim that 'the handmaidens

knew absolutely nothing of the different categories of landed estates and tenancies or of the customs and institutions of the court, and they were not able to find the volumes of records which they call *defetir*, the king agreed – and this seemed to be essential – to let the notary Matthew out of prison and recall him to his previous duties. He had had an extremely long period of court service as a notary and had always been at Maio's side, demonstrating his detailed knowledge of the customs of the entire realm, and so he was thought to be competent to compile a new set of *defetir*, containing the same material as the earlier ones.[104]

While this was happening at Palermo, Roger Sclavus, together with the duke's son Tancred and a few others who had earlier defected from Matthew Bonellus, when they saw that he was heading in the direction of an agreement on unequal terms, took occupation of Butera, Piazza Armerina and other towns of the North Italians [*Lombardi*] which his father had held.[105] He was received with relief and enthusiasm by the Lombards. When they promised that they would follow him through any danger, no matter how great, and many knights also came to join him, he first ordered their mettle to be tested against the Muslim population. There was nothing the North Italians would ever be more willing to hear, and they were not slow to put his orders into effect. They made unprovoked attacks on nearby places, and massacred both those who lived alongside the Christians in various towns as well as those who owned their own estates, forming distinct communities. They made no distinction of sex or age. The number

    and concubines in his palace are all Muslims'. It seems therefore that the kings of Sicily kept a harem.

104 *Defetir* were registers recording details of royal lands and of the rights and services owed both from the royal demesne and from fiefs held from the crown, which were kept both by the *duana de secretis* (*diwan at-tahqiq al-ma'mur*) and by the *ad-diwan al ma'mur*, Takayama (1993), 84–8, 133–5. They were often referred to by charters, e.g. *Documenti inediti*, 124–6, no. 54 (1170), which mentioned the bounds of a *casale* near Lentini (given by William II to a hermit on Mount Etna), as established in the *dafetir* of the *duana de secretis*.

105 The word *Lombardi* is always used by Pseudo-Hugo to distinguish North Italians from the *Longobardi/Langobardi*, the native inhabitants of southern Italy. We have therefore translated these two terms as 'North Italians' and 'South Italians' respectively. The North Italians had settled under the aegis of the Aleramici family (see the introduction, pp. 11–12, which discusses the significance of this episode).

of those of that community who died is not easy to reckon, and the few who experienced a better fate (either by escaping by secret flight or by assuming the guise of Christians), fled to less dangerous Muslim towns in the southern part of Sicily. To the present day they hate the North Italian race so much that they have not only refused to live in that part of Sicily again, but even avoid going there at all.

Roger Sclavus also disturbed the nearby territory of Syracuse and Catania with frequent attacks, and the man's bravery and boldness brought so much terror to the people round about that not even the king's constables could resist his onslaught, since he achieved victory despite engaging them with a very much smaller number of knights. This crisis again put the court into a sudden panic, and Count Silvester did not believe that it could be being done without the agreement of Matthew Bonellus. He thought he was all the more to be feared because he continued to be particularly close [*familiarius*] to the court; for open enemies can easily be avoided, but the enmity of *familiares* can be guarded against only with greater difficulty and not without danger. Being fearful by nature, he suspected him of preparing to ensnare himself first of all, on the grounds that he had come to the king's assistance and thereby seemed to have got in the way of his plot, and was just as much in the way now.

So when the king ordered the knights to be given their pay as he was about to lead the army out against Roger Sclavus and his associates, the count persuaded him to have Matthew Bonellus arrested and imprisoned first; for if he took him with him, he would certainly betray him and his army, and the king would not return to his palace unscathed. Nor was this the occasion for keeping his oath, since without betraying it mortal danger could not be avoided. What was done out of fear of death would easily find forgiveness. The king was pleased that the course of action he had already decided upon should be proposed by someone else, and praised the count's advice, admitting that he had long taken the same view. He was aware that Matthew could not be arrested outside the palace, and that no one would be bold enough to attempt to persuade the common people that it had to be done. Indeed, it would not even be possible to arrest him within the palace without danger, and unrest throughout the city would necessarily follow such an action. But the pattern of these popular demonstrations was that once the action had been carried out, they would run out of steam by themselves, and could be suppressed without difficulty; so the people's unrest should be ignored, and the proposed action should not be carried out any more slowly because of it.

So, on a day which they had agreed, Matthew Bonellus was summoned to court; and one of his supporters told him about the whole thing and revealed the count's deceit and his plot. But Bonellus was convinced that the king would be deterred from such audacity by fear of perjuring himself, and he did not think that (even if he did not mind breaking his oath) he would dare to do it, since he could see that the realm would be even more convulsed by it. So he ignored his friends' advice and confidently went up to the palace; but before he reached the king's presence, he was detained by the castellans and put in a most foul dungeon. Soon afterwards, with all the gates, not just of the palace but of the Galcule sector, carefully barred,[106] armed men were positioned along the circuit of the walls in order to repel any initial onslaught of the common people, should that become necessary. When rumour, that brave harbinger of disasters, broadcast this among the people, a great crowd of commoners immediately congregated together with Matthew's own knights, and headed straight for the palace to extract him from there by force and to inflict on Count Silvester the punishment that he deserved for his treachery. When they found the gates shut on all sides and saw that every approach was barred, they thought that they would set fire to the gates, piling up a great heap of firewood there. However, they could not achieve anything in this way, and were wandering around all over the place without any definite plan; the passion of their emotions at length began to cool out of despair, and fear of the king restrained their unheeding boldness. Suddenly they changed sides, just as Fortune turns her face away, which is part of the Sicilian experience, and preferred to serve the times rather than keep faith. With as much care as they had previously taken to win the favour of Matthew Bonellus, they now took pains to appear not to have been friendly towards him.

While all these friends of Fortune decamped, there still remained one spirit careless of danger that dared to embrace the name of honour and to test the freedom which suffices to win eternal glory. Ivo, one of Matthew's knights, saw the chamberlain Atenulf returning from

---

106 The *Galcule* (Arabic *Halqa*) was the small quarter next to the royal palace – Bresc estimates less than 300 m. on each side – where the royal officials lived. It was one of the six districts of medieval Palermo; Bresc (1990), 158, 163.

court, and remembered his hostility towards Matthew. Moved by grief, he bravely rode at him, and relying on the speed of his horse, he buried his sword in the skull of the fleeing man from above; then he got away through the middle of the city without being stopped by anyone. When he had already got a long way away from the city, he was captured by the king's knights and brought back to Palermo. The court ordered his right hand to be cut off. Matthew Bonellus's eyes were gouged out and he was hamstrung. He was utterly removed from the sight of the sun and thrust into a frightful dungeon, wrapped for ever in the darkness both of his own sightlessness and that of the place.[107] His cousin Matthew of Santa Lucia and his seneschal John the Roman were blinded and assigned to separate dungeons.

22 The traitors are punished in various parts of the realm; the capture of Piazza Armerina

After these events, as though all his problems had now been resolved, the king led his army out against Roger Sclavus by a hurried march. He first utterly overthrew and destroyed Piazza Armerina, the most noble city of the North Italians, located in a plain. There rioting broke out between the Muslims and the Christians in his army, a greater number of the Muslims were killed when the Christians fiercely attacked them, and they did not stop out of respect for the king, nor fear of his threats when he sent officers to help the Muslims and ordered the killing to stop.

23 How the castle of Butera was destroyed

Next he encircled Butera with a besieging ditch; his enemies had gone there when they heard of his approach. When Roger Sclavus saw that he was surrounded, he first made a short speech exhorting his associates, then warned the townsfolk to be united, not to divide into factions and not to be afraid of the king's army; if they could resist successfully for a few days, then most of Sicily and the whole

---

[107] If we can believe an interpolated charter probably to be dated to November 1173 (surviving only in sixteenth- and seventeenth-century copies), Matthew Bonellus was still alive then, and had been released and restored to favour by William II; Enzensberger (1967), 142–3, Anhang III.

of Calabria would follow their example. He reminded them of his father's many kindnesses to them, and at the same time described the king's wickedness and his tyrannical behaviour towards his subjects. They on their part promised boldly and loyally never to desert his command, nor to make any difficulty or danger an excuse for disobeying him.

Many of the knights in the army were beginning to be affected by fatigue, since they saw that the king was taking rather long over the siege, and there was no hope of capturing the town unless famine forced the townspeople to surrender, and that would hardly happen for a long while. The place was naturally well fortified, and nothing required to defend it was lacking in the courage and bravery of Roger Sclavus and the wisdom and foresight of Tancred. So the besiegers' frequent assaults did no harm to their enemies, and although the latter often came out to fight bravely and in full force, this did little or no damage to the army. This was because the king knew that his nephew Tancred was working out from astrological calculations which days would be most favourable for the besieged and the besiegers respectively. Hence he too carefully worked out the same days with his astrologers, telling his friends about any day on which he predicted that they would come down to fight, so that they could prepare the army against their surprise attacks. Thus the operation dragged on for some time, until strife between the leaders and the common people within the city resolved the situation. It was the wish and policy of Roger and Tancred to bring together all the grain in the town and hand it out to both knights and townspeople in equal rations. But the common people refused to let their food supplies be bought up, and wanted individual knights to be billeted on individual townspeople, who would provide them with what they needed in their homes. The knights were suspicious of this proposal and saw it as an indication of wavering loyalty. So a serious dispute arose between the people and the knights, with the result that the former surrendered to the king and prepared to let some of the king's knights into the town secretly. When Roger Sclavus and those with him got wind of their plan, they lost confidence in their cause. They decided that they too would come to an agreement with the king, the terms being that when he took the city he would allow them to leave safe and unharmed.

The king was ready to grant them this, since he had no expectation of gaining possession of the town so soon, and he planned to cross over to Italy immediately, under pressure of events.[108] For taking advantage of the fact that Fortune had exhausted Sicily with great unrest, Robert, Count of Loritello had invaded most of the realm and got as far as Orgeolo, a place on the borders of Apulia and Calabria.[109] All those counts who had first been turned to rebellion because of the admiral's wickedness and later despaired of being restored to the king's favour had joined him. The one exception was Count Gilbert of Gravina, who had obtained the king's favour as a result of the pleas of his relative, the queen. He had deserted the counts' party and was in command of the Apulian army, trying to delay Count Robert's advance as much as he could.[110] In Calabria the Countess of Catanzaro also defected to Robert, and had reinforced the powerful castle of Taberna with both knights and other necessities, so that if it happened that the king should cross the Straits, she could base herself there in safety together with her mother.

24 The settlement of Butera

So the king, as had been agreed, let his enemies go and captured and destroyed Butera, and prohibited it from being inhabited again in future. Not long afterwards, his army larger than before, he decided to lay siege to Taverna on his way into Apulia. But before that, so that he would find no unforeseen obstacle in the territory of Calabria, he ordered Roger of Martorana, who had quite a lot of influence among the Calabrians at that time, to be summoned to Sicily, and, charging him with treason, ordered him to be imprisoned and blinded, although he had neither been convicted nor had formally admitted guilt, as the legal rules required.[111]

---

108 In a charter of April 1162, John Malcovenant, son of Geoffrey, recorded that he had earlier gone to Messina with the king, 'to destroy traitors and his enemies'; Garufi, *Tabulario di Monreale*, 161–3, no. 1.

109 Orgeolo was near Cosenza; it had been captured by Roger II from a rebel baron, Robert de Grandmesnil, in May 1130; *Al. Tel.* I. 22, p. 19.

110 The first documentary record of Gilbert as Master Constable of Apulia and the Principality of Capua was as late as December 1162; Coniglio, *Cod. dipl. pugliese* xx, 227–8, no. 109. He seems to have been in charge of the mainland administration for the last five years of William I's reign; Jamison (1913), 289–90.

111 Nevertheless, on Pseudo-Hugo's own account he had been deeply

After he had brought his army over to Taverna and saw its superior location and how steep the approaches were, almost everyone despaired of capturing the place and thought that they should hurry on into Apulia to achieve greater things. They thought that for the time being Taverna should be left until they returned, and that they should not waste a lot of time there to no purpose. However, he inflexibly insisted that he would not leave the place until the town had been captured; and on that very day he ordered both the knights and the footsoldiers to arm themselves and climb up to attack the town by making a rush at it. But the townspeople, sending rocks down on them, and rolling down barrels which they hung down from the walls which had been covered with sharpened nails, easily threw the slow-moving column of men into confusion as they were creeping up. Many of them were killed, and the rest greatly exhausted to no effect, and many returned to camp severely wounded. After an interval of a few days, at the king's orders, all ran with one accord when the trumpet sounded that men should arm again and put Fortune to the test. First they occupied with great effort a certain hill, steep but only a little higher than the plain, which joined on to the city walls on one side; at this point they brought up ladders, and climbed on to the walls at the first attack, though not without danger. I see no explanation for how the attack on the town could have been so easy, except that the townspeople put too much reliance on the strength of the site and guarded the walls too carelessly; for there was no treachery nor any rivalry among the townsmen, and they had enough well-trained knights and leaders experienced in military affairs, who had both the courage to act daringly and the foresight to be careful. Yet what happened was that the town was wretchedly and dishonourably captured, the knights stripped, and they brought the countess and her mother, and Alferius and Thomas, the leaders of the affair and maternal uncles of the younger countess, to the king, with several other knights. Of these, Alferius was immediately handed over for punishment at the king's orders. Thomas was hanged at Messina. The other knights were punished in some cases by having their hands cut off, in others their

---

implicated in the plot to murder Maio. Roger had two sons. One Roger *Chamutus* witnessed a donation to the monastery of St Mary of Sambucina in September 1163; the other, Guido, witnessed a charter of William de Luzzi, son of Count Geoffrey of Catanzaro, in November 1170; Pratesi, *Carte latine di abbazie calabresi*, 56, 67, nos. 21, 28.

eyes put out. The countess was at once sent to Messina with her mother and then to Palermo to be kept in prison.[112]

When it was announced to the Count of Loritello that Taverna had been suddenly captured and destroyed, contrary to everyone's hope and expectation, then – although he had an army much greater than the king's in horse and footsoldiers – because he mistrusted the divided loyalties of the South Italians, which he had often experienced at great danger and cost to himself, he preferred to retreat rather than to try the fortune of war with untrustworthy soldiers. He returned to Taranto, where he left a few knights to garrison the city. From there he took a number of towns, as though trying to gain encouragement and support, and decided to turn the direction of his march towards the territory of the Abruzzi.

During these days Caid Johar the Eunuch, who was Master Chamberlain of the palace, having sustained many injuries and thrashings from the king during the military expedition which (as he claimed) he had not deserved, tried to desert to the Count of Loritello with the royal seals; but he was captured on the way and taken to the king. The king put him in a boat and ordered him to be taken out to sea and drowned there.[113]

He continued to Taranto and easily recaptured the city; he had some of Count Robert's knights, whom the citizens had handed over to him, hanged outside the city. Then he proceeded through the whole of Apulia and the Terra di Lavoro, recovering every place which his enemies had previously occupied.[114] They now rushed to join him with a fickleness as great as the foolishness with which they had previously rebelled against him. He decided to impose a stated quantity

---

112 The siege took place in March 1162; *Annales Ceccanenses*, MGH SS xix, 285. The countess's mother Segelguarda died in July 1167; *Documenti inediti*, 96–9, no. 42.

113 Johar is probably to be identified with the Master Chamberlain Theodore, whose death is recorded on 9 February 1163; Garufi, *Necrologio di S. Matteo di Salerno*, 20. Theodore was his baptismal name when he converted to Christianity; Jamison (1957), 44 and note 3. Pseudo-Hugo's use of his original Muslim name is unusual, for generally he refers to such men by their new Christian name, as e.g. Caid Martin (see below, note 117).

114 The *Annales Ceccanenses* MGH SS xix, 285 said that the royal army under the command of Richard de Say pursued the rebels into the Abruzzi.

of money as a redemption fine on all those cities and towns which had accepted the Count of Loritello or had seemed to any extent to have supported him, wishing to to make up for what his treasury had lost with this money; and he also thought it fair that while people who had fallen under an obligation regarding their homes and possessions by surrendering to their enemies should be freed from the full rigour of the law, they should at least be forced to redeem that property by a small fine.

Next Count Jonathan of Conza, Count Richard of Fondi, Count Roger of Acerra, Marius Borell and the others who had supported their party were terrified by the king's approach. Some of them fled into the Abruzzi, others to Campania. Count Roger of Avellino also thought it wise to avoid the king's anger for having recently – without the court's permission – married the daughter of Fenicia of San Severino.[115] Her son William of San Severino avoided the king's ire by fleeing with the count.[116] The countess herself, after trying to defend her besieged fortress, was captured and taken across to Palermo together with her mother Fenicia.

While this was going on in Italy, at Palermo Fortune was raging with a new kind of wickedness, and the king's absence from Sicily brought danger to many. For Caid Martin the eunuch, whom the king had left behind to guard the city and palace of Palermo, was aware that his brother had been killed by Christians in the attack on the palace; but he could not identify those who were personally responsible.[117] So he

---

115 She was called Marocta; Tropeano, *Codice diplomatico verginiano* v, 261–4, no. 474 (1167).

116 William of S. Severino came from a family which had been powerful in the Principality of Salerno since the time of Robert Guiscard. He was the son of Henry of S. Severino (d. 31 August 1150; Garufi, *Necrologio di S. Matteo di Salerno*, 124) and first cousin to Count Robert of Caserta, while he was descended on the female side from Guaimar IV (1027–52), the penultimate Lombard prince of Salerno. See Portanova (1976a, 1976b); Cuozzo (1984), 120–2; Loud (1987), 157–62, 165–6. William had been a minor when his father died, and Fenicia had then administered the S. Severino property; Cava, Arca xxx. 71 (1161). William later married a daughter of Count Silvester of Marsico; Cava, Arm. Mag. I. 41 (February 1184), L. 21 (March 1187).

117 Caid Martin was one of the Masters of the *Duana de Secretis* from 1161, when he was selling crown land outside Palermo on behalf of that office; Cusa, *Diplomi greci ed arabi*, 622–6.

started to rage viciously and secretly against all Christians, holding them collectively responsible for his brother's death. When several citizens were charged with having entered the palace along with the traitors and having taken away large amounts of money, and those who accused them claimed that they would prove their case in single combat[118] according to the tradition of the court, he accepted their accusations immediately and willingly. He praised those who won as though they had done the king a great favour, while he imposed the most frightful punishments on those who lost. He took this as a suitable opportunity to avenge his brother, and turned something that had begun as the result of the rashness of a few into a disaster for many. For there were some young men – especially those who had inherited little or nothing – whom he knew to want to achieve glory by means of their physical courage; he exhorted and incited them by the promise of rewards, boldly to keep laying charges of this kind against the citizens, saying that by this very action they would most effectively win the king's gratitude; and even if they were defeated, they would not suffer any harm, since they would be seen as fighting for the king himself.

There was now so much madness and fury in the city that anyone who had an ancient feud against anyone else, or who had verbally insulted someone in the course of litigation, immediately went to the court of Caid Martin; he was always very ready to accept lawsuits of this sort, made himself available to everyone, and was especially keen to act as judge in these cases. As for those of the accused who were defeated, he had some of them hanged with the Muslims looking on and mocking them, and had others repeatedly beaten and subjected to various tortures. He was extremely diligent in accepting these accusations, but when the parties entered the arena for the combat, he did not think it very important which of them won, since his brother's death could be avenged on either of them. The citizens were now terrorised by constant evils and punishments, with the result that prosecutors who were prepared to undergo the ordeal of single combat came forward less frequently. Hence he was ready to accept accusations from women too, and not just from respectable ones whose

---

118 *Monomachia*: the classical word for a gladiatorial combat, but used since the sixth century for a judicial duel, e.g. Cassiodorus, *Variae* 3. 24; *Annales Altahenses* ad ann. 1056, ed. E. Oefele (MGH SRG, 1891), 52; *MGH Constitutiones* ii, ed. L. Weiland (1896), 400, no. 84, c. 15 (King Henry of Germany's land peace of 1224).

reputation was untarnished, but even from shameless and dishonourable ones; and he decreed that slaves and maidservants could legally bring such charges. Their claims were often accepted in the absence of proof, and he destroyed the reputations of many, drained their material resources, and afflicted their bodies with punishments.

In the meantime, with matters settled throughout Apulia and the rebellion suppressed, the king reached Salerno. When they learnt of his impending arrival, the majority of those who had led the opposition, whom the people of Salerno call 'Capiturini', fled the city on the grounds that they had sworn support to the counts and to Marius Borell. When the elders of Salerno wished to go out to receive the king to invite him to enter their city and at the same time, announcing that all the leaders of the conspiracy had fled, to ask forgiveness for those who had stayed behind, he refused to enter the city and ordered them to be removed from his sight. He had become extremely angry towards the people of Salerno, and had decided to destroy the entire city, as he had Bari.[119]

But since the notary Matthew, *familiaris* of the court, himself came from Salerno, he addressed many entreaties to the king's other *familiares* Richard, Bishop-Elect of Syracuse and Count Silvester, to strive in every possible way to prevent such a great and noble city from being destroyed. (Henry Aristippus had been arrested at the king's orders before he had got as far as Apulia, and had been sent back to Palermo, where he reached the end of both his miseries and his life in prison not long after.)[120] So the Bishop-Elect of Syracuse and Count Silvester appealed repeatedly and earnestly to the king and tried to persuade him with many arguments that this highly regarded city, which brought considerable prestige to the entire realm, ought not to be destroyed because of the wickedness of a few. The traitors had all fled the city,

119 For the background to this episode, see Cuozzo (1996), especially 53–5. In addition, one should note that the citizens of Salerno had at first been very reluctant to accept Roger II's rule over them in 1127; *Al. Tel.* I. 5–6, pp. 8–9; though the city had remained loyal to him thereafter, notably during the German invasion of 1137. Their sense of civic identity was certainly strong; contemporary Salernitan charters recorded transactions *sicut lex et consuetudo istius civitatis*, e.g. Cava, Arca xxxii. 59 (February 1167).
120 See p. 120 above for the reasons for this; though Garufi (1942), 69 suggests that it may have been his failure to take an active role in opposing the conspiracy in March 1161 which destroyed his credit with the king.

and if it did happen to be the case that a few of them remained, then their punishment should be seen to. The people as a whole should not suffer punishment undeservedly because of the crimes of others. Although the king at first found it difficult to accept arguments of this kind, in the end he was mollified by the many points that they made, and promised that he would hold back from the destruction of the city. He gave the *stratigotus* and the magistrates orders to bring all those of the conspirators who remained in the city to him in chains. They handed a few men over to him, claiming that they had led the unrest, and he ordered them to be hanged the same day.

Among them was one man who suffered this punishment although he was innocent according to the judgement of almost the entire city. As all the citizens asserted, he had not only never taken any oath to anyone against the king, but had never been seen doing anything seditious in the city. What happened was that the notary Matthew wanted to take vicious revenge for injury done to his own relatives whom this man had insulted; so he falsely suggested to the king that he had been the head and origin of all the evil that had occurred at Salerno, although his innocence was immediately proved by unambiguous evidence, and it became apparent that something had been done that was contrary to justice and which had offended the eyes of the Just Judge of all things. For while the sky was so clear that no trace of any cloud could be seen in it, such a storm suddenly sprang up, and thunder, lightning and torrential rain followed, so that the water ran through the whole camp like a fast-flowing stream, and the gusts blew away both the king's tent and those of all the others, with their pegs torn out and ropes broken. The king and the entire army were struck by such panic that they were forced to despair for their own lives, let alone the loss of all their belongings. Many also interpreted what later happened to the notary Matthew's relatives (not without damage to the entire city) as a punishment for this matter. The same Matthew used the authority and fear of the court to force a certain young man into marriage with his niece, although the man was unwilling. Many of the city elders and their wives were invited to the engagement ceremony. But the house suddenly collapsed, crushing about sixty noble men and women, including the girl who was being given in marriage.[121] This matter upset

---

121 A similar story of the collapse of a house being the means of divine punishment, also from the Salerno region, comes in the *Vitae Quattuor Priorum Abbatum Cavensium*, ed. L. Mattei-Cerasoli (Rerum Italicarum Scriptores, Bologna 1941), 21–2, written in the 1130s. The guilty party

the spirits of the people of Salerno no less than if they were witnessing the imminent destruction of their city, with the barbarians already breaking in. Women ran this way and that with their hair loose; they filled the streets and piazzas with their wailing. Some of the citizens attempted to drag bodies out of the rubble; others wept for their own families' losses, or consoled their friends' grief. Some just stood in astonishment as they considered the frightful event that had struck the desolated city. The shops were shut, no business was done, even the schools were quiet, as though silence were being imposed; a sad and wretched holiday forced the magistrates themselves to abandon hearings into legal disputes. Given over to grief, the entire city cried out against the crimes of the notary Matthew, who had brought about these great losses. When their grief outgrew their fears, they even foolishly started saying things about the king. Let me be allowed to anticipate these events, otherwise a confused list of stories would result from a greater licence to digress.

The king returned to Sicily when he saw that everything was now peaceful again and that none of his enemies were gathering anywhere. Some of them had crossed over to Greece, others had fled to the German Emperor with the Count of Loritello, and many remained destitute in Campania. He shut himself up in his palace and decided to allow himself a peaceful and quiet holiday after his efforts. He was certain that there was little chance of any other storm erupting in his kingdom. Not long afterwards, when Count Silvester was dying, the Bishop-Elect of Syracuse and the notary Matthew monopolised the advice given to the king and the administration of the realm between them.[122] Caid Peter the eunuch was given to them as an associate; he had been appointed Master Chamberlain of the palace after the death of Caid Johar.

So the notary Matthew, since he now had the greatest power at court, decided to follow the precedent and behaviour of the admiral. He made himself likeable to everyone, fawning especially on those whom he hated, and he had already begun to sweeten the king himself with his adulation, since he knew that Maio had been his favourite for this

there was Roger of San Severino, grandfather of the William of San Severino whom 'Falcandus' discusses.

[122] Silvester was last attested alive in April 1162; Garufi, *Tabulario di Monreale*, 161–3, no. 1. His son appears not to have been allowed to succeed to his comital title until after William I's death; see below, p. 157.

reason in particular. He was hampered by his avarice from imitating Maio's liberality, nor could he display any similar rhetorical ability, since he was rather a poor speaker. In addition his spirit was mean like his background,[123] and did not suffice to raise him to the same ambition to rule which had urged Maio on, even though all his efforts appeared to be aiming at and directed towards monopolising possession of the king's friendship, so that he should more fully occupy the admiral's position, even if he could not hope to bear the title so long as this king lived. Nor did he cultivate a more loyal friendship towards his colleague the Bishop-Elect of Syracuse or show him any more outward respect than the affection the admiral had previously shown towards the Archbishop of Palermo. The bishop-elect decided not to waste too much effort on ingenuity and pretence of this kind, and spoke to the king rather more objectively, thinking it unworthy of his honest nature to flatter him by hiding the truth or impudently to substitute what was false for what was true.

At that time, when his enemies had been subdued and peace had been restored in its entirety, and the king thought that he would not have to fear anything further, a sudden occurrence taught him that Fortune often plays tricks on mortal men in such a way that anyone who thinks he has nothing to pray for encounters loss or danger all the quicker. What happened was that a few men who were still being held in prison for a variety of reasons – so that grounds for accusing the palace of tyrannical behaviour would never be lacking – despairing of being granted pardon and no longer having any wish to live, decided to devote themselves to Fortune, so that either, if she favoured their undertaking, they would escape, or if she opposed them, they preferred to meet their death rather than to go on suffering such miseries and be constantly tortured by the filth of their awful dungeon. So they corrupted the dungeon-guards with many promises and found a suitable time when the court was otherwise engaged and the palace remained unobserved. They may have been few in number, but they were outstandingly brave. They made a rush and first of all got down to the palace gate. Their plan was that if they killed the castellan

---

[123] Nothing is known about his background except that his parents were called Nicholas and Marocta. His mother died in 1173; Garufi, *Necrologio di S. Matteo di Salerno*, 14; *Romuald*, 253, note 2. The prominence of his relatives (see above note 46) was due to his influence.

Ansaldus, whom they knew to have his office there,[124] they could do the rest more easily. But when he suddenly saw them coming at him with their swords raised, he did not allow himself to be thrown off balance by fear, but cleverly and swiftly slipped out through the gate which was half-open, shut it behind him with all his force, and held it against them, establishing himself in a completely safe space between the interior and the exterior gates. So their hopes were frustrated and they went off to the lower entrance to the palace. Their intention was either to go directly to the king or to find the king's sons in the schoolroom. Their teacher Walter, Archdeacon of Cefalù, had taken them away to to the bell-tower as soon as he realised the disturbance. It also happened that there were some men with Caid Martin, whose office was in the entrance just past the first door, and when they rushed in, one of these men opposed them and parried their first strokes. This slowed down their attack and destroyed their hopes; for in the meantime Caid Martin retreated into the palace and barred the doors. So they had achieved none of their aims and were suddenly surrounded by a large number of men who had swiftly gathered with Odo, master of the stable, and every one of them was killed. The court had their corpses thrown to the dogs and refused to let them be buried.

To prevent any future danger of an incident of this kind, and so that he would not have to fear once more what had now happened to him twice, the king decided that all prisoners should be removed from the palace. He ordered some of them to be taken to the Sea Castle, and others allocated to various fortresses across Sicily. The Master of the Sea Castle, Robert of Calatabellota, was a man of extreme cruelty, particularly friendly to the eunuchs and dedicated to serving them. He had any Christians who happened to be brought to him loaded with enormous chains and tortured with constant beatings, and he locked them up in some new dungeons which he himself had constructed, full of filth and terror, in order to appear to be even more tyrannical than his predecessors. He also did the citizenry many injuries. Whenever he had any private grudge against one of them or wanted his house, vineyard, garden, or anything at all, he would lay a charge against him before Caid Peter, and he would imprison him

---

124 Cf. Cusa, *Diplomi greci ed Arabi*, 74–5 (December 1166), in which Ansaldus Μαῖστορ τοῦ ἀνακαστέλλον purchased a house in the Halqa from the baron Rainald Avenell and his sons.

and subject him to hunger, thirst and various punishments until the man was forced to hand over his property for nothing or for less than it was worth in order to escape. Wishing to earn the favour of the eunuchs even more fully, he falsely suggested to Caid Peter that many of the traitors had remained behind in Sicily, especially in the towns of the North Italians. These men were wealthy and owned large estates, and he asked to be allowed to imprison them and extort as much money as he could from them. In possession of such power, he had many innocent men from various parts of Sicily condemned. The only thing against them was that they were found to possess the means with which the unquenchable cupidity of the eunuchs could be sated. Relying on the patronage of Caid Peter, Bartholomew de Parisio and other justiciars,[125] *stratigoti*, chamberlains, and catapans also ground down the people with incalculable plundering and wrongdoing. Their main concern in any court case was to extort money from one party or the other, or even both, if it could be done. Demands for bribes raged through the whole of Apulia and the Terra di Lavoro, especially against those who had the least power to resist; it would have been better for the Kingdom of Sicily to have been laid waste by external invaders rather than being handed over to indigenous bandits to be despoiled.

25 The king's death and the accession of his son, King William

So the realm had experienced a little peace from external trouble, and the king in the meantime gave himself up to relaxation and rest. Afraid of any event that would interrupt the enjoyment of his leisure, he had given his officials orders not to bring him any news that might cause him sadness or stress, and he went on to devote himself totally to pleasure. He let his imagination run freely, and it began to occur to him that since his father had built Favara, Minenia and other

[125] Bartholomew is first attested as a witness to the exchange of fiefs by John Malcovenant to which reference has already been made several times; Garufi, *Tabulario di Monreale*, 161–3, no. 1. He held lands near Agira in eastern Sicily, and another branch of his family were minor landowners in the Capitanata. Bartholomew died between 1187 and 1194, when his son Paganus was made Count of Avellino by Henry VI; Garufi (1913b), 346–53.

enjoyable places, he too should have a palace constructed, which would be designed on a larger and better plan so as to overshadow all his father's buildings.[126] The main part of it was carried out with amazing speed, not without enormous expense, but before he could see the work completed he was affected by dysentery and began to suffer from constant ill-health. The illness continued for a space of almost two months, and then he improved; when the doctors were already assuming that he would survive, he suddenly died, overcome by a new attack.

As he was still lying on his death-bed, he summoned the great men of the court, and in the presence of the Archbishops of Salerno and Reggio, he told them his last wishes, deciding that his elder son William was to reign after him. He wanted Henry to be satisfied with the Principality of Capua, which he had granted him a long time ago,[127] and he told the queen to undertake the care and administration of the entire realm, which is commonly called *balium*,[128] until the boy should reach such discretion as would be thought sufficient to govern affairs wisely. He ordered the Bishop-Elect of Syracuse, Caid Peter, and the notary Matthew, whom he had himself appointed as *familiares*,[129] to remain in the same position of *familiares* of the court, so that the queen should decide what ought to be done on the advice of these men.

---

126 For these, see Romuald's *Chronicle* (p. 219 below), and cf. Broadhurst, *The Travels of Ibn Jubayr*, 346: 'the king's palaces are disposed around the higher parts [of Palermo] like jewels around a woman's throat'.

127 Henry, the youngest son of William I, died at Palermo on 16 May 1172, aged 12, and was buried next to King Roger in Palermo cathedral; *Romuald*, 261–2 Garufi, *Necrologio di S. Matteo di Salerno*, 84. He was thus only 6 when his father died.

128 She was Margaret, daughter of King Garcia Ramirez of Navarre, whom according to Romuald (pp. 225–6 below) William had married while he was Prince of Capua, i.e. between 1144 and 1151. She died in 1183. *Balium* was a relatively common term, e.g. Garufi, *Ryccardi di S. Germano Chronica*, 19: the Empress Constance 'left [her son] Frederick and the *balium* of the kingdom to Pope Innocent [III] in her will [1198]'. Cf. E. Winkelmann, *Acta Imperii Inedita Saeculi XIII et XIV* (2 vols., Innsbruck 1880–5), i, 413, no. 495: Manfred of Taranto exercising the *balium* for his nephew Conradin (September 1257).

129 Mathew and Richard of Syracuse were described as *familiares* in *Guillelmi I Diplomata*, 88–90, no. 33 (March 1166).

Not long after, when the crisis of the illness came, already lacking normal vision, with the others present and weeping, he resigned his life and his realm together.[130] They were afraid that if a sudden rumour spread among the common people it would cause some disorder, and ordered that he should be buried temporarily within the palace, pretending that he was still alive, until they had summoned the leaders to court and made the preparations they thought necessary for the king's coronation. That took a few days to do, and then the cries of mourning began in the palace, suddenly taken up by the grief of the entire city. After that the leaders took the body from the place where it had been buried to the royal chapel, together with the bishops and great men of the court. And all the citizens, dressed in black garments, kept the same clothes on for three days. Throughout these three days women and noble matrons – especially the Muslim ones, whose grief for the king's death was not feigned – symbolically went around in sackcloth with their hair loose day and night, in groups, with a crowd of slave-girls preceding them, and filled the entire city with their wailing and rhythmic chanting in time to the beating of drums.[131]

When the days assigned for public mourning were over, William, who had just reached his fourteenth year, was acclaimed king to the great joy of the people, and solemnly rode through the city.[132] Since he was very handsome and seemed even more handsome on that day – how, I do not know – and bore a monarchical beauty on his brow, he won the good will and support of everyone. In consequence even

---

130 William died on 15 May 1166; Garufi, *Necrologio di S. Matteo di Salerno*, 70; Inguanez, *Necrologio di Cod. Cas.* 47, 67; *Annales Casinenses* ad ann. 1166 (MGH SS xix, 312). Romuald's date of 7 May appears to be an error. The king was buried in the Palatine chapel. According to the *Liber Pontificalis* ii, 414, he made a death-bed donation to the papacy of 60,000 *tari*. Cf. also Miller and Brooke, *Letters of John of Salisbury*, ii, 116–17.

131 Cf. Broadhurst, *The Travels of Ibn Jubayr*, 349: 'The Christian women of this city follow the fashion of Muslim women, are fluent of speech, wrap their cloaks about them, and are veiled.'

132 Romuald said that William was 12 when his father died (p. 239 below). He was 36 when he died in November 1189 – therefore he was probably born in the summer of 1153, and turned 13 soon after his father died. According to the *Annales Casinenses*, MGH SS xix, 312, he was crowned in July. The discrepancies would be reconciled if his birthday was in June.

those who utterly hated his father and had never thought that they would owe any loyalty to his heirs were prepared to state that anyone who plotted anything disloyal against this boy would be passing beyond the bounds of humanity. It was enough for them that the person responsible for these evils had been removed from their midst, and this harmless boy should not be blamed for the tyrannical behaviour of his father. The beauty of this boy was indeed such that it appeared to deny the possibility of an equal rather than admit that of a superior.

So the queen, in order to make both the people and the nobles grateful towards her and her son, decided to win their support by countless good deeds, and to extract their loyalty, if possible, by granting them enormous favours. First she ordered all the prisons to be opened, and set free a great number of men, both in Sicily and in the surrounding islands. Then she decreed that the unbearable burden of redemption fees, which had shaken the whole of Apulia and the Terra di Lavoro with utter despair, should be entirely abolished, and she wrote to the Master Chamberlains that they should not demand redemption fees again from anyone on any grounds. Further, she did not wish the *familiares* of the court to remain on the same equal level of honour with one another as they used to have: for she granted supreme power over all affairs to Caid Peter, placing him in a position which overshadowed that of the others, and told the Bishop-Elect of Syracuse and the notary Matthew that as his assistants they should indeed be present at council meetings and call themselves *familiares*, but that they should obey his orders in everything.

26 The queen and her officials

Although this man Peter was not a very shrewd man and tended to keep changing his mind, he was, however, gentle, pleasant and likeable, and his actions gave no grounds for criticism. He practised liberality above all the other virtues, and thought that giving gave more satisfaction than receiving. Because of this his knights loved him dearly and followed his wishes and orders in every respect, and if the vice of his race had not cancelled out his innate peaceableness and prevented him from genuinely abandoning his hatred of Christianity, the kingdom of Sicily would have enjoyed much peace under his administration.

At that time certain archbishops were staying at the court at Palermo,

Romuald of Salerno and Roger of Reggio, as well as the bishops Gentile of Agrigento and Turstan of Mazzara. Bishop Gentile of Agrigento had for some time pretended to play the role of a devotee of religion because he was afraid of the king; under cover of that he had bought the glory of popular approval, and he had succeeded in earning royal favour by daily fasting.[133] But after the king's death, when there was nothing to fear any more, he began to take liberties, as though he had shaken off his reins; he gave up fasting and lived a less moral life, inviting his knights to join him in many splendid banquets. Sometimes he said too much in the course of these feasts, or lied boldly about things that were well known, which was a habitual weakness of his; so that those who now had experience of his behaviour just laughed at his impudence, while those who knew him less well were astonished that the bishop should elaborate such obvious falsehoods in such a foolish way. On these occasions he would boast about his background and his building works, and sometimes promise that if he became a *familiaris* of the court he would abolish every evil custom, and that there would be no place in his administration for the theft and extortion of the notaries and the ushers and the other court officials; everything would be restricted to a prescribed amount. He particularly slandered the Bishop-Elect of Syracuse and aroused the hatred of many against him. He tried to damage his reputation in the eyes of the common people and its leaders, carefully looking for every opening and thinking of a way in which he could be removed from the court at any opportunity. He hated him because he alone seemed to stand between him and what he wanted, and was trying to deprive him of something that he had greatly wanted for a long time — for the two of them were striving with all their efforts to obtain the See of the church of Palermo.[134]

---

133 Gentile was Bishop of Agrigento from 1154 to 1171. He was described by the thirteenth-century *Libellus de Successione Pontificum Agrigenti* as 'Gentile the Tuscan, who was chancellor of the King of Hungary and came as an envoy to King William I, and returned once more'. In June 1169 he and Turstan of Mazzara concluded an agreement for mutual fraternity and liturgical commemoration between their two cathedrals; Collura, *Più antiche carte*, 47–9, no. 19; 308.

134 Archbishop Hugh was perhaps still alive in 1165, if Garufi was correct in assigning the donation to the archbishopric in *Documenti inediti* 91–3, no. 39, to that year. This charter does not mention any archbishop by name, but certainly implies that there was one in office at that time.

Consequently Gentile invited the Archbishop of Reggio to many splendid banquets. This was a man whose avarice and cupidity were inexhaustible, and while he was very restrained in his own expenses, he could easily be influenced by the splendours of someone else's table. He inflamed his spirit against the Bishop-Elect of Syracuse, and made him his associate in tainting the Archbishop of Salerno with the same poison of conspiracy. He said that the pride of the Bishop-Elect of Syracuse could be tolerated no longer, and that he had gone more than far enough in providing himself with a heap of money by stealing from the poor and causing a great deal of harm, and had not even spared the bishops themselves. Now they had to make sure that he was removed from the court and at long last came to understand that those people mattered whom he had despised as though they were his subjects while he held the position of a *familiaris* of the court, stiff-necked and head held high, mouthing fine phrases, and thinking that they deserved no respect.

It was not hard to persuade the notary Matthew to join the same group; the goad of jealousy had already turned him against the bishop-elect. But he said that he would act secretly, since it would appear to be excessively cruel for him suddenly and without any clear cause to attack the man whose associate he had been for so long. In fact he was afraid that the matter might turn out differently from the way they hoped, and that was why he did not dare to reveal himself as an open enemy. Apart from the private enmities of individuals which have been mentioned, there was another factor at work to make them hate the bishop-elect. For they argued that the pride of the men from across the Alps,[135] which up till now had done much uncontrolled damage to the South Italians, supported as it was by the power of the court and the friendship of the kings, would be utterly excluded from court, if they first managed to get rid of the bishop-elect. For once he had been expelled, no one of that race would remain at court, and the king himself, once he reached the age of discretion, would rely on those *familiares* among whom he had been brought up and whom long association and custom had acquainted him with, and he

---

[135] Richard, it should be remembered, was an Englishman. Peter of Blois later wrote to him about 'the sweetness of your native English air', and said that 'England now fosters me as an old man, which fostered you as a child'; *Ep.* no. 46, MPL ccvii, 133–7, at 134 and 137. This is confirmed by the inscription on his grave at Messina; Kamp (1973–82), iii, 1013.

would not grant court dignities to foreigners and immigrants whose habits he did not like because they were strange to him.

So they began to go out riding with Caid Peter on particular days, give him frequent help and show him more honour and respect than their position as bishops should have allowed. Next they amicably advised him always to have around him friends and people he knew, and not to allow anyone he did not know to approach him, claiming that the Bishop-Elect of Syracuse, since he could suffer no superior within the court, had entered upon a conspiracy with some others to have him killed; so he should take care in order that they might thwart his trap. Peter, ready to believe anything that he might be told, praised them, and notified his friends of the affair; on their advice he decided not just to expel the Bishop-Elect of Syracuse from court, but also to choose some men to strike him down with swords at the entrance to the palace.

In the meantime he warned the king's knights and their constables that none of them should choose to go riding with the bishop-elect or follow him when he came to court. The bishop-elect, although he realised what was going on from what many people told him, nevertheless did not do anything to protect himself against their plot, and was no more reluctant to go up to the court every day, so that those who knew about the danger he was in were amazed at his feeling of security and confidence.

When he had put himself in danger of being ambushed many times by going to the palace, Caid Peter, seeing this, and having a gentle disposition, immediately abandoned the plan when he was greeted by him; he told his knights not to carry out the crime, though when he had gone, incited anew by the bishops' repeated suggestions, he promised that he was certainly going to do what they persuaded him [to do]. When the opportunity arose, he abandoned the plan again. When the bishops and the notary Matthew saw that the matter was being dragged out to no purpose, they persuaded him that since he wanted to act faithfully towards a faithless man and had decided to return good for evil, at least he should remove him from the friendship of the court and send him off to his bishopric, and appoint the Archbishop of Salerno in his place.[136] He promised that he would do this,

---

[136] Richard had not yet received consecration, despite having been bishop-elect since 1157, and had clearly rarely if ever visited his see; Millor and Brooke, *Letters of John of Salisbury*, ii, 660–1, no. 290. His would seem to

but did not follow the matter up very energetically, keeping them in a state of suspense with long waiting and uncertain hope; so the others were exhausted and tired of things being put off, and would easily have given up the plan they had embarked on, if the Archbishop of Reggio had not whipped them up with constant goading. For he began to go round their residences at crack of dawn, goading each one to finish off the business they had undertaken, and he exhorted them not to become lukewarm because nothing had been achieved, railing against their apathy and calling them sluggish, taking up the entire day with exhortations of this kind and giving hope back to their flagging spirits. For they all still respected him and willingly accepted his advice because of his reputation for sanctity, a reputation not yet unmasked by his own hypocrisy. He was now of an age that was almost advanced, of tall stature, gaunt and worn by extreme fasting; with a voice that was so weak that it sounded like a whisper; a pale colour mixed with dark marks covered his face and his whole body, so that he seemed to be more like the dead than the living, and his exterior colour gave an indication of the man within. He thought that no labour was too hard if there was any hope of gain thereby; he put up with hunger and thirst beyond human capacity, if it could cut down his expenses; he was never cheerful when he dined at home, never sad at anyone else's dinner-party; he frequently spent whole days in fasting, waiting for someone to send him an invitation (for the Bishop of Agrigento and others who knew his habits often used to invite him).

In response to this man's constant warnings, the Archbishop of Salerno and his associates, as though whipped up by goads, employed many tricks and turns against the Bishop-Elect of Syracuse. But the queen none the less continued to take his advice, even though the opposition to him did not displease her, because previously when her husband was still alive, she had appealed to the bishop-elect several times in

> be the specific case which Richard of Dover, Archbishop of Canterbury 1173–84, had in mind in a letter (actually composed by Peter of Blois) to Alexander III *c.* 1179 in which he compared the English episcopate (which had been the subject of papal criticism) favourably with that of Sicily, MPL cc; 1459–62, no. 96, at 1461: 'Furthermore, the archbishops and bishops who frequent the court of the King of Sicily do not leave that court for seven to ten years; nor does it make any difference, either for the preservation of their churches' property or for the well-being of souls, if they are alive or dead.'

matters concerning her own affairs, and he (who was always condescending when things were going well for him) had acted as though he despised her, replying proudly and ironically to her messages, and refused to take cognisance of her requests. As well as this, when John of Naples (a cardinal of the Roman Church who happened to be present) saw the deep division affecting the court, he tried to further his own interests; supporting Caid Peter, he tried to expel the bishop-elect from court. His reason for doing this was believed to have been that he thought he could persuade Caid Peter, and through him the queen, to entrust the administration of the church at Palermo to himself, and he thought that those behind the plot would be ready to agree because of their hatred of the bishop-elect.[137]

While the Bishop-Elect of Syracuse was being battered in this way by a storm of opposition, it was announced at Palermo that Count Gilbert of Gravina, the queen's relative, had heard of the king's death, was coming to the court, and had crossed the Straits. Unsettled by this rumour, the bishop-elect's opponents abandoned their conspiracy for a little, forced by necessity to think of another plan. It was clear that the reason the count had come was to be appointed Master Captain of the whole realm and undertake the administration of the business of the court in the top position after the queen.[138] But the queen's inclination would not allow her to put Caid Peter, of whom she was very fond, in second position to anyone, and the count had not come with the support of enough knights to be able to exclude the other *familiares* from the court against her wishes. So the bishop-elect sent messages to him secretly and told him about the opposition to himself and the injuries that had been done to him, and warned him to act with care and forestall the tricks of the Sicilians. He would find out that snares had without doubt been laid for him by Caid

---

137 Pseudo-Hugo's low opinion of John of Naples was echoed by John of Salisbury and other supporters of the exiled English archbishop, Thomas Becket, who considered him an ally of Henry II and a recipient of that king's bribes; Millor and Brooke, *Letters of John of Salisbury*, ii, 606–9, no. 279 (July 1168).

138 The *Chron. Casauriense*, 903, did indeed describe Gilbert as 'at this time Master Captain and governor of the whole kingdom', when he presided over a court at Foggia to hear the monastery's complaints in its long-running dispute with Count Bohemond II of Manopello, but there is no other evidence that he was anything but governor of the mainland (excluding Calabria), as he had been in William I's later years; Jamison (1913), 289.

Peter and his associates. The count wrote back to the bishop-elect that he should be confident from now on; for he himself would carefully make provision for all these matters on his own initiative.

When he had reached Palermo, the supporters of Caid Peter began to call on him quite often, and praised his care and foresight for having come to console the queen without delay as soon as he had heard of the king's death; then as they were leaving, they flattered him, and put themselves and all they had at his disposal. But at the same time they secretly slandered him to the queen, sometimes by themselves, and sometimes using the cardinal's authority. Presently she herself abandoned him, and it was made known that John of Naples had suggested to her and had been prepared to take an oath that the count had tried to take away from her the guardianship and the entire authority to govern and transfer them to himself.

When the count realised that his expectations had definitely eluded him and that the queen's attitude towards him was not favourable, he decided to use harsh words to her, and spoke to her in private (but with Caid Peter in attendance). While he was in agreement with her in most things, he added that it was something that everyone thought was like a miracle that she did not change the organisation of the court, since it could not stay any longer in the condition it was. All the leading men were already angry that she had passed over the counts and other prudent men by whose judgement the court ought to be guided, and put a castrated slave in charge of the entire realm. For the king's judgement had not been sound, and his command on this matter should not be adhered to, when he had thought that despicable persons, eunuchs indeed, sufficed to administer the realm. However, it was even more lunatic that some group of conspirators or other should have set her against the Bishop-Elect of Syracuse and considered that he should be removed from the court; he was an intelligent man who was needed by the kingdom and who constituted the only respect in which the king's foolish decrees might to some extent be excused.

The queen, however, replied that the king's final wishes would be respected in every proper way, and would never be made void by any act of hers. If he thought that Caid Peter was not good enough to administer the realm, then he should remain at court as a *familiaris* alongside him, so that his authority and wisdom might make up for any that the court lacked. Angered by this, the count said, 'How good of you to have granted the respect due to me as your blood-relative by deciding to assign me a wonderful position of honour in which you make me the equal of your slave. I know your habits and your inclinations, and know what your intention is: I know that you are going to behave in such a way that you will be shamefully ejected from the government of this kingdom – your reputation has already suffered throughout Apulia as a result of your actions, and now I have experienced something here which strongly confirms what was said there'. He attacked her with these and other equally harsh phrases, and then gradually broke into open abuse. When in the end he had made her cry, she nevertheless resisted his suggestion just as actively, so he left her, and went back to his residence in a huff.

Caid Peter had learnt the count's intentions openly from his own words (since he was present), and thought that he had to be resisted by force; so he began to bind the knights' loyalty towards him through favours and largesse. There were two noblemen who were among his advisers at the time, and whom he particularly trusted: Hugh, son of Atto, who was both intelligent and a good warrior, whom he himself had put in charge of his knights,[139] and the Master Constable Richard of Mandra, who had sweated long and hard in matters of warfare alongside Count Robert of Loritello, and had plenty of courage, but not much wisdom. So the barons and other noblemen who possessed any estates or fiefs preferred the Count of Gravina to be at the head of the court and be appointed captain, while the salaried knights (together with their constable), except for a few from north of the Alps, preferred the rewards of Caid Peter. Caid Peter, knowing that he had bound the loyalty of the Constable Richard to himself by doing him many favours, planned to have him made a count and use him as a kind of defence against the Count of Gravina, so that one count could resist the other count with full authority, as if from horseback. He appealed to the queen to grant this, and achieved it without difficulty. So he was made a count, not without resentment on the part of many, and took possession of Boiano, Venafro and all those

---

[139] Hugh was active from 1166 to 1183, and had lands and a number of vassals in Molise and Samnium on the mainland; *Cat. Bar.* 57, 138–41, arts. 340–1, 767–79; Cuozzo (1984), 80–1. In addition to the evidence cited by Cuozzo, he also witnessed a charter of a Molise baron in favour of St Sophia, Benevento, drawn up at the royal court in Barletta in May 1172; Pergamene Aldobrandini, Cartolario II, no. 25.

towns which belong to the county of Molise, with trumpets, drums and cymbals going in procession before him, according to custom.[140]

In the meantime Caid Peter started to ride about a lot with an enormous number of knights, preceded by sentries and archers. He gave considerable presents to all those who came to support him, and bound those he could to himself with oaths. The Count of Gravina pretended not to mind about all this and to be satisfied with a small number of attendants, which just made him even more suspect in the eyes of Caid Peter. He assumed that a man who was known to be ambitious was hiding some clever plan, and secretly hatching some major plot with the Bishop-Elect of Syracuse. This suspicion finally led to fear, and he carefully tried to find out about the count's plans from his friends. Many said that there was nothing to be afraid of and gave him cause for hope in order to try to restore his ebbing confidence; but several came to him privately and asserted that a secret plot was being hatched against him.

So he was shaken by different and contradictory stories, and so frightened that he thought that he would only be able to escape from the count's hands by fleeing in the night. He had a fast boat made ready with the greatest possible speed and provided with sailors, weapons and whatever else was needed. After he had had his treasure-chests carried there in the silence of the night, on the next day, after sunset, he pretended that he wanted to go to a new palace which he had recently built in the part of the city called Kemonia,[141] and went down to the sea front with a few eunuchs whom he had decided to take with him. There he sent away the horses, went on board ship and sailed across to Africa to the King of the Almohads.[142]

When news of this circulated among the people first thing in the morning, the unexpected outcome of events upset the spirits of those who had backed his side, but raised Count Gilbert and his supporters

140 The previous count, Hugh II, had died childless before October 1158; see note 60 above.
141 According to the *Letter to Peter* (p. 259 below) the Kemonia was next to the royal palace and among the mansions there were some for the eunuchs in royal service.
142 Ibn Khaldun reports the flight of an official whom he called 'Ahmed the Sicilian', who was later (1185) active as an Almohad military commander; *BAS* ii, 187, 205. Both Amari (1933–9), iii, 505 and Siragusa, *Falcando*, 99, note 1, identify him as Peter.

to the certainty of greater expectations, since they thought that their aims could now be thwarted by no possible obstacle. Many people said — and this was the view of the common people — that apart from a huge weight of gold (about which there was no doubt) Caid Peter had also taken away with him much of the insignia of the crown. But the queen firmly denied this and stated that he had touched absolutely nothing belonging to the royal treasury.

So when the bishops, counts and *familiares* of the court came to the palace following these events, and in turn discussed what had happened at length, enquiring into the reasons and the method by which it had been done, the Count of Gravina commented that he had been afraid of these and worse things before they had occurred, for it had been a lunatic idea to raise up a Muslim slave who had already betrayed one military expedition to a position of such power. It ranked as an even greater miracle that he had not secretly smuggled some Almohads into the palace and carried off the king himself with his entire treasure. He would definitely have planned to do that if he had been allowed any longer to make use of the power which he had usurped.

Count Richard of Molise was angered by these and similar utterances of the count's, and replied that Caid Peter had indeed been a slave, as he stated, but had been formally given his freedom in the late king's will, and that this grant of freedom had also been confirmed by a privilege granted by the new king and the queen. If the count or anyone else was going to behave with such audacity as to accuse the said Caid Peter of treachery, then he was ready to undertake his defence and establish the loyalty of the absent man by the test of single combat. Since the caid had not been able to escape the danger that was hanging over him and the snares that had been laid for him in any other way, it was hardly surprising that he should flee in fear of being killed, doing what he could to save his life; the fault ought to rebound on the man who had forced him to flee by threatening and terrorising him. When something like the seeds of a lawsuit had been laid in this way, the counts kept arguing against each other until things got so far that Count Richard of Molise, speaking extremely forcefully, called the Count of Gravina a coward and unworthy to be one to whom the king's army could be entrusted. If those present had not flung themselves between them, the argument that had arisen between them could not have been settled without serious damage on either side. Then on the queen's orders and the appeals of the magnates of the court, the injurious statements on both sides were

THE HISTORY OF THE TYRANTS OF SICILY 149

forgiven, and harmony was restored between them, although it could never be completely firm afterwards.

In the meantime the queen, persuaded by the arguments of Count Richard and those others who had supported Caid Peter, was looking forward to a suitable opportunity to send Count Gilbert away from court, but in such a way as not to give any impression that she was doing it because she hated him. The notary Matthew, who was more clever than any of the others, resorted to the skills Maio had perfected, and dug up old stories that had now not been told for some time, spread rumours among the people, and composed a false letter announcing as fact an invasion by the German Emperor.[143] He had this letter opened and read out in everyone's presence as though it had arrived from distant parts of the kingdom (this was one of his duties). The queen realised that this was her opportunity, and with many flattering exhortations she ordered the Count of Gravina to go to Apulia as soon as possible, since this was a crisis which could not be neglected and which he seemed to be the most suitable person to deal with. He should raise an army against the emperor, ensure that the cities would stay loyal, and see that fortresses were ready to resist. Although the count was not unaware that these tricks were coming from sources worthy of Maio, he nevertheless realised that he would be unable to achieve anything at court against the queen's wishes, and thought it better not to resist these plans; for if they saw that they had failed in the aims that they had hoped to achieve secretly, they might give up a policy of pretence and deceit and use their superior power openly to send him into exile, notwithstanding his objections.

So he was appointed Captain of Apulia and the Terra di Lavoro together with his son Bertram, who had recently been granted the county of Andria, and he crossed the Straits and returned to Apulia.[144]

---

[143] In fact anticipating Frederick Barbarossa's march on Rome in the summer of 1167; but the German Emperor's continued hostility and the attacks on the border of the Principality of Capua by Andrew of Rupecanina and Richard of Aquila, the exiled former Count of Fondi; *Annales Ceccanenses* ad ann. 1166, MGH SS xix, 285; meant that this would have seemed a very real danger.

[144] Bertram was first recorded witnessing a donation of his father to the nunnery of St Benedict of Polignano (on the Adriatic coast, 30 km. south of Bari) in December 1162, and witnessed another grant by his father to the same nunnery in January 1166, along with his (younger?) brother

In his place the queen made Richard of Mandra, Count of Molise, a *familiaris* of the court, since he had cherished great loyalty for Caid Peter, and granted him greater power than the other *familiares*. This man was greatly feared because he was a *familiaris* of the court, because of his headstrong rashness and because he was still in command of the knights in the capacity of constable.

Meanwhile the bishops recommenced their opposition to the Bishop-Elect of Syracuse, which for some time had lain dormant for fear of the count. They suggested to the queen that the flight of Caid Peter was his fault, since Count Gilbert, having been recalled to court by a letter of the bishop-elect and told what he ought to do by means of secret messages during the course of his journey, had severely hurt Caid Peter, unsettled him, and abandoned him to considerable dangers, without any attempt being made to punish this by the queen or any of the court. It was not surprising if the fact that crimes were being left unpunished gave him the confidence to undertake what he wanted. But if only she herself agreed, they would easily engineer his having to set off for Rome, summoned by a letter from the pope, and no blame of any kind for this could be pinned on her, since it did not seem to accord with her policy. After his consecration, when he would no longer be a *familiaris* of the court, he would have to return directly to his diocese.[145]

The queen agreed and said that this was in every way pleasing to her. On the day chosen, John of Naples, who was behind these schemes, was summoned to court, and after some discussions concerning the business of the Roman Church for which he had come, he finally produced a letter from the pope ordering that all bishops-elect of

---

Bartholomew; Coniglio, *Pergamene di Conversano*, 227–8, 239–41, nos. 109, 114. In neither of these documents did he have a comital title. The county of Andria had been vacant since the previous holder, Richard de Lingèvres, had been killed fighting the Byzantines in 1155; Brand, *Deeds of John and Manuel Comnenus by John Cinnamus*, 112–13; Cuozzo (1984), 24–5.

[145] Why consecration (which he only eventually received in 1169) should have debarred him from being a *familiaris* is far from clear, since other consecrated bishops were later to be *familiares* for long periods (see Takayama (1993), 119–23). This view may have based on the calculation that the pope would insist on his residence in his (hitherto neglected) diocese, and certainly once he was finally consecrated Richard ceased to be a *familiaris* for eight years, although he was to be one again from 1177 to 1184.

Sicily, whose consecration was the privilege of the Roman pontiff, should go to Rome to be consecrated. After the letter had been read out in the presence of the king and queen and of the entire court, he added that the pope had told him to decide any additional points not explicitly made in the letter; so on his own authority he was imposing on the said bishops-elect a deadline by which they would have to be consecrated. The bishop-elect replied to this that he was willing to fulfil the pope's command as soon as he could, but that he would not accept the deadline set by the cardinal, and would not do anything that the cardinal added to the import of the letter.[146] There was considerable argument about this, since the bishop-elect had cleverly thwarted the cardinal's intentions by replying to the points separately, and after most of the day had been wasted, they both left the palace.

27 Hated by many during his lifetime, they loved him after his death

Many mourned the dead king William during these days who had hated him as the most wicked tyrant when he was alive.[147] They saw that private enmities were taking precedence over the business of the realm, that the treasuries were being emptied in a variety of ways, and that many individual privileges were being exercised to the disadvantage of the reputation of court and kingdom. On one occasion, in the presence of many people, the bishop-elect wanted to signify how damaging the king's death had been, and applied to the present day Cato's words when he heard of Pompey's death: 'A citizen has died', he said, 'who was greatly inferior to our ancestors in his respect for the rule of law; he was nevertheless a model in the present age.'[148]

There was also another incident which I think I should mention: one day the great men of the court met the cardinal, with other magnates and bishops. Among them was someone with a reputation as a

---

146 The see of Syracuse was at this period directly subject to the pope, and only later, in 1188, was it made a suffragan of William II's new archbishopric at Monreale; *Documenti inediti*, 223, no. 91.
147 Something of a medieval cliché; cf. Henry of Huntingdon, *Historia Anglorum*, ed. T. Arnold (2 vols., Rolls Series 1879), ii, 256, on Henry I of England.
148 Lucan, *De Bello Civili*, 9. 190–1, cf. the introduction, p. 48 above.

chatterbox and a witty fool; his nonsense enabled him to attack the courtiers freely and sometimes extremely woundingly, and he constantly frequented the court. After having attacked everyone with his customary verbal insults, and having made some of them laugh, he finally left the rest alone and looked at John of Naples: 'Cardinal,' he said, 'how many miles do you think it is from the city of Rome to Palermo?' When he had received the reply that it was a journey of fifteen days, he said, 'When I saw you travelling such a difficult route so often in complete safety as though you didn't mind, I used to think that we could not be more than 20 miles from the Romans. But now I understand that you ignored all these dangers because you were led on by the hope of gain, when you realised that the palace treasures had fallen into the hands of such stupid people. If the elder William were still alive, you would not go home with your pockets stuffed with the gold of Sicily,[149] nor would you be returning to Palermo so often in order to stoke up rivalry and conflict in our court.' What he said pleased those who were standing round, and was quickly broadcast among the people. It excited much hostility against the cardinal, and was turned into a proverb: 'John of Naples reckons Rome to Palermo at twenty miles.'

28 The friendship between the Bishop-Elect of Syracuse and Count Richard

The legate, while continuing to accuse the Bishop-Elect of Syracuse of contempt, fixed the earliest possible date for his consecration, so that he would be forced to start his journey as soon as possible. The bishop-elect, seeing that he was implacable, was afraid that if he opposed the cardinal publicly and freely, against the opposition of the queen, whose duty it was to uphold the constitution of the realm, he would incur the displeasure of the Roman pontiff. So he adopted another plan, and by continual pressure and enormous bribes he won the favour of Count Richard, who had the greatest influence with the queen. He formed a friendship with him, considering the hatred of the others unimportant by comparision. When they all assembled at court again, they began to appeal to the cardinal with feigned requests

---

149 A reference to King William's death-bed donation to the papacy, for which see above, note 130.

to give the bishop-elect a longer period of grace. When he said that he would not do so, they replied that it was his will that had to be done, and the bishop-elect neither should nor could disobey the orders of the Roman curia. Then Count Richard, with characteristic impetuosity, suddenly broke into speech: 'I am surprised that you belittle the needs of the realm to the extent of standing by a policy which has the effect of expelling the Bishop-Elect of Syracuse, a wise man and necessary member of the court. While the king lived, he honoured him above the other *familiares*, and when he was at the point of death, he commended his sons to him in particular and before all others. I certainly cannot support this policy, and cannot see how it can be pursued while retaining our loyalty to the king. Nor should the queen suffer his departure from the court either for his consecration or for any other reason at all.'

The others were taken aback at these words of the count and remained silent. When the cardinal said that the bishop-elect would return immediately after his consecration, the queen took a different approach and replied that his presence was essential to the court, and for the time being he could not go anywhere at all. He would go at some other time, when an opportune moment presented itself.

29 The fickleness of women

Thus the plots of his enemies were confounded and their plans thwarted, and the bishop-elect remained a *familiaris* of the court. At this time Richard de Say arrived at Palermo, bringing with him his wife, the sister of Bartholomew de Parisio.[150] He wished to divorce her in order to enter into matrimony with the niece of the archbishop of Capua,[151]

---

150 Richard de Say, found as royal constable and justiciar in Calabria in 1157; Pratesi, *Carte latine di abbazie Calabresi*, 53–5, no. 20; was to be one of the key figures of the early years of William II; made Count of Fondi in 1166, transferred to the county of Gravina in 1168, and Master Justiciar of Apulia and Terra di Lavoro until 1172 (for this last, see Tescione (1990), 162–4, no. 3). Geoffrey de Say, who was perhaps his grandfather, witnessed a charter of Roger I to the abbey of Lipari in 1094; Ménager (1975), 344.

151 Alfanus, Archbishop of Capua 1153–80. Nothing is known about his family except that Florius de Camerota was his nephew; MPL cc, 332–3, ep. 303 (and see above, p. 24).

a whore of high birth with whom he had long ago fallen in love. As Captain and Master Constable for Apulia, this man had remained unshakeably loyal and never deserted the king, while others had rebelled so many times. The queen received him favourably, and invested him with the county of Richard of Aquila, Count of Fondi, who was in exile in Roman territory with no hope of being allowed to return. On the matter of the divorce, she told the *familiares* that the bishops and other clergy should be summoned to listen to what both sides had to say, and reach the decision which fairness demanded. They asked the cardinals to take part in the investigation of this affair on the grounds that they were very familiar with such matters, since the Roman Curia frequently heard cases of this kind. John of Naples was quick to assent to their request. When the Bishop of Ostia, a man of undoubted integrity, saw that his colleague had been prejudiced by bribery and favouritism and that his freedom to come to a correct judgement had thus been taken away, he could not be persuaded by any plea to take part in the proceedings.[152]

The ground on which Richard thought that his marriage ought to be dissolved was this: he claimed to have had an affair with a cousin of his wife long before the marriage had been contracted. Two knights appeared as witnesses of this who stated categorically that they had seen it. The other party denied this, and asserted that there were persons who would prove that they were giving false testimony – not that they thought that a reason of this kind, even if it were true, would be sufficient cause for divorce, but to counter the insult of the accusation levelled against their cousin. The cardinal thought it best to deal with the matter briefly, and ordered the said witnesses to take an oath. So he dissolved the marriage, made both parties swear not to have intercourse in future, enabled Richard to proceed legitimately

[152] Hubald, Bishop of Ostia, was one of the most experienced members of the Sacred College. Originally from Lucca, he was appointed Cardinal deacon of St Adrian in 1138, promoted to be Cardinal priest of St Prassede in 1141, and Cardinal Bishop of Ostia in 1158. He had been one of the negotiators of the Treaty of Benevento in 1156, and was later to be papal legate to Byzantium in 1167/8, one of the negotiators of the Treaty of Venice in 1176/7; *Romuald*, 284; and pope (as Lucius III) from 1181 to 1185; Zenker (1964), 22–5. A further pair of legates, Bernard, Cardinal Bishop of Porto, and Manfred, Cardinal deacon of St George, was present in the kingdom in December 1166, though they seem to have dealt with strictly ecclesiastical rather than political issues; Holtzmann (1926), 334–5.

THE HISTORY OF THE TYRANTS OF SICILY 155

to a second marriage,[153] and ordered her to remain without hope of a husband.

30 The cardinal's partially unjust judgement

The clerics who were present had no doubts that in this matter he had acted out of favour to Richard de Say and his friends, but they were rather more surprised that while the man who had acted wrongly had been acquitted, he had ordered the woman who had done nothing wrong to live in perpetual chastity. After criticising his disgraceful judgement among themselves, they tried to test him by asking whether they should consistently apply this precedent in cases of a similar kind; he replied that he was allowed to do what they were not, and he had not acted in this case in order to create a precedent.

31 The queen's brother and his character

At that time a certain brother of the queen's was also staying at Palermo. He had recently crossed over to Sicily from Spain when he had heard of the king's death, and had brought many Spanish knights with him in hope of wealth.[154] As several of those who came with him stated, the King of Navarre had either never believed, or never wished to admit, that he was his son, since he thought it a disgrace that someone should be called the king's son when his mother, having suffered the lust of many men, might have conceived from anyone. He had been called Rodrigo, a name which the Sicilians did not like because it was unknown to them and laughed at as barbarous; so the queen told him to call himself Henry, and she gave him the entire county of Montescaglioso and those cities of Sicily which Count Godfrey had once held, together with that county. This Henry was of stocky build, with virtually no beard, ugly because of his slightly swarthy skin, a man without discretion or speaking ability, who showed skill in nothing at all except playing knucklebones and dice, and with

153 His second wife (and the archbishop's niece) was presumably the Theodora, Countess of Gravina, mentioned in a Monreale charter of April 1179; *Documenti inediti*, 169–70, no. 70.

154 One of these was perhaps the 'John of Spain' who later (in 1182) witnessed a charter of Robert of San Giovanni; *Documenti inediti*, 173–4, no. 72.

no desire except to have a companion to play with and money which he could waste prodigally, indiscreetly and rashly.[155]

32 The various conditions of the population of Messina

After Henry had stayed at Palermo for some time and by his immoderate expenditure easily used up the vast sum of money the queen had given him, he decided to cross over to Apulia and came to Messina, where he found many people similar to himself. For this city was composed of immigrants, pirates and brigands. It held within its walls almost every type of human being, free from no kind of wickedness, rejecting no crime, thinking that nothing which it had the power to do was forbidden. So highwaymen and pirates, beggars, flatterers and those involved in other crimes flocked to him, spending their days banqueting, and entire nights in playing dice.[156] When the queen heard about this she was sharply critical of his foolishness, and ordered him to cross the Straits without delay. On his associates' advice he finally dragged himself away from there with difficulty and started his journey to Apulia.

So[157] after a period of about a year had elapsed since the king's death, and the storm had gradually died down and left the court, the leading men of the kingdom were remaining quiet for the time being, conquered by the many benefits which the queen granted to them. For quite apart from the large number of prisoners who were set free, the slaves who were awarded their freedom, the tax privileges granted to the citizens, the abolition of customs which seemed to be unjust and the estates and towns which were granted to many members of the nobility,

---

155 He was an illegitimate son of King Garcia Ramirez, and despite Pseudo-Hugo's insinuations, was probably named after the king's illustrious grandfather, El Cid (a suggestion we owe to Dr K. Thompson). He was transferred before December 1168 to the county of the Principate; Cuozzo (1979), 162. By the time that the Catalogue of the Barons was revised, probably late in 1168, the county of Montescaglioso was once again vacant and in the hands of the crown; *Cat. Bar.* 24–6, arts 135–47. Henry was last recorded alive in January 1172; Cava, Arca xxxiv. 15.

156 Cf. Sallust's description of Catiline and his associates, *Catiline* 14.1, though this is not an exact quotation.

157 This begins a new section in the early MSS.; in Recension I it is part V of the whole work, part IV of the main text.

she created eight counts in that one year: Richard of Mandra,[158] the count of Gravina's son Bertram,[159] Richard de Say,[160] Roger, son of Richard,[161] Joscelin,[162] Simon of Sangro,[163] Count Silvester's son, William,[164] and her relative Hugh of Rochefort (a man devoid of every virtue), who had recently arrived from France;[165] in addition she

158 Richard of Mandra was appointed to the County of Molise which had been vacant for about ten years, since the death of the childless Count Hugh (see above, note 60).

159 Count of Andria (see above, note 144).

160 Count of Fondi (see above, note 150). The previous count, Richard of Aquila, had died in exile. In 1168 Richard de Say was transferred to the County of Gravina when Count Gilbert was exiled, and Fondi was restored to Richard II de Aquila, the son of its previous holder.

161 Roger *filius Ricardi* was appointed to the County of Alba, vacant since the previous holder, Count Berard, had been dispossessed after being involved in the 1160 rebellion. (Andew of Rupecanina was married to his daughter; *Annales Ceccanenses* ad ann. 1160, MGH SS xix, 285). Roger subsequently (in 1168) became Count of Andria on Bertram's exile, and the County of Alba then reverted to Count Peter of Celano, the son of Count Berard. Roger was later one of the chief Sicilian negotiators of the Venice peace conference of 1176-7; *Romuald*, 270, 295-6; and in 1185 was Master Justiciar of Apulia and Terra di Lavoro; Jamison (1929), 557-9. His father Richard *filius Ricardi* was an important landholder in the region to the east of Benevento, attested between 1130 and 1146; Cuozzo (1984), 64-6, 337-9; and see above, note 25.

162 Joscelin was restored to the County of Loreto, on the kingdom's northern border, formerly held by his father Rambotus, who had died before 1163. He can have been no more than about 18 at this time. He married Adelaide, daughter of King Roger by his seond wife, and eventually died during the Third Crusade in 1189; Cuozzo (1984), 328-30.

163 He is unlikely to have been the same man as the Count Simon mentioned above p. 69. The County of Sangro had subsequently been held by a Count Philip, and probably been vacant since *c.* 1162; Cuozzo (1984), 322.

164 Restored to his father's county of Marsico, he also continued to hold the lordship of Ragusa in Sicily, for which see Pirro, *Sicula Sacra*, i, 624 (1192, 1194).

165 Nothing certain is known about him. He must have been related to the queen through the Perche or L'Aigle relations of her French mother. But there were three possible Rochefort families in northern France to whom these may have been connected: (1) the lords of Rochefort-sur-Loire (dépt. Maine-et-Loire), (2) the lords of Rochefort (Charente); a member of this family called Hugh was attested 1130-52, but was probably too old to be

restored to their previous rank Count Roger of Acerra[166] and Count Roger of Avellino,[167] who had been recalled from exile. Having experienced the queen's liberality through these and many other benefits besides, they tried hard to restrain their fierce spirits from the inborn habit of rebellion.

33 The state of the court

The real situation of the court was as follows. Count Richard of Molise, with the support of other courtiers of great power, found it easiest to obtain what he requested from the queen. The Bishop-Elect of Syracuse and the notary Matthew exercised the office of chancellor. In addition Caid Richard, who was Master Chamberlain of the Palace, and Caid Martin, who was in charge of the *diwan*,[168] played just as much a part in policy-making and dealt with the affairs of the realm jointly with the above-mentioned *familiares*. Furthermore, when Matthew the notary realised that he could not become admiral because of the hatred associated with that title, he put all his efforts into obtaining the

> the man mentioned here, (3) the descendants of Guy de Rochefort, known as the Red, seneschal to King Philip I of France. This last is most probable, for this family had Perche connections. A possible identification is Hugh, younger son of Béatrice de Rochefort and Dreux de Pierrefonds, attested in 1144; *Recueil de chartes et documents de Saint-Martin des Champs, monastère Parisien*, ed. J. Despoin, ii (Paris 1913), 152, no. 283. It is also possible that Hugh was made Count of Alife (a suggestion made to us by E. Cuozzo), since that county may have been vacant, though it is not clearly established when the previous incumbent, Count Mauger, died (for the latter, see Cuozzo (1984), 266–7).

166 Roger de Medania, previously Count of Buonalbergo (for whom see above, note 51). He died in the later part of 1167, and was succeeded by his sister's son, Richard of Aquino; Cuozzo (1984), 81–3.

167 Roger of Aquila, Count of Avellino, was restored before May 1167; Tropeano, *Cod. dipl. verginiano*, v, 261–4, no. 474, and also recovered his lands at Aderno in Sicily; Pirro, *Sicula Sacra*, ii, 934 (1177). He died in 1183. Later, c. 1170, Peter of Blois lamented that William II did not follow his sensible advice more often; MPL ccvii, 27–32 ep. 10, col. 29. See also Cuozzo (1984), 100–2 and note 80 above.

168 Caid Martin had been in charge of the *Duana de Secretis*, the office in charge of land registration and boundaries and royal property, since 1161 at the latest (see above, notes 86 and 117). He remained as a palace chamberlain until his death in 1176; Takayama (1993), 127.

chancellorship; and the bishop-elect was confident that he would be the next to preside over the church at Palermo. But the queen was in favour of a quite different policy, and reserved that position for someone else. For she had written to her uncle the Archbishop of Rouen to send her one of her relatives, preferably Robert of Neubourg or else Stephen, son of the count of Perche.[169] Since she hoped that one or other would come without delay, she spent the meantime playing off the hopes and ambitions of the Bishop-Elect of Syracuse against those of the Bishop of Agrigento. And her hope was soon realised.

34 The arrival of Stephen, son of the Count of Perche

After an interval of a few days, preceded by rumours, it was learnt that on his way to Sicily Stephen, son of the Count of Perche, had stopped with his brother's son the Count of Gravina.[170] The count

---

[169] Stephen was a younger son of Count Rotrou II of Perche (d. 1144) and his second wife, Hawise of Salisbury. Rotrou, Archbishop of Rouen from 1165 to 1183, was Count Rotrou II's nephew, son of his sister Margaret and Henry of Neubourg. He was therefore the queen's cousin rather than her uncle (*avunculus*), since she was the granddaughter of Rotrou II's sister, Juliana, by her marriage to Gilbert I, lord of L'Aigle; Thompson (1996), 182. The archbishop's blood-relationship to William II of Sicily was later noted by the English chronicler Roger of Howden; Stubbs, *Gesta Regis Henrici II* i, 116. Robert of Neubourg was Dean of Evreux from 1163 to 1175, Dean of Rouen Cathedral from 1175 to 1188 and one of the envoys sent by Henry II of England to Alexander III in 1171; *Materials for the History of Thomas Becket, Archbishop of Canterbury* vii, ed. J. B. Sheppard (London: Rolls Series 1885), 475–8, no. 751, at 476. He was one of the 'many sons' of Archbishop Rotrou's brother Robert of Neubourg, Seneschal of Normandy, who died in September 1159, for whom see *The Gesta Normannorum Ducum of William of Jumièges, Orderic Vitalis and Robert of Torigni*, ed. E. M. C. Van Houts, ii (Oxford 1995), 278–9. (See Genealogical Table II.)

[170] Gilbert of Gravina's ancestry cannot be certainly proven, and matters are complicated because Rotrou II of Perche had several illegitimate sons; Thompson (1995), 23. It is most probable that Gilbert was the son of one of these called Bertram (*Bertrandus*), which was what his own eldest son was called. He would therefore have been the brother of the Geoffrey *Bertrandi* who is attested in the French sources. This assumes that Pseudo-Hugo was correct in identifying the relationship. If he was in error, then there is another possibility. The name Gilbert was also used in virtually every generation of the L'Aigle family in Normandy; thus

gave him many gifts and carefully briefed him about the state of affairs at court, and then sent him to the healthier environment of Sicily, since he was afraid to keep him in the bad climate of Apulia any longer (it was high summer), and also because he knew that the queen anxiously awaited his arrival as soon as possible. So he crossed the Straits and approached Palermo. The *familiares*, bishops, knights and constables came to meet him, and brought him to the palace as they had been ordered. The queen received him with great honour, and addressed all who were in attendance: 'Now I see that what I have always wanted in my prayers has come true. It is impossible for me to love and honour the sons of the Count of Perche any otherwise than as real brothers. To tell the truth, it was through him that my father obtained his kingdom. For this count gave my father wide tracts of land in Spain as a dowry together with his niece, my mother. He had taken them away from the Muslims by conquest after many perils and constant exertions.[171] So you should not be surprised that I should consider that his son, my mother's cousin, should assume the role of a brother to me, and that I should receive him graciously when he has come to me from so far away; and it is my will and order that anyone who claims to love me and my son should love him diligently and respect him, so that I can measure the extent of their support for us by their loyalty and love in this.'

They all immediately replied that they would willingly do so, although there were some among them whom his arrival displeased greatly. Meanwhile the queen carefully enquired what his plans were; and when she discovered that Stephen did not intend to stay in Sicily for long, she tried very hard to change his mind about this. She repeatedly pointed out to him the glory and riches which he would have if he stayed, together with the poverty of northern Europe, and also exhorted his companions with enormous rewards to promise to stay

> Queen Margaret's mother had a brother called Gilbert, and it is just feasible that the count may have come from that side of the extended family grouping.

171 This was the lordship of Tudela on the River Ebro, along the border between the kingdoms of Navarre and Aragon. It was captured from the Muslims in 1119 and held by Rotrou II of Perche between 1123 and 1133. That it was indeed the dowry of Margaret of L'Aigle is confirmed by Roger of Howden; Stubbs, *Gesta Regis Henrici II*, i, 144, describing a dispute between the kings of Navarre and Castille in 1177.

behind with him, realising that his mind could not be changed to what she wanted in any other way.[172]

35 Stephen is appointed chancellor

With great difficulty she finally achieved this as the result of continual entreaties and many promises. On the stated day all bishops who were then present and all great men were summoned together to court, and she appointed him chancellor, and ordered that from thenceforth all court business should first of all be brought to him in the first place.[173] Not long afterwards, when the Archbishop of Salerno had ordained him subdeacon, messengers were sent to tell the canons of Palermo that the king and queen had heard the pleas they had so often uttered, and were allowing them full freedom to choose a shepherd for their church. They should come to the palace and give the court the name of the man whom they thought suitable for themselves, in accordance with custom.

36 The custom of the church of Palermo

There was no disagreement among the canons (a thing which rarely happens), and with one heart and mind they elected the chancellor, to the pleasure of the population;[174] the choice was made with the

---

[172] Peter of Blois, MPL ccvii, 155–7, ep. 46, said that he was one of the thirty-seven people who had come to Sicily with Stephen, and that at the time of writing (c. 1174 or later) he and Master Roger 'the Norman' were the only two still alive.

[173] Stephen was first recorded as chancellor in August 1167, in a charter which (surely significantly in view of the mention of the archbishop in this passage) granted the destroyed *castrum* of Montecorvino to Romuald of Salerno; Paesano, *Memorie per servire alla storia della Chiesa Salernitana* ii, 175–6. The assertion by Chalandon (1907), ii, 321, that he was chancellor from October 1166 was based on Ughelli, *Italia Sacra* x, 296, for the Bishopric of Nardo, which is a eighteenth-century forgery.

[174] He was named as archbishop-elect for the first time in November 1167; White (1938), 266–7, no. 26 (= Pirro, *Sicula Sacra*, ii, 1112) (confirming the privileges of the court monastery of St John of the Hermits), while a month earlier, in a royal charter for the Bishopric of Anglona, he was simply 'chancellor'; Ughelli, *Italia Sacra* vii, 121.

approval of William of Pavia, cardinal of the Roman Church, who had recently come to Palermo on his way across to Gaul.[175]

37 The order of the court

Having thus attained the second of the great dignities of the kingdom, he undertook the burden of the entire administration and took precedence at court after the queen. He put Odo Quarrel, Canon of Chartres, in charge of his household.[176] The latter had advised him to remain in Sicily, and had promised that he would stay with him for two years, until he should have found friends of proven reliability in Sicily, or until it should happen that some other friends or relatives with whom he could equally share his plans came from France to join him. For he loved Odo a great deal, and accepted his advice more than he ought to have done, even in the greatest matters.

175 Cardinal priest of S. Pietro in Vincoli 1158–76 and Cardinal Bishop of Porto 1176–8, one of the most prominent and active members of the papal Curia at this time; Zenker (1964), 118–23. He had played an equivocal role at the start of the papal schism, and had actually attended Frederick Barbarossa's council of Pavia in 1160; Millor, Butler and Brooke, *Letters of John of Salisbury* i, 210–11; no. 124, but was later one of Alexander III's most trusted agents, often associated with John of Naples (for whom see note 48 above). He was on his way to France to mediate in the dispute between Henry II and Archbishop Thomas Becket. He was regarded with distrust by Becket's supporters as being far too friendly to the English king; Millor and Brooke, *Letters of John of Salisbury* ii, 350–1; but his eloquence was attested by Peter of Blois; MPL ccvii, 142, ep. 48. His visit to Sicily must have been somewhat earlier than Stephen's formal election, since he was already in southern France in August 1167; Barlow (1986), 170. It seems likely therefore that, despite Pseudo-Hugo's remarks, the election was actually stage-managed and the canons had been apprised of Stephen's candidature some months earlier.

176 Chartres cathedral had a very large chapter of some seventy-six canons during the twelfth century; its surviving charters, in *Cartulaire de Notre Dame de Chartres* i, ed. E. de Lepinois and L. Merlet (Chartres 1865), reveal several Odos among them at this period, but not an Odo the subdeacon, which grade we know from his obituary notice that Odo Quarrel held (see below, note 252).

38 Odo's avarice

Odo was not marked out by any knowledge of literature, nor commended by any useful secular skill; on the other hand his avarice was such that he recognised no limit in extorting money, and selected his friends only on the basis of the quantity of gifts he received, ignoring considerations of virtue or trustworthiness. For a long time the Bishop-Elect of Syracuse had been in possession of the income from many villages and estates, the rights to which belonged to the chancellor's office, but had been temporarily granted to the bishop-elect by the king because he was employed on court business. Wishing to assuage his spirit (which he realised was extremely angry for another reason) by giving him presents, the chancellor arranged for him to have two excellent villages, which the Sicilians call *casalia*,[177] instead of those which he was holding, with the proviso that he would keep the one for as long as he was employed at court, while his heirs could possess the other in perpetuity.

39 The man who repays good with evil

But for all the care he took to anticipate the bishop-elect's request for what he wanted by doing him a good turn, the bishop-elect strove to recompense him with evil just as quickly. What happened was that some men came to court from distant parts, and when they had obtained what they requested, they offered the notary Peter, who was related to Matthew the notary, what they thought was a just gratuity for the writ they had obtained.[178] He, however, wanted a great deal more, rejected what was offered, and brought the matter to the chancellor's attention. He ordered one of the notaries in attendance to write a further writ on the same business and to dismiss the men in question on the same day. When the notary Peter saw that the men

---

177 *Casalia* were open (unfortified) villages, as opposed to *castra/castella* which had walls (but were still villages, not 'castles'). Such open villages were the norm on the island in the twelfth century; a contrast to the mainland where larger villages were often walled; Bercher, Courteaux and Mouton (1979), especially 530–1, and for the mainland, Martin (1993), 267–89.

178 This notary cannot be otherwise identified. He is unlikely to have been the same man as the notary Peter who had written royal charters back in 1145–6; Enzensberger (1967), 53.

who had earlier kept petitioning him were not coming back, he realised that they had obtained their writ from another notary, and he gathered what he thought was a suitable number of associates and kept an eye on the road along which they were to travel; when they fell into his trap, he snatched the royal writ from them, broke the seal, and tore it up, insulting and beating the men themselves. When the chancellor learnt of this, he ordered these men to present themselves before him at court, and summoned the notary Peter. When he could not deny what happened, he ordered him to be put in prison.

The Bishop-Elect of Syracuse's comment on this episode was extremely sarcastic. The sentence he had uttered was contrary to justice and right reason; perhaps it was the sort of decision that was customary in France, but such a judgement had no validity in Sicily. The notaries of the court had great authority, and they should not be condemned so easily. This affair caused the chancellor considerable worry. He saw that the same man to whom — contrary to everyone's expectations — he had freely granted two *casalia* without strings attached, was now attacking him in such harsh terms, and was not prepared to meet him at court in order to arrange some private deal or compromise on the matter. But he made no reply to him; he pretended not to mind the injury he had suffered and called Ansaldus, the castellan of the palace, and told him to send the notary Peter back to prison without delay until such time as he could look more carefully into what kind of punishment a person ought to suffer who had so patently acted in violation of the king's peace and had severely harmed and disgraced the royal majesty. But after a few days, on the pleas of the court *familiares*, he let him go free, merely banning him from exercising the office of notary in future.

40 The sums that notaries ought to accept from individual petitioners

This incident first led him to try to constrain the enormous rapacity of the notaries, and to set specified limits to the sums they ought to accept from individual litigants according to the type of business involved.[179]

> 179 The low opinion of notaries shown in this passage makes it unlikely that Pseudo-Hugo was himself one and therefore argues against Robert of S. Giovanni as the author. See the introduction, p. 32. For the *stratigoti*, see above, note 96.

He also reined in the destructive liberties of the *stratigoti* and of those who were in charge of provinces or of individual towns, since they were unrestrainedly oppressing the common people with many unjust fines. He wanted to preserve the rigour of the law to such an extent that he thought that neither his friends nor even the magnates of the court should be spared. He would not allow the subject population to be oppressed by powerful persons, and would not pass over any injury whatsoever done to the poor by pretending to be unaware of it. News of this soon spread throughout the realm, and he won the favour and support of the common people and made his name so famous that everyone was saying that he had been sent by God like an angel of mercy, who would put right the state of the court so as to restore the Golden Age. As a result it happened that such a crowd of men and women flowed to the court from every corner of the realm that there were not enough judges to examine all the cases, and the number of notaries – notwithstanding the recent increase – hardly sufficed to write out the writs.[180]

Meanwhile the deputation which had been sent to have his election confirmed returned with a most affectionate letter from the Roman pontiff, stating that he had been delighted to hear of the chancellor's promotion and that his election was in every way approved, and that he wanted it to be considered valid and settled. So when the suffragan bishops and the canons were summoned to take the oath of loyalty to the chancellor, they willingly gave their assent. After the Bishops of Mazzara and of Malta had taken the oath as it was put to them, the Bishop of Agrigento, in order to appear to give an even more heartfelt oath, swore a form of oath containing different and more forceful phrases.[181] Just as his oath was more forceful than the others', so his subsequent adherence to it fell far short. But we will discuss this elsewhere; let us now return to the sequence of events.[182]

---

[180] At least one important reforming measure preceded Stephen's arrival: Queen Margaret placed the administration of vacant bishoprics in the hands of panels of ecclesiastics rather than royal bailiffs; Prologo, *Carte di Trani*, 128–9, no. 57 (March 1167).

[181] The Bishop of Malta was John, attested from 1167 to December 1169, when he witnessed a charter of Turstan of Mazzara (see above, note 57) for the nunnery of St Mary, Palermo, which had recently been founded by the vice-chancellor Matthew; *Documenti inediti*, 115–18, no. 50. See Kamp (1973–82), iii, 1165. For Gentile of Agrigento, see above, note 133.

[182] Cf. Sallust, *Jugurtha* 4.9, 42.5, 79.10. See the introduction, p. 46 above.

41 The accusation against Robert of Calatabiano

When the people of Palermo saw that the chancellor could not be deflected from the path of justice either by bribes or by anyone's favour, they laid accusations before him against many people who had given up being Christians and become Muslims, and had long secretly been under the protection of the eunuchs.[183] He let none of those who were found guilty of this great crime get off without punishment. Encouraged by these precedents, a large group of citizens bravely came out to accuse Robert of Calatabiano. They all rushed to the chancellor; with a great cry they all demanded that this utterly wicked man should be condemned for his crimes as they deserved. Some complained that he had unjustly taken away their houses, others their vineyards, many that their brothers or other relatives had been killed in prison as a result of continual torture; one woman even stated that he had used violence to ravish her unmarried daughter, and there were those who asserted that he had restored a very ancient Muslim shrine in the Sea Castle at his own cost. There was no need for witnesses to this, since the matter itself clearly proved it. Apart from these, another accusation made against him was that several wine-merchants had hired a certain house from him for an enormous sum of money, so that under his protection Muslim people would be permitted to violate Christian women there and sexually abuse boys without fear of punishment, and carry out other enormities, from which these entrepreneurs made a great deal of dishonest profit which they shared with the owner of the house.[184]

[183] Amari (1934–9), iii, 508, note 1, suggested that these charges were probably directed against converts from Islam to Christianity who had relapsed, but cf. Broadhurst, *The Travels of Ibn Jubayr*, 342, on the women of the court.

[184] Such accusations were a stereotype of medieval Christian polemic against Muslims (and other outsiders, such as heretics). But that there was some truth in these particular allegations, or at least that they were taken seriously, is shown by a letter of Alexander III to Stephen of Perche; *Italia Pontificia* x, 232, no. 231, there dated to November/December 1167. Stephen had asked 'what should be done about Saracens who shall have seized (*rapuerint*) Christian women and boys or even killed them, and whose excesses King William of Sicily has commissioned him and the other bishops to punish'. The pope replied that while this could be punished with a fine, grave cases should be reserved to royal justice (i.e. where capital penalties might be exacted).

He was unnerved at being accused of such great crimes. At first he tried to have the matter ignored by making light of it, and threatening his accusers by promising that he would treat them badly in future, and convincing himself that the prosecution would easily be stopped. But when he saw that the bribes he was offering were being rejected, sureties had been given and the case was being properly proceeded with, he threw himself on the protection of the eunuchs. They fell at the feet of the king and queen, and with tears they begged them not to permit the condemnation of a man who was utterly essential to the realm and had always tried to serve the court most faithfully, claiming that it was not surprising that this kind of demonstration could take place against him, since it was well known that no one would ever please the people who wished faithfully to carry out the orders of the court. The queen was moved by the force of their prayers, and first asked the chancellor, and then, when he refused, ordered him not to accept anyone's accusations against Robert of Calatabiano. For the theft and the murders which he was said to have carried out were not to be ascribed to him but to Caid Peter, at whose orders he had done them. It was obvious that, while Peter was in charge of the court, Robert himself had been unable to disobey his commands.

The chancellor was caught in a difficult position, and did not know what to think or which course of action it was best for him to choose. On the one side the populace was shouting that this particularly evil man should not be allowed to go unpunished, that the business was being handled in a negligent and lukewarm way by the chancellor, and that he seemed to be deviating from his excellent intentions, corrupted by bribes or influence. From this particular case it would become quite clear whether he would keep up that love of justice, the appearance of which he had maintained to date, for ever as something innate, or whether it was something that he had deliberately made a pretence of for the occasion, in order to present to the eyes of the people a good omen for his newly acquired power. But on the other side the queen's commands pressed him to ignore the clamour of the common people, and to leave the accusations handed in to him on one side by pretending ignorance. In addition the *familiares* of the court protected Robert of Calatabiano's party as much as they could, both to appear to be as loyal as possible to the eunuchs and to the queen herself, and in order to incite the people's hatred against the chancellor.

But he chose a kind of middle way, to seem both to obey the queen's wishes and also not to disappoint the hopes and expectations of the people. He promised the queen that he would do nothing about any matters concerning the court that would require the death penalty; but he would examine most carefully any which were recognised as concerning the rights of the Church. If Robert were to be found guilty, he would be punished to the extent that the severity of ecclesiastical penalty would allow; but if she were to try to make difficulties in future, then he would rather retire into private life than let himself be deflected from his decision. So the *familiares* of the court were summoned, together with the bishops and other churchmen, and Robert was brought in with a great crowd of common people present. His thefts, rapine, injustice, the murder of citizens and the violation of an unmarried girl by force were left on one side, and investigation was made into charges of perjury, incest and adultery.[185]

42 The judgement against Robert

When the truth of the charges had become clear from many witnesses, Robert of Calatabiano was sentenced in accordance with the law to be publicly flogged and returned to prison; his property was confiscated by the treasury. Since he could not be formally paraded round the city accompanied by a herald (because the people had occupied all the narrow places to attack him with stones as he came past), he was ordered to be taken round the cathedral cloisters to cheat the waiting crowd. Even though some knights with drawn swords also followed and preceded him and guarded him on either side, nevertheless they could hardly restrain the fury of the crowd as it pressed forward. Then after a few days, when he either would not or (as others thought) could not give the court the bribe that he had promised, he was taken

---

185 These offences were deemed to pertain to canon law, hence the presence of the bishops at the trial. Adultery (which could be charged against male co-respondents) had previously been the subject of royal legislation under King Roger (in the earlier of the two versions of his assizes, Cod. Vat. Lat. 8782, clauses 28–9, 31–3), as was perjury, *ibid.*, clause 23, and judges' abuse of their position, clause 44; Monti 'Il testo'. (These last two clauses were repeated by Frederick II in *The Liber Augustalis*, Powell, 103, 142 (bk. II. 50, III. 65)). But jurisdiction in marriage cases had subsequently been surrendered to the Church; see the edition by Siragusa (1897), 117, note 1; Powell, *The Liber Augustalis*, 147–8 (bk. III. 83); Prologo, *Carte di Trani*, 134–5, no. 61 (March 1170).

to the Sea Castle and put into the dungeon into which he himself had once thrown so many. There, subject to various punishments, he died. This event gave such pleasure to all the people of Sicily, especially the North Italians, whom he had oppressed with uncounted evils, that they all promised that if it were to be necessary they would undergo the danger of death on the chancellor's behalf.

43 Jealousy directed at Stephen the chancellor

The magnates of the court and other powerful men could no longer freely behave in the tyrannical way they had been accustomed to against their subjects. When they saw that all the material advantages of the court were going to the chancellor and his friends, and that from all this wealth of gifts only a trickle was left over for them – and even that was drying up – they began to complain among themselves, informally, as though they were consoling one another. They unguardedly uttered angry words, saying that it was a disgrace that this foreign-born boy had occupied the highest position of the court and burst out into such confident audacity that he thought no one worthy to be his associate, and wanted to administer the government of this great realm on his own and tower over everyone else by virtue of his unprecedented power. They, however, who had grown old in the service of the court, who had taught it to overcome or avoid lots of difficulties and dangers through their advice, were now despised, humiliated and rejected, and thought unworthy of any respect. The queen, who was a Spaniard, was calling this Frenchman her relative, talking with him far too familiarly and looking at him as though with eyes full of desire; there was cause to fear that a forbidden liaison was hiding under the cover of a blood-relationship.[186]

---

186 Such a slander, of a supposed sexual relationship between a female ruler or consort and a powerful male adviser, was a medieval topos; see Stafford (1983), 92–6. Two other notable examples were the cases of the Empress Judith and Bernard of Septimania in the early ninth century (see here especially Ward (1990), 226–7), and Queen Melisende of Jerusalem and her cousin Hugh of Le Puiset in the early 1130s; Babcock and Krey, *William of Tyre: A History of Deeds beyond the Sea* ii, 71 (bk. XIV. 15).

44 Advice against critics

Together with the other eunuchs, Caid Richard[187] was also extremely hostile to him because he had condemned Robert of Calatabiano against his wishes. And the most noble and powerful of the Sicilian Muslims, Bulcassis [Abu-'l-Qasim],[188] also stoked up a great deal of opposition against him among the Muslims, although they had liked him a great deal at first. For he was angry that the chancellor gave audience in too friendly a way to Caid Sedictus [Siddiq], the richest of the Muslims, with whom he had a private feud, and seemed to make a great deal of his advice; consequently he thought that he himself had fallen out of favour, although he had presented him with many gifts, and that he would not be able to win his support again.

45 Note that enmities sometimes have to be covered up

When the chancellor realised all this, he began to talk to these men in a more respectful and friendly way, pretending to suspect nothing, and to try to win their support by doing them various favours; but at the same time he left nothing undone that seemed necessary for his own security. For instance, when the Master Constable Berengar went away across the Straits to visit the estate which the court had granted to him,[189]

---

[187] Master Chamberlain of the Royal Palace, who had succeeded Caid Peter in that office; Takayama (1993), 102–3.

[188] For him, see Broadhurst, *The Travels of Ibn Jubayr*, 358–60, especially 358, who referred to Abu'l-Qasim's 'great authority and exalted rank, his large household' and the houses belonging to him 'which were like lofty and superb castles', and said that he had been told that he was 'an upright man, liking good, loving his kind, full of acts of charity'. He was a patron of Arabic scholars and had a palace at Trapani, which was among the things which Henry VI promised to the Genoese in return for naval aid against King Tancred; Amari (1933–9), iii, 550–3.

[189] Probably Sarconi and Perticara in the south of the Principality of Salerno, which Berengar held in return for the service of four knights. He also possessed Viggiano in the Terra d'Otranto, which he had purchased, probably after the death of its previous holder William of Théville, c. 1165; *Cat. Bar.* 20, 91, arts. 108, 483; Cuozzo (1984), 36. Berengar was the son of a man called Giso and had succeeded Richard of Mandra as Master Constable, i.e. commander of the royal household troops; see above, note 101.

he put in his place Roger of Tiron, in whom he laid great trust.[190] Roger was powerful because of the great nobility of his ancestry, and there could be no doubt about his bravery. He also tried to maintain his loyalty so untainted that he not only never conspired against the king or ever supported any who did conspire, but also kept his word equally unshakeably towards his friends. So, since this man and Robert of San Giovanni (whom I mentioned above) had a large number of friends, nothing worthy of concern could easily happen in Palermo that did not come to their attention, and they told the chancellor about the plots of those who were conspiring, and what measures were required to forestall them. If he had preferred their warnings to the advice given by Odo Quarrel, he would easily have suppressed any plots which were being hatched right at the start. However, Odo's mind had been so overcome with avarice that he measured the trust to be put in anyone solely by the presents offered. This was why he was seduced by the splendour of gold and diamonds and took no notice of the healthy advice of his friends. He treated several enemies as real friends, as it were nurturing vipers in his bosom.

46 Note that avarice destroys loyalty

In the meantime, when it was revealed that contrary to his normal habit Matthew the notary was very frequently sending messengers with letters to his brother the bishop of Catania,[191] it was suspected

---

190 Present at the royal court in Messina in February 1168 (see below, p. 193 and note 229). He was a descendant of a family from the Perche (modern dépt. of Eure-et-Loire), who had property near Vizzini in SE Sicily. His grandfather Robert had witnessed Roger II's treaty with the Count of Barcelona in 1128; *Rogerii II Diplomata*, 22–4, no. 9. His father, another Robert, also owned land in the Stilo region of central Calabria; Trinchera, *Syllabus Graecarum Membranarum*, 198–200, no. 151 (1154) He was probably also related to Rainald of Tiron, a landowner at Calatafimi in western Sicily, who witnessed several charters of Roger II between 1112 and 1122; Ménager (1975), 381–2. In December 1172 Roger, describing himself as a royal justiciar, together with his wife Constance and daughter Tafura, gave land and a mill to the church of the Holy Cross, Buccheri, near Vizzini. Both he and his wife were dead by 1182; White (1938), 271–3, 275, nos. 30 and 33.

191 John, who had been elected in preference to Peter of Blois's brother William, Abbot of the monastery of St Mary of Matina in Calabria; the

that he was revealing the extent of the conspiracy in these letters, and stating what he wanted him to do in the territory of Catania. The chancellor wanted to have definite evidence of this, and sent Robert of Bellisina[192] with some other men to watch the routes and capture the aforementioned messengers (whom he knew had very recently been sent to Catania) on their way back, and take from them the letter they were carrying. Robert did not keep watch very well, and the man carrying the letter got through, but he captured his associate, who followed behind more slowly, and wounded him when he tried to defend himself. When this became known, Matthew the notary was very angry about the injury done to his messengers, and thought that he too had good cause to be afraid, realising that his reputation had been blemished in the chancellor's eyes.

47 How Robert of Bellisina fell ill

Not long after this, when Robert of Bellisina began to be weakened by a fever, Salernus, a physician who was a close friend of Matthew the notary and had been appointed a judge of the city of Salerno with his support, earnestly appealed to the chancellor to entrust his recovery to his expertise.[193] But the chancellor had his suspicions about him because he was a friend of the notary Matthew, and, afraid that he would use the opportunity to avenge the recent injury, he refused to

> result, so Peter alleged, of bribery; MPL ccvii, 135–6, 291, epp. 46 and 93. He is attested as bishop-elect in February 1168; Jamison (1931), 465, no. 2; and was consecrated by Alexander III in person (presumably at Benevento, where the pope was then resident) between February and July 1168, the see of Catania being directly subject to the pope; *Italia Pontificia*, x, 291–2, nos. 24–5. He was killed in the earthquake of February 1169.
>
> 192 Not otherwise attested. *Bellisinensis* may have been a derived from Bellême, in Normandy, but in Latin this was usually rendered as *Belismensis, de Belesmensa, de Belesmia*, or *de Bellismo*.
>
> 193 Salernus the judge was present, as was Archbishop Romuald, at a legal dispute in February 1159 between the abbey of Cava and the monastery of St Peter of Eboli; Cava, Arca xxx, 31. This use of the topographically-derived personal name Salernus was not unique; cf. Cava, Arm. Mag. D. 15 (1097), and the emir (admiral) Salernus, who commanded a Sicilian fleet which attacked Byzantium in 1147 and died before 1161; *Romuald*, 227; *Documenti inediti* 73–5, no. 30 (June 1155), 85–7, no. 37 (January 1161); Ménager (1960), 67–8.

let him go to him, but gave orders that other physicians should be provided for him.

48 Beware danger from physicians

But Salernus, in defiance of his wishes, decided to get to the sick man secretly, as though bringing help to a man who was refusing it. He carefully found out about the house in which he was lying, and visited him a number of times. When Robert later departed this mortal world, to the chancellor's great grief, those who were present were amazed to see his hair fall out by itself, and his mottled skin fall off at the slightest touch and easily come away from the flesh; so they concluded that poison had undoubtedly been given to him to drink. When this reached the chancellor's ears, he decided to find out the truth of the matter in any way possible. But since it was thought that this sort of thing could occur naturally in the case of some illnesses, he sent the Archbishop of Salerno, who had the widest experience of medical matters,[194] and the Bishop of Malta and some other wise and experienced men, to investigate what had happened and why. When they examined the matter they categorically stated that this kind of corruption could never have resulted from the particular illness he had been suffering from. So when there was an enquiry whether any physician had approached the deceased apart from those who had been appointed to do this, it was stated by those who were sitting by the patient that Salernus the judge had offered him something like a syrup in a glass bottle. One of them showed his hand, which was bloodstained from a deep wound, and said that he had suffered this wound from the same syrup. He claimed that it happened that when his fellow-servants had gone away and he was alone in the house, he secretly wanted to take something from the same potion (some silly people make a habit of wanting to try anything they see), since he thought that it would be of enormous help in getting rid of an illness he had just been suffering from. Fortune so had it that he first poured some

---

[194] Cf. the chronicle ascribed to Romuald (below, p. 238), and Peter of Blois, Ep. 90, MPL ccvii, 282, who described him as 'a man most practised in medical matters'. Salerno had long been a centre for medical expertise and study; e.g. *Chron. Cas.* III. 7, MGH SS xxxiv, 368; Chibnall, *The Ecclesiastical History of Orderic Vitalis*, iv, 28; Skinner (1997), 127–36.

out into his cupped hand, to rub it a little with the finger of his other hand. When he poured it on to the ground a little later, he said that his skin seemed to have broken up, with many fractures, and, as he said, it then fell off bit by bit. The notary William,[195] who had been a servant of the notary Matthew before the chancellor's arrival, also said that one of Matthew's men had frequently come up to him and kept on asking on his master's behalf that he show him the house in which Robert of Bellisina was lying. When the chancellor heard all this, he invited to his house the Bishop-Elect of Syracuse, the notary Matthew, Count Richard of Molise, Archbishop Romuald of Salerno and the other bishops and several of the nobles, revealed the whole matter to them and on their advice ordered Salernus to be summoned.

49 The arrest of Salernus, the physician who had administered the poison

When this man was questioned whether he had brought Robert any medicine, he confidently and without hesitation replied that he had never given him anything. But when the witnesses were produced and he was shown to have lied, he added that he had given him nothing that might have caused the lesion. He asserted that what he had given him was a simple rose-syrup, and that had not been prepared by him but bought the same day from a certain apothecary called Justus. So Justus was called before the court, and answered that he had sold absolutely nothing at all for the whole of the month that had just passed. Thus Salernus was found to have been a liar in everything he had said, and he greatly confirmed the suspicion that he had perpetrated what he was accused of. On the next day the court assembled and the Master Justiciars were summoned,[196] and when

195 He held small fiefs at Laviano and Nocera near Salerno; *Cat. Bar.* 88, 94, arts. 470, 511. He was probably the notary William who witnessed a legal case in January 1170; *Documenti inediti* 118–20, no. 51; wrote a royal diploma in favour of the Calabrian monastery of St Stephen de Bosco in February 1173, and acted as a notary to royal justiciars on the mainland up to 1189; Enzensberger (1967), 40, 63, 73, 110–11.

196 The Master Justiciars of the Royal Court, who should be distinguished from the two Master Justiciars, almost invariably great nobles, who oversaw the mainland administration, were the principal legal officers of the *Curia Regis*. The appointment of these specialist judges (there were

he was formally charged, he answered the accusations so weakly, hampered by consciousness of his guilt, that he gave the judges every confidence that he had indeed committed the crime.

50 Sentence passed on Salernus the physician

So sentence was passed against him, and they decreed that all his property should be confiscated and he should be subject to the penalty of death, leaving him no hope of life save only in the mercy of the court. He was thrown into prison, and many promises and threats were made to get him to confess at whose request or plans he had done it, but he could not be made to reveal it.

While Fortune[197] was arranging this development of the conspiracy in the Sicilian territories, she was weaving another conspiracy in Apulia, supported by a large party. Many of the leading men were aggrieved that Count Richard of Molise had suddenly been raised to such a pinnacle of honour, and they incited the queen's brother Henry, the Count of Montescaglioso, against him, saying that he was being labelled lazy and fearful by many, since he was either bearing the disgrace and injury brought both on himself and on the entire realm with too much patience, or pretending to approve of it. For it could not be doubted that there was a dishonourable reason why the queen, as soon as she obtained the guardianship of the realm, selected as her friend above all others Richard of Mandra, a man of no judgement, granting him the most noble county of Molise. Should Henry (whom the matter particularly called to exact revenge) wish to punish the abovementioned Richard for such great presumption, he would in no way lack support. To this, the count replied that he had hitherto been ignorant of the situation; the fact that he had not yet exacted revenge should be ascribed to ignorance, not fear. They themselves should now boldly state what they wanted to happen; he would immediately do whatever they decided, and would not suffer his sister's disgrace any longer. Their opinion was that Count Richard of Molise should

> usually two or three of them in office at any one time) was a recent innovation; the title is first found only in 1157. See Takayama (1993), 103–4 and especially the seminal study by Jamison (1967).

197 In the early MSS. a new section; in recension I, part VI (part V of the *History*) begins here.

either be killed or at least removed from court. The administration of the kingdom was rightly Henry's, since he was the queen's brother and the king's uncle. He was persuaded by their views, distributed weapons to many Spanish knights, some of whom had arrived along with himself, while others had more recently joined him, and decided to cross over to Sicily as soon as he could. He was going to take with him several of the leaders, at whose incitement he was doing this. For Count Bohemond of Manopello (an intelligent man and a good speaker),[198] William of Gesualdo,[199] Richard of Balbano[200] and several others decided to follow him, hoping that if their plan happened to succeed, they would easily obtain what they wanted from the court

198 Count Bohemond II of Manopello (1157–69) had been appointed in 1157 to replace the disgraced Bohemond of Tarsia; *Chron. Casauriense*, 897. He appears to have come originally from S. Fele in Lucania, c. 30 km. NW of Potenza. His tenure of the frontier county was troubled, and he was twice driven out and forced to take refuge in Sicily, in 1161 by Robert of Loritello and in 1167 by an imperial army led by Rainald of Dassel, Archbishop of Cologne; *Chron. Casauriense*, 897–8, 904. This latter incident explains his presence at the royal court. He was succeeded as count after his death c. 1169/70 by his son-in-law Peter. See Cuozzo (1984), 291–3.

199 Lord of Gesualdo, Frigento, Mirabella Eclano and a number of other places in the NE of the Principality of Salerno, as well as of Lucera in Apulia, for which a total of 18 knights' service was owed. He and his vassals owed in all, with the *augmentum*, 142 knights and 44 sergeants; *Cat. Bar.* 126–9, arts. 707–24. His grandfather, another William (d. 1145/1150) was the illegitimate son of Duke Roger Borsa, and was lord of Lucera from 1115 onwards (Cava, Arm. Mag. E.40), though he may only have acquired Gesualdo in the 1130s. This William (II) first appeared in 1158, when he gave his consent to a donation of his father Elias; Tropeano, *Cod. dipl. verginiano*, iv, 268–70, no. 371.

200 Son of the former Master Captain of Apulia and Terra di Lavoro, Gilbert of Balbano, an associate of the Chancellor Asclettin, who died in August 1156; Garufi, *Necrologio di S. Matteo*, 108. Richard was later (1184/1187) a royal justiciar, but died soon afterwards. His lordship comprised Lacedonia, Rocchetta S. Antonio and other places along the border between the north of the Principality of Salerno and the Duchy of Apulia, totalling twenty knights' fees; *Cat. Bar.* 78, art. 433, Cuozzo (1984), 118–20. Richard first appeared in March 1152, consenting to a donation of his father to the Cava dependency of St Stephen de Iuncarico, near Rocchetta; Carlone, *Rocchetta*, 137–8, appendix no. 8. His cousin Philip was Count of Sant'Angelo dei Lombardi c. 1156–97. See Cuozzo (1980) for an extended discussion of this family.

THE HISTORY OF THE TYRANTS OF SICILY   177

through him. For when they developed plans along these lines they had not yet realised that the chancellor's power had reached such a level that he overshadowed everyone at court. When they saw this soon afterwards with absolute certainty, they were first of all deterred a little from the project, but then they regained confidence and were prepared to carry the plan through as keenly as before, and finally arrived in Sicily.

When their arrival became known, and at the same time the reason for it was understood, Count Richard went to see the chancellor. He revealed to him what Count Henry and the Apulians were after, and pleaded with him not to allow a madman, along with those who had come with him, incited only by jealousy, to achieve the aim of his rashness. If they were allowed to unleash sedition at court with impunity, and by organising a conspiracy riot unchallenged like madmen against those who served the court, then the fault would be laid at his feet in particular, and the harm would be turned back on him, since having taken on the administration of the realm he had the obligation to suppress the insolent behaviour of wicked men. The chancellor, although the views of many people made Count Richard suspect to him, did not himself want to seem to be ignoring him, nor for the kingdom to be destabilised by this problem; so he decided to keep these rebellious troubles away from the court and take measures against the wicked plans of the Apulians. So he sent a royal letter to Count Henry (who had now got as far as Termini)[201] and ordered him to come to the city, but Count Bohemond and the others who were with him were ordered to await the court's orders at Termini for the time being. When the count came, the chancellor went up to him with a friendly look on his face, had a long conversation with him using flattering words, and began to suggest and earnestly advise him not to give many people an excuse for rebelling or to destabilise the peace of the realm (which could not easily be restored) through any movement of rebellion; he should not be moved by the tales told by the Apulians, whose intention it had always been to bring some level of instability to the kingdom. There was nothing that he ought to be angry about, since his means provided him with great wealth, and he held a position among the great leaders of the realm that was not less than theirs. He should take particular care to do nothing that

---

[201] Termini Imerese, the classical Thermae, on the north coast of Sicily, 40 km. E. of Palermo; see note 63 above.

might offend the queen, and do nothing at all contrary to her wishes, since he had attained these things through her, and might be thought to be about to obtain even more, unless his own actions were to prevent this.

In this way the chancellor defused the lunacy planned in Apulia by making all sorts of friendly statements, and in the end with some difficulty he brought Count Henry round to the simple view that accorded with his natural stupidity, restrained his anger, and summoned Count Richard in order to restore the peace and harmony between them. He also soothed the queen's anger against the same count for greatly offending her by committing so many false and rash acts in Apulia in contravention of the court's orders. Henry promised that he would follow the chancellor's advice in everything, and would not in future counter the queen's wishes in anything.

Only then did the chancellor summon Bohemond and his associates who had been waiting at Termini. He gave them a friendly welcome, and when he asked the reason for their visit, they replied that their principal purpose had been to pay him their respects, hoping that he would give them recognition and number them among his loyal knights; and also so that they could, through him, obtain certain things that they were going to request from the royal majesty. He replied that he was delighted that they had come, and that they would have his support; but it was his advice that they should not at the moment ask for anything from the court, as their petition would be more positively received on another occasion. So when they had stayed at Palermo for a few days and seen that the matter had turned out contrary to their expectations, they finally returned to Apulia. Nevertheless, Count Bohemond, who was a man whose intelligence should not be underrated, had many amicable discussions with the chancellor and won his favour and friendship, a friendship which he later consolidated with a loyalty that was undoubted and proven by events, rather than by the unreliability and empty rhetoric customary among Apulians.

Count Henry followed the chancellor's wishes and policies utterly, and became such a close supporter of his that they frequently went to the baths together. He accompanied him to court every day, and when they returned, they spent a great portion of the day talking together privately. When those who were conspiring against the chancellor saw that if the harmonious relationship between them were to persist, then their machinations would not reach the hoped-for conclusion, they looked for any possible ways in which they might break their friendship and alliance. They first tested the count's intentions by making certain insinuations that it was not right for the queen's brother to accept that anyone was superior to him at court, and that he should not go to the residence and follow the footsteps of a man by whom he should rather himself be waited upon, since the foremost position of power and the government of the entire realm ought properly to be his own. He replied to them that he was ignorant of the French language (which was an important requirement at court), and did not have the energy to be able to uphold such a burden. The role of governing ought properly to be entrusted to the chancellor, who was a man of discretion and intelligence and of the highest nobility, and equally closely related to the king and to the queen.

Not satisfied by this rebuff, they began secretly to have meetings with the Spanish knights whom they knew to be most friendly towards him, saying that the count was a man of enormous humanity and patience, since he preferred to love and respect the chancellor, whom he ought to hunt down as an enemy, rather than showing him too much reverence. He might seem to be clever in doing this, disciplining his spirit to put up patiently with everything, because he did not want to offend his sister, but in fact severe damage to his reputation ensued from this patience. All that he could now do was either to be thought to be enslaved to the queen's dishonourable wishes and to be conniving at her sexual, or more properly incestuous, liaison with the chancellor himself,[202] or to claim that he knew nothing of their illicit relationship. It was clear to all that this ignorance was, as one might put it, crass and stupid, when he alone knew nothing of what everyone was talking about.

The knights brought these stories, repeated by many, back to the count's ears. At first he was uncertain what decision to take, then when he heard this confirmed by those who had themselves invented

---

202 Until the the Fourth Lateran Council of 1215 the Church forbade marriage or sexual relationships within seven degrees of kinship, thus between even very distant cousins. However, the queen was Stephen's first cousin once removed, i.e. related to him within the third degree of kinship. Hence the alleged relationship would clearly have been incestuous (and indeed would have been deemed so even after 1215, when Innocent III relaxed the prohibition to include thereafter only those related within four degrees of kinship); Goody (1983), 134–44.

the rumours, he totally believed what he had been told, broke with the chancellor, and aligned himself with their plans, promising to do whatever they recommended in future. They had achieved the aim they had greatly desired, and did not rebuff him, but exchanged oaths and imposed the obligations they wanted on him.

This conspiracy had now reached the point where it put a great deal of fear into the chancellor's friends; for Caid Richard, who was Master of the Palace, was known to be bound to them by oaths, and gave the conspirators much additional strength. He was not content with his own knights, whom he paid himself, but had won the support of the majority of the king's knights and all the court archers through many gifts and favours, so that they would follow his wishes and commands in everything. The chancellor, however, prepared to defend himself against their traps, and decided that he would not now allow people into his presence at any time, as had been the custom, but announced particular times at which everyone would be allowed an audience, and told his own knights to be ready at these times. He also selected fifty men who would always stand guard with their weapons at the ready by the front door in the hallway of his residence, and tried to increase the number of his knights, even keeping with him some knights from north of the Alps who had recently come from France on their way through to Jerusalem. Among these was John of Lavardin,[203] whose behaviour brought the chancellor no little difficulty, as the following episode will clearly show.

51 The king sets off for Messina

Some time after the plans of his enemies had come to light, the chancellor wanted to exact punishment. After thinking carefully about

---

203 John I of Lavardin (Touraine; modern département Loir-et-Cher), the son of Geoffrey of Lavardin and his wife Marie, sister of Count Bartholomew of Vendôme, first attested 1150 x 1152; *Cartulaire de l'Abbaye cardinale de la Trinité de Vendôme*, ed. C. Metais (5 vols., Paris 1893–1904), ii, 385–6, no. 539. His family had a great Crusading tradition: his great-grandfather, Geoffrey of Preuilly, had been killed at the Second Battle of Ramla in 1101, his grandfather, another Geoffrey, had died on pilgrimage to the Holy Land in 1139, his maternal uncle Bartholomew of Vendôme died on the Second Crusade, and his paternal uncle, another John, was later (1180) also to make a pilgrimage to Jerusalem; Barthélemy (1993), 771–2, 798–9.

the matter, he decided that he did not yet have the power to dare to have the leaders of the conspiracy formally charged – that might turn their secret and hidden plotting into open rebellion. But he did not wish to cover over the matter any longer by pretending ignorance, in case they might assemble such further support that it would be difficult to confront their machinations. So he adopted another approach, and persuaded the king and queen to go to Messina and spend the coming winter there; then, if it seemed appropriate, they could cross over to Apulia as soon as the weather improved in spring. He sent a letter specifying the date and object of this journey to Count Gilbert of Gravina, writing to him that he should lay all his other business on one side for the moment, cross the Straits, and come to Messina as soon as he could. He also made sure that he never went to the court without protection, as had happened at the time of Caid Peter, but accompanied by such a force of knights and weapons that he almost gave the impression of bringing an army with him.

During these days it happened that there was more rainfall than had been experienced in Sicily for a long time; so the *familiares* of the court, exploiting the occasion, tried to persuade the chancellor to put the journey off to the following summer. When they were unable to achieve this, they nevertheless hoped that the king, the queen and the chancellor himself would be put off from their intention by the persistent rain and the difficulties of the journey. But he acted with decision, and sent a royal usher to all the towns that lay along the route with a letter from the king ordering that the narrow sections of the road should be widened and overhanging cliffs cut back, and that everything should be prepared for the king's transit, according to precedent. Then at around the stated date, contrary to everyone's expectations, the weather changed, and just as it had previously been angry with constant rain, so now a clear sky began to appear, promising pleasant weather. On the fifteenth day of November, as had been planned, the king set off for Messina, leaving a force of knights at Palermo to guard the city itself.[204]

---

204 The charter confirming the rights of the court monastery of St John of the Hermits; White (1938), 266–7, no. 26 (see above, note 174); must have been granted by the king and his mother very soon before their departure from Palermo. The first charter issued at Messina was on 7 January 1168 to the Greek monastery of SS. Elias and Anastasius, Carbone, in Lucania; Holtzmann 'Papst-, Kaiser- und Normannenurkanden', 67–9, no. 8.

52 Court personages

At that time Count Robert of Caserta[205] was at Messina with his son Roger, count of Tricarico,[206] awaiting the king's arrival there. Robert had heard that his cousin William of S. Severino, who had recently been recalled from exile, had persuaded the queen through many pleas by his friends that his own lands, which he had lost when he fled the kingdom, should be returned to him.[207] For this reason Robert had approached the court together with those who spoke for him, ready to argue that Montoro and the *castrum* of San Severino and other towns which the said William had held were legally his, and that William's own father had taken control of them illegally and by force. The chancellor, however, did not want William (whom he knew was a loyal supporter) to sustain any loss, while at the same time he was also afraid of offending Count Robert, in order not to give a man in whose loyalty he had no confidence an excuse for doing him harm.

205 Robert of Lauro, first attested in 1141, when he was seemingly still a minor and under the wardship of his stepfather Robert *Capumazza*; Inguanez, *Reg. S. Angelo in Formis*, 161–3, no. 60; was the head of the San Severino family and an important landowner in the southern part of the Principality of Capua. He was made Count of Caserta between 1150 and 1159, and was from 1171 until his death in 1183 Master Justiciar of Apulia and Terra di Lavoro; Cuozzo (1984), 271–5.

206 Probably count by 1154, certainly by 1160 (see Romuald, p. 228 below). He was the younger (?) son of Count Robert of Caserta, and after 1189 was a partisan of Count Roger of Andria in his opposition to King Tancred; Siragusa, *Liber ad Honorem Augusti di Pietro da Eboli*, 25, line 298. He died in exile on the Third Crusade; Cuozzo (1984), 32–3. For his fiefs see *Cat. Bar.*, 19–22, arts. 100–24.

207 For him, see above, note 116. William's grandfather, Roger of S. Severino (d. 1125) had been lord of Montoro, near Avellino, by 1097; Cava, Arm. Mag. D. 15; and his father Henry was recorded as lord of S. Severino and Montoro in March 1125; Cava, Arm. Mag. F. 36. William held S. Severino for the service of 8 knights, Montoro for that of 13 knights, and Rocca Cilento (in the south of the Principality of Salerno) for the service of 6 knights. With the *augmentum* he owed 44 knights and 80 infantrymen; *Cat. Bar.* 79–80, art. 438. However, Count Robert may have retained control of Montoro after 1168. William was later (1179–87) a royal justiciar and constable, last recorded in March 1187 when he confirmed the rights enjoyed by the abbey of Cava within his barony of Cilento; Cava, Arm. Mag. L. 21. Cf. Cuozzo (1984), 273; Tescione (1995), 35–45.

So he had William given back his entire inheritance, and let Robert be granted other land in the territory of Apulia,[208] on the condition that, once the argument he was having about this with William had been resolved, he would never raise any problems about it in the future.

A few days after the king's arrival the leading citizens approached the chancellor with enormous bribes, and emphatically urged him to have the privilege restored to them which king Roger had granted regarding the city's freedoms from taxation, but which he had later regretted and taken away from them.[209] The chancellor, thinking that it was in his best interests to win their support, refused to accept the gifts they offered, but fulfilled their request without taking payment.

53 The case against the *stratigotus*

In the meantime, when the people of Messina saw a large crowd of men and women gather at court from all parts of the realm, and that no one was being denied his rights, but that the strict rule of justice was being upheld in every judgement, they rose up boldly with accusations against Richard, the *Stratigotus* of Messina.[210] They drew up bills of indictment, offering them to the chancellor, and with loud cries demanded that the case should be brought before a court; some asserted that robbery, murder, theft and arson had been committed by evildoers with his agreement, in return for bribes. Others complained that their vineyards or their houses had been taken away. Many accused him of debauchery with unmarried girls or of adultery, and some of perverting the course of justice. But the chancellor, aware of the man's prudence and intelligence, thought that he would be a powerful supporter of his party if he could win over his mind by doing him a favour; he tried to restrain the anger of the demonstrators by postponing the case for a time. But their intentions were not

---

208 This land was probably Mandra and Pulcarino, *c.* 30 km. E. of Benevento, a fief of only three knights' fees; *Cat. Bar.* 48, art. 294; hardly a very adequate compensation for Montoro, so it was no wonder that Count Robert wished to retain the latter. For Mandra, see below, p. 192.

209 The only charter of Roger II for Messina now surviving is a fifteenth-century forgery; *Rogerii II Diplomata*, 29–35, no. 11+.

210 Richard of Aversa; see note 96 above. For rhetorical effect the writer shifts into the present tense for this paragraph.

deflected as a result of the delay, and when they saw that the chancellor was replying with little interest and enthusiasm, they again put their accusations in writing, and stuck them up on poles and raised an enormous clamour in front of the palace, saying that it was a shame that while all the others were obtaining their rights, only the people of Messina (who had always been utterly loyal to the king) were being made fools of, and that their voices were not being listened to at court.

The queen could not tolerate this popular demonstration, and she ordered the chancellor to receive their written petitions and bring this matter to a resolution without delay. The chancellor assigned the case to the Master Justiciars, at the same time instructing them to set a date for the *Stratigotus* Richard's trial and to see that the dispute was concluded according to law without ever leaving the path of strict justice. On the appointed day the judges carefully listened to the allegations made by both sides, and when after looking into the actual case it was clear that the *stratigotus* was guilty on a large number of counts, judgement was given, and they ordered him to be held in prison after forfeiting all his property. So the people of Messina sang the chancellor's praises, because their rights had been restored and the *stratigotus* condemned. They said that they had been restored to freedom by his good offices, and that they were ready to take up any burden of whatever difficulty for his sake.

In fact the outcome showed how shaky their loyalty was, typical both of Greek perfidy and of the reliability to be expected from pirates. For a little later, at the behest of Bartholomew de Parisio,[211] who had much influence with the people of Messina, a large proportion of the citizens secretly took an oath to Count Henry. And when many of the Calabrians who gathered at Messina heard of the king's arrival, they were ensnared in the toils of the same conspiracy, and there could be no doubt that Gentile, Bishop of Agrigento, had deserted the chancellor, breaking the oath that he had taken to him. For the moment the unexpected arrival of Count Gilbert of Gravina stopped the conspiracy's foolhardiness at the point where open indications of it were beginning to appear, and forced it to go to ground again. This was because he brought 100 knights with him of proven ability, carefully equipped with weapons as he had been instructed, men experienced in many a war, whom he had chosen from among the most

---

211 See note 125 above.

renowned warriors of Apulia and the Terra di Lavoro. The whole city now began to be restless with different rumours, and incited its common people and many of the knights against the chancellor by coming up with a local issue in addition to the conspiracy, which had already grown very strong. This was because many less significant clients had recently come to join the chancellor from France and Normandy, who were quick to make insulting remarks, as is their habit, and were unrestrainedly abusing the patronage of the court, and called the Greeks and the South Italians traitors, attacking them with much injustice.

So Count Henry, impelled by frequent advice and encouragement from those involved in the conspiracy, set a definite date on which he would suddenly attack the chancellor as he was returning from court and kill him when he was off his guard. While the day was approaching on which he had decided to do this, in the meantime he required many to take a secret oath. Among them he approached Roger, one of the judges of the the city, one night, and asked him too to swear that he would do what the count wished. When Roger replied that he would never swear such a rash oath unless he gave a clearer account of the matter, the count explained his plan to kill the chancellor to him, saying that many nobles and bishops and a large proportion of the people of Messina had agreed to the plan and taken an oath to him, and he also told him the day that had been set for the attempt by common agreement. Roger pretended that this would be welcome to him, and said that no sensible person would object to an operation approved by the judgements of so many noblemen; on the other hand it would be unwise and hasty to make such an important promise without thought and consideration. So with some difficulty he obtained a delay until the following day, having given an untertaking that he would not reveal the plan which had been entrusted to him to anyone.

First thing next morning he went to the chancellor and told him everything the count had said, stating that many of the leading persons of Sicily were conspiring against him.[212] He should quickly decide how to deal with their wicked plans. Only a single day was available for this, for it was quite certain that the following day had been set for putting their plan into effect. The chancellor summoned Count Gilbert of Gravina, Count Bohemond of Manopello and Count Roger

---

212 The revelation of the plot follows Sallust, *Catiline* 40ff.

of Avellino,[213] whom he trusted most, and briefed them on the whole affair point by point. Realising the danger that was hanging over them, they instructed Roger the judge to return to the count and do what he wished, since if he did not wish to take the oath and said anything too openly against his wishes, this might give the count some cause for suspicion against him. He should not be afraid of taking this false oath which would prevent the king from being harmed and the entire realm from being shamed and disgraced.

When he had done this just as he had been ordered, the chancellor decided to brief the king and queen on the situation and inform them of the count's intentions and actions. When the queen heard about it, she began to be overcome by worry and anxiety and to be upset by a tide of great emotion. For it certainly seemed cruel and almost tyrannical to take any harsh decision against her brother and punish his audacity in the way it deserved; but she realised that if she were to spare her brother, the chancellor would certainly risk deadly danger, and it would not be possible to deter the traitors from what they had undertaken. She thought that a man who had shown no respect for his sister, who had put out of his mind all the favours she had done him, who had decided to do only that which would clearly contribute to her dishonour and disgrace by providing many people with reasons for rebelling against her, and who was striving in every way to undermine the peace and security of the realm, was not one who deserved the love due to a brother. So the discussion resulted in well-founded anger, and she put out of her mind any desire to forgive her brother, and decided to summon the court and convict the count in formal proceedings. When he was convicted or had confessed, she would keep him for a time in one of the fortresses, until his testimony identified the other traitors.

So guards were sent and those bishops, counts and other noblemen who were *familiares* of the court were summoned to court together with the Master Justiciars. When they had been allowed in, everyone else was barred from entering the palace, except for a few of the chancellor's knights whom he had himself ordered to be brought in because he was afraid that there might be some outcry or disturbance during the court session. For he was aware that many of the noblemen who were present supported Count Henry's party, and was afraid that, once he started to take rather harsh steps against him, they

213 For the last, see notes 80 and 167 above.

would back their opposition with violence; so he put on a breastplate under his tunic[214] and had also ordered the above-mentioned knights to be ready and prepared and that a number of swords should secretly be brought in by some of his clergy.

Now that everyone had taken his seat in the court, Count Henry, as he had been advised by his associates, began to make a statement about his lack of means, saying that he was oppressed by many debts; the county of Montescaglioso could not meet his expenses and financial embarrassment, and he asked to be granted either the principality of Taranto[215] or the county which Count Simon had once held in Sicily.[216] The idea was that he would have a justified complaint against the chancellor if this request was denied him. But when Count Gilbert of Gravina was given the opportunity to reply to his speech, he said: 'This request which you are now demanding as if with your sword drawn, offering pleas, in a cowardly and shameful way, you could easily have attained long ago, if you had made it with that attitude towards the king and queen which you ought to have displayed. But as it is, you have confirmed their view of you, now no longer opinion but certainty, not only making them think that you are unworthy to be raised to a higher status, but also making them consider that they were grossly deceived in granting you what you hold, and that it is not right that you should hold anything within their realm. I will not make any mention of the huge sum of money that you have spent wastefully and prodigally on disgraceful things, or of how the towns that were granted to you are oppressed by domestic robberies and many injustices; but you have even dared to sprinkle the poison of your wickedness on the king himself and his mother, by advising the queen to fortify her castles and to bring her treasure there while it was still possible, claiming that it was not clear what the king's attitude towards her would be in the future. And as for the king, you

---

214 As Cicero had done at the consular election of 63 BC, or at least had claimed to have done in his *Pro Murena* 52, copied by Plutarch, *Life of Cicero* 14. 7. For the problems arising from these parallels, see p. 48 above.

215 For which *Cat. Bar.* 35–7, arts. 211–26. It had of course been held by William I before the death of his elder brothers, and was thus a 'traditional' appanage for a junior member of the royal family.

216 i.e. Butera and Paterno, originally granted to Roger I's brother-in-law Count Henry. This lordship remained in royal hands from its confiscation from the Aleramici family until Henry VI granted Paterno to Bartholomew de Luci in the autumn of 1194; Garufi (1913a), 161–5.

tried to persuade him to grant you the government and administration of the realm; for you claimed that the queen was following her own private interests, and making the condition of the kingdom worse; she was handing out cities and towns on a wide scale, gradually exhausting the royal treasury, and doing many things that were clearly harming the realm and detracting from the honour due to her son, and which seemed to be utterly incompatible with a mother's love. But the king saw through your insolence, and replied that if he were to harbour suspicions against his mother, then it would be even more difficult for him to trust you. How wisely you are looking after the peace of the realm – which you decry as having been harmed – by sowing discord in this way between mother and son!

'And then you had the impudence to accuse me of disloyalty! You should know that I learnt of this from information which they themselves gave me. Now both of them are here present; if you can, then deny in the presence of both what you said to each of them.

'But now you have turned to another plan and, driven by the furies of treachery, you have descended to such a depth of wickedness that you make it your intention to shed the blood of the chancellor, and choose not to be involved in such a great crime all alone, but have made many others swear the same oath as you when you swore to do this. I would like you to state openly in the king's presence what charge you would level against the chancellor, of what crime you would claim that he is guilty, what cause there ultimately is that has aroused such fierce hatred against him. Has he taken away from you the inheritance you are owed, or threatened the boundaries of your patrimony? Have you cause to complain that he ever did you any harm or injustice? Or is it not more likely that you have been aroused by envy to burn with hatred against him? You are angry that the court is too much guided by his judgement; you find it hard to bear that he rules all the peoples of the realm on the king's behalf. If you had wanted equal glory, and if you had proved yourself equal to him in courage and wisdom, we would readily let you have the honour you have solicited. But if you are unable to achieve this because of the handicap of your inborn rashness, then we for our part certainly cannot allow the fortune of the realm to be put at risk under some foolhardy governor. Perhaps you could reply to that argument of mine by saying that you would always have wise and able men at court, and that you would achieve by means of their advice what you could not do by your own efforts. You might be thought by some to be making a valid point, did not the present disastrous state of your territory, which was most flourishing when you received it, prove to us just how much trust and reliance can be placed in you. What was justly denied to you, and you have not had the courage to ask for openly, you have tried to grasp for yourself by organising a conspiracy, a rash plan. In this you have been discovered to be both a disturber of the realm and contumacious and rebellious against the royal majesty; and on those very grounds you have not only deserved to lose the territory which you used to hold, but also to suffer sentence of death, unless the royal favour should wish to grant you pardon.'

When Count Henry heard in this way that all that he had done had unexpectedly been revealed, and that he was subject to such a serious accusation, and that no opportunity was being given him to suggest any pretext for putting the trial off, he was overcome by anxiety with a mixture of fear and shock, and after some time replied cravenly that he had never organised any plot against the chancellor. But the judge Roger was brought into their midst and said that he would prove what the other had denied, stating that, under the pressure of threats, he himself had recently given him an oath to bring about the death of the chancellor. By this statement he sowed such confusion in the count's mind and wits that instead of contradicting what he said or denying what he had been accused of, the latter instead broke into insults,[217] calling the judge Roger a traitor and perjurer for having forgotten his oath and revealing the plan that had been entrusted to him. As a result the count stood condemned by his own admission, and was ordered to be kept under guard within the palace. Then a message suddenly reached the palace that Count Henry's knights were gathering, armed, at his house, and that the entire city was in turmoil, with many citizens assembling under arms. At this point the chancellor ordered the knights of the Count of Gravina and his own knights to put on their armour and assemble in front of the palace. Guards were sent through the city to order the citizens to disarm and to calm the people's fears.

The Spaniards were told through a herald that they should all cross the Straits that same day, or otherwise any of them who were found on the next day would be imprisoned. So leaving their weapons behind, as they had been ordered, they crossed over to Calabria as fast as each of them could get there. When the Greek community heard what

---

217 Cf. Catiline's behaviour before the Senate when first accused by Cicero in November 63 BC; Sallust, *Catiline* 31.4.

had taken place at Messina, they rushed to get at the fugitives in the hope of plundering them, and after beating them viciously finally let them go, without their clothing and without any of their belongings. A large number of them perished in the snow in the forest of Sila as a result of the harsh winter.[218]

When the unrest in the city had died down, Bartholomew of Luci went to the chancellor and of his own free will confessed to having taken part in the same plot,[219] asked for pardon and offered to make appropriate amends. Through the intercession of Aegidius, Abbot of Venosa,[220] he was allowed to go into exile beyond the boundaries of the kingdom for a certain period of time, until the king's mercy should recall him after all the traitors had been expelled and complete peace had been restored to the court. In the meantime his lands were to be held by this same Aegidius. Following his example, Roger Sorellus also made public the fact that he had conspired with the others, misled by many deceitful arguments;[221] but he was sent to prison without

[218] The Sila range in southern Calabria is between 1,000 and 1,500 m. in height, and can be snowbound as late as May. The population of southern Calabria remained very largely Greek until the end of the thirteenth century; Guillou (1963).

[219] He came from a Norman family, originally from near Dieppe but long established in Sicily, and was descended from Josbertus de Luci (attested 1091–1119), who had married Roger I's daughter Muriel. Anfusus de Luci, who may have been Bartholomew's brother, described himself as a relative of King William in a charter of 1171; White (1938), 267–8, no. 27. Bartholomew was made Count of Paterno by Henry VI in September 1194 and died in 1200; Garufi (1913a), 160–180, especially 168–71; Ménager (1975), 322–6. His daughter Margaret married Paganus, the son of Bartholomew de Parisio; Garufi (1913b), 353.

[220] Abbot of the important Benedictine abbey of Holy Trinity, Venosa, in southern Apulia, from 1167 to 1181. He was a Spaniard who had probably come to the kingdom in the entourage of Queen Margaret. The contemporary Venosa chronicle claimed that he had previously been cellarer of the Cistercian abbey of Fossanova in the south of the papal states, but this is improbable. In the summer of 1168 he was chosen as Abbot of Montecassino, but Alexander III refused to sanction his transfer and the election was quashed. Aegidius returned to Venosa, where he died on 28 March 1181; Houben (1995), 160–2, 440.

[221] Otherwise unattested, but probably a descendant of the William *Surel* who witnessed a charter of Bishop William of Syracuse in 1115; Ménager, *Actes latins de S. Maria di Messina*, 60–2, no. 3 (= *Documenti inediti*, 13–14, no. 5). He must also have been related to the baronial family of that name

being granted a pardon, on the grounds that his confession came too late, when all the leaders of the conspiracy had already been revealed by Count Henry's testimony.

So when he knew who all his enemies were, a huge array of worries[222] assailed the chancellor, as he wondered on whose advice it would be best for him to rely. For many of his friends, considering the number and power of the conspirators, thought it dangerous to inflict punishment on every single one of them, and thought that the threat could not be eradicated in this way. Even if they held many or indeed all of them in prison, there would always remain some relatives who would wish to avenge them. So they persuaded the chancellor to try to appease rather than persecute them. He should invite them all together to court, and forgive them in the presence of the king. He should grant them a pardon, with a few words in defence of his innocence, and should add that he certainly had the power to exact vengeance, but preferred to win by means of favours than to act in the savage manner of a tyrant against nobles whom he would rather honour.

On the other hand, Count Gilbert of Gravina, whose opinion won the day, expressed a totally opposite opinion, and thought that not one of those who were manifestly participants in such an evil plot or knew about it ought to escape unpunished, especially when he saw that a suitable time had come for vengeance against Count Richard of Molise, who had once had him expelled from court. Others who had more experience of the customs of the land of Sicily and of tyranny, looking more carefully to the future, said that they should either never have been imprisoned, or else, since they had been imprisoned, should have been drowned in the sea, or alternatively secretly murdered, or at least have had their principal limbs cut off; for that was the way in which King Roger had once most prudently brought lasting peace to his kingdom.[223] This was an effective point of view and a safe one, but the chancellor, who preferred to be merciful, balked at such cruelty.

> prominent at Aversa in the Principality of Capua since the late eleventh century, whose head at this period was Leonard Sorellus; *Cod. Dipl. Aversa*, 87–8, no. 50 (1144), 105–7, no. 61 (1151); *Cat. Bar.*, 158, arts. 876–8; Cuozzo (1984), 249–50. Another relative, Malgerius Sorellus, was later lord of Mignano in the Principality of Capua; Archivio dell'Abbazia di S. Benedetto di Montecassino, Aula III, Cap. xii, no. 16 (October 1181).

222 *Ingens cura*; cf. Sallust, *Catiline* 46.2.
223 Cf. the introduction, pp. 6–7 above.

So after a few days, when the counts and other nobles summoned to court sat down in due order, Bohemond of Tarsia, the brother of Carbonellus,[224] a young man of outstanding bravery and recognised nobility, got up in the midst of the nobles and said that Count Richard of Molise, after having become one of the *familiares* of the court by the favour of the king and queen, had acted disloyally towards them by supporting those who had conspired against the chancellor. Richard himself had not just heard of their plot from the mouth of Count Henry, but had approved of the plan, and had done nothing to protect the court from their snares. He stated that if he tried to deny it, he himself would just as readily prove this. The count, fearlessly accusing him of being a liar and answering the accusation against him with an immediate attempt to defend himself, swore that he had never even thought any evil against the chancellor, and as though incoherent with wrath, he broke into tears, ostensibly of indignation, and shouted that he was quite prepared to undertake an ordeal by combat against Bohemond, for he would fight with complete confidence either against him or against two others like him. What gave his soul a just cause for grief was that the chancellor, whom he had always tried to support loyally, could have been induced to believe this, and if he had not suffered the hatred of the Count of Gravina, he would easily have been able to win pardon from the chancellor, since there was no proof that he had either conspired, or given the conspirators any encouragement.

While these accusations were being made against the count, Count Robert of Caserta added that on his own authority he had occupied Mandra in Apulia as well as some towns belonging to the king in the territory of Troia, and was still holding them secretly, without the court knowing about it. Count Richard's reply to this was that Caid Peter, who was in charge of the court at the time, had granted him Mandra to hold for a period on condition that he send a stated quantity of money to the court each year; and as for the towns which he was said to have occupied in the territory of the Troians, these had been made over to him by Turgisius, chamberlain of that territory.[225] This

224 The son of the former Count of Manopello, who had died in disgrace in 1156/7 (see above, notes 18 and 37). Since the cause of that disgrace had been his defeat by Robert of Loritello, whose constable Richard had been, there was almost certainly an old score to settle here.

225 Troia in the Capitanata, 22 km. SW of Foggia. This passage conveys significant information on the duties of the royal chamberlains, but the only Turgisius the chamberlain who can be attested at this period,

Turgisius, who happened to be there at the time, was questioned, and denied that it was with his permission that he held these towns. Accordingly all the nobles, with the exception of the *familiares* of the court, were ordered to withdraw, in order to bring a judicial sentence on these charges which had been made against the count. The following were those who rose to give judgment: Bohemund, Count of Manopello; Robert of Lauro, Count of Caserta; his son Roger, Count of Tricarico; Roger, Count of Avellino; Simon, Count of Sangro;[226] Roger, Count of Gerace;[227] the master-constable Roger of Tiron; and Florius of Camerota;[228] as well as the judge Tarentinus[229] and Abednago, son of Hannibal,[230] who were Master Justiciars. As they were discussing the

> Turgisius de Campora, was chamberlain of the Terra di Lavoro from 1168 to 1170; Jamison (1913), 397, 401–2. It is possible that he had previously held office in the Capitanata; such a transfer from one region to another was unusual, but not unprecedented.
>
> 226 Simon II, Count of Sangro 1166–8. He died in this last year and was succeeded by his brother Richard; Cuozzo (1984), 321.
>
> 227 Otherwise unattested. Chalandon (1907), ii, 335, suggests that he was Count of Geraci in NE Sicily rather than Gerace in Calabria, but this seems unlikely, both because of the reluctance of the kings to create counts on the island, and because the Sicilian documentation is much fuller than that from Calabria; hence such an important figure would have been less likely to have escaped record there.
>
> 228 One of the longest-serving royal officials of the period. He was a justiciar in the Principality of Salerno from 1150 and in the Terra di Lavoro in 1158. He was the nephew of Archbishop Alfanus of Capua, and was exiled by William I, *c.* 1164 (discussed in the introduction, pp. 23–4). He was subsequently justiciar in the principality once more from 1172 to 1178, one of the Sicilian envoys to Henry II of England in 1176 (*Romuald*, 268) and justiciar in the Val di Crati in Calabria from 1187 to 1189; Jamison (1913), 478–80; Ménager, 'Quelques monastères' 342–53.
>
> 229 A Greek who was a Master Justiciar of the royal court from 1159 to 1171 before becoming a monk at the monastery of the Holy Saviour, Messina, in the spring of 1173; Jamison (1967), especially 301. Tarentinus, Abdenago, son of Hannibal and Roger of Tiron adjudicated in a legal case between the Calabrian monasteries of Bagnara and S. Euphemia at Messina in February 1168; *ibid.*, 331–5, no. 2. Richard's trial must have been at about the same time.
>
> 230 He seems to have been the administrator of the County of Molise when it was in the king's hands after the death of Count Hugh II, *c.* 1156 and before Richard's appointment as count in 1166; *Cat. Bar.*, 129, 133, 137–8, 147, arts. 726, 743, 761, 804–5.

case, it was the opinion of these men that Count Richard of Molise held Mandra with the approval of the court up to the moment at which Caid Peter (from whom he had received it) had fled. But after his disappearance, since he held on to it in secret, without bringing the matter to the notice of the king, as he should have done, he ought no longer to be considered as occupying it even on sufferance, but more properly as an invader.[231] He should be at the king's mercy with regard to any territory which he held, both for that reason and because it was clear that he had occupied these towns on his own authority, contrary to the loyalty he owed the king.

It was Count Bohemond, since he was a gifted speaker, who proclaimed this judgment in the presence of the king on the behalf of all and with their approval. In reply, Count Richard shouted out that he had been charged unjustly. Personal hatred was obviously being given precedence over justice, and he was ready to prove that they had brought in an unjust and false verdict. Bohemond forbade the count to reply to the court with such words, saying that this contempt reflected not on those who had delivered the verdict but primarily on the crown. So the archbishops and bishops who were present were ordered to decide a just penalty for such contempt in accordance with the severity of the law. In accordance with the laws of the kingdom of Sicily, they decreed that Count Richard was liable to the king's mercy not only with respect to the lands he held, but also his limbs and his body, on the grounds that he had presumed to claim that the court's judgment was false.[232] So he was arrested and put in the custody of some knights, and ordered to be taken to Taormina, and guarded with utmost care in the fortress which is sited on the top of the cliff, overhanging the town.

Thus these two extremely powerful men were imprisoned, and none of the conspirators now remained whom the chancellor might believe

---

[231] *non iam precario possidentem, sed invasorem rectius estimabatur.* The implication of *invasor* is clearly of illegal occupation, as opposed to rightful *possessio*: a terminology reflecting Roman law, with which the author was clearly familiar. *Precarium* could be a type of lease, but here reflects rather the classical meaning of something obtained by entreaty.

[232] Cf. King Roger's assizes, Vatican text, c, xvii, Monti, 'Il testo': 'There should be no dispute about the judgement, plans, decrees or deeds of the king, for to dispute his judgements, decrees, deeds or plans, or if he whom he has chosen or appointed is worthy, is comparable to sacrilege.' This was a Roman law maxim directly copied from Justinian's *Code* 9. 29.2.

THE HISTORY OF THE TYRANTS OF SICILY

gave cause for fear. While this was happening at court, the Bishop of Agrigento retired from the court, pretending that he was suffering a serious illness. Soon afterwards, John de Sinopoli[233] and Bartholomew de Parisio were condemned on the same charge and imprisoned in different well-fortified places in the principality of Salerno. Walter of Moac was also formally accused of being a part of the same conspiracy,[234] and agreed to single combat with his accuser – sureties were given, and he was ordered to await the date which had been set. Meanwhile Count Simon of Sangro died, and his brother Richard was appointed to his position and protected the chancellor's interests with all the strength at his disposal. Furthermore the boy Hannibal, Count Rainald's son, was made count and given all his father's lands.[235] But Count Gilbert of Gravina, considering that the chancellor had survived the attacks of all these enemies by his own help and that everything had turned out well for him and that, so he thought, no danger remained, became so bold as to put in a request to the court for the county of Loritello. He preferred to exchange his present secure position for one which held certain danger, for by doing this he provoked the jealousy of many great men and cities of Apulia against him, and created enmities that could not be appeased. By taking the county of Loritello, he appeared to have prevented a possible reinstatement of Count Robert, whose return they all very keenly wanted, and utterly removed the hope they had long been cherishing.

Although it was quite clear that several officials of the court and many others had supported the conspiracy against him, the chancellor

---

233 Otherwise unattested. Sinopoli is in southern Calabria, 7 km. E. of Bagnara.

234 Later an important financial and military official, Master Constable, i.e. commander of the household troops, in 1171 and commander of the fleet 1177–82, also one of the board who directed the *Duana de Secretis*, and in 1178–9 he was in charge of the *Duana Baronum* (the mainland financial sub-office based at Salerno, which was established *c*. 1168); Jamison (1957), 54; Takayama (1993), 131, 137–9, 149–50.

235 Rainald, son of Count Crescentius of Marsia and brother of Count Berard of Alba, had been appointed to the new county of Celano in 1143/4. He had now probably just died. Hannibal is not otherwise attested, but Rainald's illegitimate son Odo was royal justiciar of this region between 1172 and 1184. The County of Celano ultimately went to Hannibal's cousin Peter, son of Count Berard of Alba; Jamison (1933) 107; Cuozzo (1984), 335–7. For Rainald's lands; *Cat. Bar.* 214–15, arts. 1105–9.

nevertheless behaved in a conciliatory way towards them, deciding to pretend ignorance in order to appear not to be dealing with the matter too harshly. He also hoped that it would easily be possible to restrain them from their evil objective once they had been warned off by the punishment of others. With regard to Count Henry of Montescaglioso, the queen's decision was to give him 1,000 ounces of gold and send him back to her brother in Spain. So the chancellor ordered seven galleys to be armed which were to transport Odo Quarrel over to France and then take the count as far as the boundary of the territory of Arles under Odo's custody. Meanwhile he was kept in the fortress at Reggio, a city at the southernmost tip of Italy across the Straits opposite Messina, so that the galleys could pick him up from there quickly and without incident the moment the king left Messina on his way back to Palermo.

54 The king's return to Palermo

After making these arrangements, the king started his journey on the 12th of March and reached Palermo on the 20th of the same month.[236] Count Gilbert crossed the Straits with his knights and returned to Apulia. But Odo Quarrel stayed at Messina, having received detailed instructions from the chancellor and strict advice to go on board the galleys without any delay immediately after the king's departure.

55 The officers of the court

In the meantime Caid Richard, Master Chamberlain of the palace, and the notary Matthew and Bishop Gentile of Agrigento and others to whom the chancellor had given the opportunity for wickedness by pretending not to know about their plan, were striving to bring the

---

[236] (1168) Just before their departure the king and his mother gave a *casale* on the plain of Milazzo to the nuns of St Mary *de Scala* of Messina; *Documenti inediti*, 101–2, no. 44; and gave a limited customs exemption to the monks of St Mary of the Latins at Jerusalem (or rather to their Sicilian priory at Agira), and confirmed that house's possessions and privileges; Holtzmann, 'Papst, Kaiser- und Normannenurkunden', 70–2, nos. 7–8. These three documents were the last ones to be dated by Stephen as chancellor.

lunacy they had conceived to completion, and were not mollified by the favours they received from him. They thought that a great deal of support had been taken away from the chancellor as a result of the absence of the Count of Gravina, and calculated that he would be easy prey to their schemes, since he was not cautious and did not plan for the future and feared no further dangers, as though all his problems had already been overcome. So they initiated a new alliance and committed themselves with reciprocal oaths. Then a stated day was agreed for carrying out their plan, and some knights were selected who, having taken an oath, would strike down the chancellor with their swords in the middle of the crowd on Palm Sunday[237] as the king was leaving the palace according to custom. They had found that a large number of citizens both at Palermo and in some other cities were opposed to the chancellor, and by giving them much and promising them more they did not find it difficult to persuade them that if the chancellor remained at his present pinnacle of power, he would take away the freedom that they had hitherto enjoyed from all the communities of Sicily. They thought that a powerful argument in favour of this view was that John of Lavardin, who had recently been given Matthew Bonellus's estates at the chancellor's request, was injuring the townsmen under his control to the extent of demanding one-half of the movable property that they owned. He claimed that this was the custom of his own land.[238] They on the contrary asserted the liberties of the citizens and townsmen of Sicily, and stated that they owed no income and no dues, but that they did occasionally let their lords have what they asked for, on their own terms and of their own free will, when there was a pressing need; it was only those Muslims and Greeks who were classified as villeins who had to pay tithes and an annual money rent.[239]

When they got nowhere by making these claims, they brought the matter to the chancellor's attention. Ignoring the advice of Robert of San Giovanni and Roger of Tiron the Master Constable, he preferred

---

[237] 24 March 1168.

[238] John was, of course, a Frenchman (see above, note 203). The lands in question were Caccamo and Prizzi (cf. above, note 59).

[239] Their names would have been listed on the *plateae* of unfree peasants kept by landholders. Latin colonists had been attracted to Sicily by favourable terms, including personal freedom; D'Alessandro (1989), especially 309–15.

to be seduced by the arrogance of some of those he had brought with him from France. These people considered that no justice should be done for the peasants in this matter, and said that this insolence on their part was insufferable, and if the latter were ever to get what they demanded, then a precedent would be set that would be disastrous for many, in that they had shown themselves assertive and rebellious against their lords. So they achieved none of the things they hoped for, and for the time being were forced to bear their wrongs with patience.

This affair gave the chancellor's enemies maximum opportunity to arouse the hatred of many citizens and townsmen against him, claiming that it was his intention that the entire population of Sicily should be forced to pay the annual renders and exactions, as was the custom in Gaul, where free citizens did not exist. When the chancellor heard of their plans, he saw that they could not be deflected from their purpose by any feelings of humanity or gratitude. He first of all summoned the court and laid a formal accusation against the notary Matthew (who was much more intelligent than the others), and when he offered no satisfactory defence, had him remanded in prison. Several knights were imprisoned there, who had been found to have taken oaths to bring about his own murder. But the queen would in no way give her approval to the arrest of Caid Richard, who was the head and the origin of the conspiracy, and in the end the only thing the chancellor managed to obtain was that he was forbidden from leaving the palace and from talking to his knights.

With his colleagues imprisoned, the Bishop of Agrigento saw that, with so many of its members cut off, no hope remained that the conspiracy could recover sufficiently to carry out the intended crime. He decided to mobilise the population of the city of Agrigento and of surrounding towns[240] against the chancellor and openly proclaim his hostility towards him, confident that Count Roger of Gerace, who was also involved in the conspiracy, and at his exhortation many others also, would be willing to take his line. He also hoped that

---

240 Most of these would have been Muslims. The late thirteenth-century history of the bishops of Agrigento recorded that the first bishop, Gerlandus (*c.* 1092–1104), built his palace 'next to the castle for fear of the innumerable Saracens living in Agrigento, where there were few Christians until the death of William II'; Collura, *Più antiche carte di Agrigento*, 307.

William of Leluce[241] in Calabria would do the same, as had been agreed between them. So he left secretly with a few knights, without the court's permission, and reached Agrigento by a concealed route; and calling together the populace, he described to them the arrest of the notary Matthew and of the others, saying that it was the chancellor's policy first to imprison all the leaders of Sicily who did not agree with him, then to remove the king by poison and transfer the realm to himself by marrying the queen, whom he now called his relative. Things had reached such a critical stage that every Sicilian who wished to maintain his loyalty to the king ought with one mind to rise up against the traitor, and prevent the machinations of his plans before such a horrible crime was committed. He broadcast this both at a public meeting at Agrigento and in writing to the people of Messina. But he was not able to persuade the Agrigentines of any of it – the grounds for rebellion did not seem very strong. When the king and queen discovered the bishop's disappearance, they sent the justiciar Burgundius[242] to Agrigento with a royal writ, ordering the Agrigentines to send the bishop to Palermo in the custody of the same Burgundius as a traitor. When the bishop arrived at court and attempted to defend the things he had done publicly with various obfuscations, he was condemned on the evidence of many witnesses and taken to the castle of San Marco, which lies in the Val Demone, to be held there for the time being, until an account of what he had done could be submitted to the Roman pontiff.

So the fear and the difficulty presented by the affair had now been removed, and the conspiracy, utterly devoid of its supporters, would not have been able to revive, if a new incident had not occurred which brought about a new danger, and the foolhardiness of a single man had not rekindled the fuel for wickedness which had been damped down and almost extinguished by the efforts of so many wise men. For the chancellor heard that Odo Quarrel was remaining at Messina long after the date agreed for his departure. His ability to foresee events suggested to him what would happen, and he sent him a letter full of threats and insults, ordering him to leave within three days of

241 MSS. A and B have William. P (the 1550 edition) gives his name as Gilbert. *Lelucensis* may refer to Monte Lelo, near Cariati.

242 Otherwise attested only as one of the members of a court in January 1159 which dealt with a dispute over the ownership of two villeins; Ménager, *Actes latins de S. Maria di Messina*, 91–3, no. 7 (= Jamison (1967), 318–19, no. 1).

receipt of the letter and forget all thoughts of plunder or any calculation of his losses. But a fatal disaster now hung over Odo, and he was blinded by the darkness of cupidity. No threats or appeals, no type of persuasion could drag him away. He threw himself into such great danger for one reason only, because he wished to extort money from the ships leaving for Syria (otherwise he would not allow them to pass).[243]

The citizens were extremely aggrieved by this exaction, and at first began to complain among themselves in secret and then expressed their anger more freely and openly, and said that their own fear and laziness was the reason for allowing foreign-born pirates to carry off to France the treasury of the realm as well as money obtained from unjust extortions from the citizenry. But then some dependants of Odo Quarrel who made a habit of roaming drunk through the city happened to come across some Greeks gaming in a certain house, and insolently broke up their game and began to upset them with a great deal of verbal abuse.[244] Because they were afraid of the chancellor, they at first put up with this for some time and asked them to go away or at least stop doing them harm. But stoked by constant insults, their anger taught them to put aside their patience, and forgetting their fear and grabbing cudgels they attacked the men and put an end to their insulting talk with many blows.

When Odo Quarrel heard about this, he summoned the *stratigotus* and ordered that the Greeks be arrested and brought before him. The *stratigotus*,[245] however, replied that the city was shaken by all kinds of rumours and that civic opinion, ripe for sedition, ought not now to be further alienated. For the time being they should pretend

243 Messina was becoming an increasingly important entrepôt for trade between the north Italian seaports and the Crusader states. Ships often loaded Sicilian foodstuffs there for onward transmission; Abulafia (1977), 64, 92, 229–30; Abulafia (1986), 198–9; Loud (1992), 52–3. Edrisi noted both its abundant gardens and orchards, and that 'voyagers and merchants, whether from the lands of the Christians or those of the Muslims, flock there from every side'; *BAS* i. 17.

244 Much of the population of Messina was still Greek at this period, as was made clear in a contemporary account of Richard I of England's stay there in 1190–1; Appleby, *The Chronicle of Richard of Devizes*, 16–25.

245 Andrew of Limoges, in office from March 1168 to 1170 and again in 1176; Ménager, *Actes latins de S. Maria di Messina*, 41; Cusa, *I Diplomi greci ed arabi*, 368–71.

to forget about the injury done and put off punishment to an appropriate moment. But Odo, who would take no advice once he was moved to anger, went on to say that whatever action the others were likely to take, these men had to be punished for the insult offered to himself. If this incident were to go unpunished, then matters of this sort would never be properly dealt with. He had no fear of any conspiracy on the part of peasants, and it was essential for the rest to be cowed by making an example of these now. When the *stratigotus*, carrying out his wishes, went to the place where this had occurred, he found that a large number of Greeks had assembled there. When he began to address them sternly, they replied that this was not the time for a *stratigotus* to threaten the citizens, but rather to entreat them. As soon as they had said this they attacked him, and when he turned to flee, relying on the speed of his horse, they threw many stones after him.

When the Latins, who had come to hate the French because of these maritime exactions, saw that the Greeks too had been turned against them by new injustices, they started to urge them to rebel, claiming that what the French intended was to expel the whole Greek community and take over their homes, their vineyards and their other farms; and that the queen had married the chancellor, and that it was not yet quite clear what had happened to the king, but that – if indeed he was still alive – he was in great danger. So the whole city was buzzing with unfounded rumours, and giving clear indications of being about to rebel, and subject to such a storm of events that neither the *stratigotus* nor the magistrates dared to undertake any police action against the will of the common people. When it was reported to the king and the queen that the city had been deluded by false rumours and stirred up by enormous whirlpools of unrest, they sent a letter to the people of Messina written in the following manner: 'William, by the Grace of God King of Sicily, of the Duchy of Apulia and the Principality of Capua, together with the honoured queen his mother, the Lady Margaret; our greetings and love to the *stratigotus* Andrew and to the justices and to their entire loyal people of Messina. It is clear that the crime of treason is committed not only by those who are incited by such force of madness as to make a nefarious attempt on our life and well-being, but also by those who plot anything secretly or openly with a view to killing one of our *familiares*, and who plot to set up the instruments of their treason in any way against those who look after our interests, by whose help and advice our realm is happily administered.[246] Since this category of person seems to have been born for the destruction of the entire realm, they should be punished with the penalties they deserve, and the atrocities they were trying to direct against others ought justly to rebound on to their own heads. It was for this reason that we ordered Bishop Gentile of Agrigento, Caid Richard and the notary Matthew, whom we perceived on clear evidence to have conspired against our beloved relative and chancellor Stephen, having been found guilty and condemned in our presence, to be held under guard in prison. But at the request of the same Stephen, the serene light of our majesty has decided to deal leniently with them, and punishing them more lightly than the severity of the law indicates, to grant them the chance to live. We did not want this to be concealed from the loyalty you have towards us, lest you should be deceived by anyone's lying insinuations, or be made uneasy by any other rumours of any kind whatsoever, and to ensure that you should not do anything that is contrary to our will, or in any way violate the loyalty which you have until now preserved towards us unshaken. Know, consequently, that we are well and unharmed and enjoying complete peace in our palace, and put away any movements or occasions for sedition from your city, so that you may be able to earn our favour even more richly.'

When he received this letter, the *stratigotus* ordered the people to assemble at the New Church[247] in order to have it read out in the presence of the entire citizenry. When the people had to wait for quite a long time because he was delaying, they began to talk among themselves and and invent all sorts of notions. Some insisted that without doubt the chancellor Stephen had been made king, and that this letter of his that they had come to hear read out was only described as a royal letter; that King William had been killed, and that his brother Henry was surrounded in the Sea Castle with a few

246 Cf. here King Roger's laws, Vatican text, assize xviii, Monti, 'Il testo': 'Whosoever should start a plot ... or should give an undertaking or an oath to a plot, that plans or prepares the murder of one of the illustrious men who are among the counsellors and advisers – they have by their wish to commit evil chosen for themselves severe legal punishment. The culprits should be struck down by the sword as guilty of treason and all their property should be confiscated by the state.' This was derived from Justinian, *Code*, 9. 8.5.
247 The new cathedral begun by King Roger; see Romuald, p. 220 below and note 6 to that text.

knights, and cut off by siege. Others, who were more intelligent and found the obvious falsity of this unbelievable, constructed a less extreme version, that it was not the chancellor himself who was to rule but a certain Geoffrey, his brother,[248] and that in line with this Odo Quarrel was going to cross to Gaul with a vast sum of money so that this Geoffrey could sail across to Sicily with Odo's help and guidance and marry Constance, daughter of King Roger.[249] This would give him a pretext to take over the realm with an appearance of legality. So these rumours went round, and the people's anger grew as the rumours circulated, until someone began to shout out, and his voice made everyone fall silent; the only plan that remained in this whirlwind was that they should first kill Odo Quarrel and then set free Count Henry, who had always been especially kind to the people of Messina. Then all those who were present — as if they had sworn that they would obey this man's advice — rushed to storm the residence of Odo Quarrel, ignoring the orders of the *stratigotus*.

When their first onslaught achieved nothing, they quickly went down to the harbour, and finding seven galleys there, filled them with weapons and men, and sailed across the Straits to Reggio. On the advice of John Calomenus, who was the current Chamberlain of Calabria,[250]

248 Little is known of him at this period. Later, from 1174 onwards, he was a member of Henry II's court and witnessed a number of his charters, both in Normandy and in England. These included the king's peace agreement with his sons at Falaise in October 1174 the homage of William the Lion of Scotland at Valognes in December 1174, and the treaty with the King of Connaught at Windsor in October 1175; Delisle and Berger, *Recueil des Actes de Henri II* ii, 21, 23, 46, nos. 468, 471, 494; Stubbs, *Gesta Regis Henrici II*, i. 103. However, he is unlikely to have been with the king in 1168, for Henry was attacking the county of Perche in that year. Geoffrey died between April 1180 and the autumn of 1181; Delisle and Berger, *Recueil des Actes de Henri II* ii, 210, no. 616; *Pipe Roll 27 Henry II* (Pipe Roll Society, vol. 30, London 1909), 97.

249 Roger's daughter by his third wife, Béatrice of Rethel (d. 1185); *Romuald*, 231. She was born in 1154, shortly after her father's death, and would thus have now been nearly 14. However, she remained unmarried until 1186, when she married Henry, eldest son of Frederick Barbarossa, subsequently the Emperor Henry VI. After her husband's death in September 1197, Constance became sole ruler of Sicily, but died in November 1198.

250 This official is otherwise unattested. He presumably held the office of Master Chamberlain of Calabria, the Val di Crati, Val di Sinni and Val di Marsico, occupied in 1163 by Guy of Ripitella; Jamison (1913), 449–50,

the inhabitants of Reggio opened their gates to the Messinans, and took an oath to support their party. From there they went up with considerable confidence to the citadel where the count was being kept under the guard of a few knights, telling the knights (who had mounted the walls with the intention of defending it) to hand the count over to them, or else they would all be hanged on the spot as traitors once they had been captured by force. Nor would they be able to escape, for if they were indeed able to hold out for the whole of that day – which was hardly likely – sixty armed galleys would arrive from Messina on the next day and bring the siege-engines needed to capture the keep. At first they ignored their threats and actively repulsed the attackers, and they brought confusion on their piratical undertaking by firing volleys of stones. But when they considered how very few of them there were, and that in the entire citadel there was only enough food to last them for three days, they replied as follows to the Messinans' repeated demands that the count be handed over to them: that they ought not to listen to men they did not know, who had arrived without a leader or commander, regarding the demands they were putting. But if they brought the *stratigotus* or their justices or anyone at all from among the important men in the city, then they would be happy to trust their words. They immediately promised to do this, returned to Messina, and took the usher James (who had been sent by the court to prepared a fleet) to Reggio, unwillingly and reluctantly. So the knights, denied any hope or opportunity to resist further, finally handed the count over to them. After crossing the Straits he was hailed by the people of Messina at a gathering of the entire city and with much support from the common people, and they all swore that in future they would follow Count Henry's command in everything, and would not abandon him so long as he lived.

In the meantime Odo Quarrel had taken refuge with all his possessions in the royal palace, which stood next to his own residence. There he was besieged by a crowd of people who encamped around the walls, and was unable either to leave himself or to let the chancellor know

---

no. 58. There was, however, a John, Master Chamberlain of Apulia and Terra di Lavoro, in February 1167; Gattula, *Accessiones*, 262–4. Since this latter office disappeared soon after that date because its functions were taken over by the new *Duana Baronum*, it is possible that this John may have been transferred to Calabria and hence be the man mentioned here.

what had happened to him by means of a letter. The custodian of the palace, when there was no other way to ward off the violence of the attacking mob, promised that he would hold him so that he would stand trial for his life. The count sent some men along with his notary and a number of citizens to make a written inventory of all Odo's money, gold, silver, precious stones and silk clothes, with orders to keep them stored with great care inside the palace. He ordered Odo himself to be put in a skiff and taken over to the Old Castle, which stands in the harbour next to the New Church, under cover of the silence of night.

Meanwhile the people of Messina were afraid that the count was holding Odo under guard with the intention of letting him return to court so that he could intercede for him, and that he would deceitfully abandon their party. Hence they thought that the best course was to kill Odo himself. Once that was done, the count would be unable to make any excuses to the court. So they gathered together a great mob of people and went to the count demanding that he hand Odo Quarrel over to them for punishment; for he had not been taken with the intention of being kept safe, but so that he should be punished with terrible tortures for his crimes both against the king and against themselves. The count did not want to seem ungrateful for the favours he had received from them, and also saw that, even though he was unwilling, he ought not to resist the people's wishes; so he did not put any obstacle in the way of their demand, although it greatly displeased him, for he was afraid that an affair which had started so foolishly could not reach a desirable conclusion.

They quickly set off for the castle. Odo Quarrel was handed over to them by the castellan, and they brought him out and put him on the back of an ass which they had got ready for this, with his feet stretched towards the front of the ass and his head hanging down at the opposite end.[251] The entire population ran to watch, and they led him through the middle of the city to the accompaniment of enormous shouting, insulting and beating him. When they got to the city gate, one of them stuck a baker's knife into his skull with all the force he had, and in full view of everybody licked the blood sticking to the blade, to show the extent of unforgiving hatred he felt. Following his example,

---

251 Cf. the execution of Count Richard of Acerra in December 1196, as recounted by the *Annales Ceccanenses* ad ann. 1197, MGH SS xix, 294.

others tore Odo limb from limb, transfixed by countless wounds. They put his head on a spear and displayed it for some time throughout the city before finally throwing it into the public sewer, from which it was secretly extracted and handed over for burial.[252] During this time the Greeks were busy slaughtering anyone from north of the Alps they could find, until Count Henry forbade this by threatening to punish them.

In order to obstruct the route of the approaching royal army as much as they could, the people of Messina first occupied Rometta, a strong fortress,[253] after easily overcoming the castellan's loyalty with promises. Then they approached Taormina in full force but also with the greatest stealth, in order to set free Count Richard of Molise, and they were able to take control of the town itself without difficulty; but all their force could not capture the castle.[254] Nor did the loyalty of the castellan Matthew lose any of its strength and reliability, even though he was beset by many promises of rewards and many threats. Finally his wife's brother was sent out by the Messinans to beseech him with tears to abandon his cruel attitude and have mercy on his wife and children, whom the people of Messina had thrown into prison and were proposing to kill if he did not hand Count Richard over to them soon. But the castellan's reply was that not only would he be able to bear their murder, but he himself was equally ready to meet his death rather than prolong his life with treachery of this kind, a life which up till now was stained by no mark of infamy.

When the man who had been sent realised that his mind could not be moved from the position he had stated, he gave a guarantee to the *gavarettus* of the castle, whom he had known for a long time, and by making large promises he persuaded him to open the gates of the

---

252 The death of Odo Quarrel, canon and subdeacon, was recorded on 6 April (1168) by the necrology of Chartres cathedral: 'he was atrociously murdered by certain sons of Satan when he was about to return to these parts from Sicily'; *Obituaires de la Province de Sens*, ii: *Diocèse de Chartres*, ed. A. Molinier and A. Longnon (Recueil des historiens de la France, Obituaires ii, Paris 1906), 55.

253 On the north side of the Monti Peloritani, 12 km. W. of Messina.

254 That this was very strong had been shown back in 1079, when it had taken Count Roger I almost six months to capture Taormina from the Muslims; *Malaterra* III. 18, p. 67.

dungeon and set Count Richard free at the very first opportunity that presented itself. So on a particular day, while the castellan Matthew was asleep, the *gavarettus* released Count Richard from his chains as he had promised, and brought him out. They immediately went straight to the castellan. The noise of feet woke him from his sleep, and when he saw the count, he snatched a sword in terror, and would easily have been able to turn the ambush that had been laid for him on the head of the other man, had not the traitor by whose help this had been done unexpectedly grabbed him and escaped his attempt to strike him down. He struck him in the upper part of the back between the shoulders with a knife he was holding, although the count was wounded in the hand (which he held out with his raised sword). So Matthew was cut down with many wounds, and the men of Messina quickly took control of the castle of Taormina and of the count himself.

When these events were reported to the chancellor, he was overcome by the sudden misfortune, and finally he asked the advice of his friends, which he had long neglected to do. It was decided to persuade the king to summon an army and go to lay siege to Messina, and he easily and willingly granted this, after the astrologers had identified a correct date for the army to set off.[255] Meanwhile he wrote to the people of Catania to put a complete embargo on any supplies to Messina, and not to allow any Messinan ships to be loaded there, and he also ordered all Catanian ships to be beached, by having one board removed from each hull. By removing their opportunity for importing grain, this action imposed starvation on the people of Messina, since they could expect no relief from anywhere else. Calabria was suffering because that year's harvest had failed, and was hardly able to support itself.[256]

---

255 *The Travels of Ibn Jubayr*, 341, recorded that William II 'pays much attention to his astrologers'. One of them was depicted in an illustration on fo. 97r of the MS. of Peter of Eboli's poem, *Liber ad Honorem Augusti*, 121.

256 Messina's hinterland, though fertile, was very limited in extent. The town needed to import grain in most years; Abulafia (1977), 117–21; Peri (1978), 18. Cf. Broadhurst, *The Travels of Ibn Jubayr*, 339: 'Messina leans against the mountains, the lower slopes of which adjoin the entrenchments of the town.'

Meanwhile the people of Randazzo, Vicari, Capizzi, Nicosia, Maniace and other North Italian communities which were supporting the chancellor's side because of his many favours, and opposed the obvious jealousy and wickedness of the traitors, sent envoys to Palermo to appeal to the chancellor and try by every means possible to persuade him to lead out his army with confidence against the people of Messina, for whenever he gave the order, he would have 20,000 fighting men just from the North Italian towns alone.[257] The chancellor praised their loyalty and revealed to them that a date had been fixed for just this operation, and he told them to get ready with all that was needed in the meantime.

Count Roger of Gerace, who up until now had deceitfully covered up his wish to rebel, began to admit it by various public acts, since he saw that the conspiracy was unexpectedly regaining a great deal of strength. He fortified his castles and went to Cefalù to have a discussion with the bishop of that city,[258] and persuaded him to swear that he would never deny his assistance to the people of Messina against the chancellor, and he also asked that he receive the same oath from every one of his citizens. But the chancellor had already occupied the town's extremely defensible citadel, since he had seen from the outset that the bishop's loyalty was doubtful, and he had sent the royal usher Andrew to guard the citadel itself.[259]

Then the notary Matthew, who was being held imprisoned in the palace, heard what had happened at Messina and realised that the castellan Ansaldus (a friend of the chancellor) was being detained by illness in the upper part of the palace. He saw that his absence gave him the opportunity to do just what he had been hoping, and with

[257] These were in the area of SE Sicily which had seen extensive 'Lombard' immigration, encouraged by Count Henry of Paterno and his family. The figure of 20,000 men was, however, a gross exaggeration; Peri (1978), 111; Abulafia (1983), 11–13.

[258] Boso, consecrated first Bishop of Cefalù in 1166, but found as bishop-elect from 1157 onwards. His consecration had been delayed by the dubious canonical status of King Roger's foundation; White (1938), 195–8 and pp. 9–10 above. He is last attested in February 1172; Cusa, *I Diplomi greci ed arabi*, 487–8. The town of Cefalù belonged to the bishop.

[259] 'Set over the town is a mountain, on whose large circular summit is a fortress, than which I have never seen any more formidable'; Broadhurst, *The Travels of Ibn Jubayr*, 344. A castellan of Cefalù, John of S. Stephano, witnessed the February 1172 charter of Bishop Boso (see note 258).

many arguments he persuaded Ansaldus's associate Constantine, who was now solely responsible for guarding the palace, to make all the palace servants (of whom there were about forty) take an oath that on a particular day which he had announced to them they should slay the chancellor as he arrived at court, between the first and the second gate, together with John of Lavardin and Count Roger of Avellino.[260] So the conspirators were again aroused to hope and audacity, and the city suffered from division into factions and support for different sides. In addition, a number of men who were used to violence, who lived around the Via Coperta and in the upper part of the Via Marmorea, saw the fighting and disputes that arose among the *familiares* of the court and conspired among themselves, not because they were moved by support for one party or the other, but in the hope of booty. They took an oath to attack whichever side should first be under threat. They hoped that this would be the chancellor, because they thought that a great deal of money was stored in his house, and they believed that they could achieve what they wanted better and more easily there.

Caught in these uncertainties and dangers, the chancellor decided to ask the castellan Ansaldus what he thought ought best to be done in such a major crisis. His advice was this: that he should ignore the date set by the astrologers and retreat to some well-defended place in Sicily, summon both the North Italians and any others he knew to be loyal to him, assemble as large an army as possible, and wait for the king to join him there. For if he were to stay at Palermo any longer he would be unlikely to survive the serious plots his enemies were hatching.[261] But the view which prevailed was that of Count Robert of Meulan and of the other Frenchmen.[262] Because they had no idea of how clever the conspirators were or of the way the court

---

260 See above, notes 80 and 167.

261 Ansaldus himself did survive the chancellor's fall. He was in Palermo in February 1170 when Bishop Gentile of Agrigento granted him the right to build a church in his diocese; Collura, *Più antiche carte*, 49–53, no. 20; and in April 1171 he gave a house in Messina to the Holy Sepulchre at Jerusalem; Brese-Bautier, *Cartulaire du Saint Sépulcre*, 306–7, no. 157. He died later in that same year; White (1938), 172, 174, 229.

262 Robert II of Meulan in Normandy (Count 1166–1203) was the son of Count Waleran of Meulan and nephew of Earl Robert of Leicester (d. 1168), Henry II of England's justiciar, and a cousin of Archbishop Rotrou of Rouen. He may well have stopped in Sicily on his way to the Holy Land.

worked, they said that it was safer to stay at Palermo, and that the chancellor ought not to go anywhere without the king. They did not realise that traps can nowhere be laid more easily than in the palace itself, where no one is allowed to protect himself with weapons or knights.

When the planned day came the palace servants, expecting the chancellor to go up to the court that morning as usual, stood ready by the gate to let him in with a few others while keeping his knights outside. When Odo, the master of the stable, realised what they were planning, he quickly came down from the palace and told the chancellor about the danger that was hanging over him. The chancellor kept a few of his friends by him, and ordered the knights and sentries who had been assembling outside his residence in order to accompany him to court to go away. When the castellan Constantine realised that his intended plan had failed, he sent out several of the palace servants whom he knew were best known to the citizens, assigning them to the different regions of the city, and told them to make a proclamation summoning all citizens to take up arms and to lay siege to the chancellor's residence, since he had got both ships and the royal treasure ready and was planning to flee. With the city confused by these rumours, Hervey 'the Florid' (who was suspect to the palace personnel not so much because of his friendship with the chancellor as because he always talked so much about himself) and Count Roger of Avellino kept riding up and down outside the palace. When the supporters of Caid Richard and several other men who had arrived there with their weapons saw Hervey, they attacked him, threw him from his horse and stabbed him with their swords. Then they went after the count. When they got to the level area adjoining the palace outside the city gate, he had no further chance of escape, and they were already levelling their spears at him when the king, who had gone to the palace windows to see what all the noise was about, shouted out and made all sorts of threats against them if they did not bring the count to him alive and unharmed. Thus their attack was with some difficulty brought under control. Since he could not set the count free in any other way, the king ordered him to be kept under close guard in the Sea Castle.

At this point the court archers – who never seemed to be the last to appear on the scene at disorders just so long as there was any hope of gain – together with those I have mentioned above as involved in the plot, and a great crowd of other people who had gathered, were surrounding the chancellor's residence. Simon of Poitiers, into whose care the residence had been entrusted, positioned the knights and footsoldiers around the length of the wall in suitable places, protecting individual points with the appropriate defenders. But the suddenness of the mob's attack had kept the greatest part of the knights outside. When the chancellor saw how dangerous the situation had become, he retreated together with a number of noblemen whom he did not permit to leave his side through the church which stood next to his residence into the bell-tower which, towering as it did over the level ground, provided a particularly solid defence. Those who were always at his side as particularly close friends were Carbonellus and Bohemond of Tarsia,[263] William of San Severino, Alduin *Cantuensis*, Hugh Lupinus[264] and Count Robert of Meulan, with a number of French knights.

Meanwhile the Master Constable Roger of Tiron arrived with his knights, and fiercely attacked the men he came across there. But the size of the crowd which was gathering had become immense, and they took up their weapons in response and attacked him equally fiercely, forcing both him and his knights to flee. Then they began to attack the chancellor's residence – the circuit of which was great – from all sides and with all the force at their disposal. But the besieged not only fought back just as fiercely from the particular positions that had been assigned to them; they even opened the gates several times and sallied out, pushing back the entire multitude with great bravery and forcing them to position themselves further away. The notary Matthew and Caid Richard also left the places in which they had been shut up and restored themselves to their previous position of dignity, without anyone opposing them. They summoned their slave orchestra and told them to sound their trumpets and drums outside the chancellor's residence. When the entire city – both the Muslims and the Christians – heard the recognised signal for battle, they assumed that it was being made on the king's orders, and they soon ran up with a great deal of noise and shouting and began to attack with even greater violence. When they saw that they could get nowhere with further attacks, they finally piled up a great heap of firewood by the

---

263 Sons of Count Bohemond I of Manopello, cf. note 224 above.
264 Count of Catanzaro through his marriage to the heiress Countess Clementia (note 61 above). He was Master Justiciar of Calabria, the Val di Crati and Val di Sinni; Jamison (1967), 336; Takayama (1993), 218.

door of the church and decided to set it on fire. When the doors had been reduced to ashes and an entry cleared, several of the chancellor's knights, whose unqualified courage extinguished their fear of danger, took up positions against anyone who tried to enter. They fought long and with extreme fortitude; one side was supplied with strength and bravery by pressing necessity, the others were furious that so few men could resist the onslaught of such a great multitude. But in the end numbers prevailed, though with difficulty, and the knights retreated to the bell-tower in a state of exhaustion. The mob had a free passage through the church to the chancellor's residence; the knights and footsoldiers who had looked after the defence of the walls were quickly captured and handed over bound to the castellans of the palace. Any whom they still found resisting from more strongly defensible positions were made to surrender on good terms.

Thence they returned to capture the bell-tower. Many of them were now wounded, and their fierce attacks were achieving nothing. They considered various possibilities. Some thought that they should pile up an enormous mass of wood and set it alight (for the bell-tower was constructed of the kind of stones that could be easily broken up by fire); others that siege-engines should be brought up as quickly as possible; others that mantlets should be brought up and the bell-tower's foundations undermined. In the meantime the king wanted to leave the palace at his mother's behest to try to make the people end the siege; but the notary Matthew and the other conspirators who were there forbade him from setting off, telling him that it was not safe for him to go there because of the hail of arrows and stones that was flying all around. Since they saw that there was no way in which the bell-tower could be captured that day, they were afraid that if the affair were to drag on until the following day the mob's spirits would cool off, or that led by remorse they would abandon what they had started when they saw how it displeased the king.

So they decided to offer the chancellor terms: if he swore to leave Sicily alone, he would be allowed to cross the seas freely to whatever country he chose. Messengers were sent to put these conditions to him, and in the end it was agreed that the chancellor should sail to Syria in an armed galley with a few men he would choose, while the Count of Meulan and the other Frenchmen were to be given ships to cross the sea. Further, those noblemen of the kingdom of Sicily who were with him in the bell-tower were to keep their estates securely and freely, and the knights in his pay[265] were granted the choice either of remaining in the employment of the court or going to any other place they pleased. That this would be done without trickery was sworn by Richard, Bishop-Elect of Syracuse, the notary Matthew, Caid Richard, Archbishop Romuald of Salerno and Bishop John of Malta; and they had a galley made ready that very night. In the morning they brought the chancellor out of the bell-tower with a few companions and took him down to the harbour at Capo Gallo. When he was going on board the galley, the canons of the cathedral of Palermo who were present asked him to release them from the oath of loyalty they had taken to him; he pretended not to know what they meant, and said nothing. Then the courtiers[266] began with words of friendly advice, going on to demand more threateningly and violently that he should renounce his election and give the canons the opportunity to chose a new pastor. He saw that an armed multitude was seething round about him, the knights were in uproar and the great men angered; and while not giving the impression that he had abandoned hope of returning, he renounced his election under the pressure of fear.

He was soon aboard ship and ordered the galley to stand off from the shore, apprehensive of the crowd that was gathering there in vast numbers. The courtiers returned to the bell-tower and brought out the count of Meulan and the other Frenchmen. They feared a spontaneous attack by the mob as well as the arrival of the men of Messina, and forced them to stay in the two *castella* of Partinico and Carini for the time being, until they had arranged ships for them to set sail.[267] The chancellor left the harbour as soon as he could, sailed round the southern part of Sicily past the territory of Marsala, and reached Licata,[268] a fortress which lies in the territory of Agrigento. Here necessity forced him to land. He sent the Bishop of Malta (who had been given to him as a guide) on ahead to tell the townsfolk in the

---

265 *Milites stipendiarii*: paid knights had long been used in Southern Italy; e.g. the garrison of Petralia in NE Sicily was partly composed of *stipendiarii* as early as 1062; *Malaterra* II. 20, p. 35. Cf. *Al. Tel.* III. 23, pp. 71–2, for paid knights among the garrison of Naples in 1135.

266 *Curie familiares* (Siragusa edn, 160). The reference here seems not to be to the chief ministers.

267 Carini, 15 km. W. of Palermo; Partinico, 22 km. W. of Palermo.

268 38 km. E. of Agrigento. Edrisi described it as 'a fortress built on top of a rock which is surrounded by the sea and the river'; *BAS* i, 19.

king's name not to do anything to hinder him. His ship had been damaged by a storm at sea, its timbers were coming apart, and it was threatening to founder. When it could not be satisfactorily repaired in a short space of time (and the chancellor was not allowed to spend more then three days there without incurring the certain death penalty), he bought a merchant ship, which happened to be on the same shore, from the people of Genoa, hired the crew and journeyed safely to Syria.[269]

Meanwhile Bishop Gentile of Agrigento, who had been sent to the Val Demone, was recalled and made a *familiaris* of the court. Count Henry of Montescaglioso and Count Richard of Molise arrived at Palermo with twenty-three armed galleys from Messina. They used their power to change the situation at court, and appointed the following ten *familiares*: Richard, the Bishop-Elect of Syracuse; Bishop Gentile of Agrigento; Archbishop Romuald of Salerno; Bishop John of Malta; Count Roger of Gerace; Richard of Molise; Count Henry of Montescaglioso; the notary Matthew; Caid Richard; and Walter, Dean of Agrigento, who was the king's teacher.[270]

With the court constituted thus, the first decision to be taken was that Count Gilbert of Gravina should be expelled from the realm together with his son Count Bertram, safe and unharmed so long as he voluntarily obeyed these orders of the court. But if he should presume to resist, making use of force and summoning his knights, then he should be dealt with as an enemy, and attacked as a traitor with the entire force the realm had at its disposal. This matter was assigned to Count Roger of Alba and Richard de Say, Count of Fondi. They assembled an enormous army from all the cities of Apulia and besieged Count Gilbert in a certain fortress to which he had retreated together with his wife. All his knights had deserted him as soon as they heard the court's order. He had attracted a great deal of jealousy

269 The Genoese treaty with Barbarossa in 1162 had, not surprisingly, had a disastrous effect on trade with Sicily, but by 1168 negotiations had begun to end the conflict; Belgrano, *Annali Genovesi* i, 213; though a final peace was only secured in 1174; Abulafia (1977), 137. Clearly some trade was taking place before then.

270 The former archdeacon of Cefalù (cf. note 88 above). He must have been appointed to his new post before December 1166, by which time Cefalù had a new archdeacon; *Documenti inediti*, 93–4, no. 40; though the first record of him as Dean of Agrigento comes only in March 1167; Garofolo, *Tabularium* 24–5, no. 10; Kamp (1973–82), iii, 1115.

from the nobility and extreme hatred from the cities, and realised that there was no hope left to him; so he chose to submit himself and his property to Richard, Count of Fondi, on the condition of being allowed to cross over to Syrian territory with his wife and children.[271]

After his expulsion, the magnates of the court also decided to exile Count Hugh of Catanzaro, since he was a relative of the Chancellor's. But because he was a stupid and violent man whom they feared as someone who would plot in secret or else undertake some daring act on impulse, they preferred to spare him, hoping that by this very action they would do something to restrain the queen's anger a little.[272] A few days later Walter, the Dean of Agrigento, hired a mob and by frightening the canons, with the consent of the court, took over the administration of the Church of Palermo, more as a result of violent occupation than of election. More than anything else this put an end to the hopes of those who supported the chancellor, as well as of the queen herself. They had been hoping that the Roman pontiff would not accept the legitimacy of what had occurred, since it was common knowledge that the chancellor had renounced his election under pressure of threats to his life, and not of his own free will. No judge would consider what had happened as a result of force or threats as legitimate. No one doubted that there had been such cause for fear that it would have affected even the most constant person, and there was no lack of witnesses for such a public incident. Furthermore Peter of Gaeta, subdeacon of the Roman Curia, had clearly promised that the present election would be invalid, and he had accepted 700 ounces of gold to be taken to the Roman pontiff on the queen's behalf and behest. But

271 Cf. *Annales Casinenses* ad ann. 1168, MGH SS xix, 312. Richard de Say and Richard of Alba profited directly from their actions, since they acquired the counties of Gravina and Andria which had been held by Gilbert and Bertram. Richard of Alba held Andria until his death in 1190, when it escheated to the crown, and his son (who survived him) never held the comital title; Cuozzo (1981), 138–9. Gravina, however, continued in the hands of Richard de Say's descendants even after the conquest by Henry VI; his grandson William was count in 1210; Hagemann 'Kaiserurkunden aus Gravina', 196–7, no. 3.

272 His sons, Hugh and Jordan, both became counts under Tancred. Hugh the younger became Count of Conversano and Master Justiciar of Apulia and Terra di Lavoro; Zielinski, *Tancredi et Willelmi III Regum Diplomata*, 52–3, no. 22 (1191). Jordan, who was already the royal seneschal under William II (*Documenti inediti*, 214–16, no. 88 (1187)), became Count of Bovino, but was executed by Henry VI in 1197; Jamison (1957), 87–9, 157–9.

the opposite faction, whose views prevailed, stated that the Roman Curia was in a situation where it would not dare to oppose the wishes of the Sicilian nobility, and that in the critical situation it was in, would not hesitate to accept the huge sum of money offered to it to confirm the election. So after taking a few days to consider the matter, so that his decision would not appear precipitate, the pope finally declared the election valid and ordered the archbishop-elect to be consecrated by his suffragans.[273] Raised to such a great height, he immediately altered the composition of the court, keeping supreme power in his own hands, and making the notary Matthew and Bishop Gentile of Agrigento *familiares* under him.[274]

In the same year, on the 4th of February,[275] about the first hour of the same day, a terrible earthquake shook Sicily with such force that it was even felt in Calabria, around Reggio and nearby cities. The extremely wealthy city of Catania suffered such destruction that not a single house survived within the city. About 15,000 men and women

273 Pseudo-Hugo was here being economical with the truth. Alexander only ordered Walter's consecration on 22 June 1169, by which time Stephen of Perche was almost certainly dead; MPL cc. 591, ep. 620 (= *Italia Pontificia* x, 232–3, no. 32). His *pallium* (the symbol of his authority as metropolitan) was to be bestowed on him at the ceremony by Cardinal John of Naples, frequently mentioned in these pages (cf. Romuald, p. 243 below). The consecration took place on 28 September 1169; Pirro, *Sicula Sacra* i, 105.

274 Again this comment obscures the time-scale involved in such changes. In February 1169 there were seven *familiares*: Walter (as Archbishop-Elect of Palermo), Richard, Bishop-Elect of Syracuse, Gentile of Agrigento, Matthew the notary, Count Richard of Molise, Caid Richard and Caid Martin (not one of the ten mentioned earlier). In May 1169 there were still six: all of the above except Richard of Syracuse; Pratesi, *Carte latine di abbazie calabresi* 60–2, no. 23; *Documenti inediti* 109–12, nos. 47–8. The triumvirate mentioned by the *History* can only be found in the documentary sources from October 1170; and Gentile died during the summer of 1171; Takayama (1993), 120–1. Richard of Molise described himself still as a royal *familiaris* in a charter of November 1170, issued from the medicinal baths of Pozzuoli; Pergamene Aldobrandini, Cartolario II, no. 21. This is, however, the last known reference to him, and he may therefore have been in failing health and have died soon afterwards.

275 This shows that Pseudo-Hugo calculated the beginning of the year from March. By modern reckoning the earthquake was on 4 February 1169.

together with the bishop of that city and most of the monks were crushed under collapsing buildings.[276] At Lentini,[277] a fine town belonging to the Syracusans, the weight of collapsing buildings shaken by the same earthquake killed most of the townspeople. Many fortresses were also destroyed in the territory of the Catanians and Syracusans. In a number of places the earth gaped open and produced new watercourses while closing up some old ones, and that part of the summit of Etna which faces Taormina seemed to sink down a little. At Syracuse the very famous spring called Arethusa, which according to legend brings its water to Sicily by secret channels from the city of Elis in Greece, changed from a trickle to a great flow, and its water turned salty because of the amount of sea water mixed up in it.[278] A spring called Tais which rises from Piedemonte near Casale Saraceno, which has a copious outflow, was blocked up for a period of two hours, retaining all its waters, and then broke out in an enormous torrent, and for the space of one hour it presented the amazed locals with the spectacle of water the colour of blood. At Messina the sea, when it was extremely smooth, first drew back upon itself and retreated a little from the shore, then gradually returned

276 The bishop was John, the brother of Matthew the notary (see above, note 191). The see of Catania had a monastic chapter, in the Benedictine cathedral monastery of St Agatha, and a contemporary poem recorded that forty-four of the monks died in this disaster; White (1938), 115. Peter of Blois wrote exultantly to his brother, Abbot William of Matina, that 'the city of Catania was struck by an earthquake in revenge for the lord Stephen [of Perche], in which that son of pride, the brother of the notary Matthew, who fraudulently supplanted you as bishop and raised up treasonous faction against the innocent, was trapped and overthrown, and this servant of evil and slave of Satan rendered up his soul'; MPL ccvii, 293, ep. 93. It should, however, be remembered that William had been the disappointed candidate for the see. A new bishop-elect, Robert, was recorded in February 1170; *Documenti inediti*, 120, no. 52.
277 35 km. NW of Syracuse.
278 A legend, widespread in antiquity, derived from the story of the nymph Arethusa's flight from Greece to Sicily to avoid an importunate suitor, and her transformation there by the goddess Diana into a spring. The water supposedly flowing from Greece represented her suitor's continued pursuit of her. See e.g. Vergil, *Aeneid* 3.694–6; Ovid, *Metamorphoses* 5.639–41. The fountain was described by Cicero, *In Verrem* 2.4.53, who said that it would be swamped by the sea but for its protective walls. It was depicted symbolically on fo. 142r of the MS. of Peter of Eboli's poem, *Liber ad Honorem Augusti*, 147.

and crossed the previous shoreline, lapping at the city walls and even flowing in through the gates.[279] The officials of the court and their supporters were frightened by these and other portents, and they thought that these unprecedented happenings foretold great calamities for Sicily. They were afraid that the chancellor, with the support and advice of the emperor at Constantinople, who, so it was reported, had received his legates in a friendly way, would gather a force together and occupy their kingdom of Sicily. And there was no doubt that many of the king's own counts and barons keenly awaited his arrival. They also thought that Count Robert of Loritello would be certain to follow the wishes and orders of the queen, through whose efforts he had recently been recalled from exile.[280]

While they were preparing themselves with many policies and schemes against any of these eventualities, an irrefutable report suddenly reached the court that the chancellor had died,[281] which utterly depressed the queen's spirits and raised the opposition to such a sense of strength and security that they thought that they would never again have any difficulty or danger to fear. Thus the supreme power in the realm and control of its affairs was in the hands of Archbishop Walter of Palermo, who won the king's friendship (which had previously been in doubt) to such an extent that he seemed to be in control not so much of the court as of the king himself.[282]

---

[279] Cf. the *Annales Pisani* (Lupo Gentiles, 47), which also mentioned the retreat of the sea in the Straits of Messina: 'From the time of Sodom and Gomorrah, there had not occurred such amazing and incredible wonders as happened on the island of Sicily.'

[280] In March 1169; *Annales Ceccanenses*, MGH SS xix, 286.

[281] His death soon after his arrival in the Holy Land was also noted by William of Tyre, *History of Events beyond the Sea* (Babcock and Krey, 346–7) (bk. XX. 3), who described Stephen as 'a young man of fine appearance and excellent natural ability'.

[282] Archbishop Walter remained as the senior *familiaris*, whose name always appeared first in the dating clauses of royal diplomas, until the death of William II. His brother Bishop Bartholomew of Agrigento was also one of the three or four *familiares* from 1171 to 1175 and again from 1184 to 1188; Takayama (1993), 120–2.

ADDITIONAL TEXTS

Romuald of Salerno, *Chronicon sive Annales*, 1153–69[1]

Meanwhile King Roger possessed his realm in peace and tranquillity. Since in neither peace nor war did he know how to be idle, he ordered a very beautiful palace to be built at Palermo, in which he constructed a chapel floored in astonishing stone, which he covered with a gilded roof, and endowed and beautified with various ornaments.[2] And so that this great man should at no time be without the pleasures afforded by either land or water, he had a large quantity of earth excavated and removed at a place which was called Favara, and there created a delightful lake which he ordered to be stocked with different types of fish, brought from many different regions. He had another beautiful and splendid palace constructed next to this lake. He had some of the hills and woods which are round about Palermo enclosed with a stone wall, and ordered a delightful and well-stocked park made, planted with all sorts of trees, and in it he had deer, roebucks and wild boars kept. And he had a palace built in this park to which he ordered water to be brought by underground pipes from a particularly clear spring.

So this wise and careful man enjoyed these pleasures as the nature of the season suggested. For in winter, and in Lent because of its profusion of fish, he lived at the Favara palace; while in the summer he made the fiery season's heat bearable at the park, and diverted his mind from the strain of his many cares by enjoying a moderate amount of hunting. And although the king himself was possessed of great wisdom, intelligence and judgement, he also gathered men of good sense of different classes from the various parts of the earth and made them partners in his decisions. For he brought George, a man of mature wisdom, foresight and care, from Antioch, and made him great admiral [*magnus ammiratus*], and through his advice and prudence he obtained many

---

[1] Translated from *Romuald*, 232–58.

[2] The Palatine chapel was formally founded in April 1140; *Rogerii II Diplomata*, 133–7, no. 48. However, construction may have begun as early as 1132; Demus (1950), 25–6.

victories on land and sea.³ He appointed learned and prudent clerics, Guarin and Robert, in succession as his chancellor.⁴ And if he could find honest and wise men, whether from his own land or born elsewhere, laymen or clerics, he ordered them to be at his side, and promoted them to honours and riches as each man's status suggested. Finally he made Maio, a young man originating from Bari, who was both fluent of speech and prudent and careful, first *scrinarius*, then vice-chancellor and eventually chancellor. He created many new counts in his kingdom, and had the city of Cefalù built, in which he had the splendid and beautiful church of the Holy Saviour constructed at his own expense, to which he made the city subject and assigned its service.⁵

Towards the end of his life, allowing secular matters to be neglected and delayed, he laboured in every conceivable way to convert Jews and Muslims to the faith of Christ, and endowed converts with many gifts and resources. He ordered the church of St Nicholas, Messina, to be built, in large part at his own expense, although it could not be completed in his lifetime.⁶ He had a silver panel, made at his own expense, placed before the altar of St Matthew in Salerno as a memorial to his name, and every time he came to Salerno from Sicily he customarily offered one or two precious cloths to the Salernitan church. But 'since it is impossible to remain for very long at the summit',⁷ and as punishment for the sins of the whole kingdom, after so many victories and successes the most glorious King Roger died of a fever

---

3 George had previously been in the service of the ruler of Mahdia, and had emigrated to Sicily c. 1108. He was Emir of Emirs from 1132 onwards; Amari (1933–9), iii, 368–71.

4 Guarin was chancellor from 1132 and died in January 1137; *Chron. Cas.* IV.101, pp. 563–4. His successor, Robert, was an Englishman from Selby in Yorkshire, who died c. 1151. For him, see Millor, Butler and Brooke, *The Letters of John of Salisbury*, i, 57–8, no. 33, and John of Salisbury, *Policraticus*, ed. C.C.J. Webb (2 vols., Oxford 1909), ii, 173–4.

5 Most of this church was built between 1131 and 1148, although the west front was not finished until the thirteenth century; White (1938), 189, 201; Demus (1950), 3–24.

6 A new cathedral for the city, built on a different site from that founded by Roger I (for which *Malaterra*, III.32, p. 77). Roger II's foundation was only consecrated in 1197, at which time its dedication was changed to the Blessed Virgin Mary; Starrabba, *I diplomi della cattedrale di Messina*, 43, no. 32 (= Clementi, 'Calendar of the diplomas of Henry VI', 131, no. 210).

7 Lucan, *De Bello Civili*, 1.70.

at Palermo and was buried in the cathedral of that city, in the fifty-eighth year of his life, the second month and fifth day, on the 27th of February, in the twenty-fourth year of his reign, in the year from the Lord's Incarnation 1152,[8] first of the indiction. King Roger was large of stature, corpulent, leonine of face, somewhat hoarse of voice; wise, far-seeing, careful, subtle of mind, great in counsel, preferring to use his intelligence rather than force. He was very concerned to gain money, hardly very prodigal in expending it, fierce in public but in private kindly, generous with honours and rewards to those faithful to him, but inflicting injuries and punishments on those disloyal. He was more feared than loved by his subjects, dreaded and feared by the Greeks and Muslims.

On the death of King Roger his son William, who had reigned with his father for two years and ten months, succeeded him in the government of the kingdom. After the death of his father he summoned the magnates of his kingdom and was solemnly crowned at the next Easter.[9] Robert de Basonville, Count of Conversano, the king's first cousin, was present at this court. King William gave him the County of Loritello and sent him honourably back to Apulia. Afterwards he appointed the chancellor Maio as great admiral and handled almost all the kingdom's business through his advice and foresight.[10]

Meanwhile Pope Anastasius died round about Christmas in the year from the Lord's Incarnation 1154.[11] He was succeeded by Nicholas, an Englishman, who was first a canon regular and Abbot of St Ruf, and afterwards Bishop of Albano, and who was called Adrian IV.[12] On hearing this King William sent envoys to him to make peace, but was unable to obtain this. Afterwards, round about Lent, the king

8 Actually 1154.

9 Easter Sunday 1154 fell on 4 April. For William's coronation as co-king in his father's lifetime, see the *History* (above), note 8.

10 The earliest documentary evidence of Maio as Great Admiral/Emir of Emirs was in October 1154; *Guillelmi I Diplomata*, 7–8, no. 2.

11 3 December 1154; Duchesne, *Liber Pontificalis*, ii, 389.

12 Nicholas Breakespear, from Abbot's Langley near St Albans, the only English pope. He had been Abbot of St Ruf from 1147, Cardinal Bishop of Albano from January 1150 and papal legate to Scandinavia in 1152; Poole (1934), 291–5; Zenker (1964), 36–8. William of Newburgh described him as 'sharp of mind and ready of tongue' in his *Historia Rerum Anglicarum*, ed. R. Howlett (2 vols., Rolls Series 1884), i, 110.

came to Salerno and stayed there until Easter.[13] On ascertaining this, Pope Adrian sent Henry, Cardinal [priest] of SS. Nereus and Achilles,[14] to the king, but the latter refused to receive him and ordered him to return to Rome. This was because, in the apostolic letters which he was bringing to the king, the pope called him not king, but 'William lord of Sicily'. As a result Pope Adrian and the whole Roman curia were roused and much annoyed with the king.

After celebrating the Easter feast the king committed the administration of Apulia to Asclettin, Archdeacon of Catania, whom he had made chancellor, and returned to Sicily with the admiral. On the king's instructions the chancellor gathered a mighty army and besieged Benevento, devastating the territory up to the walls. The citizens of that town resisted him manfully, and they killed their archbishop, Peter,[15] whom they suspected of being a royal partisan. After the city had been besieged for some time, some of the barons rebelled and, entering the city, joined the enemy. Others left the army and returned home without permission. So the army was broken up and the city freed from siege. Count Robert of Loritello abandoned the king, regretfully and unwillingly, fearing that the monarch would have him arrested on the suggestion of the admiral, who hated him. Indeed many of the barons of Apulia rebelled, and stirred up a great war [*guerram*] there. Hearing this the Sicilian barons similarly made war against the king on the island. However, the king gathered an army and marched against them. Fearing to stand in wait for him, the rebels shut themselves up in Butera, and after he had besieged them there for some time, on the advice of Maio the admiral he pardoned them, and received them back into his grace. Then, the next summer, Frederick, the King of the Germans, came to Rome and after taking

13 Ash Wednesday 1155 was on 9 February, and Easter on 27 March.

14 A Cistercian, originally from Pisa, formerly Abbot of Tre Fontani, just outside Rome, promoted to the Curia by his fellow-Cistercian Eugenius III. He was Cardinal priest of SS. Nereus and Achilles from 1151 to 1166; Zenker (1964), 96–101. He was later legate to Germany in 1158, where Rahewin described him as a man 'of prudence in secular affairs' and well qualified to deal with matters of state; Mierow, *Deeds of Frederick Barbarossa*, 194. He and William of Pavia were legates in France in 1159, where Arnulf of Lisieux recorded that 'the people were amazed by their sanctity, and every cleric applauded their wisdom'; Barlow, *The Letters of Arnulf of Lisieux*, 48, no. 29.

15 Archbishop of Benevento 1147–55.

the customary oath, was solemnly crowned by Pope Adrian in the church of St Peter.[16] Before receiving the crown he had promised the pope that he would depose the newly created senators, and restore the City and the *regalia* of St Peter to his [Adrian's] power. But he only remained in the City for a very short time after his coronation and then returned to Germany.[17]

After having been let down in this way, the pope raised an army, entered the Terra di Lavoro along with Prince Robert of Capua and Andrew of Rupecanina, seized it by force and was honourably welcomed by the Beneventans. Meanwhile Manuel, the Emperor of Constantinople, took the opportunity to take revenge for those injuries which he had received from King Roger on the latter's son, and sent a nobleman called Palaeologos with a large sum of money to Count Robert and the barons of Apulia that they might employ knights [*milites retinerent*] with it and make war against King William. He also sent *Comminianus, Sebastos*[18] and other important men with his fleet, who arrived at Brindisi and captured all of it except the citadel in which the royal soldiers had taken refuge. Bari and the other coastal cities went over to the Greeks and Count Robert. So it occurred that the whole land was occupied, partly by Prince Robert of Capua and partly by Count Robert, except for Naples, Amalfi, Salerno, Troia, Melfi and a few other cities and fortified *castra*.

On realising this King William gathered his forces as best he could by land and sea, and came directly to Brindisi. There he found *Sebastos* and *Comminianus* and the other important Greeks along with a mighty army and fleet fiercely attacking the citadel of Brindisi and the king's people. Learning of the king's arrival, Count Robert left Brindisi and went to Benevento. King William closely besieged Brindisi by land and sea, and attacked fiercely on both sides. His sword was triumphant,

16   18 June 1155; Mierow, *Deeds of Frederick Barbarossa*, 150.
17   The emperor turned northwards on or shortly after 24 July, according to Otto of Freising because of sickness in his army, but there had previously been bitter fighting with the Romans, with heavy casualties on both sides; Mierow, *Deeds of Frederick Barbarossa*, 150–2; Güterbock, *Otto Morena*, 29–31.
18   Our author clearly had severe problems with Byzantine names and titles. The Greek commanders were Alexius Comnenus (first cousin of the Emperor Manuel and son of the historian Anna Comnena and Nicephorus Bryennius) and John Dukas. Both men held the court rank of *sebastos*; Brand, *Deeds of John and Manuel Comnenus by John Cinnamus*, 106, 126.

and he captured the Greek nobles, their fleet and war-chest, and many of the barons of Apulia and men who had rebelled against him.[19] He had many of them hanged or blinded. After doing this he came to Bari and captured it, and since the Bariots had destroyed the royal citadel, the king was filled with anger and razed the city to the ground. Then returning along the coast of Apulia he captured all the coastal cities and recovered all the land which he had lost without a battle. He himself went straight to Benevento, where his rebel enemies had fled to seek help from the pope. Prince Robert of the Capuans tried to escape because of his fear of the king, but while he was crossing the River Garigliano, Count Richard of Fondi, who was a vassal [*homo*] of this same prince, captured him in an ambush and delivered him over to the king's officers. Through this act of treachery he thereafter recovered the king's grace, which he had lost. The king sent the prince to be kept in prison in Sicily. On the pope's plea, he allowed Count Robert, Andrew of Rupecanina and the rest of his enemies who had taken refuge with the lord pope in Benevento to go free and unharmed, and to leave the kingdom with their goods.

He then came to an agreement with the pope, after many envoys had gone between them and the details of the peace-treaty had been debated back and forth. Pope Adrian and the cardinals came to the church of St Marcianus, which is near the River Calore. There King William humbly approached his feet, and the pope received him kindly. As was customary, he took an oath and became the liege man of the pope, and the pope invested him with the kingdom of Sicily with one banner, with the duchy of Apulia with another and with the principality of Capua with a third. For love of King William and on the intervention and prayers of Maio the admiral and Archbishop Hugh of Palermo, he made the churches of Agrigento and Mazzara, which belonged to the special jurisdiction of the Roman Church, subject to the church of Palermo, and granted that the bishops of these churches should be in perpetuity suffragans of this same church.[20] After doing this Pope Adrian returned to the Campagna. The king expelled many of his enemies from the kingdom, sent some to prison, and received some

19 For the capture of the Byzantine generals (28 May 1156), *ibid.*, 129–30. A royal diploma of July 1156 claimed that William I had ordered the Greek commanders to be 'laden with chains and trussed up like chickens'; *Guillelmi I Diplomata*, 36–7, no. 13.

20 Kehr, *Italia Pontificia* x, 231, no. 27 (= MPL clxxxviii, 1471, no. 103 (10 July 1156)). The Bishop of Malta was also made subject to Palermo.

back into his grace and love. Then he appointed Simon the seneschal, the brother-in-law of Maio the admiral, as Master Captain of Apulia; he himself, after securing this great triumph, returned with the admiral to Sicily.

Not long afterwards he prepared a mighty fleet and sent it with Stephen the admiral to Romania. Coming to the Euripus,[21] he found a huge fleet of the Emperor Manuel ready there. He fought manfully and defeated it, captured many of the Greeks, burnt their fleet, plundered the Euripus and the cities round about, and thus returned victoriously to Sicily.[22] Learning that many of his men had been captured by the King of Sicily and that he could not fight him on equal terms, the emperor sent a series of envoys and came to an agreement with the king, and so a treaty of peace was sworn between them.

At this time the Almohads came from Morocco and conquered all the land right up to Africa [Tunisia] at sword-point. The African city [Mahdia] was then still in King William's power, and he had placed many knights and infantry there for its guard and defence. The Almohads besieged it both by land and sea, and the Christians who were there resisted them manfully, nor were they in any way fearful of them, except that they were suffering from a great shortage of food. Realising this, King William instructed his fleet, which he had sent to Spain, to be immediately recalled, ordering it to hasten to the relief of Africa as fast as it could. Caid Peter, the king's eunuch, who was in command of the fleet, came to Africa and fought with the fleet of the Almohads, but was driven back in flight and lost many of his galleys. Since the Christians who were left in Africa could secure no assistance and were all but out of supplies, they made peace with the Almohads, abandoned the African city, and returned to Sicily with their property.

During his father's lifetime, while he was Prince of the Capuans,[23]

---

21 The strait between the northern coast of Attica and the island of Euboea. 'Romania' was the usual Western term for the Byzantine Empire in the Central Middle Ages.

22 According to the *Annales Pisani*, 17, this expedition comprised 140 galleys and 24 dromons carrying 400 knights. It began in June 1157 and returned in September. This dating is to some extent confirmed by *Guillelmi I Diplomata*, 63, no. 22 (written at Palermo in December 1157), one of the witnesses to which was the Admiral Stephen, Maio's brother.

23 i.e. between his elder brother's death in October 1144 and his coronation as co-king at Easter 1151.

King William had married Margaret, daughter of King Garcia of Navarre, by whom he had several children: Roger, whom he appointed as Duke of Apulia, Robert, whom he made Prince of the Capuans,[24] William and Henry. Hearing, however, that Pope Adrian had come to an agreement with King William and invested him with the kingdom of Sicily and duchy of Apulia, the Emperor Frederick was deeply offended. This was in the year of Our Lord 1157.

At this time the inhabitants of Milan rode against the Lombards and subjected nearly all Lombardy to their rule. As a result the Lombards were stricken by anger and grief and sent envoys to the emperor, begging humbly that he come and free them from the power of the Milanese. Heeding their petition, the emperor gathered a great army and with the King of Bohemia, the Duke of Saxony and his other princes entered Italy in full force. Nearly all the Lombards joined him, and he closely besieged Milan.[25] The Milanese, who were warlike and energetic men, surrounded their city with great ditches and resisted the emperor bravely and manfully. When the emperor had remained for some time at the siege and had been unable to achieve anything against the city by force, he took counsel, received hostages, and came to a peace agreement with them. Not long afterwards the emperor wished to appoint a governor for the city who would rule it in accordance with his will. The Milanese were unable to suffer the Germans' pride, and began to resist [him] and broke the peace-treaty. They marched on the castle [*castrum*] where their hostages were held, captured it and, rescuing the hostages, returned to their city. Hearing this, the emperor was furious, and since he could not easily meet them in pitched battle, he began to destroy their *casalia* and *castra*, to ravage as best he could the land subject to their jurisdiction, and to prevent those other Lombards who were rendering them assistance from providing them with aid. On the urgings of the inhabitants of Cremona he closely besieged the *castrum* of Crema, which the Milanese had been helping as much as they could, and which had been manfully

---

24 Robert was recorded as Prince of Capua between September 1158 and May 1159, while the king was once again ruling directly over the principality, without any nominal intermediary, in February and March 1160; Pergamene Aldobrandini, Cartolario II, no. 13; *Cod. dipl. Aversa*, 126–9, no. 73, 131–2, no. 75, 135–9 nos. 77–8. Robert had presumably died during the intervening period.

25 Frederick entered Italy in July 1158, and began the siege of Milan on 6 August; Güterbock, *Otto Morena*, 46, 53.

resisting the Cremonese, and he did not abandon the siege until he had captured it and razed it to the ground.[26]

Meanwhile Pope Adrian died at Anagni, in the fifth year of his pontificate, in the eight month, on the sixth day, in the year of the Lord's incarnation 1159, thirteenth of the indiction, on the 1st of September.[27] His body was carried to Rome and honourably buried in the church of St Peter. All the cardinals gathered with the bishops in that church, and first unanimously joined in the election of Roland, chancellor of the Roman church and Cardinal of St Mark.[28] He was a religious man who feared God, and thinking of the burden of such a great honour he resisted and refused it as best he could. The bishops and cardinals felt that it would be an insult to the priesthood if he who had been chosen was not appointed, and so they elected the said chancellor, even though he humbly resisted, and named him Pope Alexander III. But the Bishop of Tusculum, with John the Pisan, Cardinal of St Martin, and Guy of Crema,[29] and with the help of certain laymen and of the emperor's envoys the *Pfalzgraf* [Count Palatine] and the Count of Biandrate, who were then in Rome, elected

---

26 The siege of Crema lasted from early July 1159 until 27 January 1160; Güterbock, *Otto Morena*, 69–95.

27 This date is confirmed by the *Liber Pontificalis* ii, 397.

28 He came from an aristocratic Sienese family, became a canon of Pisa, then papal subdeacon from 1148. He was appointed Cardinal deacon of SS. Cosmas and Damian in 1150, had been promoted to be Cardinal priest of St Mark in March 1151 and made chancellor in 1153; Zenker (1964), 85–8.

29 Imar Cardinal Bishop of Tusculum from 1142 to 1162, a Frenchman, formerly Abbot of Montierneuf, near Poitiers. John the Pisan (or 'de Morrone') was Cardinal priest of SS. Martin and Silvester from 1152, previously Archdeacon of Tyre. He was sent by Victor as his legate to France in 1160, and died from a fall from his horse near Viterbo in 1164; Duchesne, *Liber Pontificalis* ii, 419. Guy of Crema was Cardinal deacon of S. Maria in Porticu from 1145, and promoted to be Cardinal priest of S. Maria in Trastevere in March 1158. He was elected as (anti-)pope Paschal III in April 1164. Much involved in papal diplomacy with the empire, he had been one of the leading opponents of the Curia's friendship with Sicily after 1156. See Zenker (1964), 44–6, 56–9, 92–3. Arnulf of Lisieux (a supporter of Alexander) was extremely rude about all three; he described Imar as 'observing only the hours for rest and dinner, reckoned by everyone to be another Epicurus', and Guy as 'denying nothing of the flesh, observing nothing of the sacred canons'; Barlow, *The Letters of Arnulf of Lisieux*, 44–5, no. 29.

Octavian, Cardinal of St Cecilia, and called him Pope Victor.[30] Alexander with the rest of the cardinals and bishops took refuge in the tower of St Peter's. Meanwhile Octavian began to spend a great deal of money in the City, and to call upon the senators and people to support him. With the help of Odo Frangipane[31] and other noblemen, Alexander left the City with the cardinals and bishops and came to Ninfa. There he was solemnly consecrated by Hubald, Bishop of Ostia, and the other bishops and cardinals,[32] and afterwards he came to Terracina. Octavian remained in the City for a little while, but since he was able to achieve very little there, he went into the Campania and stayed at Segni.[33] However, after hearing of Pope Alexander's election, King William sent envoys to him, and he and his kingdom received him as their father and lord.

At this time Count Jonathan of Conza, Count Gilbert of Gravina, Count Bohemond of Manopello, Count Roger of Acerra, Count Philip of Sangro,[34] Count Roger of Tricarico[35] and many barons, with the people of Melfi and Naples and various others, formed a conspiracy against Maio the admiral, alleging that he was a traitor to the king and aspired to lordship over his kingdom. On hearing this King William was extremely angry with them, since he dearly loved the admiral and had absolute confidence in him. He sent many messengers and letters ordering them to abandon this design, since he considered the admiral a faithful and loyal man. But they would not do this, saying that they were unwilling to support the admiral's rule and government any more. For this reason there was fighting and faction throughout Apulia.

30 He came from the Roman family of Monticello, a junior branch of the Counts of Tusculum, and was one of the most senior members of the College of Cardinals; he had been Cardinal deacon of St Nicholas in Carcere from 1138, Cardinal priest of St Cecilia from 1151 and papal legate to Germany in 1151 and again in 1153; Zenker (1964), 66–70, and especially Kehr (1926). The Count Palatine was Otto IV of Wittelsbach.

31 Cf. Duchesne, *Liber Pontificalis* ii, 399; Robinson (1990), 83. The Frangipane were one of the most important noble families of Rome, and Odo, closely linked with the pro-Sicilian party in the *Curia*, had been present at the Treaty of Benevento in 1156 (see below, p. 247).

32 20 September 1159; Duchesne, *Liber Pontificalis* ii, 398–9.

33 Victor IV was consecrated at Farfa on Sunday 4 October.

34 He had replaced Count Simon, for whom see above, p. 69.

35 The son of Count Robert of Caserta. See above, p. 182.

Matthew Bonellus, who had promised to take the admiral's daughter as his wife, along with certain other barons of Sicily, secretly favoured this conspiracy. For he had been promised by the counts that if he should kill the admiral then they would give him as his wife Clementia, Countess of Catanzaro. Spurred on by this expectation and their promise, he began, while pretending loyalty to the king, to plan the admiral's assassination. And although the admiral was warned of this by his friends several times, both because of the relationship which had been agreed between them and because of the many benefits which he had given him, he refused to believe this. On the vigil of St Martin [10 November], as the admiral was returning after nightfall from a visit to the Archbishop of Palermo, Matthew Bonellus lay in ambush along his route, which was next to the gate of St Agatha, came up to him and struck him down with his sword, killing him. That same night he left Palermo and fled to his home territory. On learning this King William was greatly upset and mourned, but since there was rioting in the city because of this, and Matthew Bonellus was a favourite of the mob, he disguised his grief and pretended to treat the admiral's death with equanimity. In consequence he ordered the latter's wife, sons, sisters and brother to be arrested, and all his property seized. After this, and following many people's requests, he received Matthew Bonellus back into favour to a certain extent. However, the barons and many of the people who had been associated with Matthew in this deed, knowing that the king knew all about what had happened and was furious about it, started to be very much afraid that he was waiting for an opportunity to take a savage revenge upon them for their actions. As a result they began to plot secretly among themselves and with certain others how they might seize the king or have him killed.

This is what happened. Before prime, on the fifth day of Lent,[36] as the king was intending to go to hear Mass, the dungeons were opened with the collusion of the castellan and his sergeants. Count William of the Principate, Richard of Mandra, Alexander the monk[37] and many other prisoners rushed out of the dungeons, seized weapons, and

36 9 March.
37 Perhaps the former Count of Conversano, for whom above, *History*, note 93. William III, Count of the Principate from 1146, was not named by Pseudo-Hugo. He was a shadowy figure, last recorded in 1150; Houben (1995), 361–2, no. 128; who had probably been implicated in the 1155–6 revolt.

started to storm the palace. Many of the mercenary troops and the people were associated with the prisoners in this conspiracy, and they began to assist them in attacking the palace. The king was quite ignorant and unaware of this plot, and astonished by such an unexpected event, went to a window in the Pisan tower,[38] and called out to whoever was passing by to come to his aid. But since there was nobody there who would help him, the palace was captured without resistance, and the greater part of it plundered. The king himself was arrested and put in prison, and the queen and her children were honourably guarded in a chamber. The prisoners placed the king's son, Duke Roger of Apulia, on a horse and led him all round the city of Palermo, hoping by this means to quiet the rioting of the people. After doing this the prisoners closed off the palace at nightfall, and would not let anyone enter it without their consent. In the morning, on Friday, they made Duke Roger ride round the city once again. Meanwhile heavy fighting had broken out between the Muslims and Christians of the city, and many of the Muslims were robbed and killed. That night Counts William of the Principate and Tancred of Lecce[39] hurried with certain others to Matthew Bonellus, who was the ringleader of the conspiracy and who was then at Mistretta, and they speedily brought him and his troops to Palermo. They were afraid that, if they delayed for any length of time, then the king, who had been unjustly imprisoned, would, with the help of the people, be taken from their hands, and indeed this is what did occur. On the Saturday, seeing the king unjustly imprisoned and the palace plundered, and expecting matters to get worse, Archbishops Romuald of Salerno and Robert of Messina, Richard, Bishop-Elect of Syracuse and Bishop Turstan of Mazzara started to urge the people to secure the king's release, which is what happened. With their encouragement the people took up arms and made an attack on the palace, warning the prisoners and those who were in the building that unless they freed the king all would perish by the sword. They were indeed stricken with fear, and since they could not expect help and were unable to resist the people, they flung themselves humbly at the king's feet, begging for his grace and mercy. Having obtained this, they went with the king to a window of the Pisan tower. Then the king thanked all the people for his liberation, ordering them all to return

---

38 On the north side of the palace complex.

39 Tancred was only Count of Lecce from 1169; Reisinger (1992), 24. This passage must therefore have been written after that date.

to their own homes and remain there peacefully. The archbishops, bishops and other loyal men went up into the palace and consoled the king, as best they could, for the misfortune which had occurred. Furthermore, another and no less serious cause for lamentation had been added to the king's dismay; for during the attack on the palace to free the king it had happened that his son, Duke Roger of Apulia, had been struck near the eye by an arrow. A few days later he died of this wound.

Hearing of the king's liberation, Matthew Bonellus was greatly grieved, but dissimulated and sent messengers to the king to say that he had been much distressed by his imprisonment and that he had been coming to rescue him with his troops. The king realised his ill-will and complicity, but the state of affairs was such that, concealing this, he replied kindly to these messengers and sent them back with a speech of thanks. However, those who had captured the king and plundered the palace all fled to Matthew Bonellus for fear of the king. Matthew, along with Counts William, Simon and Tancred and many others, went to Favara, and after many messengers had gone back and forth between them and the king, they came to the following agreement. The king in his liberality and grace forgave all of them the offence which they had done him, and restored to Matthew Bonellus and the other barons of Sicily his favour and their lands. He had Counts William, Simon and Tancred, and the many others who were unwilling to remain in the country taken safely and unharmed by galley to Terracina; others he permitted to go to Jerusalem. Fearing that the counts of Apulia, with whom he had been at odds because of the admiral, might rebel, the king sent Archbishop Romuald of Salerno to Apulia with messages granting these same counts his favour and love once again. Arriving there, the archbishop soothed the angry feelings of both the citizens and the counts and barons, urging them vehemently to love and fealty towards the king, to such an extent that they all wanted to travel to Sicily and avenge the injury done to him.

However, at Easter the king wrote to these counts ordering them to abjure the oaths which they had made, and this they were quite unwilling to do. But despairing of recovering the king's grace, all except Count Gilbert and Count Bohemond went to Count Robert of Loritello, did homage to him, and with him began the invasion and occupation of the king's land. Roger Sclavus, along with the North Italians, started to stir up sedition in Sicily, invading the land of the royal demesne and killing Muslims wherever he could find them. On hearing of this King William first had Matthew Bonellus arrested and thrown into prison, and then raised an army, went to Piazza [Armerina] and destroyed it, putting the North Italians to flight. Fleeing from the king, Roger Sclavus took refuge in Butera, along with many of the North Italians. The king followed them to Butera, where he and his army besieged them from every side. And since King William had [also] been informed of the war which had arisen in the Terra di Lavoro and Apulia, he despatched Aquinus of Moac[40] to the Terra di Lavoro to engage knights and to resist the enemy, for Andrew of Rupecanina had already invaded part of that area. Count Robert, however, had occupied Apulia without meeting any resistance. He arrived at Salerno, believing that it would be his, but the Salernitans remained faithful to the king, as was their custom, and refused to receive him. Then he went to Benevento, and was received with honour by its inhabitants. After this he returned to Apulia and went as far as Taranto. However, King William was detained for almost the whole summer at the siege of Butera. But since he was unable to capture it, guarded as it was by its strong site and a large number of brave men, an agreement was made and he permitted Roger Sclavus and the North Italians to depart by sea unharmed. Then, totally destroying Butera, he pacified the whole of Sicily and returned in triumph to Palermo.

Meanwhile Pope Alexander had stayed for a time at Anagni and Terracina.[41] Then he took the advice of Archbishop Villanus of Pisa, who had journeyed to him with one galley, and, being sent some royal galleys, he sailed to Genoa with the cardinals and was received by the Genoese with the utmost devotion.[42] Afterwards he sailed on with

40 Garufi, *Romuald*, 249, note 1, suggested that he was perhaps the father of Geoffrey of Moac, later Master Justiciar of the Val di Noto in 1172 and Master Chamberlain of the Palace in 1180 (for whom see Cusa, *Diplomi greci ed arabi*, 287–8; *Diplomi Inediti*, 152; Takayama (1993), 136). He must also have been related to the admiral Walter of Moac.

41 Alexander was at Anagni from 13 November 1159 until April 1161. He briefly returned to Rome, then went to Praeneste and Ferentino before spending the autumn at Terracina. The *Liber Pontificalis* (Duchesne, ii, 403) said that almost all the papal state except for Anagni, Terracina and Orvieto was in the hands of the schismatics (i.e. Victor's supporters).

42 The archbishop sailed to Terracina on 18 December and spent Christmas with the pope there; Lupo Gentile, *Annales Pisani*, 24. Alexander arrived

their galleys to Provence. When Octavian, who had remained at Segni, heard of Alexander's departure, he went to the emperor in Lombardy, and was honourably received by him. Then the emperor called a solemn council of bishops at Pavia, and there he openly recognised Octavian, who called himself Victor, as the rightful pope, promising publicly and bindingly that neither he nor his successors would ever obey Alexander or his successors.[43]

After waging war against Milan for five years and being unable to conquer the city because of the resistance of its warlike inhabitants, at length the emperor came to an agreement with them, promising to allow the city itself and its citizens, together with their property, to remain unharmed.[44] But afterwards he forgot his promise, destroyed the city and ordered the citizens whom he had expelled from it to settle in villages. Having secured this victory, the emperor began to rule Lombardy arbitrarily, appointing his own officials and governors in *castella* and cities, exacting regalian rights and tribute, and turning the greater part of Lombardy into his demesne land. So it occurred that the Lombards, who had rejoiced in a liberty unknown to other nations, were brought down along with Milan by their envy of that city, and imposed upon themselves a wretched bondage to the Germans.[45]

Hearing that Pope Alexander had gone to France and fearing that he would be welcomed by the King of the French, the emperor immediately sent an envoy to the latter, requesting a meeting at Dijon to decide what to do about Popes Alexander and Victor and how they might settle this issue through the judgement of churchmen. This

> in Genoa on 21 January 1162 (with four Sicilian galleys); Duchesne, *Liber Pontificalis* ii, 404; and remained there until 25 March; Belgrano, *Annali Genovesi* i, 63.
>
> 43 The chronology of this paragraph is very confused. Frederick recognised Victor IV as the legitimate pope on 11 February 1160; Holder-Egger, *Gesta Frederici I in Lombardia*, 39. Victor had always been closely linked with the emperor, who in 1159 had invested him and his brother with the County of Terni; Kehr (1926), 65.
>
> 44 Milan surrendered at the beginning of March 1162. Its destruction was ordered on 26 March; Güterbock, *Otto Morena*, 152–7.
>
> 45 Cf. Duchesne, *Liber Pontificalis* ii, 411: 'the emperor reduced the whole of Lombardy to such servitude that not only did he violently seize the other property of its people, but his officials also kidnapped their wives and daughters'.

message was very agreeable to King Louis of the French, who arrived with a few knights on the appointed day and time at the place arranged, but he did not find the emperor there. The latter was careful to turn up at this same place on another day, along with Octavian and a huge force of knights and footmen. When the King of France heard of this, he refused to come to meet him, fearing his cunning.[46] The emperor was angered by this and returned to Germany with Octavian. However, after staying in Germany for a little while and not being treated with respect by the Germans, Octavian returned to Italy and went to Lucca, where he remained until the end of his life.

Meanwhile Pope Alexander was staying at Savigny. There, first of all, the King of England came to him and, along with his whole kingdom, received him as lord and father.[47] After this the King of France and the whole French church recognised him as universal pope, and the king brought him honourably to Paris. Pope Alexander summoned the kings of France and England and arranged peace and concord between them. Not long afterwards he celebrated a universal council at Tours, where archbishops, bishops and abbots from England, Scotland, Ireland, Spain and the whole of Gaul foregathered.[48] At that time a certain noble German cleric, Conrad, a relative of the emperor, who was Archbishop-Elect of the church of Mainz and was unwilling to be a party to the schism of Octavian and the emperor, abandoned his church without the emperor's knowledge and hurried to Pope Alexander in France. The pope received him kindly, and afterwards took him with him to Rome; then he promoted him to be a cardinal

---

46 Late August 1162. Other sources suggest that Louis was the one who deliberately did not turn up at the correct time; Munz (1969), 231–2.

47 The monastery of Savigny was in the diocese of Dol, on the border between Normandy and Brittany. It had been founded by the hermit Vitalis of Mortain *c.* 1112 and affiliated to the Cistercian Order in 1149. Alexander met Henry II there in early September 1162. According to the *Liber Pontificalis* (Duchesne, ii, 407–8) the latter treated the pope with such respect that he declined the stool which was offered to him and was happy to sit on the ground at the pope's feet. Arnulf of Lisieux claimed (mendaciously?) that Louis VII had delegated the choice between the two rival popes to Henry; Barlow, *The Letters of Arnulf of Lisieux*, 49, no. 29.

48 The council met on 19 May 1163; Duchesne, *Liber Pontificalis* ii, 408 (which claimed that there were 17 cardinals and 124 bishops present). For its decrees, see William of Newburgh, *Historia Rerum Anglicarum* i, 136–9. Alexander had been in Paris from 6 February to 25 April 1163.

and Bishop of Sabina, finally raising him to be Archbishop of Mainz.[49] Hearing this the emperor was furious, and had Christian the chancellor elected to the church of Mainz and consecrated by his suffragans.[50] And while Pope Alexander was staying in France, exercising his canonical rights in the churches of God, Octavian died at Lucca. Through the command of Rainald, the emperor's chancellor, he was succeeded by Guy of Crema, who was called Paschal by his followers.[51]

In the meantime King William, with Sicily under his control, gathered his forces by land and sea and came to Apulia. First he captured Taverna at sword-point and destroyed it. Then he came to Taranto and besieged it, and when it was captured wreaked his revenge on those who had betrayed him. After this he led his army towards the coast of Apulia. Hearing this, Count Robert, who was then based at Salpi[52] with his army, fearing that the barons of Apulia would, as was their custom, abandon him, retreated to the Abruzzi. Learning of this King William sent Richard de Say after him with a great army.[53] But Count Robert, a wise and astute man, took care to leave the kingdom before his arrival. King William came to San Germano with his army, expelled Count Richard of Aquila from the kingdom, and had Monte Arcano, which the count had recently built, captured by his galliots[54]

---

49 Conrad of Wittelsbach, son of the Count Palatine Otto IV, chosen as archbishop in June 1161 at Lodi after a disputed election to fill the see of Mainz, vacant after the murder of Archbishop Arnold. In fact he remained loyal to Victor, but on the latter's death advised Frederick not to allow a new election and to be reconciled with Alexander, whom he joined in October 1164. He was finally consecrated as Archbishop of Mainz (in exile) in December 1165, translated to Salzburg in 1177 and died in 1200. See Ganzer (1963), 104–14.

50 Christian of Buch, Archbishop of Mainz 1165–83, who had become imperial chancellor in 1162.

51 Victor died on 20 April 1164; Lupo Gentile, *Annales Pisani*, 31. Guy was elected as Paschal III two days later, and died on 20 September 1168. The 'chancellor' was Rainald of Dassel, Archbishop of Cologne from 1159 to 1167, who had been imperial chancellor from 1156 to 1162.

52 Salpi, now abandoned, was on the Apulian coast, below the Gargano peninsula and about 15 km. NW of Barletta.

53 Cf. *Annales Ceccanenses*, MGH SS xix, 285.

54 The Latin is *a galiotis*. *Galiotae* were small, fast galleys, widely used in the medieval Mediterranean for scouting and by corsairs; Pryor (1988), 67;

and destroyed, capturing there also his wife and son. And so, after recovering all his land, he came to Salerno. Since he was indignant with the citizens of Salerno, he refused to enter the city, but pitched his tents outside. He demanded a huge sum of money from the citizens, and, when they were unable to pay it immediately, he was furious, using it as an excuse to have some of them hanged, telling the others that unless they promptly paid over the money he would destroy their city. However the apostle St Matthew, who has been given by God as the patron and defender of the city of Salerno, did not abandon his city in such a crisis. For, since the king was determined to inflict this great harm on Salerno, at midday, when the air was so completely still that not a cloud appeared in the sky, suddenly a great wind sprang up from the north with driving rain and turbulence, blowing down all the army's tents and uprooting and blowing away the king's tent from the hill on which it was placed, all but killing the sleeping king. On waking up, he was astonished by such a deluge and fled, invoking the apostle's help, and was just able to take shelter in a little tent. Although the king disguised the fear that this caused in his mind, nevertheless the magnates of the court and men of prudence knew clearly that this miracle had been caused by the power of the apostle. For in this event the apostle clearly acted both for the people committed to him and for the king, in saving the people entrusted to him from danger and preventing the king for carrying out his evil plan. The king thought over what had happened, and fearing the anger of the apostle he, changed his plan. Although he had been intending to stay in the Salerno area for some time, he boarded his galleys the next day and hastily returned to Sicily.

Meanwhile, hearing of the death of Octavian, the Romans sent envoys to Alexander in France, begging him to return to the City and visit the people entrusted to him, who would receive him with honour and devotion.[55] Believing this to be both to his advantage and to that of the Church, Alexander went to Magalonne and a great ship was prepared, belonging to the Hospital, on which nearly all the cardinals embarked, while Alexander and a few cardinals set out in a galley of

> but the word also occurs with reference to the oarsmen or marines who manned the royal fleet of the kingdom of Sicily. Monte Arcano has not been identified (the text is uncertain), but is likely to have been on the coast of the Principality of Capua.

55 Alexander had stayed at Sens from October 1163 to April 1165.

the people of Narbonne, with the intention of transferring to this same ship. Suddenly Pisan galleys which had been lying in ambush for him appeared. On seeing them, the pope and his galley hastily returned to Magalonne.[56] The galleys of the Pisans surrounded the ship in which the cardinals were, but not finding the pope there, they allowed it to go on in peace, and with the help of a following wind it reached first Palermo and then Messina. Not long afterwards Pope Alexander and the remaining cardinals, along with the Archbishop of Mainz, boarded a smaller ship, committed themselves to the deep and although menaced by storms came by divine guidance safely and with all their followers to Messina. Hearing this, King William, who was then at Palermo, sent envoys with gifts to the pope, and ordered him to be conducted with five galleys to Rome. Coming to Salerno, he was welcomed with proper honour and reverence by Archbishop Romuald and the whole populace of the city. Afterwards he continued with these same galleys to the Tiber, and from there with all the cardinals along the river to St Paul's.[57] The clergy and the Roman people went out to meet him, and together brought him with great honour and glory to the Lateran. At that time King William had a large and marvellously designed palace built near Palermo, which he called the Zisa,[58] surrounding it with beautiful fruit-trees and delightful pleasure-gardens, furnished with many streams and splendid fishponds.

However, in Lent King William was afflicted with pain and diarrhoea. For some time he concealed this illness, but around the middle of Lent, feeling his sickness growing worse and believing himself about to die, he made confession and received penance, freed some of his prisoners, remitted the fine he had imposed on Apulia and made his

---

56 The Pisan ships may actually have been in Provençal waters to fight the Genoese. Oberto the Chancellor, the contemporary Genoese annalist, claimed that the Pisan squadron fled from Marseilles for fear of the Genoese, and that thirteen Pisan ships then sank in a storm; Belgrano, *Annali Genovesi* i, 187.

57 They arrived at the mouth of the Tiber on 23 November 1165; Duchesne, *Liber Pontificalis* ii, 413 (which confirms the number of ships, and added that Archbishop Roger of Reggio accompanied the pope to Rome). Alexander had granted Roger his *pallium* (the symbol of his metropolitan authority) at Gaeta on 19 November; *Italia Pontificia* x, 23, no. 20.

58 From the Arabic *al Aziz*, 'the glorious'; Amari (1934–9), iii, 500–1.

will, in which he made his eldest son William heir to his whole kingdom. He confirmed to his other son Henry the Principality of Capua, which he had already conceded to him, and left a huge sum of money to be spent for the salvation of his soul. He appointed his wife Queen Margaret both governor of his kingdom and guardian of his sons, and ordained that Richard, Bishop-Elect of Syracuse, and Matthew, master of his notaries, careful and discreet men skilled in the law, should be the counsellors and *familiares* of her and their sons. As his illness grew worse, King William ordered Archbishop Romuald II of Salerno, who was extremely well-versed in matters medical, to be summoned to him. He arrived about Easter, and was well received by the king, to whom he brought timely medical assistance.[59] But though confident in his own considerable skill, he only employed those medicines which seemed acceptable to the king. Thus it happened that, on the Saturday before the octave of Easter, he was stricken with a tertian fever. His suffering grew worse and he died. He was buried in St Peter's chapel in his palace. King William passed away in the forty-sixth year of his life, having ruled both with his father and by himself for fifteen years and ten months, in the year from the incarnation of the Lord 1166, fourteenth in the indiction, on 7 May at about the ninth hour.[60] King William was of fine appearance and handsome of face, stout of body and very tall.[61] He was proud and desirous of honour, victorious in war on land and sea, hateful to his kingdom and more feared than loved, very active in collecting money but not very generous in dispensing it. He lavished honours and wealth on those faithful to him, but inflicted savage punishments on those who were unfaithful, and exiled them from his kingdom. He was assiduous in listening to the divine office and greatly respected churchmen. He had the chapel of St Peter in his palace painted with marvellous pictures, covered its walls with different sorts of valuable marble and greatly enriched and ornamented it with gold and silver

---

59 Cf. the *History*, note 194. The archbishop was by no means the only contemporary Salernitan cleric skilled in medicine; cf. Cava, Arca xxviii.104, the will of a deacon Romuald *medicus* (August 1154).

60 All the other sources give 15 May; see above, *History*, note 130. His body was reburied at Monreale between 1183 and 1189; Deér (1959), 14–15.

61 The *Chron. Ferrariae* (Gaudenzi, 29) described the king as having a black beard and being of prodigious strength, and adds that 'he was greatly feared and held in hatred by many'.

vessels and precious vestments.[62] He instituted many clerics and prebends there and arranged for the divine office to be properly and carefully celebrated in reverence and fear of God.[63]

On his death his eldest son William, who was 12 years old, succeeded him in the kingdom. On the second day after his father's death he was installed as king, on the queen's orders and with the advice of the archbishops, bishops, barons and people. For on that day he came in glorious and regal state to the church of St Mary at Palermo,[64] and with many archbishops, bishops and barons assisting, was anointed and crowned as king by Archbishop Romuald II of Salerno. Afterwards he returned in great state to the palace wearing his crown, amid the joy and rejoicing of the people. The queen, a wise and sensible woman, knew very well that her people had been greatly upset by the evils which they had suffered from King William, but she believed that they could be encouraged to love and be loyal to her son by good deeds. That was why, on the best possible advice, she opened the prisons, freed many captives, restored their lands to those freed, forgave debts, recalled to the kingdom the counts and barons who had been exiled and restored to them the lands which had been confiscated. With royal liberality she granted many lands to churches, counts, barons and knights. By these and many other benefits she kindled loyalty and love for her son in the minds of everyone, making the loyal more loyal and the devoted more devoted. At this time the eunuch Caid Peter, the Master Chamberlain of the palace, along with certain others, sought flight and went to the King of Morocco, taking a lot of money with him.

Hearing of the death of King William, Manuel, the Emperor of Constantinople, sent envoys to King William the younger in Sicily, saying that he would willingly conclude peace with him, and give

62 Demus (1950), 51–8, suggests that the additional mosaics in the chapel commissioned by William I led to considerable alterations to the original decorative scheme of King Roger's reign, and indeed the destruction of some of the original mosaics. There were then further alterations in the early years of William II. See also Borsook (1990), 17–41, for a detailed description.

63 His provisions for the Palatine chapel were later confirmed by Henry VI, but no charters now survive; *Guillelmi I Diplomata*, 128–9 deperdita nos. 52–3.

64 The cathedral.

him his only daughter and heiress to his empire along with the empire itself. The king and queen took counsel and sent a series of ambassadors about this matter to the emperor and received them from him. They concluded a new peace-treaty with him, but the business about the marriage remained unconcluded owing to many details which had not been settled.[65] However, because of the many benefits which he and the queen had brought to the people, King William was much loved by his men and ruled his kingdom in peace and tranquillity. At this time the queen's natural brother Henry came to the king in Sicily, and the latter gave him the county of Montescaglioso and one of the daughters of King Roger as his wife. In this same period Stephen, son of the Count of Perche, a cleric and blood-relation of the queen, came to Sicily, and the king and queen first made him chancellor and afterwards had him elected to the church of Palermo. In a very short space of time he had become so favoured and close to the king and queen that he ran the whole kingdom as he wished.

At this time Frederick, the Emperor of the Germans, entered Italy once again, and came through the Marches to Ancona, which he besieged. He sent his chancellor Rainald and Andrew of Rupecanina with part of his army to Tusculano to make war on Pope Alexander and the Romans.[66] The proud and confident Romans, trusting overmuch in their own strength, rushed carelessly and in disorder against the Germans. Placing ambushes on the flank, the Germans defeated the Romans, and many of the latter were captured or killed. The rest fled and were only just able to regain the City.[67] What had happened greatly disturbed Pope Alexander and all the Roman citizens, and struck them all with fear. The chancellor sent envoys to the emperor, requesting him to come speedily to the City, which would be at his mercy. So although he had captured Ancona, and was just on the point of invading the land of King William, he nevertheless returned in haste to the City in August and pitched his camp near the church

---

[65] Parker (1956) provides a detailed discussion of, and context for, these negotiations. The marriage between William II and Maria Comnena was finally agreed in 1172, and the king went to Barletta to await his bride's arrival. However, Manuel changed his mind and called the marriage off, which greatly offended the Sicilian court; *Romuald,* 261–2.

[66] The *Annales Ceccanenses,* MGH SS xix, 285, add Count Richard of Fondi to the leaders of this force.

[67] 29 May 1167; Güterbock, *Otto Morena,* 197.

of St Peter.[68] The Romans, both because of the death of their relations and because many of them were held prisoner by the emperor, were unable to resist him. The emperor thus took advantage of the opportunity and stormed into the church of St Peter with his troops. He had the portico which was in front of the church burned down,[69] brought Guy of Crema into the church and had him sing mass there.[70] Hearing of this, Pope Alexander, who was then staying in the Cartularia tower,[71] left the city dressed as a pilgrim with a few followers and went to Gaeta. There he resumed his pontifical robes and went on to Benevento where he was honourably received by the citizens.[72] God, however, imposed condign punishment for the injury done to the apostle Peter and the violation of his church, for a terrible sickness suddenly broke out among the emperor's army, and in a short time the chancellor, Charles [*sic*], son of Conrad, many nobles and the greater part of the army died.[73] Seeing this and realising that it was clearly God's punishment, the emperor left a prefect in the City and, sad and grieving, returned to Germany with only a few men.

King William was, however, as we have said, much loved by his men because of the many benefits which he and his mother had conferred on his kingdom, and manfully held his kingdom in peace. Stephen the chancellor first showed himself humble and kindly to all, but afterwards grew proud and through the counsel of wicked men began to harbour

68 His army pitched camp on Monte Mario, just outside Rome, on 19 July; Duchesne, *Liber Pontificalis* ii, 416, or 24 July; Güterbock, *Otto Morena*, 202.

69 Actually the church of S. Maria in Turri, to the left of the atrium of St Peter's.

70 He also crowned Frederick and his wife, on Tuesday 1 August, having himself been enthroned there two days earlier; Güterbock, *Otto Morena*, 202–4; Lupo Gentile, *Annales Pisani*, 43.

71 Near the Arch of Titus in the Forum area; the name was derived from its use for storing the papal archives.

72 He had arrived in Benevento by 22 August 1167, and remained in exile there for three and a half years.

73 The epidemic, probably amoebic dysentery, broke out during the afternoon of Wednesday 2 August. Rainald of Dassel died on 14 August, and Frederick of Swabia, son of King Conrad III, on 19 August. Four other bishops, and at least six counts, as well as Welf VII of Bavaria, also died; Herde (1991), especially 139–43.

both hatred and suspicion for the natives of the land. Around Christmas he came with the king and queen and the magnates of the court to Messina. Count Gilbert of Gravina, a blood-relation of the queen and the chancellor, who was then the Captain of all Apulia, arrived at Messina with a large force of knights. After taking counsel with him, the chancellor had Count Henry, the queen's brother, arrested and imprisoned at Reggio, charging that he and many others had plotted the chancellor's and Count Gilbert's deaths. For this reason too Count Richard of Molise, Bartholomew de Parisio, John de Sinopoli and many others were arrested and put in prison. What had happened greatly disturbed the men of the kingdom. After this, on the advice and with the help of the chancellor, Count Gilbert of Gravina obtained from the king the county of Loritello with everything belonging to it, and returned in state to Apulia. At Easter the chancellor returned to Palermo with the king and queen, and there, only a few days later, 'he had Matthew, a citizen of Salerno, the master of the lord king's notaries and his *familiaris*, arrested without cause. What had been done seemed wrong and evil to everybody, for this said Matthew was a wise and discreet man, and had been raised from boyhood in the king's hall, and had been found of proven loyalty in the king's business. During the Easter octaves the people of Messina rose in riot and, going to Reggio, took Count Henry from his prison; they freed Count Richard, who was being held in prison in Taormina, and they killed Odo Quarrel, the chancellor's cleric and chosen familiar, who was at that time in Messina. When they heard this, the people of Palermo similarly rose in rebellion, made an attack on the chancellor and besieged him and all his men in the Tower of the Bells for a full day. The next day, on the orders of the king and queen, he and some of his men boarded a galley, but when it had come to Licata the galley was wrecked. Afterwards he boarded a ship and sailed to Jerusalem, and after being there a little while he died. Count Gilbert of Loritello with his son Count Bertram of Andria and all their men swore to leave the land and went to Jerusalem. On leaving prison, Counts Henry and Richard, along with the men of Messina, came to Palermo with twenty galleys. The king received them back into his grace and restored their lands to them, and after the chancellor and Count Gilbert had left the country, the land remained in peace and tranquillity. Rejecting the chancellor, the clergy of the church of Palermo unanimously chose as their pastor Walter, canon of this same church and Dean of Agrigento, the king's teacher. Since Walter was busy with the affairs of the kingdom, and could not on this account easily leave the king's side, Pope Alexander was most earnestly requested by the king, for love of and favour to him, to permit the archbishop-elect to be consecrated by his suffragans and to be sent his *pallium* by the hands of Cardinal John of Naples. After receiving the oath of obedience from him, the pope conceded the *pallium* to him, as was customary.[74] Count Robert of Loritello, who had often begged for King William's grace and been unable to secure it, now once again sent a series of letters and envoys to King William the younger, humbly begging that the latter restore his love and grace to him. The king and queen, with their customary compassion, took pity on him and granted their grace to him, and the king, with his usual generosity, restored to him the county of Loritello, as had once been granted to him by his father, and out of the abundance of his grace added to this the county of Conversano.[75]

At that time there was a great earthquake in Sicily, which in large part demolished the castle of Syracuse. The city of Catania was razed to the ground. The church of St Agatha collapsed, killing the bishop and forty-five monks. Lentini and Mohec and many other *castra* in Sicily collapsed in the tremor. At Messina too there was a great and terrible earthquake. This happened in the year 1168 from Our Lord's incarnation, second of the indiction, in the month of February, on the vigil of St Agatha.[76]

II From Boso's *Life of Pope Adrian IV*

[This official biography of Adrian was written by one of his closest associates, whom he appointed as his chamberlain – the *Curia*'s principal financial officer – at the beginning of his pontificate. Boso was

---

74 Alexander III confirmed his election on 22 June 1169; *Italia Pontificia* x, 232–3, no. 32. He was consecrated on 28 September; Pirro, *Sicula Sacra* i, 105. Cf. the *History*, above, note 273.

75 March 1169, *Annales Ceccanenses*, MGH SS xix, 286. The earliest documentary record of his restoration as count was, however, only in February 1173; Camobreco, *Regesto di S. Leonardo di Siponto*, 50, no. 79; Petrucci (1959), 117. In March 1175 Count Robert was in office as Master Justiciar; Gattula, *Accessiones*, 265–6.

76 4 February, *recte* 1169.

a Tuscan, a former regular canon of Bologna, who was an important figure in the papal chancery from 1149 onwards, though he had already been in Rome for some years before that. Adrian appointed him Cardinal deacon of SS. Cosmas and Damian in January 1157. He played an important part in the election of Alexander III, and the latter promoted him to be Cardinal priest of St Prudentia in 1165/6. He died after July 1178.[77] Boso began the recording of papal rights and revenues which was later to be consolidated by Cencius Savelli into the *Liber Censuum* of 1192. He also wrote the official biographies of both Adrian and Alexander, as well as producing new or revised biographies of their predecessors from Leo IX (1048–54) onwards. His authorship was proclaimed in a postscript appended to the biography of Adrian, which was probably written soon after 1165.[78]

The following extracts have been translated from Duchesne, *Liber Pontificalis* ii, 389–90, 393–5.]

At this time King William of Sicily insolently raised up his horns against his mother and lady, the most Holy Roman Church, and after levying an army had the land of St Peter invaded with hostile intent. His troops besieged the city of Benevento for quite some time and set fire to its suburbs; then he violently crossed the frontiers of the Campagna and burned the town of Ceprano,[79] the *castrum* of Bauco and other places, even though they were unfortified. For these and other offences the said Pope Adrian then drew the sword of St Peter and struck the king with its point – excommunication.

In the meantime King Frederick entered Lombardy with a great army and for a long time besieged the city of Tortona.[80] Once that had been conquered and made subject to him, he hurried on to the City, showing such haste that one might indeed have thought that he was its enemy, not its patron. [A long account follows of Frederick Barbarossa's visit to Rome and his imperial coronation in 1155.]

---

77 Zenker (1964), 149–52; Robinson (1990), 254–7.

78 Duchesne, *Liber Pontificalis* ii, 397.

79 Ceprano on the River Liri was on the border between the Principality of Capua and the papal state. Robert Guiscard had sworn fealty to Gregory VII there on 29 June 1080.

80 February–April 1155; Güterbock, *Otto Morena*, 20–3.

[...]

At this same time, after he had been struck down by the sentence of excommunication, the above-mentioned King of Sicily was held in contempt by his own men. He rejected the wise advice of his own faithful subjects that he should make satisfaction [to the Church], and remained all but alone in his foolish pride. When his great men, the counts and barons, along with the principal persons of the cities of Apulia, were totally unable to persuade him from this utter folly, they abandoned him. They sent envoys to Pope Adrian as their principal lord, requesting that he deign to travel to that region and receive that land, which was recognised as belonging to the jurisdiction of the Blessed Peter, and their persons and property into his hands and his power. The pope took the advice of his brothers on these issues, raised a suitable military force from the counts and other nobles both of the City and of the Campagna, as well as from other places round about, and then went down to S. Germano at about the [time of the] Feast of St Michael.[81] There he received the fealty and homage of Prince Robert of Capua, Count Andrew and the other nobles of those parts. He urged them in a personal meeting that they prepare the way for him, 'making straight in the desert a highway and every mountain low'.[82] After some days he journeyed via the *castrum* of Mignano[83] and the city of Capua, and with the Lord as his companion reached Benevento. While he was in that city he recalled all the barons of the area, their lands and the surrounding towns to fealty to the Blessed Peter and himself as their principal lord.

Meanwhile the Emperor of the Greeks sent one of his princes called Palaeologus to Ancona with a large sum of money from the treasury. He also wrote to the pope, asking and beseeching him that he grant to the emperor three cities in the coastal district of Apulia, on condition that he provide the pope with both adequate supplies of money and a large enough force of knights and other troops to drive the said king right out of Sicily; he promised to provide not less than 5,000 pounds of gold for the pope and his court. The king was stricken with terror by these projects being daily set in motion against him,

---

81 29 September.

82 Isaiah, 40.3–4.

83 Half-way between Ceprano and Capua, *c.* 35 km. SE from Ceprano and NE from Capua, it was the site of Innocent II's recognition of King Roger on 27 July 1139; *Italia Pontificia* viii, 42, no. 159.

and repenting of his sin decided to return in all humility to the bosom of his mother, the most Holy Roman Church and to obedience to his lord and father, this same Roman pontiff. So he sent the Bishop-Elect of the church of Catania[84] and some others from among the great men of his court to Salerno, to go on to meet the pope. He gave them full power humbly to seek on his behalf the pope's grace and peace, and to make plenary satisfaction (as described below) and to pledge security to him. First of all, he sought to be absolved according to the Church's custom; then he promised to do fealty and homage to the pope; he would restore full liberty to all the churches in his land; furthermore, in return for the harm he had caused he would give to the Blessed Peter and the Roman Church three *castra*, Paduli, Montefusco and Morcone,[85] as hereditary possessions; and he would provide arms and money to subjugate Rome, which was then in rebellion against the pope, to the latter's rule; after he had recovered the grace of the lord pope and the Church he would grant them as large a sum of money as the Greeks had given.

On hearing these concessions, and on the unanimous advice of his brothers, the pope sent the venerable man Hubald, then Cardinal priest of St Prassede and now Bishop of Ostia, to Salerno.[86] He was to inquire from the envoys as to the truth of what had been offered and to report back what he had ascertained. This the cardinal did, and on his return it was found that the terms which had been promised on the king's behalf were genuine and ready for completion. It seemed to the pope therefore right to sanction an agreement so advantageous to the Church and so much to its credit. But since the majority of the brothers, who felt very strongly and were very dubious about this, were quite unwilling to agree, the whole offer was spurned and rejected outright. And since, according to the words of the Gospel, 'everyone that exalteth himself shall be abased, and he that humbleth himself shall be exalted',[87] after the king had humbled himself in this way and yet his satisfaction had not been accepted, he marched out

---

84 Bernard, attested in December 1157 and April 1162; *Guillelmi I Diplomata*, 60–4, no. 22, at 63; Garufi, *Tabulario di Monreale*, 161.

85 All within 10 km. of Benevento. As the former chamberlain, Boso was particularly interested in the property of the Roman Church; Robinson (1990), 30–1.

86 See the *History*, note 152.

87 Luke 18.14.

with his army against the Greeks and the Apulians who had occupied his land, came to Brindisi where they were gathered and fought a battle with them. Finally they were overcome, totally defeated, and fled, and the king won a complete and triumphant victory over them. As a result such fear and trembling quickly spread right through Apulia that thereafter nobody dared to resist him, everyone fled from his presence, and its strongest cities and fortresses immediately returned to his lordship without a fight or any sort of coercion.

As a result of this, the pope realised that he had been deceived and totally abandoned by all those who had sworn to stand resolutely by him. He sent the majority of his brothers to the Campagna, while he himself with just a few of them remained at Benevento, waiting for the king's arrival. A few days later the king marched with his army from northern Apulia and approached to some two miles from the city of Benevento. Then the previously mentioned pope sent to the king these venerable men, the cardinal priests Hubald of St Prassede (already mentioned), Julian of St Marcellus[88] and Roland of St Mark, the chancellor of the Apostolic See,[89] to warn him carefully on behalf of the Blessed Peter to cease from all his offences, to make satisfaction for the harm he had caused, and to respect the rights of his mother, the most Holy Roman Church. They were welcomed and well treated, and, after some argument between them about various of the clauses, the king made peace with the pope through their mediation. He came to the church of St Marcianus, situated right next to Benevento, humbly prostrated himself at the pope's feet and did liege homage and fealty to him, in the presence of a large number of bishops, cardinals, counts, barons and a host of other people, with Odo Frangipane[90] drawing up [*computante*] the oath. The king therefore received the kiss of peace, gave many presents to the pope, his brothers and his whole court, of gold, silver and silken cloths, and both sides were happy. They then departed joyfully.

88 Cardinal priest of St Marcellus 1144–58 and Cardinal bishop of Palestrina 1158–64; legate to Hungary 1160–1 and papal Vicar in Rome 1162–4; Zenker (1964), 42–3.
89 The later Alexander III; see above, note 28.
90 Cf. above, note 31.

The Treaty of Benevento, 1156

[The original manuscript of this important document still exists (Archivio segreto vaticano, AA. Arm. I-XVIII.4421), as well as two near contemporary copies, in the *Liber Censuum* and the letter book of Thomas of Gaeta. The division into paragraphs is the work of modern editors, but is retained for ease of reference.][91]

In the name of God the eternal and our Saviour Jesus Christ, amen. To Adrian, by the grace of God Supreme Pontiff of the Holy Roman Church, his dearest lord and his reverend father and to his successors, William, by the same grace King of Sicily, of the Duchy of Apulia and of the Principality of Capua.

(1) It has always been our custom to show ourselves humble at heart at moments of triumph and greatest success, and then to devote ourselves more carefully to thanking Almighty God and to the exercise of clemency. Since we seem to have come to greater prosperity and glory, and we wish therefore to bring thanks to our Redeemer that our affairs are now so peaceful and prosperous, that we should not appear ungrateful for the benefits which we have received from the King of Kings, and that we may equally hope for greater successes and victories with the help of God's power.

(2) Thus, because of this our custom, and considering that, to the praise and glory of God, the Greeks and barbarous nations who sadly entered our kingdom, not through their own strength but because of traitors to us, have been killed or captured in battle, and the disturbers of the peace and traitors have been driven in flight from the borders of our kingdom, we have decided that we must bow down in humility before the hand of Almighty God and intend to devote ourselves more humbly to the exercise of humility.

(3) Desiring to put a suitable end to those disputes which have arisen between the Roman Church and ourselves, when we came to the city of Benevento and our enemies had fled in the face of our wrath, we received with proper honour your venerable cardinals, namely the Cardinal priests Hubald of St Prassede and Julian of St Marcellus, and with them your chancellor, Roland, Cardinal priest of St Mark,

---

[91] Translated from MGH *Constitutiones* i, 588–90, no. 413, and following the paragraph numbering there; also in *Guillelmi I Diplomata*, 34–5, no. 12.

whom you have directed into our presence, and willingly listened to them conveying your wish and instructions for a good peace. Through them, and through the mediation of Maio, Great Admiral of Admirals, our beloved and faithful subject and *familiarissimus*, and the venerable Archbishops Hugh of Palermo and Romuald of Salerno, Bishop William of Troia[92] and Abbot Marinus of Cava,[93] our faithful subjects, we have through them come to a peace agreement with you, in the following way, namely that these clauses which have been written below shall be observed with regard to those matters which have caused controversy between your majesty and ourselves.

(4) Of appeals, thus: If any cleric in Apulia and Calabria, or from those other lands which border Apulia, shall have a dispute with another cleric about ecclesiastical matters, and the matter cannot be dealt with by the chapter or bishop or archbishop or any other ecclesiastical person of his province, then if he wishes he shall freely appeal to the Roman Church.

(5) There shall be translations between churches, if it is necessary and useful to the Church for someone to be called from one church to another, and if you and your successors shall wish to allow this.[94]

(6) The Roman Church shall freely hold consecrations and visitations in the whole of our kingdom.

(7) The Roman Church can certainly celebrate councils without challenge in whatever city it chooses in Apulia or Calabria or those areas that border on Apulia, except for those places in which we or our heirs shall be residing at that time, unless that should be with our or our heirs' consent.

(8) The Roman Church shall freely send legations to Apulia, Calabria and those areas bordering on Apulia. However, those who have been

92 William III, Bishop of Troia (in northern Apulia, 22 km. SW of Foggia) 1155–74; *Italia Pontificia* ix, 209. Immediately after the treaty was concluded he received privileges from both the pope and the king; Martin, *Chartes de Troia*, 237–41, nos. 74–5 (the royal diploma also in *Guillelmi I Diplomata*, 38–41, no.14).

93 Marinus, Abbot of the abbey of the Holy Trinity, Cava dei Tirreni, north of Salerno, 1146–70. This was one of the most important and prestigious monasteries of the kingdom, for which see Loud (1987).

94 The translation of a bishop from one see to another was becoming more common than hitherto in the twelfth-century Church, but canonically had to have papal permission.

sent by the Roman Church for this purpose shall not waste the possessions of the Church.

(9) In Sicily the Roman Church shall also have consecrations and visitations, and if it summons any persons in ecclesiastical orders from Sicily, they shall go. Our Majesty and that of our heirs shall, however, retain free from bad faith whatever it considers necessary to retain for promoting Christianity and for upholding the crown. The Roman Church shall have everything else there that it has in the other parts of our kingdom, except appeals and legations, which shall not occur except at the request of us and our heirs.[95]

(10) About those churches and monasteries of our land concerning which inquiry has been raised by the Roman Church, it shall be thus: You and your successors shall have in them what you have in the rest of the churches which lie under our power. Where they are accustomed to receive consecrations and blessings [*benedictiones*] from the Roman Church they shall furthermore pay the due and customary census to it.[96]

(11) With regard to elections let it indeed be thus: the clergy should agree on a suitable person and keep that secret among themselves until they have nominated that person to our Excellency. And after that person has been designated to our Eminence, if that person is not among the traitors or enemies of us or our heirs, or does not appear hateful to our Magnificence, or there is no other reason why we should not assent, we shall give our assent.[97]

(12) You shall moreover concede to us, and to Duke Roger our son and to our heirs who shall succeed to the kingdom by our designation

---

[95] The treaty thus recognised the special status of Sicily established by Urban II's grant of quasi-legatine powers to Count Roger I in 1098; *Malaterra*, IV.29, p. 108.

[96] The clause refers to monasteries like Montecassino and Venosa which were canonically exempt from normal diocesan jurisdiction, or to bishoprics such as those of Sora, Troia and (until 1183) Catania, which were not part of a normal metropolitan province. They were in consequence directly subject to the pope.

[97] This clause refers to the canonical election of bishops and abbots. The best-documented example of the operation of the procedure decreed here is the election of an abbot by the monks of St Bartholomew of Carpineto in 1180–1; Holtzmann, 'Norman royal charters', 99, nos. 3–4. Cf. Enzensberger (1980), 402–12.

the Kingdom of Sicily, the Duchy of Apulia and the Principality of Capua with all that appertains to them, Naples, Salerno and Amalfi with their appurtenances, Marsia and those other properties beyond Marsia which we ought to have,[98] and the other tenements which we hold from our predecessors who were the men of the Holy Roman Church, in full right, and you should help us honourably to maintain them against all [other] men.

(13) For all these we have sworn fealty to you and your successors and the Holy Roman Church and we have done liege homage to you, as is detailed in two identical documents, one of which, sealed with our gold seal, shall be held by your majesty, and the other, sealed with your seal shall be held in our possession. And we and our heirs obligate ourselves to pay every year to the Roman Church a census of 600 *schifati* for Apulia and Calabria, and 400 *schifati* for Marsia, or its equivalent in gold and silver,[99] unless by chance some impediment shall intervene, and once that no longer applies the census shall be paid in full.

(14) All the above which you have granted to us, you also grant to our heirs as you have to us. We decree of our own free will that they will do fealty to you and your successors and to the Holy Roman Church as we do, and shall willingly observe what is stated above.

(15) So that everything which has been stated above shall remain in force in perpetuity for you and your successors, and so that neither in our time nor in that of our heirs shall any of it be disturbed by anyone's presumption, we have ordered this present document to be written by the hand of Matthew our notary,[100] and to be sealed with our golden seal stamped with our image, and to be adorned by our sign manual.

Given before Benevento by the hand of Maio, Great Admiral of

---

98 The region in the Abruzzi north of the River Sangro, comprising the six bishoprics of Chieti, Forcone, Marsia, Penne, Teramo and Valva, conquered by Roger II's sons in the early 1140s; Deér (1972), 234–5, 249–50.

99 *Schifatus* was a south Italian name for the Byzantine *solidus*, equivalent to 4 *tari* in local money. It was derived from the Arabic *shafah*, meaning a coin with a border. However, by this period it was simply a notional unit of account, not an actual coin in circulation, and the census would almost certainly have been paid in gold *tari* or silver pennies, as the text suggests; Travaini (1995), 10, 218.

100 The later vice-chancellor who plays such a prominent part in the *History*.

Admirals, in the year of the Lord's incarnation 1156, in the month of June, fourth of the indiction, in the sixth regnal year of lord William, by the grace of God magnificent and most glorious King of Sicily, of the Duchy of Apulia and the Principality of Capua, happily, amen.

IV A letter concerning the Sicilian tragedy to Peter, Treasurer of the Church of Palermo[101]

My dearest Peter,

Now that the harshness of winter has been tempered thanks to a milder breeze, I had intended to write something pleasant and light-hearted, and dedicate it to you so to speak as the first-fruits of reborn spring. But after hearing of the death of the King of Sicily, I gave thought to what a great disaster this political change would bring about, how greatly the most peaceful state of that realm would be shattered either by the blast of enemy invasion, or by the heavy storm of internal conflict; my mind was stunned, and I abandoned my undertaking; my lyre turned to grief, I preferred to begin tearful tunes, a sad song of lamentation, even though the clear brightness of a cleansed sky and the pleasant appearance of gardens and orchards bring a happiness to my mind that is out of place, and attempt to divert me in another direction and impede my intention to mourn and weep. For what place can there be for weeping or complaint, and who would not feel offended by the untimely shedding of tears, now that the year has had the greyness of frosty old age wiped away, and once again flowers into welcome youthfulness, with the season of spring replacing the cold of winter and inviting the long-idle voices of the birds to the sweet melodies they had given up?

However, since it is hard to persuade a child not to mourn the death of its nurse,[102] I admit that I am not able to restrain my tears. I cannot pass over in silence or talk about with dry eyes the desolation

---

101 A real person, 'Peter, canon and treasurer of Palermo', who witnessed a charter of Archbishop Walter in January 1188; *Documenti inediti*, 216–21, no. 89, at 221.

102 Jamison (1957), 220–3 argues that *nutrix* ('nurse'/'nursing mother') is used in the sense of 'born and brought up', and thus shows that the author was a native Sicilian. Cf. note 105 below.

of Sicily, who took me in her gracious lap and gave me such kind support. I seem to imagine the disorderly columns of the foreigners occupying her with that impetus with which they are borne forward, destroying with fear wealthy cities and places flourishing as a result of a long period of peace, devastating them with slaughter, wasting them with plunder and sullying them with rape. The vision of the tragedy to come forces itself upon me, and makes me shed tears in spite of myself. On the one hand I imagine citizens cut down by the sword for resisting, or forced to surrender into wretched slavery; on the other, unmarried women violated before the very eyes of their parents, respectable ladies – after all their different kinds of valuable jewellery have been snatched from their head, neck and breast – treated with insolence and, their eyes fixed on the ground, weeping inconsolably that the matrimonial oath which ought to be respected had been violated by the lust of that disgusting race. For the madness of the Germans has no experience of being ruled by the guidance of reason, or being deflected from its aims by human sympathy, or deterred by religious scruples. Its inborn fury urges it forward, greed goads it, lust drives it on.

Granted that it is a sad and dreadful crime that this should happen in Apulia and the neighbouring provinces, and it should regretted with great sadness that anyone should think it bearable that the beastliness of the foreigners should rage even in the areas beyond the Straits. But if the force of the raging storm were to strike that blessed island which deserves above all kingdoms the privilege of wonderful gifts and great deserts, if the inexorable clash of weapons were to disturb its pleasant peace and quiet, made more attractive by every type of enjoyable thing, who then could bid his mind not to exceed the proper measure of grief? Who would not dissolve completely into tears, when confronted by the destruction of cities, the slaughter of citizens, the grey hairs of old men, which deserve respect, instead besmirched with dust; respectable women clad in sackcloth instead of silk; young boys and girls terrified by the grating sounds of a foreign language; and all the inhabitants of every class cast down from a wealth of possessions to utter destitution, from happiness to mourning, from glory to dishonour, from the highest summit of happiness to the extreme price of wretchedness?

I wish that when Constance enters the borders of Sicily with her German king she might not have the constancy to continue, and that she should not be given the opportunity to go further than the fields of the people of Messina or the limits of Mount Etna – for that race would most appropriately stay in those places, where the savagery of the Germans could join up with the cruelty of pirates, and that hard and stony people could burn itself out in the blazing of angry rage among the scorched rocks and fires of flaming Etna. For it would be an abomination, and like a portent, for the interior parts of Trinacria,[103] and especially that area upon which the light of its most noble city shines, a city which deserves the unique privilege of rising above the entire kingdom, either to be polluted by the entry of foreigners, upset by the fear of invasion, exposed to the rapine of pirates, or in any way at all to be disturbed by the barbarity of laws imposed by outsiders.

Now I would like you to explain the following to me: what direction do you think the political situation will take in this crisis, what line will the Sicilians follow? Will they decide that they ought to choose a king for themselves, and fight against the foreigners with united strength? Or will they be creatures of circumstance, and prefer to accept the yoke of slavery, no matter how severe, rather than act to protect their reputation and honour and the freedom of their country, out of lack of confidence in their cause and distaste for unaccustomed effort? In silence I think over these issues, unclear in my own mind, driven by various arguments in one direction or the other, and disagree with myself; nor is it sufficiently clear to me which of the two policies I ought to think preferable. Certainly if they were to choose themselves a king of undoubted virtue, and if the Muslims were not to take a different line from the Christians, then the king who was elected could come to the aid of the situation even if hope had almost been abandoned and the situation virtually lost; and if he acted wisely, he could repel the enemies' onslaughts. For if he were to win the support of the knights by offering them higher pay and court the feelings of the ordinary people by conferring benefits, if he fortified the cities and coastal towns carefully and posted garrisons in suitable places in Calabria as well, then he would be able to protect both Sicily and Calabria and prevent them from falling under the authority and power of the foreigners. For I do not think that any hope of reliance ought to be placed in the Apulians, who constantly plot revolution because of the pleasure they take in novelty; if you ordered them to go out to battle with all their

---

103 The island of 'three promontories' (τρεῖς ἄκραι): a name used for Sicily in classical poetry, e.g. Vergil, *Aeneid* 3.429, 3.440, 3.582; Ovid, *Metamorphoses* 5.476, 13.724–7, where the term is explained.

A LETTER CONCERNING THE SICILIAN TRAGEDY 255

forces, they would generally turn in flight before the signal to fight was given; if you put them in charge of defending fortifications, each would betray a different one and allow the enemy in without the knowledge or against the opposition of their allies. Furthermore, because it would be difficult for the Christian population not to oppress the Muslims in a crisis as great as this, with fear of the king removed, the Muslims, worn down by many injuries at the hands of the Christians, would begin to take a different line from them and perhaps occupy forts along the coast or strongholds in the mountains;[104] so it would be necessary both to fight the Germans with all one's strength and also deal with frequent attacks from the Muslims. What do you think the Sicilians should do, caught up in these narrows, placed in great danger, so to speak, between the hammer and the anvil? The Muslims will certainly do what they can in their wretched situation to surrender to the foreigners and hand themselves over to their power. How I wish that the hopes of both the Christian and the Muslim communities and their leaders would coincide, so that they would choose a king for themselves by common agreement and fight to resist the foreign invaders with all their power, all their effort and all their will.

You are an island whose condition is wretched, and fate damned. You have nurtured and educated your children to the end that when they grow up to the hoped-for strength, they first tested that strength on you, and then – fattened on the abundance of your breasts – trample upon and tear your womb! Many who were once nursed in your lap and by your goodness have later harmed you in this way with many injuries and in many battles. Constance too, brought up from her first cradle for many years in the riches of your delights, educated and moulded by your instruction and manners, later left to enrich foreigners with your wealth, and now returns with huge forces to repay you with a disgraceful recompense, so as to violently tear apart the apparel of her most beautiful nurse[105] and stain with foreign filth the elegance with which you exceed all other realms.

104 Either reflecting what had already happened, or anticipating what was going to occur. After a riot in Palermo, the Muslims did indeed flee to the mountains and rebel; *Annales Casinenses* ad ann. 1189, MGH SS xix, 314. This led to a guerrilla war in western Sicily which was to last more than thirty years. See Peri (1978), 116–28.

105 Since Constance was undoubtedly Sicilian by birth, this passage supports the view that if a land was someone's *nutrix*, then that person was therefore a native. For the significance of this, cf. note 102 above.

Come now, city of Messina, powerful and outstanding in the great nobility of your citizens, what plan do you think would secure your safety so that you may escape the initial onslaught of the foreigners and prevent the enemy forces from crossing the Straits? It is essential that you consider what you should do in good time, for you are the first port of call for ships that cross to Sicily after they have traversed the Straits, and you are forced to sustain the initial attacks of the invaders and experience the first beginnings of the fighting. If you consider the bravery and courage of your citizens, your old men are experienced in devising plans and your young men accustomed to warfare; the circuit of your walls is entrenched with towers close together; if you look carefully at your power, with which you have so often defeated the arrogance of the Greeks, with which you have plundered Africa and Spain and so often brought back home from there immense booty and rich spoils,[106] then a great deal of strength and confidence, a great deal of hope and security should certainly accrue to you from these factors. So the barbarity of that lawless people should cause you no fear or terror. If you are able to sustain its initial attack by resisting bravely, then you should be able to shake the harshest yoke from off your neck and gain yourself immortal glory and a famous reputation.

I weep for you, city of Catania, who have so often experienced bad fortune, and have not been able to restrain or turn back her savagery by any of the disasters you have suffered! When we unroll the ancient accounts contained in historical annals, we will find that you have frequently both been destroyed by deadly fumes and – while laid low by dreadful disaster in war – that fire has flowed down upon you several times in the form of a river from the cavernous craters of Etna. But if we wish to recall the disasters of our own age and those we have seen ourselves, then recently a great earthquake shook you with such violence that all your buildings collapsed, and the weight of wood and stone crushed a multitude of both sexes, whose number was not easy to estimate.[107] And now that Fortune's wickedness relents in that respect, you will finally be

---

106 A reference to the naval expeditions against Mahdia and the Balearic Islands in 1178 and 1181–2, as well as to the earlier campaigns of Roger II, Chalandon (1907), ii, 398; Abulafia (1985).

107 In 1169; see pp. 216–17 above and note 276 to the *History*.

A LETTER CONCERNING THE SICILIAN TRAGEDY

assigned to the most disgraceful slavery after many disasters of different kinds.[108]

May you now be dissatisfied with constant peace, city of Syracuse! Now, if you can, you should restore your strength for war, lift up the spirits of your citizens with that eloquence with which you once flourished, strengthen the circuit of your walls with many defensive bastions, and hasten to build defensive towers to protect that narrow space which by lying between your two harbours begrudges you the title of an island, if you are by any chance to resist the invasion of the foreigners. But in fact, regrettably, you do not have the resources for this, and your attempts are thwarted both by your lack of citizens and paucity of fighting men. That ancient nobility of the Corinthians will be forced into slavery to the foreigners; a long time ago they left their ancestral homes and crossed to Sicily, where they looked for a suitable place to found a city, and finally constructed your walls on a particularly safe site in the best and most beautiful part of Sicily, in between your harbours of different sizes.[109] What help is it to you now that you once flourished through the teaching of philosophers, and that the mouths of your poets overflowed with the nectar of the fount of inspiration? What help is it that you threw off from your neck the hateful yoke of Dionysius and others like him?[110] It would have been better and safer for you still to suffer the savagery of Sicilian tyrants than to experience the tyranny of a barbarous and repellent nation. I weep for you, Arethusa, fountain with a famous and celebrated name, who have fallen to such a degree of wretchedness that you who used to inspire the songs of poets will now have to calm the drunkenness of Germans and serve their revolting manners! What a dreadful misfortune it is for you to be fleeing back to your natal land, to be flowing in long currents underneath great tracts of sea to raise your head in the city of Syracuse and there flow into the nearby sea – where Alpheus (whom you fled before) mixes himself

---

108 This was a singularly accurate prediction. After the rebellion against Henry in 1197, Catania was sacked and its bishop imprisoned in Germany; Jamison (1957), 158.

109 The Corinthians founded Syracuse *c.* 734 BC on the peninsula of Ortygia, which faces south, with the 'greater harbour' to the west and the 'lesser harbour' to the east.

110 The tyrants Dionysius I and his son Dionysius II controlled Syracuse from 405–367 and 367–357 BC respectively. The former in particular was represented by ancient tradition as an archetypal tyrant.

with you in the greater of the two harbours.[111] Your situation, Cianus,[112] is a much better one, since after flowing a little way you trickle away and reach that same harbour as hardly even a small stream, hiding away your waters secretly to avoid being polluted by contact with the foreigners.

What point is there in my weeping for the calamity in store for the people of Agrigento? Why describe the disaster hanging over the people of Mazzara? I will pass over the new city-walls of Cefalù, destined to wretched and dishonourable slavery; I will keep quiet about how exposed the fields of the people of Patti[113] are to pillage by that raging nation. I must turn to you, most celebrated city, the head and glory of the whole realm of Sicily. Even though I do not have the ability to praise you as you deserve, yet I just cannot keep silent, both remembering the benefits I received from you and challenged by the miracle of your unparalleled fame. Is there anyone who would not fail in such a massive task, or who would not later regret such great boldness as to sing the praises of Palermo or to attempt to match its glory with words? But because I cannot keep the speech I have conceived barred within my breast, I will try with what ability I have to say a few brief words in praise of the city; so that from that very fact I may give some impression of how much lamentation will be needed to mourn her, how enormous the glory with which she has been endowed.

This city, then, lies in a plain: on one side she is subjected to the frequent lashings of the sea, the beating of whose waves is, however, checked by the former palace (called the Sea Castle) and by walls armed with a large number of towers. The New Palace sits on the opposite part of the other side, built with amazing effort and astonishing skill out of squared stones; the outer side has walls which

---

111 Cf. above, the *History*, note 278. Alpheus was the Greek river from whom Arethusa was said to have fled. Contemporary interest in the fountain can also be seen from a letter of Henry VI's chancellor, Conrad of Querfurt, Bishop-Elect of Hildesheim, included in the *Chronica Slavorum* of Arnold of Lübeck; MGH SS xxi, 195.

112 The River Ciane, which flows into the sea at Syracuse.

113 On the north coast of Sicily, 50 km. W. of Messina. The see of Lipari was transferred there at about this time, probably between 1186 and 1194, to judge by the charters of Bishop Stephen; White (1938), 278–9, no. 36; Jamison (1957), 321–3, no. 3.

wind far and wide, while the inner side is remarkable for its great splendour of gems and gold. On one side it has the Pisan Tower, assigned to the protection of the treasury, on the other the Greek Tower overlooks that part of the city which is called Kemonia. That part of the palace called Joharia glorifies the middle section;[114] it is particularly beautiful, sparkling with the glory of many kinds of adornment, and the king used to spend his time there intimately when he wanted to enjoy peace and quiet. Over the rest of the site there are spread various mansions placed all around for the married ladies, the girls of the harem, and the eunuchs who are assigned to serve the king and queen. There are some other smaller palaces there, shining with great beauty, where the king either discusses the state of the realm in private with his *familiares*, or invites the powerful when he is going to talk about the great public affairs of the realm. Nor is it appropriate to pass over in silence the high-quality workshops which belong to the palace, where the threads of silkworms are spun most finely into separate threads of different colours before being knitted together to make multiple strands.[115] Here you can see how single-stranded, double-stranded and triple-stranded thread is finished with less skill and expense; and there six-stranded thread is pressed together using richer material; here the red thread meets your eyes with the gleam of fire; and there the colour of green thread gives pleasure to the eyes of onlookers with its pleasant aspect; over there damask cloth marked by circles of different kinds requires greater application from the craftsmen and richness of raw material, and is consequently finished at greater cost. You may see many other adornments of different colours and types there, among them gold threaded into the silk, and a variety of different-shaped representations made by sparkling gems. Pearls too, either complete ones encased in gold, or perforated ones strung together on a thread and engraved by means of some elegant work of arrangement, are made to demonstrate the level of craftsmanship. Further on, for those who enter the palace from the side that overlooks the city, the Royal Chapel first meets the eye, paved

114 Probably from the Arabic *Jawhariyya*, 'the Jewel Room'.
115 Cultivation of mulberry-trees and silkworms (and therefore presumably silk-weaving) took place in eleventh-century Calabria, but the royal workshop at Palermo was probably begun after the Sicilian fleet which raided Thebes and Corinth in 1147 kidnapped a number of silkworkers; Chalandon (1907), ii, 136–7, 703–4. However, in 1184 one of the embroiderers was a male Muslim; Broadhurst, *The Travels of Ibn Jubayr*, 341.

with a floor of costly craftsmanship and with walls whose lower level is decorated with plates of precious marble, and the higher one with mosaic stones, some gold and others of different colours, with representations of the story of the Old and New Testaments. The uppermost level is adorned by an outstanding elegance of carvings and an amazing variety of sculpture, with the splendour of gold shining all around.[116]

Just as the head rises above the rest of the body, so the palace, arranged and adorned in this way, anointed by the grace of every kind of delight, overlooks the whole of the city, which is divided into three sections and (I might almost say) contains three separate cities within it. That which lies in the middle between the two outside ones has the more nobly constructed buildings. It is divided from both the one on its left and the one on its right by walls of enormous height. It is not so wide, but stretches very much further in length, as if someone were to put together in a single segment the two lesser portions of two equal circles.[117] Three major streets divide this city, stretching along the whole of its length. The one in the middle, called the Via Marmorea and allocated to marketing activities, leads from the top part of the Via Coperta straight down to the Arab Palace and from there to the Lower Gate by way of the Forum of the Muslims. The second goes from the Pisan Tower past the Via Coperta to the archbishop's residence, next to the Greater Church, then to the Gate of Saint Agatha and then on past the residences of the admiral Maio to the above-mentioned Forum of the Muslims, where it meets the Via Marmorea. The third goes from the Royal Hall which is next to the palace past the residence of Siddiq the Muslim[118] to the house of Count Silvester and the chapel of the admiral George,[119] and then

---

116 A very accurate description of the still-surviving decoration of the Palatine Chapel; while the sanctuary is vaulted in stone, itself decorated with mosaic, the nave and aisles have an elaborately carved wooden roof. For a detailed description of the mosaics, including an elaborate cycle from the book of Genesis, see Borsook (1990), 20–41, and especially the plan in her fig. 16.

117 The description is of the Halqa and Cassaro districts (see map II).

118 Cf. p. 170 above. But nothing else is known about him, except that a garden formerly belonging to him (which may have been attached to this house) was given to Palermo cathedral by the royal chancellor, Walter of Palearia, in 1209; Amari (1933–9), iii.510.

119 The church of St Mary of the Admiral, which served a Greek nunnery founded by George of Antioch in 1143. In 1433 this house was combined

turns across to the neighbouring city gate. The right-hand part of the city, however, which begins near the monastery of Saint John built next to the palace in the Kemonia quarter, is surrounded by walls which go right down to the sea. The left-hand part also stretches from the edge of the palace down to the Sea Castle and finishes there. It too is protected by an enormous circuit of walls.[120] The area in between the centre of the city and the harbour, where the two other parts of the city come together, contains the Amalfitan colony. It is rich from the resources of imported goods, and clothes of different colours and prices made both from silk and from wool from Gaul are offered for sale there.

Who is able to admire as they deserve the astonishing buildings of this marvellous city, the sweet richness of the fountains that gush up everywhere, the pleasant appearance of the trees that are always green or the aqueducts that abundantly serve the needs of its citizens? Who can match with due praise the glory of that unparalleled plain which stretches for about four miles between the city walls and the mountains? Blessed plain, to be extolled in all future centuries, which holding in its lap every sort of tree and fruit alone produces everything that is delightful, which offers every enticement to indulge the eyes, so that anyone who has once seen it can hardly ever look away from it whatever the inducement.[121] For there you may admire vines revelling both in the richness of their fertile clumps and the excellence of their remarkable tendrils. There you can see orchards which evoke praise for the astonishing variety of their fruits, and towers made ready to guard the orchards as well as for enjoyment, and there you can also see wells being emptied, and the cisterns next to them being filled, by buckets which rise and fall as the water-wheel turns round; and the water being drawn from them through canals to different places so that the irrigated plots may become green.[122] Citrus groves

      with a nearby Benedictine nunnery founded by Geoffrey of Martorano – hence it is now known as the Martorana. For a contemporary description, see Broadhurst, *The Travels of Ibn Jubayr*, 349; see also Demus (1950), 73–90.

120 The Seralcadi district.
121 The fertility of the plain of Palermo is attested by its more modern nickname of the Conca d'Oro.
122 This irrigation around Palermo was noted by the Muslim traveller Ibn Hawqal when he visited Sicily in 977 and by Edrisi *c.* 1150; *BAS* i, 6, 16.

grow in confined spaces, cucumbers of enormous length are produced, and melons which are almost perfect spheres in shape, and gourds growing all over the place on lattices of reeds. Here, if you turn your eyes to the different kinds of trees, you will see both sour and sweet pomegranates, their pips hidden within them, protected on the outside against intemperate weather by a hard skin. And you will see citrus fruits made up of three different substances, with their external skin indicating warmth through both its colour and its odour; the centre giving evidence of coldness through its sour sap, and what is in between is acknowledged to be more temperate. And there you can see limes whose acidity makes them suitable for adding savour to food, and oranges filled on the inside with just as much sourness, so that they rather delight the eye with their beauty than seem to be useful for anything else.[123] They drop from the tree they grow on with great difficulty even when they have ripened, and the mature ones refuse to fall even when a new crop appears; for fruit from two seasons ago, now ruddy, and those still green from last year and the flowering fruit of the current year, can be found together on the same tree. This tree revels in the signs of constant youth, and is not unsightly in the sterile old age of winter, nor is it deprived of its greenery by the harshness of unwanted cold; but with its green foliage it always represents the springtime. Why need I list walnuts or different types of figs or olives that provide oil both for preserving food and allowing the flames of lamps to burn? Why need I mention the husks of the carob-tree and its rather vulgar fruit which attracts the palates of peasants and children with its insipid sweetness? You would rather admire the lofty crowns of the palms, and the branches that hang down from the very top of a clipped tree. If you were to turn your eyes in the other direction, you would see amazing crops of reeds which are called honeycane by the inhabitants; they select this name from the sweetness of the sap within. When this sap is partially cooked, it changes into the appearance of honey; and when it has been fully cooked, it condenses into the form of sugar. I have thought it unnecessary to add to these the common kinds of fruits and those which are cultivated in our country.[124]

123 Bitter, or Seville, oranges; Jamison (1957), 233, note 1.
124 Jamison (1957), 233, argues that this phrase should not be taken to imply that the author was a non-Sicilian. She suggests that this interest in botany was also to be found in the poems of Eugenius, and is therefore another indication of his authorship of the *Letter*.

A LETTER CONCERNING THE SICILIAN TRAGEDY

I have described these things in a short digression so that the wisdom of the sympathetic reader may understand much from a few words, and important things from small; and also so that, however it has been stated, it may become clear what need there would be for how much lamentation and for what a great quantity of tears if the tragedy facing this city were to be properly mourned.

May you live long, dearest Peter, may you long be happy and not grudge to send me a letter about the situation of the realm, as a substitute for your own self.

BIBLIOGRAPHY

Manuscript sources (charters)

Cava dei Tirreni, Archivio della Badia di S. Trinità

Armarii Magni D. 15 (1097), E. 40 (1115), F. 36 (1125), H. 21, H. 22 (both 1155), H. 28 (1157), H. 32 (1158), I. 41 (1184), L. 21 (1187).
Arcae xxviii.104 (1154), xxx.31 (1159), xxx.71 (1161), xxxii.59 (1167), xxxiv.15 (1172).

Montecassino, Archivio dell'abbazia di S. Benedetto

Aula III, Capsula xii, no. 16 (1181)

Vatican City

Archivio segreto vaticano, Archivio Boncompagni Ludovisi, Prot. 270, no. 9 (1168)
Archivio segreto vaticano, Archivio S. Angelo, Arm. I. xviii.118 (1173)
Biblioteca apostolica vaticana, Pergamene Aldobrandini, Cartolario II, nos. 13 (1158), 21 (1170), 25 (1172) (these documents were examined by GAL in the Vatican Library in 1990; we are informed that they have now been returned to their owners, the Principi Aldobrandini, at Frascati)

Salerno, Archivio diocesano, Mensa Archiepiscopalis

Arca I, no. 53 (1144)

Printed primary sources

Amari, M., *Biblioteca Arabo-Sicula*, 2 vols., Turin, 1880.
Appleby, J. T., *The Chronicle of Richard of Devizes*, London, 1963.
Babcock, E. A. and Krey, A. C. (trans.), *William of Tyre: A History of Deeds done beyond the Sea*, 2 vols., New York, 1943.
Balducci, A., *Archivio della curia arciscovile di Salerno*, i *Regesto delle pergamene (945–1727)*, Salerno, 1945.

BIBLIOGRAPHY

Barlow, F., *The Letters of Arnulf of Lisieux*, London, 1939.
Bartoloni, F., *Le Più antiche carte dell'abbazia di San Modesto in Benevento (secoli VIII–XIII)*, Rome, 1950.
Belgrano, L. T., *Annali Genovesi di Caffaro e de' suoi continuatori* i (Fonti per la storia d'Italia 11), Rome, 1890.
Brand, C. M. (trans.), *Deeds of John and Manuel Comnenus by John Cinnamus*, New York, 1976.
Bresc-Bautier, G., *Le Cartulaire du chapitre du Saint Sépulcre*, Paris, 1984.
Broadhurst, R. J. C., *The Travels of Ibn Jubayr*, London, 1952.
Brühl, C-R., *Rogerii II Regis Diplomata Latina* (Codex Diplomaticus Regni Siciliae, Ser. I. ii(1)), Cologne, 1987.
Camobreco, F., *Regesto di S. Leonardo di Siponto*, Rome, 1913.
Carlone, C., *Documenti cavensi per la storia di Rocchetta S. Antonio*, Altavilla Silentina, 1987.
Chibnall, M. (ed. and trans.), *The Ecclesiastical History of Orderic Vitalis*, 6 vols, Oxford, 1968–80.
Chibnall, M., *The Historia Pontificalis of John of Salisbury*, Edinburgh, 1956.
Chronicon Casauriense auctore Johanne Berardi, in L. A. Muratori, *Rerum Italicarum Scriptores*, ii(2), Milan 1726, 775–1018.
Clementi, D. R., 'Calendar of the diplomas of the Hohenstaufen Emperor Henry VI concerning the kingdom of Sicily', *Quellen und Forschungen aus italienischen Aarchiven und Bibliotheken* xxv (1955), 86–225.
Collura, P., *Le Più antiche carte dell'archivio capitolare di Agrigento (1092–1282)*, (Documenti per servise alla stonà di Sicilia, Ser. I. xxv), Palermo, 1960.
Coniglio, G., *Le Pergamene di Conversano* i (901–1265), (Codice diplomatico pugliese xx), Bari, 1975.
Cusa, S., *I Diplomi greci ed arabi di Sicilia*, Palermo, 1860.
Deér, J., *Das Papsttum und die süditalienischen Normannenstaaten 1053–1212*, Göttingen, 1969.
Delisle, L. and Berger, E., *Recueil des Actes de Henri II, Roi d'Angleterre et Duc de Normandie, concernant les provinces françaises et les affaires de France*, 4 vols, Paris, 1906–27.
De Nava, L., *Alexandrini Telesini Abbatis Ystoria Rogerii Regis Siciliae, Calabriae atque Apuliae* (Fonti per la storia d'Italia 112), Rome, 1991.
Duchesne, L., *Liber Pontificalis*, 2 vols, Paris, 1886–92.
Ellis, G. M. and Munz, P., *Boso's Life of Alexander III*, Oxford, 1973.
Enzensberger, H., *Guillelmi I Regis Diplomata* (Codex Diplomaticus Regni Siciliae, Ser. I. iii), Cologne, 1996.
Gallo, A., *Codice diplomatico normanno di Aversa*, Naples, 1927.
Garofolo, A., *Tabularium Regiae ac Imperialis Capellae Collegiatae divi Petri in Regio Panormitano Palatio*, Palermo, 1835.
Garufi, C. A., *Catalogo illustrato del tabulario di S. Maria Nuova di Monreale* (Documenti per servire alla storia di Sicilia, Ser. I. xix), Palermo, 1902.
Garufi, C. A., *I documenti inediti dell'epoca normanna in Sicilia* (Documenti per servire alla storia di Sicilia, Ser. I. xiii), Palermo, 1899.

# BIBLIOGRAPHY

Garufi, C. A., *Necrologio del Liber Confratrum di S. Matteo di Salerno* (Fonti per la storia d'Italia 56), Rome, 1922.

Garufi, C. A., *Romualdi Salernitani Chronicon* (Rerum Italicarum Scriptores), Città di Castello, 1935.

Garufi, C. A., *Ryccardi de Sancto Germano Notarii Chronica* (Rerum Italicarum Scriptores), Bologna, 1938.

Gattula, E., *Accessiones ad Historiam Abbatiae Casinensis*, Venice, 1734.

Gaudenzi, A., *Chronicon Ignoti Monachi Cisterciensis S. Mariae de Ferraria*, Naples, 1888.

Güterbock, F., *Ottonis Morenae et Continuatorum Historia Frederici I* (MGH SRG, n. s. vii), Berlin, 1930.

Hagemann, W., 'Kaiserurkunden aus Gravina', *Quellen und Forschungen aus Italienischen Archiven und Bibliotheken* xl (1960), 188–200.

Hoffmann, H., *Chronica Monasterii Casinensis* (MGH Scriptores xxxiv), Hanover, 1980.

Hofmeister, A., *Ottonis de Sancto Blasio Chronica* (MGH SRG), Hanover, 1912.

Hofmeister, A., *Ottonis Episcopi Frisingensis Chronica, sive Historia de Duabus Civitatibus* (MGH SRG), Hanover, 1912.

Holder-Egger, O., *Gesta Frederici I Imperatoris in Lombardia auctore cive Mediolanensi* (MGH SRG xviii), Hanover, 1892.

Holtzmann, W., 'Die ältesten Urkunden des Klosters S. Maria del Patir', *Byzantinische Zeitschrift* xxvi (1926), 32–46.

Holtzmann, W., 'Kanonistiche Ergänzungen zur Italia Pontificia', *Quellen und Forschungen aus Italienischen Archiven und Bibliotheken* xxxviii (1958), 67–175.

Holtzmann, W., 'The Norman royal charters of S. Bartolomeo di Carpineto', *Papers of the British School at Rome* xxiv (1956), 94–100.

Holtzmann, W., 'Papst-, Kaiser- und Normannenurkunden aus Unteritalien I', *Quellen und Forschungen aus Italienischen Archiven und Bibliotheken* xxxv (1955), 46–85.

Houben, H., *Il libro del capitolo del monastero della SS. Trinità di Venosa (Cod. Casin. 334); una testimonianza del Mezzogiorno normanno*, Galatina, 1984.

Inguanez, M., *I Necrologi Cassinesi*, i: *Il Necrologio del Cod. Cassinese 47* (Fonti per la storia d'Italia 83), Rome, 1941.

Inguanez, M., *Regesto di S. Angelo in Formis*, Montecassino, 1925.

Jaffé, P., *Monumenta Corbeiensia* (Bibliotheca Rerum Germanicarum, i), Berlin, 1864.

Jamison, E. M., *Catalogus Baronum* (Fonti per la storia d'Italia, 101), Rome, 1972.

Kehr, P. F., *Italia Pontificia*, 10 vols., Berlin, 1905–74 (vol. ix: *Apulia–Samnium*, ed. W. Holtzmann (1963); vol. x: *Calabria–Insulae*, ed. D. Girgensohn (1974)).

Leccisotti, T., *Le colonie cassinesi in Capitanata*, iv: *Troia* (Miscellanea Cassinese 29), Montecessino, 1957.

Lupo Gentile, M., *Gli Annales Pisani di Bernardo Maragone* (Rerum Italicarum Scriptores), Bologna, 1936.

Martin, J. -M., *Les Chartes de Troia* i (1024–1266) (Codice diplomatico pugliese xxi), Bari, 1976.
Mathieu, M., *Guillaume de Pouille, La Geste de Robert Guiscard*, Palermo, 1961.
Ménager, L. -R., *Les Actes latins de S. Maria di Messina*, Palermo, 1963.
Ménager, L. -R., 'Notes critiques sur quelques diplomes normands de l'archivio capitolare di Catania', *Bollettino del archivio paleografico italiano* n. s. ii/iii (1956/7), 145–74.
Ménager, L. -R., 'Quelques monastères de Calabre à l'époque normande', *Byzantinische Zeitschrift* i (1957), 7–30, 321–61.
Mierow, C. C. (trans.), *The Deeds of Frederick Barbarossa, by Otto of Freising and his Continuator Rahewin*, New York, 1953.
Millor, W. J., Butler, H. E. and Brooke, C. N. L., *The Letters of John of Salisbury*, i: *The Early Letters (1153–1161)*, London, 1955.
Millor, W. J. and Brooke, C. N. L., *The Letters of John of Salisbury*, ii: *The Later Letters (1163–1180)*, Oxford, 1979.
Minio-Paluello, L., *Phaedo Interprete Henrico Aristippo* (Warburg Institute, Plato Latinus ii), London, 1950.
Monti, G. M., *Codice diplomatico brindisiano* i (492–1299), Trani, 1940.
Monti, G. M., 'Il testo e la storia esterna delle assise normanne', *Studi di storia e di diretto in onore di Carlo Calisse* i, Milan, 1940, 295–348.
Nitti di Vito, F. and Nitto di Rossi, G. B., *Codice diplomatico barese*, i: *Le Pergamene del duomo di Bari (952–1264)*, Bari, 1897.
Nitti di Vito, F., *Codice diplomatico barese*, v: *Le Pergamene di S. Niccola di Bari (1075–1194)*, Bari, 1902.
Paesano, G., *Memorie per servire alla storia della chiesa Salernitana*, 4 vols., Naples, 1846–57.
Pertz, G. H., *Annales Casinenses*, MGH SS xix (1866), 303–20.
Pertz, G. H., *Annales Ceccanenses*, MGH SS xix (1866), 275–302.
Peter of Blois, *Epistolae*, in MPL ccvii, 1–560.
Petrucci, A., *Codice diplomatico del monastero benedettino di S. Maria di Tremiti, 1005–1237*, 3 vols (Fonti per la storia d'Italia), Rome, 1960.
Pirro, R., *Sicula Sacra*, 2 vols., Palermo, 1733.
Pontieri, E., *De Rebus Gestis Rogerii Calabriae et Siciliae Comitis auctore Gaufredo Malaterra*, (Rerum Italicarum Scriptores), Bologna, 1927–8.
Powell, J. M. (trans.), *The Liber Augustalis or Canstitutions of Melfi Promulgated by the Emperor Frederick II for the Kingdom of Sicily in 1231*, Syracuse, NY, 1971.
Pratesi, A., *Carte latine di abbazie calabresi provenienti dall'archivio aldobrandini*, Vatican City, 1958.
Prologo, A., *Le carte che si conservano nello archivio dello capitolo metropolitano della città di Trani (dal IX secolo fino all'anno 1266)*, Barletta, 1877.
Siragusa, G. B., *La Historia o Liber de Regno Sicilie e la Epistola ad Petrum Panormitane Ecclesie Thesaurium di Ugo Falcando* (Fonti per la storia d'Italia 22), Rome, 1897.
Siragusa, G. B., *Liber ad Honorem Augusti di Pietro da Eboli* (Fonti per la storia d'Italia 39), Rome, 1906.

Starraba, R., *I diplomi della cattedrale di Messina* (Documenti per servire alla storia di Sicilia, Ser. I. i), Palermo, 1876–90.
Stubbs, W., *Gesta Regis Henrici II Benedicti Abbatis*, 2 vols. (Rolls Series), London, 1867 (actually by Roger of Howden).
Trinchera, F., *Syllabus Graecarum Membranarum*, Naples, 1865.
Tropeano, P. M., *Codice diplomatico verginiano*, 10 vols, Montevergine, 1977–86.
Ughelli, F., *Italia Sacra sive de Episcopis Italiae*, 2nd. edn by N. Colletti, 10 vols., Venice, 1717–21.
Zielinski, H., *Tancredi et Willelmi III Regum Diplomata* (Codex Diplomaticus Regni Siciliae, Ser. I. v), Cologne, 1982.

Secondary sources

Abulafia, D. S. H. (1977), *The Two Italies: Economic Relations between the Norman Kingdom of Sicily and the Northern Communes*, Cambridge.
Abulafia, D. S. H. (1979), 'The reputation of a Norman king in Angevin Naples', *Journal of Medieval History* v, 135–47.
Abulafia, D. S. H. (1983), 'The crown and the economy under Roger II and his successors', *Dumbarton Oaks Papers* xxxvii, 1–14 (reprinted in Abulafia (1987)).
Abulafia, D. S. H. (1984), 'Ancona, Byzantium and the Adriatic, 1155–1173', *Papers of the British School at Rome* lii, 195–216 (reprinted in Abulafia 1987).
Abulafia, D. S. H. (1985), 'The Norman kingdom of Africa and the Norman expeditions to Majorca and the Muslim Mediterranean', *Anglo-Norman Studies* vii, 26–49 (reprinted in Abulafia 1987).
Abulafia, D. S. H. (1986), 'The merchants of Messina: Levant trade and domestic economy', *Papers of the British School at Rome* liv, 196–212.
Abulafia, D. S. H. (1987), *Italy, Sicily and the Mediterranean*, London.
Amari, M. (1933–9), *Storia dei musulmani di sicilia*, 2nd edn by C. A. Nallino, 3 vols, Catania.
Ameling, W. (1986), 'Tyrannen und schwangere Frauen', *Historia* xxxv, 506–7
Barlow, F. (1986), *Thomas Becket*, London.
Barthélemy, D. (1993), *La Société dans le comté de Vendôme de l'an mil au XIVe siècle*, Paris.
Bercher, H., Courteaux, A. and Mouton, J. (1979), 'Une Abbaye latine dans la société musulmane: Monreale au XIIe siècle', *Annales, Economies, Sociétés, Civilisations* xxxiv, 525–47.
Berschin, W. (1988), *Greek Letters and the Latin Middle Ages. From Jerome to Nicholas of Cusa*, trans. J. C. Frakes, Washington, DC.
Bloch, H. (1972), 'Monte Cassino's teachers and library in the High Middle Ages', *Settimane di studio del centro italiano di studi sull'alto medioevo* xix, 563–605.
Borsook, E. (1990), *Messages in Mosaic. The Royal Programmes of Norman Sicily, 1130–87*, Oxford.

Bresc, H. (1990), 'In ruge que arabice dicitur zucac les rues de Palerme (1070–1460)', in H. Bresc, *Politique et société en Sicile, XIIe-XIVe siècles*, Aldershot, chapter 8 (pp. 155–86).

Brown, T. S. (1992), 'The political use of the past in Norman Sicily', in *The Perception of the Past in Twelfth-Century Europe*, ed. P. Magdalino, London, pp. 191–210.

Brühl, C. R. (1978), *Urkunden und Kanzlei König Rogers II von Sizilien*, Cologne.

Capitani, O. (1977), 'Specific motivations and continuing themes in the Norman chronicles of southern Italy in the eleventh and twelfth centuries', in *The Normans in Southern Italy and Sicily. The Lincei Lectures 1974*, Oxford, pp. 1–46.

Caravale, M. (1966) *Il Regno normanno di Sicilia*, Rome.

Cavallo, G. (1975), 'La Trasmissione dei testi nell'area beneventano–cassinese', *Settimane di studio del centro italiano di studi sull'alto medioevo* xxii, 357–414.

Chalandon, F. (1907), *Histoire de la domination normande en Italie et en Sicile*, 2 vols., Paris.

Clementi, D. (1967), 'The circumstances of Count Tancred's succession to the Kingdom of Sicily, Duchy of Apulia and Principality of Capua', *Mélanges Antonio Marongiu*, Palermo, 57–80.

Clementi, D. (1968), 'The relations between the papacy, the western Roman empire and the emergent kingdom of Sicily and south Italy (1050–1156)', *Bullettino del istituto storico italiano per il medio evo* lxxx, 191–212.

Cooper, K. (1992), 'Insinuations of womanly influence: an aspect of the Christianization of the Roman aristocracy', *Journal of Roman Studies* lxxxii, 150–64.

Cuozzo E. (1979), '"Milites" e "testes" nella contea normanna del Principato', *Bullettino del istituto storico italiano per il medio evo* lxxxviii, 121–63.

Cuozzo E. (1980), 'Prosopografia di una famiglia feodale normanna: I Balvano', *Archivio storico per le provincie napoletane* xcviii, 61–87.

Cuozzo E. (1981), 'Ruggiero, conte d'Andria. Ricerche sulla nozione di regalità al tramonto della monarchia normanna', *Archivio storico per le provincie napoletane* xcix, 129–68.

Cuozzo E. (1984), *Catalogus Baronum. Commentario* (Fonti per la storia d'Italia), Rome.

Cuozzo, E. (1985), 'La Contea di Montescaglioso nel secoli XI-XIII', *Archivio storico per le provincie napoletane* ciii, 7–37.

Cuozzo, E. (1989), *"Quei maledetti normanni". Cavalieri e organizzazione militare nel mezzogiorno normanno*, Naples.

Cuozzo, E. (1996), 'A propos de la coexistance entre normands et lombardes dans le royaume de Sicile. La révolte féodale de 1160–1162', *Peuples du Moyen Age. Problèmes d'identification*, ed. C. Carozzi and H. Taviani-Carozzi, Aix-en-Provence.

D'Alessandro, V. (1989), 'Servi e liberi', in *Uomo e ambiente nel Mezzogiorno normanno–svevo* (Atti delle ottave giornate normanno-svevi, Bari, 20–23 ottobre 1987), Bari, 293–318.

BIBLIOGRAPHY 271

Deér, J. (1959), *The Dynastic Porphyry Tombs of the Norman Period in Sicily*, Cambridge, Massachusetts.
Deér, J. (1972), *Papsttum und Normannen. Untersuchungen zu ihren lehnsrechtlichen und kirchenpolitischen Bezeihungen*, Cologne.
Demus, O. (1950), *The Mosaics of Norman Sicily*, London.
Duby, G. (1977), 'Youth in aristocratic society', in his *The Chivalrous Society*, London, 112–22.
Enzensberger, H. (1967), *Beiträge zum Kanzlei- und Urkundenwesen der normannischen Herrscher Unteritaliens und Siziliens*, Kallmünz.
Enzensberger, H. (1980), 'Der "böse" und der "gute" Wilhelm. Zur Kirchenpolitik der normannischen Könige von Sizilien nach dem Vertrag von Benevent (1156)', *Deutsches Archiv für Erforschung des Mittelalters* xxxvi, 385–432.
Enzensberger, H. (1981), 'Il documento regio come strumento di potere', in *Potere, società e popolo nell'età dei due Guglielmi* (Atti del centro di studi normanno-svevi 4), Bari, 103–38.
Epstein, S. (1996), *Genoa and the Genoese, 958–1528*, Chapel Hill.
Falkenhausen, V. von (1987), 'Il popolamento: etniè, fedi, insediamenti', in *Terra e uomini nel Mezzogiorno normanno–svevo* (Atti delle settime giornate normanno–sveve, Bari, 15–17 ottobre 1985), Bari, 39–73.
Fuiano, M. (1956), 'La fondazione del Regnum de Siciliae nella versione di Alessandro di Telese', *Papers of the British School at Rome* xxiv, 65–72.
Fuiano, M. (1960), *Studi di storiagrafia medioevale*, Naples.
Ganzer, K. (1963), *Die Entwicklung des auswärtigen Kardinalats*, Tübingen.
Garufi, C. A. (1910), 'Gli Aleramici e i normanni in Sicilia e in Puglia. Documenti e ricerche', *Centenario della nascità di Michele Amari*, Naples, vol. i, 47–83.
Garufi, C. A. (1912), 'Per la storia dei sec. XI e XII. Miscellanea diplomatica, ii: I conti di Montescaglioso', *Archivio storico per la Sicilia orientale* ix, 324–65.
Garufi, C. A. (1913a), 'Per la storia dei sec. XI e XII. Miscellanea diplomatica, iii: La contea di Paternò e i de Luci', *Archivio storico per la Sicilia orientale* x, 160–80.
Garufi, C. A. (1913b), 'Per la storia dei sec. XI e XII. Miscellanea diplomatica. iv: I de Parisio e i de Ocra nei contadi di Paternò', *Archivio storico per la Sicilia orientale* x, 346–73.
Garufi, C. A. (1942), 'Roberto di San Giovanni, maestro notaio e il "Liber de Regno Sicilie"', *Archivio storico per la Sicilia* viii, 33–128.
Goody, J. (1983), *The Development of the Family and Marriage in Europe*, Cambridge.
Guenée, B. (1973), 'Histoires, annales, chroniques. Essai sur les genres historiques au Moyen Age', *Annales, Economies, Sociétés, Civilisations* xxviii, 997–1016.
Guillou, A. (1963), 'Inchiesta sulla populazione greca della Sicilia e della Calabria nel medio evo', *Rivista storica italiana* lxxxv, 53–68 (reprinted in A. Guillou, *Studies on Byzantine Italy*, London 1970).

BIBLIOGRAPHY

Hartwig, O. (1883), 'Re Guglielmo e il suo grande amiraglio Maione di Bari', *Archivio storico per le provincie napoletane* viii, 397–485.
Haskins, C. H. (1927a), *The Renaissance of the Twelfth Century*, Cambridge, Massachusetts.
Haskins, C. H. (1927b), *Studies in the History of Medieval Science*, 2nd edn, New York.
Herde, P. (1991), 'Die Katastrophe vor Rom im August 1167. Eine historisch–epidemiologische Studie zum vierten Italienzug Friedrichs I. Barbarossa', *Sitzungsberichte der wissenschaftlichen Gesellschaft an der Johann-Wolfgang-Goethe-Universität Frankfurt am Main* xxvii, 139–66.
Hoffmann, H. (1967), 'Hugo Falcandus und Romuald von Salerno', *Deutsches Archiv für Erforschung des Mittelalters* xxiii, 117–70.
Hoffmann, H. (1978), 'Langobarden, Normannen und Päpste. Zum Legitimitätsproblem in Unteritalien', *Quellen und Forschungen aus italienischen Archiven und Bibliotheken* lviii, 137–80.
Houben, H. (1992), 'Barbarossa und die Normannen. Tradionelle Züge und neue Perspektiven imperialer Süditalienpolitik', *Friedrich Barbarossa. Handlungsspielräume und Wirkungsweisen des Staufischen Kaisers*, ed. A. Haverkamp, Sigmaringen, 109–28.
Houben, H. (1994), 'Möglichkeiten und Grenzen religiöser Toleranz im normannisch–staufischen Königreigh Sizilien', *Deutsches Archiv für Erforschung des Mittelalters* l, 159–98.
Houben, H. (1995), *Die Abtei Venosa und das Mönchtum im normannisch–staufischen Süditalien*, Tübingen.
Jamison, E. M. (1913), 'The Norman administration of Apulia and Capua, more especially under Roger II and William I, 1127–66', *Papers of the British School at Rome* vi, 211–481 (reprinted as a separate volume, Aalen 1987).
Jamison, E. M. (1929), 'The administration of the county of Molise in the twelfth and thirteenth centuries, I', *English Historical Review* xliv, 529–59.
Jamison, E. M. (1931), 'Note e documenti per la storia dei conti normanni di Catanzaro', *Archivio storico per la Calabria e la Lucania* i, 451–70.
Jamison, E. M. (1933), 'I conti di Molise e Marsia nei secoli xii e xiii', *Convegno storico Abruzzese–Molisano, 25–29 marzo 1931: atti e memorie* (Casalbordino 1933), i, 73–178.
Jamison, E. M. (1951), 'La carriera del logotheta Riccardo di Taranto e l'ufficio del logotheta sacri palatii nel regno normanno di Sicilia e d'Italia meridionale', *Archivio storico pugliese* iv, 1–23.
Jamison, E. M. (1957), *Admiral Eugenius of Sicily. His Life and Work and the Authorship of the* Epistola ad Petrum *and the* Historia Hugonis Falcandi Siculi, London.
Jamison, E. M. (1959), 'The significance of the earlier medieval documents from S. Maria della Noce and San Salvatore di Castiglione', *Studi in onore di Riccardo Filangieri* i, Naples, 437–66.
Jamison, E. M. (1967), 'Iudex Tarentinus', *Proceedings of the British Academy* liii, 289–344.

BIBLIOGRAPHY 273

Jamison, E. M. (1971), 'Additional work on the *Catalogus Baronum*', *Bullettino del istituto storico italiano per il medio evo* lxxxiii, 1–63.
Johns, J. (1993), 'The Norman kings of Sicily and the Fatamid Caliphate', *Anglo-Norman Studies* xv, 133–59.
Johns, J. (1995), 'The Greek Church and the conversion of Muslims in Norman Sicily', *Byzantinische Forschungen* xxi, 133–57.
Kamp, N. (1973–82), *Kirche und Monarchie im Staufischen Königreich Siziliens*, 4 vols., Munich.
Kamp, N. (1980), 'Der unteritalienische Episkopat im Spannungsfeld zwischen monarchischer Kontrolle und römischer "libertas" von der Reichsgrundung Rogers II. bis zum Konkordat von Benevent', *Società, potere e popolo nell'età di Ruggero II* (Atti delle terze giornate normanno–svevi, Bari, 23–25 maggio 1977), Bari, 99–132.
Kamp, N. (1994), 'Die Bischöfe Siziliens in der Normannenzeit: ihre soziale Herkunft und ihr geistlicher Bildungsweg', *Abhandlungen der Braunschweigischen Wissenschaftlichen Gesellschaft* xlv, 81–103.
Kehr, K. A. (1902), *Die Urkunden der normannisch–sizilischen Könige*, Innsbruck.
Kehr, P. (1926), 'Zur Geschichte Viktors IV (Oktavian von Monticelli)', *Neues Archiv für ältere deutsches Geschichtskunde* xlvi, 53–85.
Le Tourneau, R. (1969), *The Almohad Movement in Spain and North Africa*, Princeton.
Liebeschütz, H. (1950), *Medieval Humanism in the Life and Writings of John of Salisbury*, London.
Loewenthal, J. A. (1972), 'For the biography of Walter Offamil, Archbishop of Palermo', *English Historical Review* lxxxvii, 75–82.
Loud, G. A. (1982), 'Royal control of the Church in the twelfth-century kingdom of Sicily', *Studies in Church History* xviii, 147–59.
Loud, G. A. (1983), 'The Church, warfare and military obligation in Norman Italy', *Studies in Church History* xx, 31 45.
Loud, G. A. (1985), *Church and Society in the Norman Principality of Capua 1058–1197*, Oxford.
Loud, G. A. (1987), 'The abbey of Cava, its property and benefactors in the Norman era', *Anglo-Norman Studies* ix, 143–77.
Loud, G. A. (1992), 'Norman Italy and the Holy Land', in *The Horns of Hattin*, ed. B. Z. Kedar, Jerusalem, 49–62.
Loud, G. A. (1993), 'The genesis and context of the chronicle of Falco of Benevento', *Anglo-Norman Studies* xv, 177–98.
Loud, G. A. (1996), 'Continuity and change in Norman Italy: the Campania in the eleventh and twelfth centuries', *Journal of Medieval History* xxii, 313–43.
Loud, G. A. (1998), 'William the Bad or William the Unlucky? Kingship in Sicily 1154–1166', *The Haskins Society Journal* viii.
Lowe, E. A. (1980), *The Beneventan Script*, 2nd edn by V. Brown, Rome.
Martin, J.-M. (1993), *La Pouille du VIe au XIIe siècle*, Rome.
Matthew, D. J. A. (1981), 'The chronicle of Romuald of Salerno', in *The Writing*

of *History in the Middle Ages. Essays Presented to Richard William Southern*, ed. R. H. C. Davis and J. M. Wallace-Hadrill, Oxford, 239–74.

Matthew, D. J. A. (1992a), 'Maio of Bari's commentary on the Lord's Prayer', in *Intellectual Life in the Middle Ages. Essays Presented to Margaret Gibson*, ed. L. Smith and B. Ward, London, 119–44.

Matthew, D. J. A. (1992b), *The Norman Kingdom of Sicily*, Cambridge.

Ménager, L. -R. (1960), *Amiratus – Αμερασ L'Emirat et les origines de l'amirauté (XIe–XIIIe siècles)*, Paris.

Ménager, L. -R. (1969), 'La Législation sud-italienne sons la domination normande', *Seltimane di studio del Centro Italiano di Studi sull'alto Medioevo* xvi, 439–96.

Ménager, L. -R. (1975), 'Inventaire des familles normandes et franques émigrées en Italie méridionale et en Sicile (XIe–XIIe siècles)', in *Roberto il Guiscardo e il suo tempo* (Relazioni e communicazioni nelle prime giornate normanno–sveve, Bari, maggio 1973), Rome, 259–390.

Munz, P. (1969), *Frederich Barbarossa*, London.

Norwich, J. J. (1967), *The Normans in the South*, London.

Norwich, J. J. (1970), *The Kingdom in the Sun*, London.

Olsen, B. M. (1982–9), *L'Etude des auteurs classiques latins aux XIe e XIIe siècles*, 3 vols. in 4, Paris.

Parker, J. (1956), 'The attempted Byzantine alliance with the Sicilian Norman kingdom, 1166–1167', *Papers of the British School at Rome* xxiv, 86–93.

Patch, H. R. (1927), *The Goddess Fortuna in Medieval Literature*, Cambridge, Massachusetts.

Peri, I. (1978), *Uomini, città e campagne in Sicilia dall XI al XIII secolo*, Bari.

Peters, E. (1970), *The Shadow King. Rex Inutilis in Medieval Law and Literature*, New Haven.

Petrucci, A. (1959), 'Note di diplomatica normanna, I: I documenti di Roberto di "Basunvilla", II Conte di Conversano e III Conte di Loritello', *Bullettino del istituto storico italiano per il medio evo* lxxi, 113–40.

Poole, R. L. (1934), 'The beginning of the year in the Middle Ages', in his *Studies in Chronology and History*, Oxford, 1–27.

Portanova, G. (1976a), 'I Sanseverino dalle origini al 1125', *Benedictina* xxii, 105–49.

Portanova, G. (1976b), 'I Sanseverino dal 1125 allo sterminio del 1246', *Benedictina* xxii, 319–63.

Poso, C. D. (1988), *Il Salento normanno. Territorio, istituzioni, società*, Galatina.

Pryor, J. H. (1988), *Geography, Technology and War. Studies in the Maritime History of the Mediterranean 649–1571*, Cambridge.

Reisinger, C. (1992), *Tankred von Lecce, normannischer König von Sizilien 1190–4*, Cologne.

Reynolds, L. D., ed., (1983), *Texts and Transmission. A Survey of the Latin Classics*, Oxford.

Reynolds, L. D. and Wilson, N. G. (1974), *Scribes and Scholars. A Guide to the Transmission of Greek and Latin Literature*, Oxford, 2nd. edn.

Robinson, I. S. (1990), *The Papacy 1073–1198. Continuity and Innovation*, Cambridge.
Rowe, J. G. (1969), 'Hadrian IV, the Byzantine Empire and the Latin Orient', in *Essays in Medieval History Presented to Bertie Wilkinson*, ed. T. Sandquist and M. Powicke, Toronto, 3–16.
Schanz, M. and Hosius, C. (1935), *Geschichte der römischen Literatur*, ii (4th edn), Munich.
Schütz, W. (1995), *Catalogus Comitum. Versuch einer Territorialgliederung Kampaniens under den Normannen von 1000 bis 1140 von Benevent bis Salerno*, Frankfurt.
Siragusa, G. B. (1929), *Il Regno di Guglielmo I in Sicilia*, 2nd. edn, Palermo.
Skinner, P. (1997), *Health and Medicine in Early Medieval Southern Italy*, Leiden.
Smalley, B. (1971), 'Sallust in The Middle Ages', in *Classical Influences in European Culture, AD 500–1500*, ed. R. R. Bolgar, Cambridge, 165–75.
Stafford, P. (1983), *Queens, Concubines and Dowagers. The King's Wife in the Early Middle Ages*, London.
Stroll, M. (1987), *The Jewish Pope. Ideology and Politics in the Papal Schism of 1130*, Leiden.
Takayama, H. (1985), 'The financial and administrative organisation of the Norman kingdom of Sicily', *Viator* xvi, 129–57.
Takayama, H. (1989), '*Familiares regis* and the royal inner council in twelfth-century Sicily', *English Historical Review* civ, 357–72.
Takayama H. (1993), *The Administration of the Norman Kingdom of Sicily*, Leiden.
Tescione, G. (1990), *Caserta medievale e i suoi conti e signori*, 3rd edn, Caserta.
Thompson, K. (1995), 'The Counts of Perche, c. 1066–1217' (unpublished Ph.D. thesis, University of Sheffield).
Thompson, K. (1996), 'The Lords of Laigle: ambition and insecurity on the borders of Normandy', *Anglo-Norman Studies* xviii, 177–99.
Travaini, L. (1995), *La Monetazione nell'Italia normanna*, Rome.
Ward, E. (1990), 'Caesar's wife. The career of the Empress Judith, 819–829', in *Charlemagne's Heir. New Perspectives on the Reign of Louis the Pious (814–840)*, ed. P. Godman and R. Collins, Oxford, 205–27.
White, L. T. (1938), *Latin Monasticism in Norman Sicily*, Cambridge, Massachusetts.
Wiedemann, T. E. J. (1979), 'The figure of Catiline in the *Historia Augusta*', *Classical Quarterly* xxix, 479–84.
Wiedemann, T. E. J. (1993), 'Sallust's *Jugurtha*: concord, discord, and the digressions', *Greece and Rome* xxxix (2), 150–9.
Wieruszowski, H. (1963), 'Roger II of Sicily. *Rex tyrannus* in twelfth-century political thought', *Speculum* xxxviii, 46–78.
Zenker, B. (1964), *Die Mitglieder des Kardinalkollegiums von 1130 bis 1154*, Würzburg.

INDEX

Abednago, son of Hannibal, Master Justiciar of the Royal Court, 193
Abruzzi, 9, 64, 74, 77, 128–9, 235
  see also Marsia
Abu-'l-Qasim, 170
Adelaide, Countess of Sicily, mother of King Roger, 86
Adelaide, daughter of King Roger, 86–7
Adelicia of Adernò, 31, 105, 111, 119–20
Admirals (Emirs)
  see Eugenius, Admiral; George of Antioch; Maio of Bari; Stephen, Admiral; Walter of Moac
Adrian IV, Pope (1154–9), 2, 10, 19, 221–4, 227, 243–5, 248
Aegidius, Abbot of Holy Trinity, Venosa 190
Africa, 78–81, 225
  see also Mahdia
Agrigento, 198–9, 258
  bishopric of, 224
  Bishop, see Gentile
Alan, Bishop of Chieti, 77
Alduin *Cantuensis*, 211
Aleramici family, 11, 83, 121, 187, 208
  see also Henry, Count of Paterno; Roger Sclavus; Simon, Count of Policastro
Alexander, Abbot of Telese, 4–5
Alexander, Count of Conversano, 8, 115–16, 229
Alexander III, Pope (1159–81), 15, 19–20, 22, 24, 39, 81, 166, 172, 190, 216, 227–8, 232–7, 240, 243, 247–8
Alexius Comnenus, cousin of Emperor Manuel, 66, 223
Alfanus, Archbishop of Capua (1153–81), 24, 153, 193
Alferius, uncle of the Countess of Catanzaro, 127
Alife, county of, 26
Almagest, 33, 98–9
Almohads, 53, 78–9, 81, 147, 225
Amalfi, 82, 85, 223, 251
Anacletus II, anti-pope (1130–8), 4, 10, 19
Anastasius IV, Pope (1153–4), 221
Andrew, eunuch, 99
Andrew, usher, 208
Andrew of Limoges, *stratigotus* of Messina, 200–3
Andrew of Rupecanina, 8, 23, 26, 84, 149, 223–4, 232, 240, 245
Andria, county of, 149–50
  counts of, see Bertram, Roger
Anfusus, Prince of Capua (d. 1144), 9, 59
Ansaldus, palace castellan, 134–5, 164, 208–9
Aquinas of Moac, 232
Arethusa, fountain of, 217, 257–8
Ariano, county of, 4, 10
Aristippus, Henry, Archdeacon of Catania and chancellor, (1156–61), 16, 18, 39, 48, 98–9, 108, 120–1, 131
Asclettin, Archdeacon of Catania (1145–56) and Chancellor, 63–5, 73, 222
astrologers, 125, 207

INDEX

Atenulf, chamberlain 96–7, 102–4, 123–4
Avellino, 26
Aversa, 6, 191

Balium, 137
Bari, 3, 41–2, 73–4, 131, 223–4
  nunnery of St Scholastica, 17
Bartholomew de Luci, 187, 190
Bartholomew de Parisio, 136, 153, 184, 190, 195, 242
Bartholomew of Garsiliato, 71
Benevento, 4, 20, 222–4, 232, 241, 245, 247
  Treaty of (1156), 2, 18–20, 52, 81, 154, 247–52
Berengar, Master Constable, 170
Bernard, Abbot of Clairvaux, 6
Bernard, Bishop-Elect of Catania, 246
Bertram, Count of Andria, son of Count Gilbert of Gravina, 26, 149, 157, 214–15, 242
Bertrandus II, Archbishop of Trani, 119
Boccaccio, Giovanni, 51
Boethius, 37, 39
Bohemond I (of Tarsia), Count of Manopello (1140–57), 64, 75, 176, 192
Bohemond II (of S. Fele), Count of Manopello (1157–69), 21, 144, 176–8, 185, 193–4, 228, 231
Bohemond of Tarsia, son of Count Bohemond I of Manopello, 192, 211
Bonellus, Matthew, 21, 86, 92–104, 107–8, 110–12, 115–20, 122–4, 197, 229–32
  blinded, 124
  family of, 86
Borell, Marius, 83, 129, 131
Boso, Bishop of Cefalù, 19, 31, 208
Boso, Cardinal priest of St Prudentia, 263–4
Bracciolini, Poggio, 48
Brindisi, 66, 73, 78, 85, 223, 247

Burgundius, justiciar, 199
Butera, 71–2, 121, 124–6, 187, 222, 232
Byzantine Empire, 3, 7–8, 19, 73, 223–5
  see also John Comnenus; Manuel Comnenus

Caccamo, 97, 100, 112, 116–19, 197
Caiazzo, county of, 10
Calabria, 3–4, 11, 15, 85, 87, 92–3, 100, 125–6, 189, 190, 207, 254
Calomenus, John (Master?)
  Chamberlain of Calabria, 203
Capua, 3, 63–4, 66, 126, 245
  sack of, 6
Carbonellus, son of Count Bohemond I of Manopello, 192, 211
Catalogue of the Barons, 9
Catania, 122, 172, 207, 216–17, 256–7
  Bishop of, *see* John, Bishop of Catania
  earthquake in (1169), 216–17, 243, 256
Catanzaro, Countess of, *see* Clementia
Catiline
  Conspiracy of Catiline (Sallust), 43, 45, 47–8, 156, 185, 189
  In Catilinam (Cicero), 39, 46
Cava, abbey of Holy Trinity, 182
  see also Marinus, Abbot
Cefalù, 208, 220, 258
  bishopric of, 9, 19
  bishops of, *see* Boso; Guido
  cathedral of Holy Saviour, 220
Celestine II, Pope (1143–44), 9
Ceprano, Treaty of (1150), 10, 19
Chancellor, *see* Aristippus; Ascletin; Guarin; Robert of Selby; Stephen of Perche
Charlemagne, 45, 82
Christian, Archbishop of Mainz, 23, 235

INDEX

Cicero, Roman politician and writer, 37–9, 44–50, 187, 189, 217
Clement III, Pope (1187–91), 37
Clementia, Countess of Catanzaro, 89–90, 92, 126, 128, 211, 229
Conrad, Archbishop of Mainz (later Archbishop of Salzburg), d. 1200), 234–5, 237
Conrad III, King of Germany (1138–52), 8, 66, 241
Consolation of Philosophy (Boethius), 37, 39
Constance, daughter of King Roger and empress, 2, 8, 27, 35, 203, 253, 255
Constantine, palace castellan, 209–10
Constantinople, 98
see also Byzantine Empire
Crusade, Second, 7–8, 180

Darius, usher, 35, 114
defetir/defetarii 29, 49, 121
duana, 29, 49, 109–10, 121, 158
  Baronum, 33–5, 195, 204
  de Secretis (*diwan-at-tahqiq-al ma'mur*), 110, 121, 129, 158, 195
Dukas, John, 66, 223

earthquake (1169), 216–18, 243
Edrisi, Arabic geographer, 68, 71, 93, 213, 261
Eugenius, Admiral (Emir), 32–40, 262
Eugenius III, Pope (1145–53), 10, 19–20, 87
eunuchs, 100–3, 109, 136, 145, 166–7, 170, 225, 239
  Andrew, 99
  see also [Caid] Johar; [Caid] Martin; [Caid] Peter
Eustochia, Abbess of St Scholastica, Bari, sister of Maio, 17

Everard, Count of Squillace, 15, 61, 71–2, 76–7, 81

Falco of Benevento, chronicler, 7
familiares, 18, 27, 29, 120, 131, 137, 139–41, 145, 148, 150, 154, 158, 160, 164, 167–8, 181, 186, 201, 214, 216, 242, 259
Favara palace, 136, 219, 231
Fenicia of San Severino, 129
Florius of Camerota, 24, 153, 193
Fortune, 37, 70, 89–90, 94, 123, 126–7, 129, 134, 173, 175, 256
  Wheel of, 37–8, 55, 94
Frangipane, Odo, 228, 247
Frederick I (Barbarossa), German Emperor (1152–90), 2, 8, 19–20, 22–3, 203, 214, 222–3, 226, 233, 240, 244
Frederick II, King of Sicily and German Emperor (1220–50), 28, 52–3, 63, 149, 168

Gallipoli, 70
gavarettus, 106, 108, 207
Genoa, 7, 18, 20, 22, 105, 214, 232, 237
Gentile, Bishop of Agrigento (1154–71), 30, 140–1, 143, 159, 165, 184, 195–7, 199, 202, 214, 216
Geoffrey of Perche, 203
George of Antioch, Great Admiral, 12, 219–20, 260
Gilbert, Count of Gravina, cousin of Queen Margaret, 21–2, 26, 83, 126, 144–50, 159, 181, 184–5, 187, 189, 191–2, 195–7, 214–15, 228, 231, 242
Godfrey, Count of Montescaglioso, 26, 67–70, 72–3, 75–6, 135
Gregory I 'the Great', Pope (590–604), 17
Gregory VII, Pope (1073–85), 3, 82, 244

Grimoald, Prince of Bari (1119–32), 3–4
Guarin, Chancellor (d. 1137), 220
Guido, Bishop of Cefalù, 32
Guiscard, Robert, *see* Robert Guiscard
Guy of Crema (anti-pope Paschal III 1164–8), 227, 241

Hannibal, son of Count Rainald of Marsia, 195
Henry, Cardinal priest of SS. Nereus and Achilles, 222
Henry (Rodrigo), Count of Montescaglioso, brother of Queen Margaret, 26, 48, 155–6, 175–9, 184–7, 189, 191–2, 195, 203–6, 214, 240, 242
Henry, Count of Paterno, 4–5, 61, 187, 208
Henry, Prince of Capua (d. 1172), 137, 202, 226, 238
Henry II, King of England (1154–89), 144, 162, 193, 203, 234
Henry VI, German Emperor (1190–7), 2, 8, 27, 33, 35, 105, 109, 170, 187, 203, 215, 253, 257
Hervey, Bishop of Tropea, 99
Hervey 'the Florid', 210
Hoffman, Harmut, 39–42
Honorius II, Pope (1124–30), 4–5
Horace, Roman poet, 30
Hubald, Cardinal Bishop of Ostia (Pope Lucius III, 1181–5), 154, 246–8
Hubald, Cardinal priest of St Prassede, *see* Hubald, Cardinal Bishop of Ostia
Hugh, Archbishop of Palermo, 16–18, 61–2, 65, 71, 90–2, 94–5, 102–3, 118, 134, 140, 224, 229, 249
Hugh (Lupinus), Count of Catanzaro, 90, 211, 215
Hugh, Count of Molise, 86–7, 104, 147
Hugh, son of Atto, 146
Hugh of Rochefort, 157–8

Ibn al-Athir, historian, 11–12, 79–80
Ibn Jubayr, Muslim traveller, 12, 92–3, 96, 110, 120–1, 137–8, 166, 170, 207–8
immigrants in Sicily, *see* North Italians
Innocent II, Pope (1130–43), 8, 245
Ivo, knight of Matthew Bonellus, 123–4

Jacquintus, Prince of Bari (d. 1139), 6
James, usher, 204
Jamison, Evelyn (1877–1972), 16–17, 28, 34–7, 40
Jerusalem, 169, 180, 231, 242
[Caid] Johar, the eunuch, 128, 133
John, Bishop of Catania (d. 1169), brother of Matthew the notary, 81, 171, 217
John, Bishop of Malta, 165, 173, 213–14
John Comnenus, Byzantine Emperor (1118–43), 6
John of Lavardin, 180, 197, 209
John of Naples, cardinal, 21, 82, 144–5, 150–4, 216, 243
John of Salisbury (d. 1180), 29, 38, 43, 48, 87, 144
John of Sinopoli, 195, 242
Jonathan, Count of Carinola and Conza, 83, 129, 228
Joscelin, Count of Loreto, 25, 157
Justinian, Emperor (527–65), 17, 49, 194, 202
Juvenal, Roman poet, 38, 47

Kemonia, district of Palermo, 147, 259, 261

Letter to Peter, 29–30, 32, 34, 40, 50, 252–63

INDEX 281

Liber Pontificalis, 21, 233–4, 243–7
Lipari, abbey and bishopric, 9, 19, 85, 258
Livy, Roman historian, 46
Loritello, county of, 10, 195
 Count, *see* Robert IV
Lothar III, German Emperor (1125–37), 6, 8
Louis VII, King of France (1137–80), 22, 24, 233–4
Lucan, Roman poet, 38, 43, 48, 151, 220
Lucius II, Pope (1144–5), 20
Lucius III, Pope (1181–5), *see* Hubald, Cardinal Bishop of Ostia

Mahdia, 15, 78–81, 225, 256
Maio of Bari, Great Admiral, 12–18, 21–3, 25, 31, 35–6, 39, 45–6, 60, 62, 64–5, 67–8, 70–1, 75–7, 80–2, 85–102, 104, 118–19, 121, 133–4, 149, 220–2, 224–5, 228–9, 249, 251
 houses of 99, 260
 murder of, 94–7, 229
Malaterra, Geoffrey, chronicler, 38, 43, 49, 53
Malta, 9
 Bishop of, *see* John, Bishop of Malta
Mansellus, Philip, 103
Manuel Comnenus, Byzantine Emperor (1143–80), 7, 10, 23–4, 66, 78, 218, 223, 225, 239–40, 245
Margaret of Navarre, Queen of Sicily, wife of William I, 13, 24–5, 42, 98, 101, 126 137, 139, 143–6, 148–51, 153–62, 165, 167–9, 175–6, 179, 181–2, 184, 186–8, 190, 196, 198–9, 201, 215, 226, 238, 240
Marinus, Abbot of Cava, 249
Marsia, 19–20, 195, 251

Marsico, counts of, *see* Silvester; William
Martianus Capella, late Roman poet and satirist, 38
[Caid] Martin, 49, 129–31, 135, 158, 216
Master Chamberlains
 of Apulia and Terra di Lavoro, 33, 204
 of Calabria d the Val di Crati, 203–4
 of the Royal Palace, 128, 133, 158, 170, 196, 239
 see also [Caid] Johar; [Caid] Peter; [Caid] Richard
Master Constables of the Royal Palace, 120, 146, 170, 193, 197, 211
 see also Berengar; Richard of Mandra; Roger of Tiron
Master Justiciars (Captains and Constables) of Apulia and Terra di Lavoro, 22, 27, 76–7, 110, 119, 126, 144, 149, 154, 176, 225, 242
 see also Gilbert, Count of Gravina; Peter of Castro Nuovo; Richard de Say; Robert, Count of Caserta; Roger, Count of Andria; Simon the Seneschal; Tancred, Count of Lecce
Master Justiciars of the Royal Court, 174–5, 193, 199
 see also Abednago; Tarentinus
Matthew, castellan of Taormina, 206–7
Matthew, the notary (later vice-chancellor), 27, 35, 46, 81, 90, 96–7, 99, 121, 131–4, 137, 139, 141–2, 149, 158, 163, 171–2, 174, 196–7, 199, 202, 208, 211–14, 216, 238, 242, 251
 family of, 81, 134
Matthew of Santa Lucia, 103, 124

Mauger, palace castellan, 106
Mazzara, bishopric of, 224, 258
   Bishop of, see Turstan
Melfi, 85
Ménager, Leon-Robert, 33–4
Meno, 98
Messina, 3, 14, 20, 41, 72–3,
   117–18, 127–8, 156, 181,
   183–5, 190, 196, 199–201,
   204–8, 213, 217, 237, 242,
   254, 256
   Archbishop of, see Robert,
   Archbishop of Messina
   archbishopric of, 9–10
   monastery of the Holy Saviour, 193
   New Church (St Nicholas), 202,
   205, 220
Milan, 226–7, 233
Mistretta, 107
Molise, county of, 25, 146–7, 193
   counts of, see Hugh, Count of
   Molise; Richard of Mandra
Monomachia (judicial duel), 105
Monreale, abbey and archbishopric,
   151, 155, 238
Montecassino, abbey of St Benedict,
   22, 38, 48–9, 62, 250
   Monte Cassino (the mountain), 84
   Montecassino Chronicle, 49
Montescaglioso, county of, 26, 187
   counts of, see Godfrey; Henry,
   Count of Montescaglioso
Muslims, 11–13, 27, 53, 109–10,
   121–2, 124, 130, 138, 166,
   170, 197–8, 211, 220–1, 230,
   232, 254–5

Naples, 85, 223, 228, 251
Nicholas, Logothete, 92
Nicholas II, Pope (1059–61), 2
Normans, 2–3, 58
North Italians, 12, 53, 121–2, 136,
   169, 208–9, 231–2
Noto, 3, 67–8

Octavian of Monticelli, Cardinal
   priest of St Cecilia (anti-Pope
   Victor IV, 1160–64), 20, 228,
   233–6
Odo, master of the stable, 98, 135,
   210
Orderic Vitalis, Anglo-Norman
   chronicler, 37
Otto, Bishop of Freising, German
   chronicler, 5, 8, 37, 58
Ovid, Roman poet, 50, 254

palace, 106–7, 109, 111–12, 123,
   134–5, 142, 210, 212, 219,
   229–31, 258–61
   castellans, see Ansaldus;
   Constantine; Mauger
   concubines, 120–1, 259
   'Greek' tower, 107, 259
   'Johar' tower, 112, 259
   Palatine chapel of St Peter, 138,
   219, 238–9, 259–60
   'Pisan' tower, 230, 259–60
   see also, Favara; Zisa
Palaeologus, Michael, 66, 223, 245
Palermo, 3, 5, 12, 14, 17, 50, 58,
   63, 67, 72–3, 76, 80, 92–4, 97,
   115, 117, 119, 128–9, 145,
   152, 155, 160, 178, 181,
   196–7, 199, 208–10, 219, 229,
   237, 242, 258–61
   archbishopric of, 9, 25
   archbishops, see Hugh,
   Archbishop of Palermo;
   Stephen of Perche; Walter,
   Archbishop of Palermo
   cathedral of St Mary, 213, 239
   papal Curia, see Roman Curia
Papyrus Lake, 110
Pavia, Council of (1160), 162, 233
[Caid] Peter, 12, 78–9, 133, 135–7,
   139, 142, 144–50, 158, 167,
   181, 192–3, 225, 239
Peter, Archbishop of Benevento, 222
Peter, notary, 163–4
Peter, Treasurer of the Church of
   Palermo, 252

INDEX

Peter of Blois, 27, 111, 143, 161–2, 171, 217
Peter of Castro Nuovo, Master Captain of Apulia, 119
Peter of Eboli, 34–5, 141, 207, 217
Peter of Gaeta, subdeacon of the Roman Curia, 215
Petrarch, Francesco, 51
Phaedo, 16, 98
Philip, Count of Sangro, 69, 228
Philip of Mahdia, 11
Piazza Armerina, 121, 124, 232
Pisa, 7, 22, 237
Villanus, Archbishop of Pisa, 232
Plato, 16, 98
see also *Meno*; *Phaedo*
Plutarch, Greek historian, 48
Ptolemy, Claudius, 35
see also *Almagest*

Quarrel, Odo, Canon of Chartres, 162–3, 171, 195, 199–201, 203, 205–6, 242
Quintilian, Roman rhetorician, 38, 50

Rainald of Dassel, Archbishop of Cologne (1159–67), 176, 235, 240–1
Rainulf, Count of Caiazzo (d. 1139), 6–8, 26
Reggio Calabria, 196, 203–4, 216
Archbishop of, see Roger, Archbishop of Reggio
[Caid] Richard, 158, 170, 180, 196–7, 202, 211, 213–14, 216
Richard, Bishop-Elect of Syracuse (later Archbishop of Messina, 1183–95), 30, 115, 120, 131, 133–4, 137, 139, 140–5, 147, 150–3, 158–9, 163–4, 174, 213–14, 216, 230, 238
Richard de Say, Count of Fondi (1166–8), later Count of Gravina, 23, 26, 128–9, 153–5, 157, 214–15, 235

Richard I, Prince of Capua (1058–78), 3
Richard I of Aquila, Count of Fondi (d. c. 1166), 26, 74–5, 83, 149, 224
Richard II of Aquila, Count of Fondi, 23, 26, 154, 240
Richard of Aversa, *stratigotus* of Messina, 117, 183–4
Richard of Balbano, 176
Richard of Mandra, Count of Molise (1166–70), 15, 25, 77, 109, 120, 146, 148–50, 152–3, 157–8, 174–8, 191–2, 194, 206–7, 214, 216, 229, 242
Robert, Archbishop of Messina, 96, 230
Robert, Count of Caserta (d. 1183), 182–3, 192–3
Robert, Count of Meulan, 209, 211–13
Robert of Selby, Chancellor, 220
Robert, Prince of Capua, son of William I (d. 1159), 226
Robert II, Prince of Capua, 5, 66, 74–5, 223–6
Robert IV, Count of Loritello and Conversano (d. 1182), 3, 11, 26, 61–6, 73–5, 77, 85, 109, 126, 128–9, 133, 146, 176, 195, 217, 221–4, 231–2, 235, 243
Robert Guiscard, Duke of Apulia (1058–85), 2, 6, 20, 37, 48, 56, 117
Robert of Bellisina, 172–4
Robert of Bova, 76, 109
Robert of Calatabellotta, 135
Robert of Calatabiano, 166–8, 170
Robert of Neubourg, Dean of Evreux, 25, 159
Robert of S. Giovanni, 14–15, 31–2, 47, 118–19, 155, 164, 171, 197
Robert of Sorrento, see Robert II, Prince of Capua

Roger, Archbishop of Reggio, 15, 137, 140–1, 143, 237
Roger, Count of Alba (1166–8), Count of Andria (1168–90), 26, 40, 52, 69, 157, 214
Roger, Count of Ariano, 8
Roger, Count of Gerace, 15, 193, 198, 208, 214
Roger, Count of Tricarico, son of Count Robert of Caserta, 21, 182, 193, 228
Roger (Borsa), Duke of Apulia (1085–1111), 3, 105
Roger, Duke of Apulia, eldest son of King Roger (d. 1148), 9, 16, 39, 59, 67, 110, 113–14
Roger, Duke of Apulia, eldest son of William I (d. 1161), 39, 113, 226, 230–1, 250
Roger, judge, 185–6, 189
Roger, King of Sicily (1130–54), 1, 4–5, 8, 10, 12, 15–16, 25, 31, 38, 45, 56–7, 58, 63, 66, 86, 105, 110, 168, 191, 203, 219–21, 223, 245
Roger I, Count of Sicily (d. 1101), 56, 117, 190, 206
Roger II, Count of Sicily (1105–28), see Roger, King of Sicily
Roger of Acerra (de Medania), Count of Buonalbergo, 26, 83, 129, 158, 228
Roger of Aquila, Count of Avellino (1152–83), 21, 27, 105, 120, 129, 158, 186, 193, 209–10
Roger of Creon, 84
Roger of Martorano, 87–90, 126–7
Roger of Rupecanina, Count of Alife, 26
Roger of Tiron, Master Constable of the Royal Palace, 171, 193, 197, 211
Roger Sclavus, illegitimate son of Count Simon of Policastro, 115–16, 120–2, 124–5, 231–2

Roland (Bandinelli), Cardinal priest of St Mark, papal Chancellor, see Alexander III, Pope
Roman Curia, 20–1, 153, 215–16
Roman law, 29, 49, 194, 202
Rome, 20, 150–2, 228, 237, 240–1
Romuald II, Archbishop of Salerno (1153–81), 2, 27, 51, 137, 139–43, 161, 172, 173–4, 213–14, 219, 230–1, 237–9, 249
Chronicle attributed to Romuald, 11, 14, 21, 23–4, 51–3, 217, 219–43
Rotrou, Archbishop of Rouen, 159, 209

Salerno, 3, 62, 83, 131–3, 172, 220, 223, 232, 236–7, 251
Salernus, physician, 172–5
Sallust, Roman historian, 14, 18, 28, 37–8, 40, 43–7, 49, 56, 156, 165, 185, 189, 191
see also Catiline
Sea Castle, 109, 135, 166, 169, 202, 210, 258, 261
Sfax, 57
[Caid] Siddiq 'the Muslim', 170, 260
Silvester, Count of Marsico, 84, 98–9, 120, 122–3, 131, 133, 260
Simon, Count of Policastro, 61, 63–5, 72–5, 115–16, 187
Simon, illegitimate son of King Roger, 23, 104, 108, 111, 115, 120, 231
Simon I, Count of Sangro (1140–56?), 69–70
Simon II, Count of Sangro (1166–8), 157, 193, 195
Simon of Poitiers, 211
Simon the seneschal, brother-in-law of Maio, 18, 77, 85, 225
Sorellus, Roger, 190
'Stephanites and Ichnelates', 16, 35–6

INDEX

Stephen, Admiral, brother of Maio, 77, 85, 99, 225
Stephen, King of England (1135–54), 25, 32, 38
Gesta Stephani, 32, 49
Stephen, son of Maio, 17, 99
Stephen of Perche, Chancellor, 13–15, 22, 25–7, 30–2, 41, 46, 48, 159–62, 164, 166–70, 177–82, 184–9, 194, 197–9, 202, 208–10, 212–14, 241–2
 appointed Chancellor and elected Archbishop of Palermo, 161
 death of, 218
 family of (Counts of Perche), 159
stratigotus, 117, 132, 136, 165, 183–4, 200–4
Suetonius, Roman historian, 18, 45, 47, 102
Suger, Abbot of St Denis (1122–52), 37
Syracuse, 50, 122, 257
 Bishop-Elect of, *see* Richard, Bishop-Elect of Syracuse
 bishopric of, 151
 earthquake at, 217, 243
Syria, 200, 212, 214

Tacitus, Roman historian, 31, 37
Tancred, Count of Lecce (1169–90), King of Sicily (1190–4), 26–7, 33–6, 37, 40, 67, 69, 76, 81, 104–5, 108, 115, 121, 125, 215, 230–1
Taormina, 194, 206–7, 217, 242
Taranto, 128, 187, 235
 principality of, 15–16, 105
Tarantinus, Master Justiciar of the Royal Court, 193
Tarì (coin), 99–100, 102, 251
Taverna, 53, 126–7, 235
Terence, Roman playwright, 43
Termini Imerese, 92–3, 177–8
Thomas, uncle of the Countess of Catanzaro, 127
Tours, Council of (1163), 234

Tremiti, monastery of St Mary, 48–9
Tripoli, 57
Troia, 52, 192
 bishop of, *see* William III
 bishopric of, 250
Turgisius, chamberlain, 192–3
Turstan, Bishop of Mazzara, 85, 140, 165, 230

Urban II, Pope (1088–99), 9

Venice, 7, 18, 118–19
 peace conference at (1177), 7, 23, 52
Venosa, monastery of the Holy Trinity, 18, 81, 190, 250
 see also Aegidius, Abbot
Venosa, sack of town, 7
Vergil, Roman poet, 43, 47–8, 254
Via Coperta, 94, 96, 103, 209, 260
Via Marmorea, 209, 260

Walter, Archbishop of Palermo (1169–90), 15, 27, 37, 110–11, 135, 214–17, 242–3
Walter, Archdeacon of Cefalù (1156–66?), *see* Walter, Archbishop of Palermo
Walter, Dean of Agrigento (1166–8), *see* Walter, Archbishop of Palermo
Walter of Moac, 35, 195
William, Count of Lesina, 75, 108, 115
William, Count of Marsico, 25, 99, 157
William, Count of the Principate, 229–31
William, Duke of Apulia (1111–27), 3–4, 57, 103
William, son of Duke Roger and brother of Tancred, 76
William I, King of Sicily (1154–66), 1–2, 11–13, 15–16, 18, 20–3, 27, 35, 41–2, 46, 59–60, 64,

66–7, 70, 75, 78, 80, 90–1, 98, 100–1, 103, 105, 109–10, 112–14, 117, 119, 123–5, 131, 136, 151–2, 187, 201, 221, 223–6, 228–9, 232, 235, 237, 244–8, 252
  death of, 136–8, 237–8
  sons of, 226
William II, King of Sicily (1166–89), 1, 8, 12, 14, 19–20, 27–8, 33, 35–6, 39–41, 52, 81, 111, 113, 124, 136, 166, 180–3, 187–8, 196–7, 199, 201–3, 210–11, 218, 226, 238–41, 243
  coronation of, 138–9
  death of, 252
William III, Bishop of Troia, 249
William of Blois, Abbot of Matina, 171–2, 217
William of Gesualdo, 176
William of Leluce, 199
William of Pavia, cardinal priest of S. Pietro in Vincoli, 162, 222
William of San Severino, 129, 133, 182–3, 211

Zanobi della Strada, humanist (c. 1312–61), 50
Zisa palace, 237